# IMMIGRATION

# Contemporary Issues

Series Editors: Robert M. Baird
                        Stuart E. Rosenbaum

Other titles in this series:

# IMMIGRATION

## DEBATING THE ISSUES

**Edited by**
# Nicholas Capaldi

 Prometheus Books

59 John Glenn Drive
Amherst, NewYork 14228-2197

Published 1997 by Prometheus Books

01 00 99 98 97    5 4 3 2 1

Library of Congress Cataloging-in-Publication Data

Immigration : debating the issues / edited by Nicholas Capaldi.
        p.    cm. — (Contemporary issues)
    Includes bibliographical references.
    ISBN 1–57392–142–4 (pbk. : alk. paper)
    1. United States—Emigration and immigration. 2. United States—Emigration and immigration—Government policy. I. Capaldi, Nicholas. II. Series: Contemporary issues (Buffalo, N.Y.)
JV6465.I475    1997
325.73—dc21                                                    97–6542
                                                                  CIP

Printed in the United States of America on acid-free paper

# Contents

# PART III: THE ECONOMICS AND POLITICS OF IMMIGRATION

# PART IV: CULTURAL CHALLENGE OF IMMIGRATION

# PART V: SHOULD ENGLISH BE THE NATIONAL LANGUAGE?

## APPENDIX

# Introduction

## Nicholas Capaldi

Immigration in one form or another has been a widely debated public policy issue since the founding of the United States. The form and content of the debate has varied from one historical period to another. Some sense of the evolution in that debate is reflected in our historical survey appendix. Our focus is on the contemporary debate about immigration, a debate that originated in the discussion preceding the Immigration Act of 1965. Why the year 1965 fixes the origin of our debate is something we shall discuss below.

The debate about immigration is important and interesting because it is first and foremost a debate about national identity. It is, as well, a debate among conflicting philosophical political visions. Lastly, it is a debate that challenges political stereotypes.

There are two dimensions to the contemporary debate: factual and normative. The factual debate concerns the following issues:

1. What is immigration? Who or what is an immigrant? What is the difference between a legal and an illegal immigrant? Who or what is a refugee? Who or what is an alien? What is "political asylum"?

One thing that would help our understanding of the debate is to know what the terms of the debate mean. The largest category is encompassed by the term "alien." An *alien* is any person who is not a citizen of the United States. A *citizen* of the United States, according to the Constitution, is any person born in the United States (including Puerto Rico, Guam, Virgin Islands, Northern Mariana Islands) or who has been *naturalized*. Additionally, a person may have *derivative* citizenship if at least one parent was a citizen.

Aliens may be of two types, temporary residents or permanent residents. Temporary aliens include tourists, students, and the like. More importantly, temporary aliens include refugees and asylees. *Refugees* are persons currently outside of the United States and who are unable or unwilling to return to their country of nationality because of fear of persecution on account of race, religion,

9

membership in a particular social group, or because of political opinions. *Asylees* are refugees who are already in the United States or at its borders.

*Immigrants* are aliens who have been granted permanent residency. That is, they can reside in the United States, work without restriction, and are protected by law. Asylees and refugees may in due course apply to become immigrants or permanent residents through *naturalization*. Immigrants may become citizens by fulfilling the following six requirements: be at least eighteen years of age, achieve basic literacy in English, demonstrate a knowledge of United States history (by answering ten to twelve questions from a prepublished list of one hundred questions), have resided in the United States for five years, reflect sound moral character, and take an oath of allegiance.

2. How many people presently fit into the above categories both in absolute numbers and relative to the population as a whole? How does this compare with the past? What demographic trends are suggested by the present numbers?

3. What is the present impact of immigration, specifically in the areas of economics, the environment, unemployment, welfare, crime, education, culture, family life, religion, race relations, and domestic politics in general? How does this vary by origin (understood as ethnic group, religion, national origin, etc.)?

4. What has been the law concerning immigration? Refugees? Political asylum? What is the present law and how did it evolve out of previous law? What have been the respective roles of the judiciary, the executive and legislative branches of government?

The normative debate concerns the following issues:

5. Is there a set of fundamental values that defines what the United States is or should be? To what extent should immigration policy reflect these values? To what extent should immigrants be required to "assimilate" or reflect these values?

6. What has been the traditional role(s) of immigration in the history of the United States?

7. What should be the *present* immigration policy of the United States? To what extent should the foreign policy of the United States influence immigration policy? To what extent should the approach to other domestic public policy issues influence immigration policy?

The fundamental issue in this debate is issue 5. Who we think we are and what we think we are trying to do as a nation determines what kind of immigration policy we should have. Even a consensus on the factual issues only becomes relevant once the fundamental normative issue is resolved. That is, once we have identified the norms we can discuss the conditions that promote or realize those norms.

There are two kinds of disagreement possible here. First, there may be disagreement about the fundamental norms; second, there may be disagreement about which policies best promote or realize those norms. We shall begin by sketching one view of the fundamental norms and indicate what implications it has for immigration. We shall then engage in a two-fold review: first, we shall indicate which of these norms has been challenged and what implications the challenges have for immigration; second, we shall indicate what kind of disagreements have emerged about policies that promote the norms even where there may be agreement on the norms.

## A SKETCH OF THE FUNDAMENTAL NORMS

The United States is a nation-state subscribing to the fundamental norms of liberal culture. *What is liberal culture?* By liberal culture, we understand the kind of culture that emerged in western Europe in the post-Renaissance and post-Reformation period and eventually spread to North America and beyond. The most distinctive institutions of liberal culture are individual rights, the rule of law, a republican or representative form of government, and a free market economy. Liberal culture is the greatest force in the modern world; it has transformed and continues to transform the moral landscape by improving the material conditions of life and by institutionalizing individual freedom. Classical articulations of liberal culture are to be found in Hobbes, Locke, Montesquieu, Adam Smith, and Hume. These authors, in turn, are major influences on the founding fathers such as Jefferson, Madison, Hamilton, and Jay (the latter three are the authors of the Federalist Papers).

The moral framework of liberal culture has three key components:

1. a claim to *universality*;

2. the assertion of the fundamental moral worth of the free and responsible *individual*; and

3. the recognition of the role of the *family* as the key institution in nurturing a free and responsible individual.

The claim to universality is the claim that liberal culture embodies "a" or "the" fundamental moral truth that is universally applicable to all human beings in every culture. This is the assertion of the existence of a form of *natural law.* The claim to universality has two components: one formal and the other substantive.

The *formal component* consists in the recognition that if there were no universal truth there would be no rational basis for resolving disagreements or even for discussing them. Without a universal truth neither the validity nor the invalidity of a particular cultural matrix could be an issue. The recognition of this formal or logical component of universality allows both for self-criticism and for cross-cultural criticism. To fail to recognize this logical or formal component is to exclude oneself and one's culture from consideration within the substantive debate. To be a legitimate contender requires recognition of the formal component. Historically, the formal component is articulated *only within Western civilization*; it originated in those eastern Mediterranean societies that saw themselves as instantiating a cosmic order, most specifically in the Judaic monotheism of the Old Testament, in classical Greek drama, and most clearly in Socrates,

Plato, and Aristotle. One of the things the reader should keep in mind is that neither China nor Japan permits immigration.

It is, however, not enough to recognize the formal component. Recognizing the need for a universal moral truth is not the same thing as having identified in any substantive way the actual universal moral truths. Logic can take us only so far. The *substantive moral truth* that is embodied in liberal culture is the inherent worth and dignity of the free and responsible individual. This is a substantive claim inherent in all of Western civilization. Let me spell out the content of this claim before discussing its history.

Individuality means:

1. that human beings possess the rational capacity to recognize the universal moral truth;

2. that human beings have the internal capacity to be unconstrained in their decision to act in accordance with the universal truth, i.e., *free will*;

3. that true freedom and dignity consist in the inner or self-discipline that comes with the exercise of these capacities.

This conception of individuality has evolved throughout the history of Western civilization from the Greek philosophers through the Stoics, Cicero, and Christianity. What needs to be identified here is the specifically *Christian component.* It is important to call attention to this component in order to emphasize that liberal culture depends upon moral presuppositions and cannot therefore be understood from the perspective of either social science or an outside disengaged observer.

What Christianity added to or made explicit within the conception of individuality is the recognition that human beings have self-destructive impulses as well as wholesome ones, that the self-destructive impulses can be overcome only by conscious self-discipline, and that we are not fit to assume responsibility for ourselves or others unless we have developed the inner discipline of self-restraint. It is this moral dimension that is needed to supplement the rational insights of classical philosophy. Integrally related to Western civilization, therefore, is some conception of the human person and its spiritual dimension.

The essence of the Christian insight is that the locus of freedom is within the individual. How significant is this point? Consider the following example. Take two identical maps of Europe; draw a line on one of the maps. On one side of that line are all of the communities that have been defined historically by Western Christianity; on the other side are all of the others even including non-Western versions of Christianity and Islam. Then take the second map of Europe and draw a line through it. On one side of that line are all of the communities that easily embrace market economies, republican government, and the practice of toleration; on the other side are all those who define themselves by hatred and intolerance of others. You won't have to look very far, for such maps appear every day in the newspapers telling us of new ethnic conflict. What may surprise the reader is that the two lines neatly coincide.

The point of the example is that respect for the individual, market economies, and limited or republican government exist as an integrated trio only in communities historically defined by Western Christianity. Christianity has encouraged the development of the inner-directed individual; such individuals thrive in market economies; and republican government maximizes respect for the inner spiritual domain.

It is with regard to individuality that the family takes on a special significance within liberal culture. For most of history and in most cultures the human being has had a collective identification; in modern liberal cultures the attitude of the family to its members is remarkably different: *a child is perceived as a subject of cultivation,* not as the inadvertent by-product of a biological process, nor as an object of utility.

These three moral presuppositions, namely, universality, individuality, and family, inform *major practices within liberal culture,* specifically:

1. a market economy;

2. a representative government;

3. toleration;

4. civic virtue; and

5. a conception of world order.

There are two ways of defending a market economy, one instrumental and one moral. Some will defend the market economy on the basis of its greater productivity and power. Others choose to defend a market economy on moral grounds. *Wealth is a good thing because*:

1. It enhances the human condition. Income is not merely a means to consumer satisfaction, nor merely an incentive. Rather, income is a *means to accomplishment.* Participation in a market economy informed by an individualist moral culture actually promotes a variety of forms of virtuous behavior.

2. Wealth liberates us from the culture of poverty. Whereas in the medieval world it was wealth that created a scandal, the scandal of the modern world is the existence of poverty.

3. Private wealth provides a check on the power of the government, and leads to the expansion of individual liberties.

4. Finally, wealth provides the dynamic of social reform.

*The family is the key institution in a market economy understood as the expression of an individualist moral culture. It is the family that provides the cultural context of individuality.* It has performed this function in a number of ways:

1. The family is not a means to another end, it is "the" end of a good society. Getting married, setting up house, raising children, struggling to bring oneself and one's family to the greatest degree of accomplishment is what a liberal culture is all about. This does not preclude the existence of a wider net of institutions within society or other forms of community, but it does define their relative importance.

2. The family is a private social security system.

3. The family provides support for mobility, a common pattern being that the first established member creates a base to which other family members can come later and thus ease the burden of transition; in poorer families the pattern is one of concentrating savings on giving a special advantage, such as education, to one member; and surely the most common pattern is seen in the sacrifices parents make for the education of their children.

4. One of the greatest motivations that energetic and creative people bring to the marketplace is not only the desire to found a fortune but the desire to have a durable and substantial legacy to pass on to their children.

The second most important institution in the development of liberal culture has been the concept of republican or representative or limited government. Limited government is a good thing. It is a good thing because it maximizes respect for the inner spiritual domain. One of the great and lasting contributions of Christianity is that it has *de-divinized the state,* that is, it has transferred the locus of the ultimate good from the state to the spiritual domain of the individual.

The dichotomy between the purely private life and the communal life is a false one. Every practice is connected in some way with a community. But, just as the view that serving God is possible only within a religious order was a false view, so too is the view that political activity is the only adequate expression of communal interests.

Modern liberal culture operates without the notion of a collective social teleology; it therefore operates without the assumption that the state, political institutions, and political activity are fundamental. It is, in Oakeshott's words, a civil association and not an enterprise association. As a civil association, its public good is a series of collective interests rooted in history (Hume). Political activity is not the cultivation of a collective interest but the negotiation of conflict among those evolving interests; the conflict is not resolved by appeal to a mythical teleology (mysteriously accessed through democratic dialogue) but by appeal to a moral consensus (grounded in a religious vision and whose secular expression is Kant's categorical imperative and J. S. Mill's conception of individuality and liberty) and historically rooted procedure (law).

The notion of republican or representative government is that no one person, regime, or group determines the public good. Rather, representatives of all the interests determine or negotiate the public good. In this sense, government is limited by or defined by these other interests.

The most obvious feature of a liberal culture is its formal commitment to and practice of tolerance. The most obvious feature of an illiberal culture is the lack of toleration, usually seen as strife between or rejection of what is different. The ethnic strife we see today in Eastern Europe or tribal strife in Africa are examples. The justification of this tolerance is not relativism or the lack of a belief in any truth. On the contrary, the basic truth of individuality is that individuals must come to agreements by the exercise of their own rationality and free wills. This was the basis of the argument for religious toleration in Milton's *Areopagitica,* Locke's *Letter Concerning Toleration,* and Mill's essay *On Liberty.* Toleration is possible only if there is universal agreement on another level about why we should tolerate. More than any other issue, this underscores the cultural context that informs our political and social practices.

What does *civic virtue* mean in liberal culture? First, it is a misunderstanding of individuality to see it as opposed to the notion of a cultural whole. You cannot be an autonomous individual on your own; rather, individuality requires the support of a liberal culture in general, and family life in particular. In seeking this context for myself, I seek it necessarily for others. To the extent that others do not share it, my own is less secure. Second, the only public business worthy of the name is the business of providing the context within which individuals can have greater and greater control over their own lives. It is a contradiction in terms to think that giving greater and greater control to public agencies increases individual freedom. While relief is an unquestionable social obligation which the demise of traditional communities, responsible aristocracies, and church wealth has devolved onto the state for want of any other agency, it is open to discussion whether policies of *redistribution* can be effective, whether they are the best means of dealing with the problem, and whether policies of *redistribution* conflict with other legitimate social objectives.

A truly autonomous individual is one who defines himself or herself. The perception we have of ourselves as self-defining cannot be sustained if we are constantly dealing with those whom we think of or have to treat as inferiors. The double standards that prevail in many institutions, standards that demand less of some than of others, invariably reconfirm the perception that we are dealing with inferiors. It takes an enormous act of bad faith to ignore this. A true individual can maintain his autonomy only by interacting with other autonomous beings, that is by interacting with equals. It follow from this that *civic virtue in a modern liberal culture requires us to help others, and we can only help others by helping them to achieve autonomy.* Equality has to be understood as the moral capacity for being autonomous, not as an equal division of the spoils or redistribution of social badges of prestige.

The foregoing conception of civic virtue not only makes room for traditional communities such as religion but provides for forms of communal cooperation (solidarity if you wish) that have no analogue in premodern Europe. We shall mention three. First, autonomous individuals can come together in a risk-sharing venture such as buying insurance. This form of solidarity is generated out of market concerns. Second, large commercial republics allow for the pursuit of public goods on a much larger scale than the traditional closed community. Third, the global market economy leads to the creation of forms of solidarity that transcend conventional national borders. Long ago, Aristotle, in his analysis of friendship, delineated the different kinds of friendship that are possible in a variety of different regimes. That analysis is still important for suggesting that what is at issue is not whether community or solidarity be taken seriously but what kinds of community are meaningful in different contexts.

What we have discovered so far is that the major moral concept of a liberal culture is individual autonomy. We have also seen that the economic system most compatible with an individualist moral culture is a market economy, and that the political system most compatible with it is a republican form of government. What would happen if every society in the world were to adopt a market economy and a republican form of government based upon an individualist moral culture? Immanuel Kant asked this question at the end of the eighteenth century, two hundred years ago. His answer, which is our answer, is that there would be world peace. Rather than present a detailed argument for this thesis, *we raise one simple question: how many of the major international conflicts in the last two hundred years have occurred between two sides both of which had market economies and republican forms of government based upon an individualist moral culture?*

The reader may be tempted to ask at this point, what right do we have to proffer our views as a model for others? That is a good question. How do we know that our ideas of freedom are the right ones? Shouldn't we allow others to decide for themselves how they want to understand freedom?

Merely stating this objection shows that the objector already accepts our notion of freedom as individual autonomy. To let others decide for themselves is precisely to treat them as ends and not as means. When we talk about others deciding for themselves we most certainly do not mean letting a self-appointed elite decide for all. Is there anyone here who believes that when one person, one economic interest group, one gender, one religion, one race, one ethnic group does the deciding for others that it makes sense to call this letting "them" decide for themselves? "Deciding for themselves" means, if it means anything at all, allowing each autonomous individual to decide for himself or herself, and when applied to a state this has to mean a public and free election with universal suffrage and without reprisals. That is, it means a republican form of government.

The issue we face today is not whether there should be some kind of global culture. Events are already pushing us in that direction. *The issue is, what kind of global culture,* what kind of unity, and what will be the parameters of diversity within that unity. *There is no serious competitor to liberal culture* as the model; liberal culture is self-critical, characterized by its striving for universality, has as its great strength the power of assimilation, and is a fertile source of adaptation of what has been and still can be absorbed from other historical cultures.

# IMMIGRATION WITHIN THE FRAMEWORK OF THE FUNDAMENTAL VALUES

What are the implications for immigration of the foregoing vision of the United States of America?

1. The United States is a nation-state with a double mission:

   A. to preserve and foster liberal culture within its own borders, and

   B. to promote liberal culture in the world at large.

Legal immigrants are welcome to the extent that they can serve that double mission. With regard to A, legal immigrants are welcome to the extent that (1) they already subscribe to and practice the fundamental values of liberal culture; (2) they seek to leave a place which prohibits or inhibits the practice of such values; and (3) accepting those immigrants does not undermine or inhibit the ability of current U.S. citizens to practice such values. With regard to B, legal immigrants are welcome if (1) their potential success in practicing the fundamental values of liberal culture can serve as a positive example to their previous nation and culture to join the family of liberal cultures, and (2) accepting them does not undermine or inhibit the ability of current U.S. citizens to practice such values.

2. It is understandable that in the beginning of U.S. history preference would be given to those from northern and western Europe, most especially those from Great Britain, since these people are most likely to have instantiated liberal cultural values. Given the historical and geographical origin of liberal culture, this is no accident.

From 1820 to 1860, over ten million immigrants entered the United States. They were mostly Irish and German Catholics. Since 1850 Catholics have been the single largest religious denomination in the United States. There was an anti-immigration movement within the Protestant Anglo-Saxon community in the cities of the Northeast. This is reflected in the riot which occurred in Philadelphia in 1844 and in the rise of the Native American Party of the 1850s (from which we get the expression "nativist"). Some sense of the lingering effects of this confrontation between WASPs and Irish Catholics can be seen in Edwin O'Connor's novel *The Last Hurrah*. It is all too easy today to give in to the temptation to characterize WASP opposition as prejudicial. However, it is important to keep in mind that the attitude of the Catholic church toward liberal culture was very different, perhaps one would even say hostile, in the last half of the nineteenth century from its present more supportive attitude. Even today there is a debate within Catholic circles, with writers such as Father Neuhaus and Michael Novak emerging as the outstanding defenders of liberal culture whereas others such as Archbishop Roger Mahony of Los Angeles maintain that "the right to immigrate is more fundamental than that of nations to control their borders."

Throughout its immigration history, the United States has looked with suspicion on certain groups. When a consensus emerged that members from that group or area were hostile to liberal culture or could not or would not adapt to it, the United States has excluded them from immediate consideration for immigrant status. One might question whether these judgments were always as well informed as they should have been, or one might have reservations about the motives (as opposed to the reasons) of some of the supporters of the exclusion, but it would be tendentious to dismiss this as a symptom of racism. The assumption that everybody naturally wants to be like us or would have no difficulty in becoming like us is highly suspect. More to the point, the United States has always modified its policy by lifting exclusions when circumstances changed.

Immigrants have often brought with them political and economic attitudes hostile to liberal culture. For example, Daniel DeLeon, the man responsible for pushing the Socialist Labor Party in the direction of Marxism was born in Curacao; the *Jewish Daily Forward* founded in 1897 as a Yiddish (it did not represent the entire Jewish community in America) newspaper, was a long-time proponent of socialism.

3. Liberal culture is the greatest force in the modern world; it has transformed and continues to transform the moral landscape by improving the material conditions of life and by institutionalizing individual freedom. As liberal culture expands internationally, preference can be expanded to accommodate those who come from newly emerging liberal cultures. It is understandable, for historical reasons, that southern and eastern Europeans would be the immediate beneficiaries of this expanded preference.

4. As the economic and technological success of liberal culture succeeds in creating a global market, talented individuals from around the world seek to emulate its values in advance of their culture or nation. Sometimes this entails studying or doing business within the United States. Preference can now be expanded to individuals, regardless of national origin, who have demonstrated their precocious adoption of liberal values.

5. As the net of preference evolves and expands geographically, strains begin to appear in the capacity to absorb individuals who   differ in some degree from the "native" stock broadly understood. To take a simple example, many individuals who aspire to live in a liberal culture might not speak English or they may not adapt easily to "native" mores or the current mores that have evolved from the "native" mores. There are costs to acculturating such individuals. New dimensions of preference might now be introduced such as the possession of a large amount of capital, high levels of education, and the presence of other family members who have already made the transition. What these new dimensions share is that they increase the probability of a smoother transition not only for the immigrant but also for the host country.

6. The United States sees as part of its foreign policy the promotion of liberal cultural values around the world. Sometimes liberal culture establishes tem-

porary "beachheads" or "enclaves" in other countries only to see them collapse for political or military-political reasons. Subscribers to liberal culture become endangered within their own homeland. Such individuals or groups may become refugees. The United States may feel a special obligation to grant these individuals asylum or immigrant status. Middle-class Cubans who fled Castro's Cuba or the Southeast Asian "boat people" would be examples. The dilemma of the success of liberal culture is that during an age of transition the number of these cases may increase. If so, the strains of accommodating such people increases and, consistent with the policy of not undermining those who are already here, this may require numerical limits based upon our capacity for successful absorption.

7. The United States has not always acted consistently with its own principles. It has sometimes permitted, condoned, and even encouraged illegal immigration. It has not seriously followed up the progress of immigrants once they are here. Politicians at every level of government have for a variety of motives exercised certain prerogatives with regard to immigration to encourage the granting of immigrant status to those who might not otherwise qualify. The consequence is the presence of a large number of immigrants who do not subscribe to the values of liberal culture. At present no program or policy exists for dealing with the acculturation of those indifferent to or hostile to liberal culture as opposed to those who would like to make the transition but are having difficulties.

8. The costs, both material and social, of having immigrants should not be underestimated. There is a federal department or bureaucracy that must oversee this matter. This costs tax dollars. Keeping track of legal immigrants might require some form of national identification that could conceivably violate traditional notions of privacy. Conflicts of an economic and cultural nature with groups already here entail other costs.

## CHALLENGES

Challenges to the foregoing view of U.S. immigration policy may be distinguished into two categories: normative and factual. Normative challenges reflect disagreement with the foregoing account of the fundamental values of the United States.

### Arguments to Eliminate Immigration

1. *Isolationist.* It has been argued that the United States is a sovereign nation in a world of nation-states and that its primary overriding obligation in a hostile world is to protect itself and advance its own national interest. That is, it is arguable that the United States has no obligation to promote liberal culture anywhere but within its own borders. Using immigration to solve some of the world's problems undermines the United States.

2. *Nativist.* It has been argued that the United States has achieved a fragile domestic balance of liberal culture at great cost. Immigration is to be opposed because the costs, stresses, and strains (primarily cultural, political, and economic) of immigration threaten that delicate balance.

## Arguments to Augment Immigration

1. *Reform.* The United States is failing to live up to the goals of liberal culture in one or more ways. In order to realize those goals in a more complete fashion, immigration of certain categories of people should be increased. For example, some racial, ethnic, or religious groups already within the United States are routinely penalized because they are a minority, and increasing their numbers will gain for them the respect they deserve.

2. *Multiculturalist.* Aside from democracy and toleration, liberal culture is a bad thing. Individualism, the rule of law, free market economies, and limited government are values that reflect accidental historical features of northwest Europe used to dominate and oppress peoples both within the borders of the United States and throughout the world. If the United States has a mission it is to disappear as a sovereign entity to be replaced by a world government, such as the United Nations but without a Security Council, in which all cultures, not nations, are to be respected. Immigration should be permitted and encouraged in order to change totally the composition of the current population to reflect and better implement planetary heterogeneity. From this point of view, there may be no such thing as "illegal" immigration.

There is a second category of challenge, namely, challenges about the best ways of implementing the norms, however one construes them.

The historical demographic pattern for immigrants has been for newly arrived immigrants to cluster in selected cities (for economic opportunities) and neighborhoods (for maintaining some kind of cultural continuity, e.g., Chinatown, Little Italy, Little Havana, etc.). The existence of ethnic neighborhoods both eases the transition and exacerbates the difficulties of making the transition. It eases the transition by allowing newly arriving immigrants to benefit from the experience of older immigrants. It exacerbates the transition by allowing some members to use the ethnic neighborhood to immunize themselves from change. Sometimes the immunization takes the form of rejecting the host culture either by engaging in criminal activity (every major immigrant wave brought with it a serious increase in crime including organized crime) or by the demagogic organizing of voting blocks that promote group identity rather than individual autonomy and assimilation.

The questions raised by the process of acclimatization are:

A. What aspects of the immigrant cultures (religion, family life, mores, etc.) positively promote the fundamental values of the host culture?

B. What aspects of the immigrant cultures ease the transition to the fundamental values of the host culture? For example, bilingual education as opposed to immersion does not directly promote the speaking of English but it may, in the opinion of some, ease the transition to speaking and dealing in English.

C. What aspects of the immigrant cultures are serious obstacles to promoting the transition to the fundamental values of the host culture? For example, is the religion of Islam incompatible with liberal culture?

D. Are there aspects of the host culture that not only are not necessary for the promotion of the fundamental values but also inhibit the transition of immigrants toward practicing those fundamental values? For example, is unilinguism necessary?

So far we have discussed the immigration debate by identifying the major issues internal to the issue of immigration itself. But the contemporary immigration debate does not exist in an intellectual vacuum. Rather, we are living during a time when there is a larger debate in the background, or a series of larger debates. The larger context consists of competing visions of how to conceptualize public policy issues, whether those issues are immigration, poverty, family values, abortion, and the like.

For the sake of argument, we shall identify three broad positions and how they respond to immigration in particular. Our description of these positions is broad and abstract, and we do recognize that many participants in the debate might not fit neatly into one of these three categories, or that they might vary from issue to issue. However, keeping in mind that this is just a model, we think it helps to frame and clarify the debate.

*Liberal Position.* The term "liberal" is used in so many different ways that it is a source of confusion. At the same time, it is a word that we can hardly escape using. In order to avoid confusion, we shall introduce a distinction between "liberal culture" and "liberalism." So far we have been talking about liberal culture as a complex series of practices informed by certain values including individual rights, rule of law, a free market economy, and limited government. "Liberalism" is a particular philosophical account (i.e., an understanding and a justification) for liberal culture. Liberalism is not the only philosophical account for "liberal culture"; there can be libertarian and conservative philosophical accounts of liberal culture.

As a philosophical account for liberal culture, liberalism consists of the following set of beliefs:

1. The ultimate goal of human existence is happiness in this life (secularization), and all human beings naturally pursue an autonomous life.

2. Human beings, basically, are not sinful but good (rejection of the traditional Christian conception of "sin").

3. Hence, evil behavior is exclusively the result of environmental forces; freedom is compatible with environmentalism only where *freedom is construed as the absence of arbitrary external constraints,* and where constraints are found to be arbitrary relative to the end enumerated in belief 1. By subscribing to internal determinism, *no distinction exists between "freedom" and "liberty."* These terms refer interchangeably to

environmental constraints. This conception of freedom leads to a political conception of ethics based on external social sanctions instead of morality (which involves the inner sanction of autonomous agents).

4. Social engineering can create a utopia by the control of external forces; Social policy consists in the removal of external constraints.

5. The end of human action is happiness; rights are means to the achievement of the ends. As such, rights are only *prima facie,* may be overridden, and may be possessed by any entity, not just individual human beings. Such rights can be welfare rights, i.e., they may be such that others have a positive obligation to provide such goods, benefits, or means.

*What are the implications of liberalism for immigration?* Adherents of liberalism have a tendency to lump together aliens of all kinds (legal immigrants, illegal immigrants, asylees, etc.). Once here, there is no difference between someone who entered legally and someone who entered illegally. Moreover, *adherents of liberalism have a tendency to assimilate aliens to the poor or underclass.* Since adherents of liberalism believe that all people are naturally autonomous, that is, are motivated to achieve their own ends, any problems that aliens have are the result of structural barriers in the host nation such as discrimination. All aliens should be given full access to all welfare benefits. Adherents of liberalism tend to look on critics of immigration the same way they look upon critics of welfare rights—as mean-spirited people standing in the way of progress.

An important part of the liberal case is the rejection of the notion of limited government as a fundamental value. While granting that this may have been part of the original intent of the founding fathers, liberals argue that times have changed largely for economic reasons. Hence greater government involvement is needed, specifically in the area of welfare rights. This also means that voting in elections becomes more important in order to provide broad-based support for the liberal legislation that will promote social reform. As a consequence, liberals tend to view immigration as part of a larger domestic agenda to enhance the welfare state. Immigrants are looked upon as potential converts to this political agenda (in keeping with the liberal assimilation of immigrants to the poor). Illegal immigrants cannot vote. Therefore, liberals favor an amnesty and any other program that will increase the number of immigrants or aliens who will stay and who can be naturalized as citizens and thereby become eligible to vote.

The liberal position is reflected, in part, by the American Civil Liberties Union. The ACLU, among its many activities, helps refugees and immigrants facing deportation. The liberal position is also reflected by the American Friends Service Committee. This Quaker organization opposes sanctions on employers of illegal immigrants and documents what it identifies as human rights violations committed by law enforcement agents against immigrants. The foremost liberal think tank on immigration issues is the Brookings Institution. The liberal position is represented in this anthology by Pete Hamill.

*Libertarian Position.* Adherents of the libertarian (or classical liberal) position, share with adherents of liberalism the assumptions 1 through 3 above. The difference is with 4 and 5. Whereas adherents of liberalism as a social philosophy view the state as the superagency for removing environmental obstacles (internal or external) to the realization of our "rights," adherents of libertarianism view the state as one of these environmental obstacles. This is because adherents of libertarianism have a traditional Lockean conception of rights. In its Lockean formulation, the ends (e.g., life, liberty, property) are designated as "rights" (qualified as "natural," "human," etc.); these ends are teleological. Rights, so understood, are absolute, do not conflict, and are possessed only by individual human beings. Rights are morally absolute or fundamental because they are derived from human nature and as such cannot be overridden; the role of these rights is to protect the human capacity to choose. Finally, such rights impose only duties of noninterference.

*What are the implications of libertarianism for immigration?* Like liberalism, libertarianism is generally favorable to immigration. But the similarities end here. Adherents of libertarianism do insist upon a distinction between legal and illegal immigration. They do so because a free market economy requires the rule of law. These *adherents also tend to assimilate all immigrants to entrepreneurs,* not to the poor or dispossessed. It tends to believe that all or most immigrants can be great successes if only the welfare state does not corrupt them once they are here. If we do away with the welfare state and allow free markets to operate, then the poor and the immigrants will all succeed. Every success story of immigrants who become successful entrepreneurs in America is an argument about the failure of liberal social engineering as a domestic policy.

Some doctrinaire libertarians advocate totally open borders both to allow the market to determine success and to undercut the notion of a sovereign state, which they see as a constant threat. Other libertarians, those who recognize that the world is not at present a totally free market, advocate controlled immigration but stress that economic benefits be the sole or major criterion for admission.

The libertarian position is best represented by the Cato Institute. Cato's most influential publication on immigration has been Julian Simon's seminal book *The Economic Consequences of Immigration.* Cato is also represented in this anthology by Stephen Moore.

*Conservative Position.* What distinguishes the conservative from both the liberal and the libertarian is that adherents of the conservative position deny that autonomy is a natural condition. Individual autonomy is a cultural achievement. (1) Human beings are born with self-destructive impulses as well as wholesome ones (i.e., an acceptance of the Christian doctrine of original sin with or without a theological framework); (2) antisocial behavior is the natural result of a lack of self-discipline, and self-discipline is learned behavior but it is not totally induced from the outside, because while outside example and support is important, the final result depends upon free will; and (3) in order to make people whole, we must provide them not only with good examples (i.e., examples of self-discipline) but also with opportunities to learn in an internal sense self-control and personal responsibility by holding them responsible for what they do. This is not a political or technical task but a moral one. Notice that the conservative paradigm does not deny the importance of environmental influence, but it does stress that there is something more fundamental than the environment, namely human free will, and it has a different conception of what constitutes a benign environment. The conservative paradigm is a call not for inaction but for action; however, it denies that there is a guaranteed utopian resolution of the human predicament. The types of policy or action conservatives advocate are (a) termination of the welfare state as we know it (shared view with libertarians) and (b) having the government and/or other social agencies take control of the lives of dysfunctional people (directly opposed to libertarianism; negative statism as opposed to liberal positive statism). Whereas both liberals and libertarians see something on the "outside" holding people back, conservatives maintain that what goes on "inside" is what holds people back.

What is crucial for us to remember is that even within our own liberal culture going back as far as the Renaissance and the Reformation *many people have not made the transition to individuality.* There is a whole complicated history behind this, but what is important is to recognize that the most serious problem within modern liberal societies is the presence of the dysfunctional or *incomplete individual.* Being an incomplete individual is a state of mind. It is not directly correlated with income, intelligence, or how articulate you are. Some incomplete individuals are highly intelligent. Either unaware of or lacking faith in their ability to exercise self-discipline, the incomplete individual seeks escape into the collective identity of communities insulated from the challenge of opportunity. These are people focused on avoiding failure rather than on achieving success. Phenomenologically speaking, the incomplete individual can identify himself or herself by feelings of envy, resentment, self-distrust, victimization, and self-pity, in short, an inferiority complex. What really inhibits these people, according to conservatives, is *not* a lack of opportunity, not a lack of political rights, and *not* a lack of resources but a character defect, a *moral inadequacy.*

What happens when a nonindividualist culture comes into contact with liberal culture, as for example in the transition from feudalism to capitalism, the advent of colonialism, the transition of former Iron Curtain countries or Third World communities to a market economy, the current detribalization in Africa, or the entrance into the United States of poorly educated immigrants from a Third World country? A frequent result, as detailed by Oscar Lewis, is the *culture of poverty.*[1] The culture of poverty is marked by social, moral, and economic disintegration and perpetual dependence. Finally, other things that contribute to the perpetuation of the culture of poverty are government policies of paternalism, and most especially the dominance of the liberal paradigm. All of these fail to promote the sense of personal responsibility. I hasten to add that this factor is not a particular social structure but the failure to promote or encourage a change in psychological makeup.

Conservatives share with libertarians a distrust of the liberal welfare state. Conservatives, like libertarians, distrust liberal immigration policies because they see such policies as intended to increase political support for the liberal welfare state. They do not trust liberal affirmations about ending illegal immigration as sincere since liberals always call for amnesty of those already here and oppose returning illegal aliens to their country of origin. Conservatives will point out that in the 1996 election, the more liberal President Clinton got 72 percent of the Hispanic vote as compared to 21 percent for the more conservative Dole; Clinton also got 84 percent of the Black vote but only 42 percent of the Asian-American vote as compared to Dole's 49 percent.

But conservatives do not share the libertarian belief that a free market economy solves every social problem. It is only, according to adherents of the conservative position, when the free market operates within a larger social and cultural context of individual responsibility that the market is successful. Although a free market may be a necessary condition, it is not a sufficient condition.

*What are the implications of the conservative position for immigration?* Conservatives tend to favor tighter control over immigration and greater stress on criteria that reflect cultural support for individual responsibility. Conservatives argue among themselves about which factors (national origin, religion, family, etc.) are most relevant. Conservatives also call, from time to time, for a moratorium on immigration in order (a) to better assimilate those who are already here and (b) to inhibit the massive naturalization of supporters of the liberal welfare state.

The conservative position is most notably reflected in work of the Heritage Foundation and the Rockford Institute. It is represented in this volume by Peter Brimelow.

\*     \*     \*

This brings us back to the question of *why 1965 is the watershed date in the contemporary debate on immigration.* Nineteen sixty-five marks the high tide of the liberal position in defining public policy debate. The Civil Rights Act of 1964 with the seeming introduction of affirmative action was its most controversial achievement. It was also the 1965 Immigration Act that ended national origin quotas. The advocates of the new act accused the defenders of national origin quotas of being racists. It is the consequences of the 1965 Immigration Act among other things that have galvanized conservative opposition. The liberal position seems, at least at present, to be in retreat. Conservative and libertarian views can now vie to replace it. All of this is what makes the contemporary debate about immigration such a lively one. You, the reader, are now invited to enter that debate and draw your own conclusions.

## CHRONOLOGY

The Founding Fathers debated the immigration issue. Jefferson's concern was that immigrants from monarchies would not support republican government; Washington and the authors of the *Federalist* were concerned that immigrants would challenge the idea of a federal government. Benjamin Franklin was concerned that the large numbers of Germans in Pennsylvania would lead to German becoming the official language of the state. Immigration has always been, in part, a debate about national identity and the American experiment. Individual states had immigration laws.

| | |
|---|---|
| 1789 | Jedidiah Morse used the word "immigrant" in his book *American Geography.* |
| 1790 | Immigrants could become citizens after 2 years of residence and the renunciation of former allegiance. |
| 1795 | Immigrants could become citizens after 5 years of residence and the renunciation of former allegiance. |
| 1798–1800 | Alien and Sedition Acts—President John Adams can expel suspected subversives. |
| 1839 | Pennsylvania permits public schools to teach in German if 30 percent of parents request it. |
| 1849 | Passenger cases—U.S. Supreme Court declares state head taxes on immigrants to be unconstitutional; only Congress has power to regulate immigration under commerce clause of the Constitution. |
| 1870 | Naturalization Act—limits citizenship to white persons and those of African descent only. Asians are excluded. |
| 1875 | In *Henderson* v. *Mayor of New York,* the U.S. Supreme Court rules that immigration is a federal jurisdiction. Its ruling is based on the implied power to regulate foreign commerce and the "inherent power of sovereignty." This decision has been upheld in subsequent rulings but never unanimously. It is still a bone of legal contention. |
| 1882 | Congress passes the first national immigration act. It bars the indigent, criminals, the mentally ill, polygamists, those convicted of crimes of moral turpitude, and those with contagious diseases (cholera and tuberculosis). It also banned further Chinese immigrants. Part of the motivation behind this legislation was pressure from labor to protect jobs and wages. |
| 1886 | Statue of Liberty given to the United States as a gift by France. |
| 1892 | Ellis Island immigration center opened. |
| 1903 | Excluded anarchists (in response to President McKinley's assassination), epileptics, the insane, and "professional beggars." |
| 1906 | Naturalization Act required applicants for citizenship to speak English and to be able to write their own name on official documents. |

| 1907 | Congress—Expatriation Act—American women lose their citizenship if they marry a foreigner. |
|---|---|
| 1907 | Congress establishes Dillingham Immigration Commission; 1911 report favored restricting immigration. |
| 1908 | Israel Zangwill's play *The Melting Pot.* |
| 1917 | Immigration Act excluded most Asians and Pacific Islanders and imposed a literacy test for incoming immigrants. It also contained a provision for the deportation of aliens who preached revolution or overthrow of the government. The issue of deportation continues to be a bone of legal contention. |
| 1921 | Quota Act—established overall numerical restrictions. It created the *national origin system* to maintain the present ethnic and cultural balance; the annual limit of immigrants from a given nationality was set at 3 percent of numbers already present (as of the 1910 census). |
| 1922 | Cable Act repeals 1907 Expatriation Act except for women who marry aliens ineligible for citizenship. |
| 1924 | Border Patrol created (response to illegal immigrants from Europe attempting to enter via Mexico); Congress passes National Origins Act and sets the 1890 census as base year for quotas; it reduces the quota to 2 percent. |
| 1940 | Alien Registration Act provides that all immigrants must register and be fingerprinted; further it permits the deportation of criminals and subversives. |
| 1942 | Foreigners are permitted to enter temporarily to work (mostly Mexican farmworkers); extended in the 1951 U.S.-Mexican Migrant Labor Agreement (Bracero program); repealed in 1964. |
| 1943 | Wartime legislation eliminated racial exclusions and permitted immigrants from China, India, and the Philippines to become U.S. citizens. |
| 1948 | Displaced Persons Act for wartime European refugees. |
| 1952 | Immigration and Nationality Act (McCarran-Walter Act)—preserved the quota system, repealed Japanese exclusion, added a quota for Asians, expanded the political grounds for denying entry, and added skilled workers and relatives of citizens and resident aliens as special categories. |
| 1964 | The repeal of Bracero program was followed by an increase in illegal immigration from Mexico. |
| 1965 | Congress abolished national origin quotas and established a series of preferences for relatives of present citizens or resident aliens: un- |

married adult sons and daughters (54,000); spouses and children (70,200); those with important professional skills (27,000); married sons and daughters (27,000); brothers and sisters (64,000); needed unskilled labor (27,000); any unused slots in the order of application. In addition, there are limits on any one country of 20,000, a numerical ceiling for immigrants from the Eastern Hemisphere of 170,000.

1968    Congress sets a quota for immigration from the Western Hemisphere at 120,000 annually.

1980    Refugee Act limits the number of refugees and establishes rules for granting refugees permanent resident status.

1986    The Immigration Reform and Control Act (IRCA) provided for an amnesty to undocumented aliens who could prove they had lived in the United States since before January 1, 1982. It also prohibited employers from hiring undocumented aliens and imposed penalties.

1990    Immigration Act increased number of immigrants allowed in each year; reaffirmed preference to relatives of U.S. citizens and resident aliens; and identified as priority workers professors, researchers, executives, professionals, and their immediate relatives. This act also introduced the Diversity Program or "lottery visas" to correct the consequences of the quota system with regard to underrepresented countries.

1996    Illegal Immigration Reform and Immigrant Responsibility Act (Simpson Act) specified grounds for removing illegal aliens, restricted public benefits for aliens and immigrants, imposed sanctions on employers of illegal aliens, and tightened controls on entering the United States.

## CURRENT GROUNDS FOR EXCLUSION

1. Communicable diseases including HIV (under review by the Clinton administration)
2. Physical or mental disorder dangerous to others
3. Mentally retarded
4. Insane
5. Psychopathic personality
6. Drug addiction or drug trafficking
7. Chronic alcoholic
8. Convicted of crime of moral turpitude (theft, fraud, child abuse, violence, prostitution, polygamy)
9. Convicted of crimes totaling more than five years of prison sentencing
10. Paupers, beggars, or likely to become a public charge
11. Illiterate

12. Espionage, sabotage, or terrorism
13. Member of a Communist or Totalitarian political party
14. Participated in Nazi persecutions
15. Graduates of foreign medical schools planning to practice medicine
16. Previously deported
17. Convicted of immigration fraud
18. Stowaway
19. Draft evader in the United States
20. Violated a child custody order.

## SELECTIONS

The contemporary immigration debate began as a response to the changes that were introduced by the Immigration Act of 1965. Until that time there were immigration quotas that reflected the origin of the present population, mostly northern and western European. It was maintained (e.g., John F. Kennedy) that such quotas discriminated against people from the rest of the world, many of whom were people of color. This way of conceptualizing the problem ("discrimination against people of color") reflected some of the political concerns and movements of the 1960s, issues to which we shall return. The changes in the law (quotas to increase the percentage of people from areas other than northern and western Europe as well as family reunification) raised fundamental questions about both the desirability and nature of immigration to the United States. Should we allow immigration? How much? For what purposes? By whom? The initial debate is reflected in the selections by John F. Kennedy and Marion Moncure Duncan.

A second factor contributing to the debate was the increase in illegal immigration, especially across the California and Texas borders from Mexico. Compounding the problem of its illegality were the facts that illegals (a) did not reflect any rational policy of who should be allowed to come, (b) did not assimilate easily both because of their illegal status and because they often spoke a different language, mainly Spanish, and (c) seemed to exacerbate growing social problems of crime and welfare dependency. Once more this raised questions: Should we allow immigration? How much? At what rate? For what purposes? By whom?

The reassessment sparked by illegal immigration is reflected in the selection from Peter Brimelow. Brimelow's article and subsequent book, *Alien Nation,* are at the center of the current immigration debate and sparked a national discussion. Peter Schuck's article is a critical response to Brimelow's book. The questions raised in this debate were:

1. What is the historic role of immigration in the United States?
2. Is that role still valid?
3. If so, what policies best serve it?
4. How many immigrants (legal and illegal) are there? How does this compare demographically with immigration in the past?

5. What is the economic impact of immigration? the environmental impact? the social and political impact?

The article by Nadia Nedzel examines the actual law, its history, and the consequences of changes introduced, and current legal debate.

The articles by Stephen Moore and George J. Borjas examine the demographic and economic impacts, from different points of view; the article by Leon F. Bouvier addresses the environmental impact.

Up until this point, we have tried to present the historical background and the facts about immigration in as objective a manner as possible. Even the tendentious articles serve merely to set the stage by identifying issues and problems.

What is most important about the debate is that it reflects conflicting views about America, America's problems, and how to address those problems. The rest of the anthology attempts to indicate the major positions on those conflicts.

On the one hand, we have those (e.g., Peter Brimelow, Richard John Neuhaus, Arthur M. Schlesinger Jr.) who identify America with a specific set of values (personal autonomy, individual rights, free market economy, rule of law, limited government) historically originating in Protestant northern and western Europe, especially Great Britain. Consequently, America has absorbed and can continue to absorb immigrants who subscribe to those values or who can assimilate those values without disrupting the conditions that permit those values to continue to flourish among those who are already here. Brimelow insists that it is important to identify the cultural background of potential immigrants, that rates of immigration are important to the absorption process, that speaking the English language is a crucial part of the absorption process (Linda Chavez, Christine H. Rossell), and that changing economic circumstances influence the capacity of those who can absorb the values. The arguments of Chavez and Rossell are challenged by the National Association for Bilingual Education and by the American Civil Liberties Union.

On the other hand, we have those (Peter Hamill) who identify America's problems (racism, bigotry, economic exploitation, crime, welfare dependency, etc.) as the result of a lack of democracy resulting from the domination of America by the descendants of western Europeans. Greater or true democracy will come about when the population is demographically altered, and immigration is one way to achieve that end.

We include a brief interview with Doris Meissner, current head of the Immigration and Naturalization Service, who comments from her perspective on the impact of recent changes in immigration legislation.

## NOTE

1. Oscar Lewis, *Five Families: Mexican Case Studies in the Culture of Poverty* (New York: Random House, 1959). See also Oscar Lewis, *La Vida* (New York: Random House, 1966).

# PART I

# WHY IS THERE A DEBATE ABOUT IMMIGRATION?

# 1.

# Time to Rethink Immigration?

## Peter Brimelow

Dante would have been delighted by the Immigration and Naturalization Service waiting rooms. They would have provided him with a tenth Circle of Hell. There is something distinctly infernal about the spectacle of so many lost souls waiting around so hopelessly, mutually incomprehensible in virtually every language under the sun, each clutching a number from one of those ticket-issuing machines which may or may not be honored by the INS clerks before the end of the Civil Service working day.

The danger of damnation is perhaps low—although a Scottish friend of mine once found himself flung into the deportation holding tank because the INS misunderstood its own rules. And toward the end of my own ten-year trek through the system, I whiled away a lot of time watching confrontations between suspicious INSers and agitated Iranians, apparently hauled in because the Iran hostage crisis had inspired the Carter Administration to ask how many of them were enrolled in U.S. universities. (The INS was unable to provide an answer during the 444 days of the hostage crisis—or, as it turned out, at all.)

Nevertheless, you can still get a pretty good blast of brimstone if you dare suggest that it might be another of those misunderstandings when, having finally reached the head of the line, you are ordered by the clerk to go away and come back another day with a previously unmentioned Form XYZ.

Your fellow huddled masses accept this treatment with a horrible passivity. Perhaps it is imbued in them by eons of arbitrary government in their native lands. Only rarely is there a flurry of protest. At its center, almost invariably, is an indignant American spouse.

Just as New York City's government can't stop muggers but does a great job ticketing young women on Park Avenue for failing to scoop up after their lap-

From the *National Review* (June 22, 1992): 30–46. Copyright © 1992 by Peter Brimelow, reprinted with the permission of the Wylie Agency, Inc.

dogs, current U.S. immigration policy in effect enforces the law only against those who obey it. Annual legal immigration of some 950,000—counting the 140,000 refugees and the 100,000 granted political asylum—is overwhelmed by the 2 to 3 million illegal entries into the country every year, which result in a net annual increase of perhaps 250,000 illegal aliens. (A cautious estimate—again, no one really knows.)

The INS bureaucracy still grinds through its rituals. But meanwhile the U.S. has lost control of its borders As it turned out, I could have avoided my INS decade by the simple expedient of staying here after I graduated from Stanford in 1972 and waiting to be amnestied, along with some 3.2 million other illegal immigrants, by the 1986 Immigration Act.

There is another parallel with New York: Just as when you leave Park Avenue and descend into the subway, on entering the INS waiting rooms you find yourself in an underworld that is almost entirely colored. In 1990, for example, only 8 percent of 1.5 million legal immigrants, including amnestied illegals, came from Europe. (And a good few of those were on-migrants from Asia or the Caribbean.)

Only the incurious could fail to wonder: Where do all these people get off and come to the surface? This is: What impact will they have on America?

## WHERE WILL THEY SURFACE?

American liberals, of course, are determinedly, even devoutly, incurious about this subject. You quickly learn not to raise such matters with them at all.

The silence of American conservatives has a more complex cause. To a significant degree, it's due to sheer ignorance. In the early 1970s, a battle-scarred Goldwater veteran brushed aside my news from the INS waiting rooms. The U.S., he said, was far too big for immigration to have any but the most marginal effect. When later I showed him a news report that the inflow from the former British West Indies had quintupled during the previous decade, he was astonished. (These numbers add up. By 1973, over 220,000 West Indians lived in the New York area alone. And it was just the beginning. The number of Jamaicans immigrating to the U.S. between 1951 and 1980 amounted to more than a tenth of the island's population. By 1990, almost another tenth of Jamaica had arrived in the U.S., the highest proportion from any country in the world.)

Very few people can absorb new realities after the age of 21. And conservative leaders now in their fifties spent their formative years in one of the greatest lulls in the history of American immigration—the result of restrictive quota legislation designed to favor Northern Europeans in the 1920s, followed by the Depression and World War II. Amazingly, only about 500,000 legal immigrants entered the U.S. in the whole of the 1930s. (In those days, there was virtually no illegal immigration.) And only about a million entered in the 1940s—including World War II refugees. By contrast, of course, the U.S. accepted over 1.5 million immigrants, counting only legals, in the single year of 1990 alone.

The Great Immigration Lull was ended dramatically by the 1965 Immigration Act. Typical of so many Great Society reforms, it was passed amid much moralizing rhetoric and promptly had exactly the opposite of its advertised effect.

U.S. immigration policy was not transformed without debate. There was a debate. It just bore no relationship to what subsequently happened. In particular, staunch defenders of the national-origins quota system, like the American Legion, allowed themselves to be persuaded that the new legislation really enacted a sort of worldwide quota, no longer skewed toward Northern Europe— a policy easily caricatured as "racist" in the era of the civil-rights movement— but still restricting overall immigration to the then-current level of around 300,000. (A detailed account of Congress's deluded intent and the dramatic consequences appears in Lawrence Auster's devastating *The Path to National Suicide: An Essay on Immigration and Multiculturalism,* published by AICF.\*)

Today, it is astonishing to read the categorical assurances given by supporters of the 1965 Immigration Act. *"What the bill will not do,"* summarized Immigration Subcommittee chairman Senator Edward Kennedy:

> First, our cities will not be flooded with a million immigrants annually. Under the proposed bill, the present level of immigration remains substantially the same. . . . Secondly, the ethnic mix will not be upset. . . . Contrary to the charges in some quarters, [the bill] will not inundate America with immigrants from any one country or area, or the most populated and deprived nations of Africa and Asia. . . .

Every one of these assurances has proved false. Immigration levels *did* surge upward—they *are* now running at a million a year. Immigrants *do* come predominantly from one sort of area—85 percent of the 11.8 million legal immigrants arriving in the U.S. between 1971 and 1990 were from the Third World, 44 percent from Latin America and the Caribbean, 36 percent from Asia—*and* from one country: 20 percent from Mexico. And about 33,000 Africans arrived in 1990, which looks small only by comparison.

Above all, the American ethnic mix *has* been upset. In 1960, the U.S. population was 88.6 percent white; in 1990, it was only 75.6 percent white—a drop of 13 percentage points in thirty years. (Indeed, the proportion of "European-Americans" is probably a couple of percentage points lower than that, because the Census Bureau counts all Middle Easterners as "white.") The demographer Leon Bouvier has projected that by 2020—that is, easily within the lifetimes of many *National Review* readers—the proportion of whites could fall as low as 61 percent. Among children under 15, minorities could be approaching the point of becoming the majority.

These projections put into context the common claim that—as Professor Julian Simon put it in *The Economic Consequences of Immigration* (1990), a

---

\*The American Immigration Control Foundation, P.O. Box 525, Monterey, Va. 24465; price: $3 for a single copy; $2 apiece for two or more.

book that has been widely accepted by conservatives as their bible on the subject—"contemporary immigration is not high by U.S. historical standards." In fact, immigration is high, in terms of absolute numbers, by comparison with all but the peak decade of 1901–10, when about 8.7 million immigrants arrived, part of the great wave from Southern and Eastern Europe. And counting illegals, the 1981–90 decade probably matched and may have exceeded that total. Furthermore, this latest wave shows no sign of receding. Nor, given the Third Word's demographic structure, is there any particular reason to suppose it will.

Of course, immigration is lower in relative terms than in the first decade of the twentieth century—the total U.S. population at that time was less than a third of today's. However, this was not a proportion that could extend indefinitely. Immigration has never been *relatively* higher than when the second Pilgrim Father came down the gangplank, increasing the Plymouth Colony's population by 100 percent. As it is, the U.S. takes half of all the emigrants in the world.

But it also is crucial to note a point always omitted in pro-immigration polemics: in 1900, the U.S. birthrate was much higher than today. American Anglos' birthrates, for example, are now below replacement levels. So immigrants have proportionately more demographic impact. By the early 1980s, immigration was running at the equivalent of about 16 percent of native births—including births to immigrants—and rising. This is eminently comparable to the 19.9 percent of 1901–10. Hence the steadily shifting ethnic balance.

"The government should dissolve the people and elect another one," quipped the Communist playwright Bertolt Brecht after the East German riots of 1953. For good or ill, the U.S. political elite seems to be acting on his advice.

## IMMIGRATION SLEIGHT OF HAND

Perhaps because the 1965 Immigration Act was slipped through in such a deceptive way, many Americans, and many conservatives, just do not realize that it is directly responsible for this transformation of their country. They tend to assume that a kind of natural phenomenon is at work—that Hispanics, for example increased from 4.5 percent of the U.S. population in 1970 to 9 percent in 1990 because they somehow started sprouting out of the earth like spring corn.

But no natural process is at work. The current wave of immigration, and America's shifting ethnic balance, is simply the result of public policy. A change in public policy opened the Third World floodgates after 1965. A further change in public policy could shut them. Public policy could even restore the *status quo ante* 1965, which would slowly shift the ethnic balance back.

It's often said that Europeans no longer want to emigrate. But in fact the 1965 Act cut back a continuing flow: the number of British immigrants, for example, had been running at around 28,000 a year and was immediately reduced by about half. Along with other Europeans, the British seem simply to have been diverted to the countries that compete with the U.S. for skilled immigrants: above all Australia and Canada.

And all such dogmatic assertions about immigration are dangerous. Witness the sudden influx of more than 100,000 illegal Irish immigrants in the late 1980s—and the wholly unexpected unfreezing of a sea of potential immigrants from Eastern Europe in the early 1990s.

Since 1965, moreover, U.S. public policy has in effect actively discriminated against Europeans. This is because, in another reversal, the 1965 Act placed a higher priority on "family reunification" than on admitting immigrants with skills. And "reunification" meant relatives no matter how remote. So the new immigrants arriving from countries that had not been traditional sources were able to sponsor so many additional immigrants that they crowded out European applicants with skills but no family connections from the "overall quota"— before spilling over into the special category of admissions outside the "overall quota," which turned out to be vastly larger than predicted.

As a result, the post-1965 immigration is not only much bigger than expected: it is also less skilled. And it is becoming even less so—one economist, Professor George J. Borjas, himself a Cuban immigrant, has gone so far as to say, in his 1990 *Friends or Strangers: The Impact of Immigrants on the U.S. Economy,* that "the skill level of successive immigrant waves admitted to the U.S. has declined precipitously in the past two or three decades." For example, in 1986 less than 4 percent of the over 600,000 legal immigrants were admitted on the basis of skills.

Paradoxically, Borjas says, the U.S. attracts disproportionate numbers of unskilled people from Third World countries because the income distribution there is so unequal. The poor have the most to gain. Conversely, it is skilled workers who have the most to gain by leaving egalitarian Western Europe—if they could get in here.

Some more skilled immigrants will be coming to America as a result of legislation in 1990, which—initially as a result of pressure from Irish groups— increased the skill quota by rather less than 100,000. But the price of this, extracted by other, post-1965 ethnic lobbies, was a substantial overall increase in family-reunification immigration.

## COME, ALL YE HUDDLED MASSES

Just as conservatives tend to think immigration is a natural phenomenon, they also assume vaguely that it must have been ratified by some free-market process. But immigration to the U.S. is not determined by economics: it is determined— or at least profoundly distorted—by public policy. Inevitably, there are mismatches between skills supplied and skills demanded. Which helps explain why—as Borjas demonstrated in *Friends or Strangers*—welfare participation and poverty rates are sharply higher among the post-1965 immigrants, with some groups, such as Dominicans and other Hispanics, approaching the levels of American-born blacks.

Borjas's findings, although well understood among specialists, will be surprising to many conservatives. They contrast sharply with some of Julian Simon's more familiar conclusions. The basic reason: Simon's data were old, reflecting earlier, more traditional immigrant groups—another danger in this rapidly changing area.

Such is the grip of the American elite's pro-immigration consensus, however, that book reviewers simply assumed Borjas must be pro-immigration too. They failed to pick up what he described as his "worrisome" evidence that problems were developing with the post-1965 immigrant flow. Thus *Business Week*'s Michael J. Mandel reviewed both Borjas's and Simon's books under the drumbeating heading "DOES AMERICA NEED MORE 'HUDDLED MASSES'? YES." Possibly provoked by such total misreadings, Borjas the following year spelled out his position in the preface to his paperback edition:

> it is almost certain that during the 1990s *new immigrants will make up at least a third of all new labor market entrants*. In view of the available empirical evidence, there is *no economic rationale* to justify this huge increase in the size of the foreign-born population. [Italics added!]

On close examination, at least some pro-immigration enthusiasts turn out to be perfectly well aware that current policy is deeply flawed. Ben J. Wattenberg has popularized the idea that the U.S. can become "The First Universal Nation," as his 1991 book is titled, drawing its population from every corner of the globe. This romantic vision has entranced quite a few conservatives. But they don't seem to have noticed that in that book, Wattenberg actually calls for "designer immigration"—radically reoriented toward skills rather than family reunification, keeping out illegals and ending what he describes as the "odd situation" whereby Europeans are effectively discriminated against. Of course, he hastens to add, this will not cut back on Third World immigrants as such. (Wattenberg tells me that the 1990 Act was merely "a good solid half-step forward" and that he still advocates designer immigration.")

## "A NATION OF IMMIGRANTS"

Everyone has seen a speeded-up film of the cloudscape. What appears to the naked eye to be a panorama of almost immobile grandeur writhes into wild life. Vast patterns of soaring, swooping movement are suddenly discernible. Great towering cumulonimbus formations boil up out of nowhere, dominating the sky in a way that would be terrifying if it were not, in real life, so gradual that we are barely aware that anything is going on.

This is a perfect metaphor for the development of the American nation. America, of course, is exceptional. What is exceptional about it, however, is not the way in which it was created, but the speed.

*"We are a nation of immigrants."* No discussion of U.S. immigration policy gets far without someone making this helpful remark. As an immigrant myself, I

always pause respectfully. You never know. Maybe this is what they're taught to chant in schools nowadays, a sort of multicultural Pledge of Allegiance.

But it secretly amuses me. Do they really think other nations sprouted up out of the ground? ("Autochthonous" is the classical Greek word.) The truth is that *all* nations are nations of immigrants. But the process is usually so slow and historic that people overlook it. They mistake for mountains what are merely clouds.

This is obvious in the case of the British Isles, from which the largest single proportion of Americans are still derived. You can see it in the place-names. Within a few miles of my parents' home in the north of England, the names are Roman (Chester, derived from the Latin for camp), Saxon (anything ending in -*ton,* town, like Oxton), Viking (-*by,* farm, like Irby), and Norman French (Delamere). At times, these successive waves of peoples were clearly living cheek by jowl. Thus among these place-names is Wallesey, Anglo-Saxon for "Island of the Welsh"—Welsh being derived from the word used by low-German speakers for foreigners wherever they met them, from Wallonia to Wallachia. This corner of the English coast continued as home to some of the pre-Roman Celtic stock, not all of whom were driven west into Wales proper as was once supposed.

The English language that America speaks today (or at least spoke until the post-1965 fashion for bilingual education) reflects the fact that the peoples of Britain merged, eventually; their separate contributions can still be traced in it. Every nation in Europe went through the same process. Even the famously homogeneous Japanese show the signs of ethnically distinct waves of prehistoric immigration.

But merging takes time. After the Norman Conquest in 1066, it was nearly three hundred years before the invaders were assimilated to the point where court proceedings in London were again heard in English. And it was nearly nine centuries before there was any further large-scale immigration into the British Isles—the Caribbean and Asian influx after World War II.

Except in America. Here the process of merging has been uniquely rapid. Thus about 7 million Germans have immigrated to the U.S. since the beginning of the nineteenth century. Their influence has been profound—to my British eye it accounts for the odd American habit of getting up in the morning and starting work. About 50 million Americans told the 1980 Census that they were wholly or partly of German descent. But only 1.6 million spoke German in their homes.

## WHAT IS A NATION?

So all nations are made up of immigrants. But what is a nation—the end-product of all this merging? This brings us into a territory where words are weapons, exactly as George Orwell pointed out years ago. "Nation"—as suggested by its Latin root *nascere,* to be born—intrinsically implies a link by blood. A nation is an extended family. The merging process through which all nations pass is not merely cultural, but to a considerable extent biological, through intermarriage.

Liberal commentators, for various reasons, find this deeply distressing. They regularly denounce appeals to common ethnicity as "nativism" or "tribalism." Ironically, when I studied African history in college, my politically correct tutor deprecated any reference to "tribes." These small, primitive, and incoherent groupings should, he said, be dignified as "nations." Which suggests a useful definition: tribalism/nativism is nationalism of which liberals disapprove.

American political debate on this point is hampered by a peculiar difficulty. American editors are convinced that the term "state" will confuse readers unless reserved exclusively for the component parts of the United States—New York, California, etc. So when talking about sovereign political structures, where the British would use "state," the Germans *Staat,* and the French *l'état,* journalists here are compelled to use the word "nation." Thus in the late 1980s it was common to see references to "the nation of Yugoslavia," when Yugoslavia's problem was precisely that it was not a nation at all, but a state that contained several different small but fierce nations—Croats, Serbs, etc. (In my constructive way, I've been trying to introduce, as an alternative to "state," the word "polity"—defined by Webster as "a politically organized unit." But it's quite hopeless. Editors always confuse it with "policy.")

This definitional difficulty explains one of the regular entertainments of U.S. politics: uproar because someone has unguardedly described America as a "Christian nation." Of course, in the sense that the vast majority of Americans are Christians, this is nothing less than the plain truth. It is not in the least incompatible with a secular *state* (polity).

But the difficulty over the N-word has a more serious consequence: it means that American commentators are losing sight of the concept of the "nation-state"—a sovereign structure that is the political expression of a specific ethno-cultural group. Yet the nation-state was one of the crucial inventions of the modem age. Mass literacy, education, and mobility put a premium on the unifying effect of cultural and ethnic homogeneity. None of the great pre-modern multinational empires has survived. (The Brussels bureaucracy may be trying to create another, but it has a long way to go.)

This is why Ben Wattenberg is able to get away with talking about a "Universal Nation." On its face, this is a contradiction in terms. It's possible, as Wattenberg variously implies, that he means the diverse immigrant groups will eventually intermarry, producing what he calls, quoting the English poet John Masefield, a "wondrous race." Or that they will at least be assimilated by American culture, which, while globally dominant, is hardly "universal." But meanwhile there are hard questions. What language is this "universal nation" going to speak? How is it going to avoid ethnic strife? dual loyalties? collapsing like the Tower of Babel? Wattenberg is not asked to reconcile these questions, although he is not unaware of them, because in American political discourse the ideal of an American nation-state is in eclipse.

Ironically, the same weaknesses were apparent in the rather similar concept of "cultural pluralism" invented by Horace M. Kallen at the height of the last great immigration debate, before the Quota Acts of the 1920s. Kallen, like many of today's pro-immigration enthusiasts, reacted emotionally against the calls for

"Americanization" that the 1880-to-1920 immigrant wave provoked. He argued that any unitary American nationality had already been dissipated by immigration (sound familiar?). Instead, he said, the U.S. had become merely a political state (polity) containing a number of different nationalities.

Kallen left the practical implications of this vision "woefully undeveloped" (in the words of the *Harvard Encyclopedia of American Ethnic Groups*). It eventually evolved into a vague approval of tolerance, which was basically how Americans had always treated immigrant groups anyway—an extension, not coincidentally, of how the English built the British nation.

But in one respect, Kallenism is very much alive: he argued that authentic Americanism was what he called "the American Idea." This amounted to an almost religious idealization of "democracy," which again was left undeveloped but which appeared to have as much to do with non-discrimination and equal protection under the law as with elections. Today, a messianic concern for global "democracy" is being suggested to conservatives as an appropriate objective for U.S. foreign policy.

And Kallenism underlies the second helpful remark that someone always makes in any discussion of U.S. immigration policy: *"America isn't a nation like the other nations—it's an idea."*

Once more, this American exceptionalism is really more a matter of degree than of kind. Many other nations have some sort of ideational reinforcement. Quite often it is religious, such as Poland's Roman Catholicism; sometimes cultural, such as France's ineffable Frenchness. And occasionally it is political. Thus—again not coincidentally—the English used to talk about what might be described as the "English Idea": English liberties, their rights as Englishmen, and so on. Americans used to know immediately what this meant. As Jesse Chickering wrote in 1848 of his diverse fellow-Americans: "English laws and institutions, adapted to the circumstances of the country, have been adopted here. . . . The tendency of things is to mold the whole into one people, whose leading characteristics are English, formed on American soil."

What is unusual in the present debate, however, is that Americans are now being urged to abandon the bonds of a common ethnicity and instead to trust entirely to ideology to hold together their state (polity). This is an extraordinary experiment, like suddenly replacing all the blood in a patient's body. History suggests little reason to suppose it will succeed. Christendom and Islam have long ago been sundered by national quarrels. More recently, the much-touted "Soviet Man," the creation of much tougher ideologists using much rougher methods than anything yet seen in the U.S., has turned out to be a Russian, Ukrainian, or Kazakh after all.

Which is why Shakespeare has King Henry V say, before the battle of Agincourt, not "we defenders of international law and the dynastic principle as it applies to my right to inherit the throne of France," but

*We few, we happy few, we band of brothers.*

However, although intellectuals may have decided that America is not a nation but an idea, the news has not reached the American people—especially that significant minority who sternly tell the Census Bureau their ethnicity is "American." (They seem mostly to be of British origin, many generations back.) And it would have been considered absurd throughout most of American history.

John Jay in *The Federalist Papers* wrote that Americans were "one united people, a people descended from the same ancestors, speaking the same language, professing the same religion, attached to the same principles of government, very similar in their manners and customs." Some hundred years later, Theodore Roosevelt in his *Winning of the West* traced the "perfectly continuous history" of the Anglo-Saxons from King Alfred to George Washington. He presented the settling of the lands beyond the Alleghenies as "the crowning and greatest achievement" of "the spread of the English-speaking peoples," which—though personally a liberal on racial matters—he saw in explicit terms: "it is of incalculable importance that America, Australia, and Siberia should pass out of the hands of their red, black, and yellow aboriginal owners, and become the heritage of the dominant world races."

Roosevelt himself was an example of ethnicities merging to produce this new nation. He thanked God—he teased his friend Rudyard Kipling—that there was "not a drop of British blood" in him. But that did not stop him from identifying with Anglo-Saxons or from becoming a passionate advocate of an assimilationist Americanism, which crossed ethnic lines and was ultimately to cross racial lines.

And it is important to note that, at the height of the last great immigration wave, Kallen and his allies totally failed to persuade Americans that they were no longer a nation. Quite the contrary: once convinced that their nationhood was threatened by continued massive immigration, Americans changed the public policies that made it possible. While the national-origins quotas were being legislated, President Calvin Coolidge put it unflinchingly: "America must be kept American."

Everyone knew what he meant.

## "PULLING UP THE LADDER"

Another of those helpful lines exactly describes what Americans did in the 1920s: *"Pulling up the ladder."* But pulling up the ladder may be necessary—if the lifeboat is about to capsize.

And the American lifeboat undeniably did stabilize after the 1920s. It took time. As late as 1963, when Nathan Glazer and Daniel Patrick Moynihan published *Beyond the Melting Pot,* the ethnic groups that had arrived in the 1880-to-1920 wave appeared not to be assimilating into the American mainstream. At best, as Will Herberg argued in Protestant, Catholic, Jew, there was a "triple melting pot" working within the major religious communities—for example, Irish Catholics marrying Italian Catholics; German Jews marrying Russian Jews.

But then, just when the media-academic complex had tooled up an entire industry based on the "unmeltable ethnics," they started to melt. The figures are dramatic. According to Robert C. Christopher in his 1989 *Crashing the Gates: The De-Wasping of America's Power Elite,* half of all Italian-Americans born since World War II married non-Catholics, mainly Protestants; some 40 percent of Jews marrying in the 1980s chose Gentile spouses, a phenomenon rare if not unknown only twenty years earlier.

Christopher, a former *Newsweek* writer and political liberal, naturally saw this development as an emerging cultural synthesis free (at last!) of any nasty ethnic connotations at all. But there is a simpler interpretation: the American nation was just swallowing, and then digesting—Wasping, to adapt Christopher's terminology—an unusually large and spicy immigrant meal.

This pattern of swallowing and digesting has recurred throughout American history. Waves of immigration have been followed by lulls right back into colonial times. After the turmoil of the Revolutionary War, there was a Great Lull remarkably similar to the one earlier this century. For nearly fifty years, there was practically no immigration at all. The U.S. grew rapidly through natural increase. But the make-up of the white population remained about what it had been in the 1790 Census: largely (60 percent) English, heavily (80 percent) British, and overwhelmingly (98 percent) Protestant. This was the nation Alexis de Tocqueville described in *Democracy in America* (1835)—an irony, since his name has now been adopted by Gregory Fossedal's pro-immigration lobby. That Tocqueville's analysis still has relevance is a tribute to that nation's powers of assimilation and cultural transmission.

Thereafter, immigration relative to U.S. population peaked about every fifteen or twenty years: in 1851–54, 1866–73, 1881–83, 1905–07, and 1921–24. In between it plunged, by as much as three-quarters or more. And the ethnic composition continuously changed. Earlier in the century, the largest element was Irish; in the middle, German; by the end, from Southern and Eastern Europe. After 1924, immigration was reduced to a trickle—but that trickle was from Northern and Western Europe. These variations in the magnitude and make-up of immigration were vital to the process of digestion.

And this pattern of variation puts a different perspective on the immigration debate. For example, it is conventional to dismiss all concerns about immigration with the argument that such fears have proved groundless in the past. Of course, this is illogical. Just because a danger has been averted in the past does not mean it cannot happen in the future. Many passengers might have climbed aboard the lifeboat safely; one more may still capsize it.

But in fact these concerns, which have been expressed by the most eminent Americans going right back to colonial times, were perfectly reasonable. They were rendered moot only by changing circumstances. Thus Benjamin Franklin worried about German immigration in 1751: "Why should Pennsylvania, founded by the English, become a Colony of Aliens, who will shortly be so numerous as to Germanize us instead of our Anglifying them . . . ?" Franklin was not proved wrong: instead, German immigration was halted—in the short run, by the Seven Years' War (1756–63); in the longer run, by the post-Revolution Great Lull.

Similarly, the nativist anti-Catholic "Know-Nothing" insurrection, which had seized six state governments and elected 75 congressmen by 1855, was the reaction, harsh but human, of a Protestant nation that had forgotten immigration to its apparently imminent inundation by Irish Catholics fleeing the 1846 potato famine. Subsequently, Know-Nothingism receded, partly because of the Civil War, but also because the supply of Irish Catholics turned out to be finite after all. The Irish made up nearly half of the 1851–54 wave. They were perhaps a fifth or less of the subsequent trough. The public policies that excluded Asian immigration for nearly a hundred years also appear rather different in this historical perspective. The California Legislature's 1876 report on immigration complained that the Chinese "have never adapted themselves to our habits, mode of dress, or our educational system. . . . Impregnable to all the influences of our Anglo-Saxon life, they remain the same stolid Asiatics that have floated on the rivers and slaved in the fields of China for thirty centuries of time." Whatever its dark motive, this is on its face a very specific complaint about the difficulty of assimilating immigrants from a pre-modern society. In the interim, the Orient has modernized. Today, immigrants from the area are often viewed (perhaps naïvely) as the most, well, "Anglo-Saxon," of the current wave.

## ASK A STUPID QUESTION . . .

Historical perspective also discredits another conventional ploy in the immigration debate: *"How can X be against immigration when the nativists wanted to keep his own great-grandfather out?"* This, of course, is like arguing that a passenger already on board the lifeboat should refrain from pointing out that taking on more will cause it to capsize.

But let's assume, for the sake of argument, that X is Irish-American. Disqualifying him from the debate overlooks the long and painful adjustment to America that the Irish, like every immigrant group, had to make. The Irish too came to the U.S. from what was still basically a pre-modern agricultural society. Throughout the nineteenth century, they displayed social pathologies strikingly similar to those of the current black ghetto: disease, violence, family breakdown, drug addiction (alcohol in those days), and, perhaps not surprisingly, virtually no intermarriage.

Slowly, over generations, America changed the Irish—and they changed themselves. Today, in terms of measures like income, education, and political affiliation, Irish-Americans are more or less indistinguishable from the mainstream, with which they have extensively intermarried. (Well . . . alcoholism is a little higher. But so are incomes.) In his book *The Economics and Politics of Race: An International Perspective,* the Hoover Institution economist Thomas Sowell describes this as "historically . . . one of the great social transformations of a people." Irish-Americans have earned the hard way their right to opinions about who and how many their country can absorb.

The Irish changed themselves with a great deal of encouragement from a notably stern clergy. But the Roman Catholic Church itself made an adjustment to America. Indeed, the word "Americanization" was invented in the 1850s by a Vermont Yankee convert to Catholicism, Orestes A. Brownson, who argued in his *Brownson's Quarterly Review* that the nativists had a point: the Irish should assimilate to the American nation that had already been formed; the Church should not identify itself with Old World autocracy—as Pius IX, after the 1848 Revolutions in Europe, was inclined to do. Brownson provoked a ferocious controversy. But, today, his view can be seen to have prevailed.

In politics as elsewhere, if you ask a stupid question, you get a stupid answer—or at any rate a terse answer. And asking people if they want their communities to be overwhelmed by weird aliens with dubious habits is a stupid question. The answer is inevitable. Until now in America, chance circumstances and changes in public policy have always combined to change this question before the inevitable answer became too embarrassing. But the greater the number of immigrants, and the greater their difference from the American mainstream, the louder and ruder the answer will be.

The political elite may choose not to hear. Others, however, will.

## CLOSING THE FLOODGATES

At the moment, the political elite shows every sign of choosing not to hear. The immigration floodgates were opened by accident in 1965. Opinion polls show most Americans want them shut—for example, in a recent poll by FAIR,* 84 percent wanted Congress to take a more active role in decreasing immigration and stopping the entry of illegal aliens. But the elite's reaction is unexpectedly odd: it stands around idly, alternately ignoring the situation, denouncing anyone uncouth enough to mention it, and, most frequently, indulging in romantic rationalizations *("The more the merrier!" "Diversity is strength!")*.

This sort of after-the-fact rationalization infests U.S. immigration history. Thus the much-loved lines on the base of the Statue of Liberty—

> . . . Give me your tired, your poor,
> Your huddled masses yearning to breathe free,
> The wretched refuse of your teeming shore . . .

—are not part of the Declaration of Independence or some other pronouncement of the Founding Fathers. Instead, they are the reaction of a young Zionist, Emma Lazarus, to the Russian pogroms following the assassination of Czar Alexander II in 1881. They were added years after the dedication of the statue, which was a gift from France to commemorate the U.S centennial and originally supposed to symbolize, not "The Mother of Immigrants" in Miss Lazarus's phrase, but "Liberty Lighting the World"—"liberty *under law*," adds FAIR Chairman Dan Stein, thinking grimly of recent amnesties for illegals.

And they aren't even true. American immigration has typically been quite selective, if only because the cost of passage was (until recently) an effective filter. ". . . even throughout the early history of the U.S.," admits Julian Simon, "immigrants did not arrive with less education than natives had—contrary to popular belief and contrary to the famous poem by Emma Lazarus. . . ." Early English settlers included Royalist gentry who went to Virginia, like George Washington's ancestors, and Puritan gentry who went to New England, as Oliver Cromwell and his family once planned to do. And, whatever Yankees may have thought, the Irish immigrants of the 1850s were not the bottom of the barrel. Three-quarters of them were literate; their fares were commonly paid by established extended families.

It was thirty years from the founding of the Immigration Restriction League in 1894 to the passing of the restrictions in the 1920s. FAIR was founded in 1979 and the AICF in 1983. So there are some years to go.

Still, there can be little doubt that, this time around, the political elite has been notably more inhibited about responding to the issue. One important reason has been pointed out by Katherine Betts in *Ideology and Immigration,* her study of the parallel Australian situation. Using polling data, Professor Betts showed that while non-traditional immigration was viewed with increasing hostility among ordinary Australians, the university-educated were inclined to favor it. Favoring immigration, she concluded, was "part of a cluster of values defining social status for Australian intellectuals."

The "New Class," as Irving Kristol has called the confluence of educators, bureaucrats, and media professionals, has everywhere emerged as the key sociological fact of late-twentieth-century political economies. Dogmatic attitudes on immigration and race have become a badge of New Class superiority to ordinary people—and a route to power, since the social stresses resulting from non-traditional immigration are a splendid excuse for further government programs.

Deference to these elite values explains to a significant degree the silence of American conservatives about the current immigration wave—in such striking contrast to the aggressive Americanism of Republicans from Henry Cabot Lodge to Theodore Roosevelt last time around.

In his first volume of his autobiography, *Making It,* Norman Podhoretz describes the "brutal bargain" by which he says the children of Eastern European Jews were accepted into WASP society at the price of repressing their ethnic *mores.* Similarly, American conservatives have reached what might be called a "bland bargain" with their country's ruling establishment.

Conservatives are now somewhat more likely to be allowed into public debate than in the dark years of the 1950s. But they still must not say anything that impinges upon the truly sacred liberal taboos—above all anything that might be remotely connected with ethnicity or race. And immigration, of course, is inextricably so connected.

Slaves naturally try to curry favor with their masters. Some conservatives, fixated on the issue of economic growth, have apparently calculated that, by emphasizing the (assumed) need for more immigration, they can establish their non-racist credentials and even advance their limited agenda with the liberal elite.

Slaves can even grow to love their chains. Some conservatives have internalized the prohibitions under which they must operate. An example, alas, seems to be Paul Gigot, the otherwise estimable Washington columnist of the *Wall Street Journal* editorial page. Writing about the question, which became an issue early in the 1992 presidential election cycle, of whether a million Englishmen or a million Zulus would assimilate more easily into Virginia, Gigot expressed good inside-the-Beltway distaste. Then he added an economic-growth twist: *"The Zulus . . . would probably work harder than the English."*

This comment reveals an utter innocence about the reality of ethnic and cultural differences, let alone about little things like tradition and history—in short, the greater part of the conservative vision. Even in its own purblind terms, it is totally false. All the empirical evidence is that immigrants from developed countries assimilate better than those from underdeveloped countries. It is developed countries that teach the skills required for success in the United States. As Borjas puts it ". . . the per capita GNP in the United Kingdom is more than six times greater than [that of] the Dominican Republic. It is not surprising that immigrant households originating in the Dominican Republic are about five times more likely to be on welfare than those in the United Kingdom."

But it should not be necessary to explain that the legacy of Shaka and Cetewayo—overthrown just over a century ago—is not that of Alfred the Great, let alone Elizabeth II or any civilized society.

Let's spell it out with an anecdote. Recently, the South African police were perplexed by an epidemic of murders on the black commuter trains between the townships and Johannesburg. Naturally, Nelson Mandela's African National Congress blamed the government. But the victims were from all factions. Now it has emerged that the black operators of the semi-legal private cab services competing with the railroad had paid gangs of those hard-working Zulus to influence consumer preferences by going on board and throwing passengers from the moving trains.

## ASKING THE RIGHT QUESTIONS

Supposing America's political elite suddenly decided to notice immigration. What questions should they consider?

### Is Immigration Really Necessary to the Economy?

Audiences always burst out laughing at one apparently gagless scene in the hit movie *Back to the Future*: the time-transported hero drives up to a gas station in the 1950s, and an army of uniformed attendants leaps forth to pump the gas, clean his windshield, fill his tires, polish his hubcaps, offer him maps, and so on.

---

*The Federation for American Immigration Reform, Suite 400, 1666 Connecticut Avenue, N.W., Washington, D.C. 20009.

The joke was in the shock of self-recognition. It was only yesterday—and yet completely forgotten, so accustomed is everyone now to self-service.

*"We need immigrants to meet the looming labor shortage/do the dirty work Americans won't do."* This further item from the pro-immigration catechism seems to be particularly resonant for the American conservative movement, deeply influenced by libertarian ideas and open, somewhat, to the concerns of business.

But it has always seemed incongruous, given persistent high levels of unemployment among some American-born groups. Since these groups obviously eat, it would appear that public policy is subsidizing their choosiness about work, thus artificially stimulating the demand for immigrants.

And if there is a looming labor shortage (hotly disputed), it could presumably be countered by natalist policies—encouraging Americans to step up their below-replacement birthrate. Even the current high immigration inflow is exceeded by the 1.6 million abortions in the U.S. each year.

For example, the federal income-tax code could be adjusted to increase the child allowance. In 1950, this provision exempted the equivalent (in 1992 dollars) of $7,800 for each child; now, after inflation, it exempts only $2,100. Or the "marriage penalty"—by which a couple pay more in taxes if they marry than if they live together out of wedlock—could be abolished. Or the public-school cartel could be broken up, reducing the crushing costs of educating a child.

But *Back to the Future* makes a more fundamental point: labor is not an absolute. Free economies are infinitely ingenious at finding methods, and machinery, to economize on labor or any other scarce resource.

The implicit assumption behind the economic argument for immigration appears to be something like this:

$$Labor \times Capital = Economic\ Growth$$

So, for any given capital stock, any increase in labor (putting aside the question of its quality) will result in at least some increase in output.

This assumption is just wrong. Typically, technical studies that attempt to account for economic growth find that increases in labor and capital account for at most half and often much less of increases in output. Simon Kuznets's survey of the growth of the West over the last two centuries concluded that increases in labor and physical capital together were responsible for less than 10 percent of the greatest output surge in human history. The rest seems to be attributable to changes in organization—to technological progress and ideas. Or:

$$Economic\ Growth = Labor \times Capital \times (???)$$

And (???) is dominant.

*Back to the Future* illustrates this process in action. On the face of it, gas stations have simply substituted capital (the self-service pumps) for labor (gas jockeys). But actually what has happened is more complex: the cost of making the pumps, and of designing the computer system behind them, is far exceeded by the savings on labor, which extend indefinitely into the future. It is reorganization that has resulted in a permanent increase in productivity.

From an economist's standpoint, the factors of production are not absolutes, but a fluid series of conditional interacting relationships. This insight won Julian Simon one of the famous debating victories of our age. In 1980, he bet the well-known liberal doomster Paul Ehrlich that several commodities Ehrlich claimed were running out would in fact be lower in price in 1990, the economy having adjusted in the meantime. They were, and Ehrlich had to pay up. Paradoxically, however, when it comes to immigration, Simon seems to revert to a classic non-economic view: Labor is good, more labor is better.

The economic view of labor has influenced the current immigration debate only in one direction: it is triumphantly produced by the pro-immigration side to refute any unwary critic of immigration who assumes that native-born workers must inevitably be displaced. They aren't, necessarily, in aggregate, because the economy adjusts; and because the increase in the factors of production tends to create new opportunities. "Immigrants not only take jobs," writes Julian Simon, "they make jobs."

Maybe. But missing from the current immigration debate is the fact that this effect operates in the other direction too. On the margin, the economy is probably just as capable of getting along with less labor. Within quite wide boundaries, *any* change in the labor supply can be swamped by the much larger influence of innovation and technological change.

The historical importance of immigration to the U. S. can be exaggerated. Surprising as it may seem, demographers agree that the American population would be about half its present size—that is, much bigger than Germany's and about as big as Japan's—even if there had been no immigration after 1790. Even more significantly, the *Harvard Encyclopedia of American Ethnic Groups* estimates that immigration did not increase U.S. per-capita output at all. Indeed, both France and Germany outstripped the US. in growth of per-capita output in the hundred years after the mid nineteenth century.

Absolute size can be useful while seizing a continent or fighting wars. But in the end it is output per capita that determines living standards. And both proportionately and absolutely, in an increasingly technical age, what will count is not the quantity of people but their quality—and the quality of their ideas.

The (???) factor is the explanation for the great counter-factual episode hanging like the sword of Damocles over contemporary pro-immigration polemics: the success of Japan since World War II. Despite its population of only 125 million and virtually no immigration at all, Japan has grown into the second-largest economy on earth. The Japanese seem to have been able to substitute capital for labor, in the shape of factory robots. And they have apparently steadily reconfigured their economy, concentrating on high value-added production, exporting low-skilled jobs to factories in nearby cheap-labor countries rather than importing the low-skilled labor to Japan.

It is highly significant of the false nature of the American immigration debate that, despite all the public hysteria about Japan, no attempt is ever made to look for lessons in its immigration policy. Incredibly, although his book is called *The Economic Consequences of Immigration,* Julian Simon simply ignores the subject altogether. Asked about it by *Forbes* magazine's Jim Cook, he in effect struck out: "How Japan gets along I don't know. But we may have to recognize that some countries are *sui generis.*"

However, Simon's view of the impact of immigrants does include important qualifications, which his enthusiastic acolytes often miss. Simon believes that native-born workers are not *necessarily* displaced *in aggregate.* In his book, he frankly and repeatedly acknowledges that "Any labor-force change causes some groups to suffer some harm in the short run. . . . It is true that some particular groups may be injured by a particular group of immigrants. . . ." (This works in reverse. Agribusiness lobbies for cheap immigrant labor rather than mechanize itself, regardless of the overall cost to the economy. Ironically, agribusiness is itself often subsidized—for example, by federal water projects.)

As it happens, the U.S. contains one particular group that is clearly vulnerable to competition from immigration: blacks. This question has attracted attention for years. Immigration from Europe after the Civil War is sometimes said to have fatally retarded the economic integration of the freed slaves. Conversely, no less an authority than Simon Kuznets felt that the Great Immigration Lull after the 1920s enabled Southern blacks to begin their historic migration to the cities and the economic opportunities of the North.

Blacks themselves take a dim view of immigration, according to opinion polls. In the FAIR poll cited above, 83 percent of blacks thought Congress should curb immigration. But George Borjas found that blacks living in areas of immigrant concentration did not appear to have suffered significantly reduced incomes compared with those elsewhere. The reason, he theorizes, is that during the years in question—the 1970s—the effect of immigration was overwhelmed by the effects of baby-boomers and women entering the labor market. Now, of course, these factors no longer apply. Additionally, studies of high-immigrant areas may fail to capture a tendency for native-born workers to relocate because of the increased competition. Across the entire country, the wages of native high-school dropouts fell by 10 percent in the 1980s relative to the wages of more educated workers. Borjas calculates that about a third of that decline is attributable to immigration.

Borjas, moreover, was perturbed by the tendency of low-skilled recent immigrants, not necessarily to displace American blacks, but to join them in swelling the ranks of the underclass: "Few issues facing the U.S. are as important, and as difficult to resolve, as the persistent problem of poverty in our midst. . . . The empirical evidence presented here suggests that immigration is exacerbating this problem."

Since the Great Society, a significant part of the black community has succumbed to social pathology. There is at least a possibility that this is related to the simultaneous opening of the immigration floodgates. In which case, it is perhaps to current policy, and not to critics of immigration, that the over-used epithet "racist" might best be applied.

Another important Simon qualification, unnoticed by his acolytes, is his concept of "negative human-capital externalities." Most recent immigrants have lower skill levels than natives, he notes. If enough of them were to arrive, they could overwhelm and render less effective the higher skills of the natives. "In other words, if there is a huge flood of immigrants from Backwardia to Richonia, Richonia will become economically similar to Backwardia, with loss to Richonians and little gain to immigrants from Backwardia. . . . So even if *some* immigrants are beneficial, a *very large* number coming from poorer countries . . . may have the opposite effect."

This is a crucial theoretical concession. Coupled with the fact that the numbers and type of potential immigrants are unknown, it is the reason Simon quietly declines to follow the logic of his other arguments and endorse completely open borders (as, for example, the *Wall Street Journal* editorial page has done). Of course, he insists that immigration levels could be *much* higher than at present. But Richonians in California, Florida, and New York City might not agree.

*"You have to accept the free movement of people if you believe in free trade/free markets."* You do? It's a more radical proposition than appears at first sight. Third World populations are very large and their wage levels very low—Mexican wages are a tenth of those north of the border, and Mexico is relatively advanced. So calculations of the market-clearing wage in a U.S. with open borders necessarily imply that it must be some fraction of its present level. This arrangement might optimize global economic utility. But it can hardly improve American social harmony.

However, a calculation of this sort requires impossible assumptions. The fact is that a belief in free markets does not commit you to free immigration. The two are quite distinct. Even Julian Simon, although he favors immigration, says explicitly that immigration's benefits are not from "trade-like effects":

> Contrary to intuition, the theory of the international trade of goods is quite inapplicable to the international movement of persons. There is no immediate large consumer benefit from the movement of persons that is analogous to the international exchange of goods, because the structure of supply is not changed in the two countries as a whole, as it is when trade induces specialization in production . . . the shifts due to international migration benefit only the migrant.

On a practical level, free trade actually tends to operate as a substitute for immigration. Hence the Japanese have factories in the Philippines rather than Filipinos in Japan. And Victorian Britain, with its grand strategy of "splendid isolation" from the quarrels of Europe, combined total free trade with almost no immigration, a policy that satisfied Liberal "Little Englanders" and Tory Imperialists alike.

In theory, free trade with Mexico should help reduce the current immigrant flood by providing work south of the border. In practice, however, "free-trade negotiations" (a paradox: what's to negotiate?) often get captured by political elites seeking to favor client constituencies. Rumors that the current talks with Mexico might lead, absurdly, to an *increase* in immigration suggest this insidious process is well under way.

A commitment to free trade and free markets does not mean that you would sell your mother if the price was right. The free market necessarily exists within a social framework. And it can function only if the institutions in that framework are appropriate. For example, a defined system of private property is now widely agreed to be one essential precondition. Economists have a word for these preconditions: the "metamarket." Some degree of ethnic and cultural coherence may be among them. Thus immigration may be a metamarket issue.

At the very least, a diverse population increases what in economics-speak are called "transaction costs." Dealing with people whom you don't know and therefore can't trust requires expensive precautions. I suspect this is one factor behind the legalism infesting business practices in the U.S., as compared to Britain. Beyond this, capitalism generates inequality and therefore envy. And such emotions can be much more intense across ethnic and racial lines—witness the fate of the Korean storekeepers in Los Angeles.

This is not an unprecedented insight. Friedrich von Hayek, the first classical liberal to win the Nobel Prize for economics, used to advance a sort of sociobiological argument for the apparently immortal appeal of socialism. Cities and civilization have come very late in human history, he pointed out. Almost all mankind's experience has been in small hunter-gatherer bands. Face-to-face relationships are still much more comprehensible to us than impersonal ones. Thus an increase in rent is blamed on the greed and obnoxiousness of the individual landlord, and provokes an irresistible urge to bash him with rent controls, despite all the evidence that this leads merely to shortages and inequity. And, to extend Hayek's argument, it is obviously easier to demonize a landlord if his features are visibly alien.

Another classical liberal Nobel Laureate, Milton Friedman, has speculated that the culture of the English-speaking world itself may be, from an economic standpoint, *sui generis* . . . in Simon's phrase. I interviewed him for *Forbes* magazine in 1988:

> FRIEDMAN: . . . The history of the world is the history of tyranny and misery and stagnation. Periods of growth are exceptional, very exceptional.
>
> BRIMELOW: You've mentioned what you see as the institutional prerequisites for capitalism. Do you think there might be cultural prerequisites too?
>
> FRIEDMAN: Oh, yes. For example, truthfulness. The success of Lebanon as a commercial entrepot was to a significant degree because the merchants' word could be trusted. It cut down transaction costs.
>
> It's a curious fact that capitalism developed and has really come to fruition in the English-speaking world. It hasn't really made the same progress even in Europe—certainly not in France, for instance. I don't know why this is so, but the fact has to be admitted.

Eschewing these more subtle considerations, George Borjas focuses on the quantifiable. His conclusion is stark. "The economic arguments for immigration simply aren't decisive," he told me recently. "You have to make a political case—for example, does the U.S. have to take Mexican immigrants to provide a safety valve and keep Mexico stable?"

Put it another way: for the U.S., immigration is not an economic necessity. It is a luxury. Like all luxuries, it can help—or it can hurt.

## Is Immigration Really Beneficial to Society?

Forty-four years ago, Richard Weaver published a book the title of which, at least, convinced the conservative movement: *Ideas Have Consequences*. It is now time to recognize a further truth: *Immigration Has Consequences*.

The crudest consequences relate to political power. Because many libertarians and economic-growth conservatives are so reluctant to admit this logical possibility, it is worth emphasizing that there are plenty of examples of immigrants and their descendants threatening the political balance of a state (polity), from the *Uitlanders* in the nineteenth-century Boer Republics to the Indian politicians recently elected to govern Fiji and promptly deposed by the ethnically Fijian army. And how about this chilling comment from the *Harvard Encyclopedia*?

> In obtaining land grants in Texas, Anglo immigrants agreed to become Mexican citizens, obey Mexican laws, accept the official Catholic faith, learn Spanish, and take other steps to become fully assimilated as law-abiding citizens. However, over the years, it became clear that these settlers, now Anglo-Mexicans, were not becoming integrated into the nation and that Anglo immigration had become a problem. . . . The strains and disagreements ultimately led to the Texas Revolution in 1835.

Er, quite.

These political consequences need not threaten the integrity of the state (polity)—just its foreign policy. Thus domestic ethnic-group pressure clearly plays a role in Washington's essentially contradictory attitudes to the white settler communities of southern Africa and the Middle East.

But probably the most important consequences are cultural. "The most obvious fact about the history of racial and ethnic groups," writes Thomas Sowell in *The Economics and Politics of Race*, "is how different they have been—and still are." Sowell's work, carried on in *Ethnic America: A History*, conclusively demonstrates that cultural patterns are pervasive, powerful, and remarkably persistent, even after generations of living under common institutions, as in the United States. (Similarly, David Hackett Fischer's monumental *Albion's Seed* recently traced America's dominant folk-ways all the way back to four distinct waves of colonial immigration from different regions of Britain.)

*"But aren't these consequences good?"* Naturally, there isn't anything in the pro-immigration script about cultural consequences. However, this is the usual reaction if you insist on raising the point. It's embarrassing, of course. In the current climate, it is impossible to discuss the failings of any ethnic group.

But look at it this way: Thomas Sowell's work shows that cultural traits, such as attitudes to work and education, are intrinsically related to economic success. Germans, Japanese, and Jews are successful wherever they are in the world. Conversely, the work of George Borjas and others shows that national origin, a proxy for culture, is an excellent predictor of economic failure, as measured by propensity to go on welfare. In a recent paper, Borjas has demonstrated that disparities among the 1880-to-1920 immigrant groups have persisted for as much as four generations. Thus there can be absolutely no question that the cultural characteristics of current immigrant groups will have consequences for the U. S.—in this case, economic consequences—far into the future.

The same argument applies to crime. Random street crime, the great scandal of American cities since the 1960s, is clearly related to impulsiveness and present-orientation, a key cultural variable. More significant, however, is organized crime. This has typically been ethnically based, partly because it reduces the criminals' transaction costs and because such groups are difficult to penetrate.

In recent years the Mafia or *Cosa Nostra* has been in decline, not least because of the acculturation of Italian-Americans. But this is "dirty work" that some of the post-1965 immigrant groups are positively anxious to do—more violently, particularly in the burgeoning drug business, than the Mafia ever was. There are several such new "mafias," staffed by Russian Jews, Hong Kong Chinese, Colombians, and even less well-known communities like the Chaldeans—Iraqi Christians whose convenience stores in the Detroit ghetto are centers of criminal activity.

Today such news would be judged unfit to print regardless of its accuracy. Researchers find that official figures on immigrant and ethnic crime patterns are rarely collected. That certain ethnic cultures are more crime-prone than others, however, must be considered a real possibility.

Curiously, Congress appears to have shaken off its general paralysis to recognize that immigration can have cultural consequences—for Pacific Islanders. Five U.S. territories, American Samoa, Micronesia, the Marshall Islands, the Northern Marianas, and Palau, have been given control over immigration to protect their ethnic majorities. In American Samoa and the Northern Marianas, U.S. citizens cannot even own land unless they are Samoan, Chamorro, or Carolinian.

This double standard has incensed an extremely erudite and energetic professional writer in Rye, New York, Joseph E. Fallon. Fallon argues that controlling immigration is simply a question of American self-determination. And he is attempting to organize a class-action law suit challenging current policy on the grounds of the 1948 Genocide Convention, which banned "deliberately inflicting upon a [national] group conditions of life calculated to bring about its physical destruction in whole or in part."

Which, after all, is no crazier than much liberal litigation.

## Is Immigration Really Good for (Ahem) the Republicans?

The fate of the Republican Party may not be of concern to the political elite as a whole. But it should worry those aspiring members of the elite who also consider themselves conservatives.

Ethnicity is destiny in American politics. This point was made definitively in Kevin Phillips's brilliant *The Emerging Republican Majority* (1968), which demonstrated that ethnic settlement patterns had an amazingly persistent influence on voting patterns. Phillips predicted on the basis of demography that the Republicans would replace the Democrats as the majority party. And he was undeniably right in the presidential contest, even if timid and unimaginative leadership has squandered the opportunity on the congressional level.

As a glance around any of their meetings will tell you, the Republicans are the party of the American majority; the Democrats are the party of the American minorities. On its WASP foundation, the Republican Party has been able to add the children of each immigrant wave as they assimilate. This was the unmistakable subtext of the 1988 presidential election. With a Greek-American nominee, and implicitly anti-WASP attacks on George Bush's "preppie-ness," the Democrats hoped to hold the 1880-to-1920 immigrant wave. But they failed, just as nominating John F. Kennedy in 1960 did not prevent the continued defection of Irish-Americans.

The post-1965 immigrants, however, are overwhelmingly visible minorities. These are precisely the groups that the Republican Party has had the most difficulty recruiting. And, Jack Kemp please note, this is not necessarily a question of the Republicans' making nice, or nicer, to minorities. It may reflect the more divergent minorities' different values, and their more radical feeling of alienation from white American society. Current immigration policy is inexorably reinforcing Jesse Jackson's Rainbow Coalition.

The strained sound you hear is the conservative leadership whistling as they pass by the rainbow. Prohibited by the Bland Bargain from discussing the problem, they have indulged in a frenzy of wishful thinking. *"We get quite a good vote from some Hispanic groups."* Well, Hispanics are not quite as Democratic as blacks—that's a statistical impossibility—but the Republicans still face an uphill struggle. Even the much-lauded Cuban vote has actually been quite split, electing the likes of Claude Pepper and Dante Fascell to Congress. And Republican success with Hispanics, as with other minorities, is often at the expense of conservative principles. *"West Indians are different."* Some West Indians do appear to have been more economically successful than American blacks, although it must be said that nowadays part of their enterprise goes into drug "posses" and car-theft rings. However, the skill level of the post-1965 wave of West Indian immigrants has deteriorated sharply. Caribbean immigrants are now the most prone of all to welfare dependency. And anyway, the political consequences were always illusory. Shirley Chisholm and Stokely Carmichael are both of West Indian descent. *"The Asians are small-business types, education-minded, family-oriented—they're natural Republicans."* So were the Jews, and look how they vote—still overwhelmingly and outspokenly Democratic despite the best efforts of a brilliant generation of conservative Jewish intellectuals. And Hawaii, where Asians predominate, is a Democratic stronghold. The truth is that no one really knows how the Asians will vote. But since 1965 they have become a minority twice as large as the Jews, and potentially at least as influential.

## Is Immigration Really Good for the Environment?

American liberalism has survived the loss of its traditional issue, economic management, by improvising new ones. And environmentalism is one of the most important, both because it particularly appeals to the vocal upper middle class and because it appears to necessitate an interventionist government. Yet the single biggest problem for the environment is the fact that the U.S. population, quite unusually in the developed world, is still growing quickly. Immigration is currently an unusually large factor in U.S. population growth.

Like the impact of immigration on native workers, the relationship between population and pollution is subtler than it looks. A primitive band of slash-and-burn agriculturalists can cause more devastation than a much larger community of modern ex-urbanites with sealed sewage systems and manicured horse farms.

But only within limits. Something has clearly got to give if the population of California grows from 20 million in 1970 to 60 million by 2020, which is Leon Bouvier's upper-limit projection. (His lower-limit projection: a mere 44 million. Phooey!) The fragile desert ecologies of the Southwest may not be utterly destroyed. But they must be transformed. California will cease to be the Golden State and become the Golden Subdivision.

This prospect is presumably anathema to true environmentalists, who value wilderness in itself. But although a few were active in founding FAIR, most of the professional environmentalist community in Washington avoid the issue. Which is a measure of the extent to which they have been co-opted by the liberal establishment—just like the civil-rights lobby, which never voices the anti-immigration sentiments widespread among the black masses.

No reason, however, why conservatives should not use the immigration issue to wrong-foot them all.

## IS THE U.S. STILL CULTURALLY CAPABLE OF ABSORBING IMMIGRANTS?

Let's be clear about this: The American experience with immigration has been a triumphant success. It has so far transcended anything seen in Europe as to make the application of European lessons an exercise to be performed with care.

But in the late twentieth century, the economic and political culture of the U.S. has changed significantly—from classical liberalism to an interventionist welfare statism. In the previous two hundred years of U.S. history, a number of tried-and-true, but undeniably tough, techniques of assimilation had been perfected. Today, they have been substantially abandoned. Earlier waves of immigrants were basically free to succeed or fail. And many failed: as much as a third of the 1880-to-1920 immigrants returned to their native lands. But with the current wave, public policy interposes itself, with the usual debatable results.

*"You can't blame the immigrants for our bad policies."* Of course you can't.

But if there's a shower when you've got pneumonia, you don't blame the rain. You just stay indoors.

Some of public subsidies to immigrants are direct, like welfare. Others are indirect, such as the wholly new idea that immigrant children should be taught in their own language, thus transferring part of the costs of immigration from the immigrant to the American taxpayer. New York's public-school system now offers courses in more than a hundred languages—and is hunting for teachers of Albanian, who will probably themselves be immigrants.

Pro-immigration advocates are fighting furiously to defend the proposition that subsidies to immigrants are not a net cost to native-born Americans because of the taxes immigrants pay. But they are clearly losing.

George Borjas's most recent estimate is that immigrants' cash welfare benefits alone cost about $1 billion more than is paid in taxes each year. (Tellingly, immigrants prone to welfare dependency seem to get more addicted as they assimilate.) And he points out that there is no guarantee that any increase in total economic output from immigration will compensate those specific Americans paying taxes in high-immigrant areas.

Whatever the academic argument, Wall Street in its unideological, money-grubbing way is already pulling back its snout. As the investment firm Sanford C. Bernstein commented tersely in downgrading California's bond rating last year: "The primary reasons for the State's credit decline are above-average population growth and shifting demographics . . . the degree of public assistance required by two of the fastest growing groups, Latinos and political/ethnic refugees, is substantially higher than that of the general population." Governor Pete Wilson has been trying to control welfare and get more remedial federal aid. But he has only himself to blame. As a U.S. senator, he worked hard for the 1986 amnesty for illegal immigrants favored by agricultural interests.

Ultimately, however, any overall break-even calculation is irrelevant. The nature of averages dictates that many immigrants must get more than they give. And any public subsidies must affect whatever demand/supply balance exists for immigrants. A year for one student in the New York City public-school system, for example, involves an average taxpayer expenditure greater than the per-capita national income of Haiti. National health care, if enacted, could be an even greater magnet.

And it's not just the American economic culture that has changed. So has the political culture. Ethnically fueled "multiculturalism" taught in the public schools, as described by Lawrence Auster and by the eminently establishmentarian Arthur Schlesinger in his best-seller *The Disuniting of America,* raises the question of whether there is still an "American Idea"—and if so, what is it?

Actually, the outlines of what might be described as the new American Anti-Idea are already appallingly clear. It's a sort of neosocialism, derived from what Thomas Sowell calls "the Civil Rights Vision" and amounting to a sort of racial spoils system. Government power is used not to achieve economic efficiency, which traditional socialism can no longer promise, but ethnic equity—most importantly, the extirpation of "discrimination."

That's private discrimination, of course. Government-sponsored discrimination is not merely acceptable but mandatory, in the form of "affirmative action" quotas. "Quotas were originally supposed to be remedial," says Professor Frederick R. Lynch of Claremont College, author of *Invisible Victims: White Males and the Crisis of Affirmative Action.* "Now they are being justified by affirmative-action professionals as a way of 'managing diversity.' " That "diversity," needless to say, is being substantially introduced into the U.S. by current immigration policy.

Indeed, absurd as it may appear, all brand-new immigrants from the right "protected class"—black, Hispanic, Asian—count toward government quota requirements that were allegedly imposed to help native-born Americans. Hence a number of the African Ph.D.s teaching at American colleges. The 1986 Immigration Act prohibited discrimination against legalized "undocumented" aliens and set up an office in the Justice Department to enforce this new law.

Symptomatic of the American Anti-Idea is the emergence of a strange anti-nation inside the US.—the so-called Hispanics. The various groups of Spanish-speaking immigrants are now much less encouraged to assimilate to American culture. Instead, as a result of ethnic lobbying in Washington, they are treated by U.S. government agencies as a homogeneous "protected class," even though many of them have little in common with one another. (Indeed, some are Indian-language speakers from Latin America.) And they have been supplied with "leaders" financed to a significant extent by the Ford Foundation.

In effect, Spanish-speakers are still being encouraged to assimilate. But not to America.

Many current public policies have an unmistakable tendency to deconstruct the American nation. Apart from official bilingualism and multiculturalism, these policies include: multilingual ballots; defining citizenship so as to include all children born here—even the children of illegals; the abandonment of English as a prerequisite for citizenship; the erosion of citizenship as the sole qualification for voting; the extension of welfare and education benefits as a right to illegals and their children; congressional and state legislative apportionment based on legal and illegal populations.

Finally, there is a further ominous change in American political culture since 1910: a peculiar element of emotionalism that has entered intellectual life.

Julian Simon in *The Economic Consequences of Immigration* makes an admirable effort to be honest about his underlying motives: "Perhaps a few words about my tastes are appropriate. I delight in looking at the variety of faces I see on the subway when I visit New York . . . [telling innocent visiting schoolgirls] about the Irish in New York—and about other groups too—I get tears in my eyes, as again I do now in recalling the incident." This is obviously somewhat different from my own reaction to the New York subway, although presumably we are both also studying those faces to see if their owners plan to mug us.

But in debate Professor Simon is notably quick to attribute unattractive motives if anyone dares raise America's shifting ethnic balance—although logically the onus should be on him to show why the balance should be shifted, and what he has against the American nation. To *Forbes* magazine, Simon was flatly dogmatic: "The notion of wanting to keep out immigrants in order to keep our institutions and our values is pure prejudice." This intense reaction surely goes beyond "taste."

Even more significant was this recent column from A. M. Rosenthal in the *New York Times*:

> Almost always now, when I read about Haitians who risk the seas to get to this country but wind up behind barbed wire, I think of an illegal immigrant I happen to know myself, and of his daughters and his son.
> Then a shiver of shame and embarrassment goes through me. . . .

The illegal immigrant was—Rosenthal's father. He came here from Russia via Canada.

> Many years later, when his children told the story of their father and his determination to find work in America, to hell with borders, people smiled in admiration of this man. And always, his children were filled with pride about him . . .
> I know that if he had been born in Haiti or lived there, he would have broken every law that stood between him and work in the U.S.

In short, because one generation of Americans failed to catch an illegal immigrant, their children must accept more, transforming their nation into a charity ward.

> Imagine what a quick pickup [a] lobby, or parade, demanding succor for the Haitians could do if it were headed by a few Irish-American cardinals, a batch of rabbis, and the presidents of Eastern European, Greek, Italian, Arab, and Turkish organizations. American Blacks and Wasps welcome too!
> . . . Even reluctantly recognizing some economic limitations, this country should have the moral elegance to accept neighbors who flee countries where life is terror and hunger, and are run by murderous gangs left over from dictatorships we ourselves maintained and cosseted.
> If that were a qualification for entry into our golden land, the Haitians should be welcomed with song, embrace, and memories.

Be careful about those embraces. A significant proportion of Haitians are reported to be HIV positive.

The search for an explanation for the paralysis of the American immigration debate, and the drive to transform America from a nation into a charity ward, need go no further than this fretful psychodrama in the mind of the man who, as editor of the *New York Times,* substantially set the national media agenda.

Actually, Rosenthal is unfair to Jewish organizations. They have generally supported immigration. FAIR's Director of Media Outreach, Ira Mehlman—who like his chairman, Dan Stein, is himself Jewish—looks depressed at the thought. "They still think it's 1939," he says. "But even if we took all the Soviet Jews, and all the Israelis, that would still only be 6 million people." As it is, FAIR expects 15 million immigrants in the 1990s.

## END OF CHAPTER

[Nineteen ninety-three saw] the hundredth anniversary of Frederick Jackson Turner's famous lecture on "The Significance of the Frontier in American History." The Superintendent of the Census had just announced that there was no longer a continuous line of free, unsettled land visible on the American map. Closing with the frontier, said Turner, was "the first period of American history." A century later, it may be time to close the second period of American history with the announcement that the U.S. is no longer an "immigrant country."

Because just as the American nation was made with unusual speed, so it is perfectly possible that it could be unmade. On speeded-up film, the great cloud formations boil up so that they dominate the sky. But they also unravel and melt away.

And why do I, an immigrant, care? For one reason, I am the father of a nine-month-old American, Alexander James Frank. He seems to like it here. A second reason: just as Voltaire said in the eighteenth century that every man has two countries, his own and France, so in this century no civilized person can be indifferent to the fate of America.

Beyond this . . . I have an infant memory, more vivid even than my later purgatory in INS. I am playing with my twin brother in the back yard of my aunt's home in a Lancashire cotton town. Suddenly, great whooping giants in U.S. Air Force uniforms (although with the crystal-clear recollection of childhood, I now realize that they had the lithe figures of very young men) leap out and grab us. We are terrified and struggle free.

Which always made me feel bad in subsequent years. They were far from home, lodging with my aunt. And they just wanted a souvenir photograph.

They were the cold-war tail of that vast host that had come to Britain during World War II, when the whole town had resounded night and day to the roar of B-24 engines on the test beds at the great Burtonwood air-base, and everyone had been glad to hear them. They were, as Robert E. Lee once described his troops, not professional soldiers, but citizens who had taken up arms for their country. However, Housman's "Epitaph on an Army of Mercenaries" applies to them:

> Their shoulders held the sky suspended;
> They stood, and earth's foundations stay.

I don't know what happened to them, although I remember one young wife showing us the first color slides we had ever seen, of Southern California, and explaining that they hoped to move to this breathtaking paradise when they got out of the service. They will be old now, if they are still alive. I don't know what they or their children think of the unprecedented experiment being performed, apparently by accident and certainly with no apprehension of the possible consequences, upon the nation they so bravely represented.

I do know, however, that they ought to be asked.

POSTSCRIPT: "At a Cabinet meeting today, Attorney General William P. Barr said nearly one-third of the first 6,000 [Los Angeles] riot suspects arrested and processed through the court system were illegal aliens, according to a senior Administration official. Barr has not proposed any special effort to have them deported, a Justice Department spokesman said."

—*Washington Post,* May 6, 1992

# 2.

# Alien Rumination

## Peter H. Schuck

It's a damn good thing for Peter Brimelow and his son, Alexander James Frank Brimelow, that Alexander was born in this country in 1991. Peter, a recently naturalized Briton, obviously loves the boy and wants him to live in the United States with Peter and his Canadian wife. But if Alexander had been born elsewhere, he would not be an American citizen, and if his dad had his way with our immigration policy, perhaps *none* of the Brimelows, dad included, could have entered as immigrants. The Brimelows are fortunate that the law did not and does not reflect Peter's radically anti-immigration prescriptions. And so, I shall argue, are the rest of us.

Part of the allure of this high-spirited,[1] chatty, often personal,[2] but otherwise uncharming book is that the author acknowledges such ironies. Indeed, he skillfully exploits them to construct a case for radical reform of immigration policy that verges on total elimination of immigration to the United States. Thus, he ruefully tells us that he feels "slightly, well, guilty that [Alexander's] fellow Americans had so little choice" in conferring a citizenship that Alexander, like many children of illegal aliens and temporary visitors, acquired through the fortuity of birth on American soil.[3] He shrugs off the prospect (now happily hypothetical in his own case) that when Congress adopts his proposal to cut off legal immigration entirely, even the nuclear family of an American citizen could not immigrate to the United States. Had that been the law when he came, he says in his amiable, no-big-deal style, "I would probably be writing a book on Canadian immigration policy right now."[4]

Although it is tempting to dismiss this book as another ideological tract, one

Book review of *Alien Nation: Common Sense about America's Immigration Disaster*, by Peter Brimelow (New York: Random House, 1995). Reprinted by permission of the Yale Law Journal Company and Fred B. Rothman & Company from *The Yale Law Journal*, Vol. 105, pp. 1963–2012.

to which only the already-converted will attend, that would be a mistake.[5] The book must be taken seriously, first, because it is already influencing the public debate on immigration.[6] *Alien Nation* has grand ambitions. It not only raises fundamental questions about immigration's effect on the past, present, and future of American society (which is common enough in this era of apocalyptic politics) but also proposes to *answer* them (which is more unusual). Brimelow wishes to jettison the basic structure of our immigration policy established by the Immigration and Nationality Act Amendments of 1965.[7] The 1965 law abolished the national origins quotas, which had been in effect since 1921,[8] replacing them with a system that allocated hemisphere-specific limits among seven preference categories (based on skills, family relationships, and refugee status) and in which all countries of origin in the eastern hemisphere were subject to the same 20,000-immigrant limit.[9] The immigration reform laws enacted in 1978, 1986, and 1990 preserved the essential structure (while altering the details) of this system.[10]

Brimelow proposes to end this system in favor of "a drastic cutback of legal immigration."[11] This proposal is perhaps the only instance of understatement in a book suffused with hyperbole. Calling his plan a drastic cutback is rather like calling Jack the Ripper unfriendly. Brimelow would stop all immigration immediately (but temporarily) and seems to propose a permanent termination of all family-based, refugee, and asylee immigration.[12] Presumably, he would permit only skills-based immigration, but he does not indicate how many of these immigrants he would admit. Of all the reform proposals advanced during this season of discontent, Brimelow's are surely among the most radical."[13]

Another reason to take *Alien Nation* seriously is its assertion that "race[14] ought to matter in immigration policy. In the superheated environment in which racial issues are debated (and often evaded) today, they continue to be perhaps the most divisive and incendiary in American society. In the immigration policy context, they are explosive. Until the 1950s, racism pervaded and polluted American public law. Until only thirty years ago, it defined the very structure of our immigration law. Even today, the major receiving nations, all democracies, have embedded ethnocultural favoritism in their immigration and citizenship policies.[15] In Europe, even more virulent forms of racism and xenophobia increasingly taint immigration politics.[16]

Racism in the United States has declined dramatically in recent decades, despite frequent denials of this fact.[17] I believe—although the point is certainly arguable[18] and much turns on difficult definitions—that racism as such no longer plays a crucial role in immigration law; certainly it plays a less significant role than it did before 1965. Even so, immigration fundamentally shapes a number of racially charged policy questions, such as the future level and composition of the population, affirmative action, multicultural education, and legislative districting.[19]

Indeed, when commentators discuss how immigration affects labor markets, public budgets, urban development, political strategy, population growth, and the environment, they frequently refer to statistical data that break down the empirical effects of immigration, such as welfare utilization or fertility rates, by race. The public does not need experts to inform it that the proportion of nonwhites in the population is growing; the "browning" of America is obvious to anyone who walks down the street, rides a subway, or visits a classroom in almost any large city.

Nevertheless, the immigration debate has carefully elided discussion of the normative questions raised by these current and future demographic shifts: Are these changes good or bad for American society? Should they be slowed, accelerated, or left undisturbed? Which kinds of arguments support these evaluations? Our delicate discursive etiquette in matters of race consigns such questions largely to outspoken nativists such as Patrick Buchanan and to those who wish to pursue eugenic goals through immigration restriction.[20]

In more polite, punctilious company, these issues are left to evasive innuendo—or utter silence. Yet if the immigration debate is to have intellectual integrity and contribute to sound policy, this void must be filled. We must somehow learn to discuss racial questions candidly and fearlessly, but also with respect, sensitivity, and humility. This need is especially compelling in the immigration policy debate. After all, three decades after the national origins quotas were repealed, we still select most immigrants according to their national origins. We do so explicitly in our refugee, "diversity," and nation-specific (e.g., Cuban) programs, and implicitly in our family-based and legalization programs.[21] And individuals' national origins, of course, are highly correlated with race.[22]

Brimelow wishes to advance this debate but doubts that he will receive a fair hearing. He expects to be labeled a racist, which he archly defines *"anyone who is winning an argument with a liberal."*[23] His prediction, if not his definition, is surely correct. Race is very much on his mind.[24] But is he a racist? Since Brimelow himself raises the question of his own racism and draws the reader's attention to it, a reviewer is tempted to seek an answer. The issue of his motivation, however, is an unwelcome diversion from the merits of Brimelow's claims, and I relegate it to a long footnote.[25]

In the end, the more interesting, significant, and policy-relevant issue is not the attitudes that underlie Brimelow's claims but the validity of those claims. If Brimelow's argument that the 1965 Immigration Act has been a national calamity were correct, we would be extraordinarily myopic and perverse to ignore or deny that fact—even if his argument were infected by racism. For reasons that I shall explain in the remainder of this Review, I believe that his claim is false—or at least premature. But while *Alien Nation* is a bad book, it is also a valuable one—all the more so because it is so seductively easy to read. On the way to its erroneous conclusions, it makes many important points that are easily overlooked or have been driven underground in current immigration debates. It forces us to think more clearly about how and why his arguments are wrong. And it reminds us to resist the patriotic smugness and national self-delusion that come so easily to Americans and to be vigilant to assure that Brimelow's dire prophecies are not fulfilled.

The book's argument can be reduced to five distinct but related empirical claims whose significance can only be understood in the light of certain normative assumptions about the nature and purposes of American society. The first is a claim about *demography*; it asserts that immigration to the United States has reached unprecedented levels that are problematic in part because of the racial composition of the post-1965 flow. The second is a claim about *carrying capacity*; it holds that these high immigration levels are stretching American society's environmental resources (broadly defined) beyond the breaking point. The third is a claim about *economic impacts*; it contends that the post-1965 immigrants fail to pull their weight in the labor market and drain off scarce fiscal resources. The fourth is a claim about *cultural assimilation*; it states that the post-1965 immigrants are not embracing American values as completely or as swiftly as their predecessors did. The fifth is a claim about *politics*; it maintains that the post-1965 immigrants are altering the terms of political discourse in ways that weaken the American polity and call into question its viability as a nation-state. I shall discuss each of these claims in turn.

# I. DEMOGRAPHY

Brimelow emphasizes that total immigration to the United States, legal and illegal, is "at historic highs."[26] As Brimelow recognizes, the significance and truth of this assertion turn on several issues.[27] Should immigration be measured in absolute terms or relative to something else, such as the total or foreign-born population? Is it more meaningful to measure immigration on an annual basis or over longer periods of time? How many illegal aliens are being counted? Should immigration be measured net of permanent departures by aliens and U.S. citizens, and if so, how many departures are there? Except for legal admissions, which require the Immigration and Naturalization Service (INS) to issue visas, none of these indices is based on hard, reliable data; all can be, and often are, contested.

In absolute terms, legal immigration in 1995, the most recent year for which statistics are available, was 720,000.[28] This represents a decline of 10 percent from the 1994 figure of 804,000, which in turn represented a decline of 11 percent from the 1993 total of 904,000.[29] The 1993–1995 decline represents the largest two-year drop in legal immigration since the Depression.[30] This decline, moreover, was a broad one, occurring in five major categories: employment-based admissions, dependents of aliens previously legalized under the amnesty provisions of the Immigration Reform and Control Act of 1986 (IRCA), family-based admissions, asylees adjusting to permanent status, and certain special programs (Amerasian children, Indochinese and Soviet parolees, and registered nurses).[31] The 1995 total was the lowest total since 1988, when 643,000 were admitted.[32]

These figures might seem to refute Brimelow's "historic highs" claim, blurring his apocalyptic vision of America being deluged by immigrants. Before reaching that conclusion, however, we must examine the data more closely and from different angles. Admissions figures tend to fluctuate from one year to another, confounding efforts to discern significant trends on the basis of short-term changes. For example, the admissions total in 1991 was approximately 1.8 million;[33] it then declined over the next four years to 720,000 in 1995[34] (when the INS had expected the total to increase again[35]). These fluctuations often reflect temporary special factors, including the evolution of particular short-term programs. The most important example is the legalization program under IRCA. This one-time spike in the admissions totals produced dramatic increases in the admissions totals beginning in 1989 but leveling off in 1992. IRCA legalizations, however, have had little effect on the figures since 1993,[36] and, for political reasons, such a legalization is unlikely to be repeated in the foreseeable future.

Brimelow, then, is right to focus on longer-term trends. He is also correct to include illegal aliens in the total. Data on the number of illegal aliens are controversial and inexact, although expert estimates have narrowed considerably in recent years.[37] Estimates are based largely on extrapolations from the number of aliens apprehended at the Mexican border and from census surveys. Both methods are problematic.[38] Moreover, the gross category of illegal aliens must be broken down into subgroups for more precise, meaningful policy analysis. For example, different policies are needed to deal with the two, roughly equal, categories of illegal aliens: those who enter the United States illegally ("entrants without inspection" [EWIs]) and those who enter legally on temporary visas but then become illegal when they violate the terms of their visas ("overstays"). As another example, illegal aliens differ in how long they remain in the United States. Many illegals are temporary sojourners," the duration of whose stays in the United States depends on seasonal, family, and economic factors, or are "commuters" who cross the border frequently. A growing share of the illegal flow from Mexico, however, now consists of "settlers"—mostly women and children planning to live with their families in the United States more or less permanently.[39] Because settlers' prolonged, illegal residence in the United States affects American society in more complex and significant ways than does the residence of sojourners, they pose the greatest challenges to politicians and policymakers.

In discussing illegal aliens, Brimelow is somewhat sloppy with the data, such as they are. Noting both the 1.3 million illegals apprehended by the Border Patrol in 1993[40] and estimates that it catches about one-third of those attempting to cross, he suggests that "a remarkable *2 to 3 million* illegal immigrants may have succeeded in entering the country in 1993."[41] But this suggestion ignores two well-known phenomena: multiple apprehensions of the same individuals who make repeated attempts until they cross successfully and sojourners who travel back and forth across the border repeatedly but are sometimes apprehended. Both of these common situations inflate the number of illegals. More important, he cites a "cautious" INS estimate that "300,000 to 500,000" net illegals remain each year.[42] His source for this estimate, however, is an unnamed INS spokesman, and the estimate is higher than the published estimates—300,000 is the figure most commonly used by researchers in the field, including INS researchers[43]—that he could have readily cited.

A similar slippage occurs when he discusses *emigration* by U.S. citizens and permanent residents, which of course bears on the total of *net* immigration. The best estimates are that 1.6 million emigrated during the decade of the 1980s, an outflow that has been steadily increasing since the 1940s and equaled the number emigrating during the 1920s.[44] Emigration seems to be accelerating during the 1990s.[45] He seeks to minimize this factor by stating that the post-1965 immigrants are less likely to emigrate than their pre-1920 predecessors, a trend that he attributes to the growth of the welfare state.[46] He may be correct, but the data do not establish his claim. First, the emigration data do not distinguish between noncitizen emigrants who were once immigrants and emigrants who were U.S. citizens (some of whom were never immigrants). Second, the decline in emigration began in the 1930s (if measured in absolute terms) and in the 1940s (if measured as a proportion of immigration).[47] It thus began long before the late 1960s, when Brimelow's two *bêtes noires*—the post-1965 immigration and the major growth in the welfare state—occurred. This chronology casts some doubt on his welfare-state explanation for declining emigration rates.

In a sense, however, these are mere details; they do not contradict Brimeow's position that the current level of net legal immigration is, by historical standards, quite high in absolute terms. The 1994 net legal immigration of just over 600,000 (804,000 immigrants minus 195,000 emigrants) is almost three times higher than the annual figures during the 1950s (for Brimelow, the last halcyon period before the Fall), when net legal immigration averaged just over 209,000.[48] It is also almost twice the level recommended by the politically astute, blue-ribbon Select Commission on Immigration and Refugee Policy only fifteen years ago.[49] Even the figure of 600,000 immigrants understates recent growth, of course, because it fails to *include* illegal immigrants, of whom there presumably were relatively few prior to the mid-1960s and almost none in the early decades of the century.[50] Adding 300,000 *resident* illegal aliens to he immigrant population each year[51] produces a grand total of at least 90,000 new resident immigrants each year, net of emigration. This number is high indeed, at least in absolute terms.

If we consider current immigration in relative, rather than absolute, terms—that is, new admissions or total foreign-born as a percentage of the total U.S. population—Brimelow's claim that immigration is at historically high levels must be qualified somewhat, as he acknowledges.[52] But even when viewed in these relative terms, the recent inflows have been substantial. Although the legal immigrants who entered in recent years constituted only 3.1% of the total U.S. population during the 1980s (the comparable shares for the first three decades of this century were 10.4%, 5.7%, and 3.5% respectively),[53] the steady accumulation of immigrants over time has produced a growing cohort of foreign-born in the United States. In 1994, over 22 million people, 8.7% of the total US. population, were foreign-born.[54] Although the percentage of the foreign-born remains far below the 13.2% share it comprised in 1920, it is the highest percentage since then, and the foreign-born share has almost doubled since 1970, when it was 4.8%.[55] The fact that one out of every eleven persons in the United States is a first-generation immigrant gives immigration a much higher political and media profile today than it possessed only a quarter-century ago, when fewer than one in twenty were foreign-born.

Brimelow, however, does not simply ground his demand for drastic restriction on the size of the post-1965 cohort. He also claims that this newer immigration is fundamentally different from that which preceded it in two other respects: its continuity and its racial composition.

*Continuity.* One of the book's principal themes is that America has not always been a country that admitted immigrants. The traditional notion that there has been a steady stream of immigrants to the United States is one of those hoary, politically useful (to some) myths. The truth is that immigration to the United States has always come in waves—that is, until Congress unleashed the *tsunami* of 1965.[56] Beginning in the colonial period, immigration exhibited recurrent cycles of growth and decline. The many peaks and valleys were sensitive to conditions in Europe and job opportunities in the United States. When jobs were plentiful, immigrants came, many only as sojourners; when jobs were scarce, many of the earlier immigrants returned to the old country, and few new immigrants arrived. This punctuated pattern of immigration—occasional spurts followed by short-term "pauses" or longer "lulls"[57]—resulted mostly from the convulsions of war and the business cycle.[58] This pattern was also socially benign. Like the period between meals, the pauses and lulls facilitated digestion, a process that would have been far more dangerous and uncomfortable had the newcomers entered America's maw in large and constant gulps. Americans could more readily accept immigrants, who in turn had the time, space, and incentive to assimilate swiftly into American society.

Like almost every other good thing in Brimelow's account, however, this Edenic paradise of leisurely assimilation ended abruptly in (you guessed it!) 1965. Far from being wave-like, the post-1965 immigration has waxed but never waned; even now it shows no sign of receding.[59] The flow has been both continuous and continually rising (short-term fluctuations aside). In particular, the business cycle has had little effect on this immigration flow.[60] Brimelow has a ready explanation for this new development: In addition to jobs, the welfare magnet both attracts immigrants and keeps them here.[61] If Brimelow is correct about this—if immigrants' motives have changed and the business cycle no longer disciplines immigration flows—the implications for both immigration and welfare policy would be far-reaching. But is it true?

Brimelow seeks to persuade us with strong assertions and vivid charts that draw our attention to the contrasting peaks and valleys before 1965 and the continuous ramping upward thereafter.[62] The unwary reader, however, should be forewarned: There is less to this evidence than meets the eye.[63] First, the major declines in immigration occurred during periods of either world war (1915–20, 1940–45) or deep economic depression (after 1873 and 1893, and during the 1930s).[64] Because we have managed since 1965 to avoid both of these evils—a point to which I shall return in the Conclusion—Brimelow cannot show that the historical responsiveness of immigration to the business cycle no longer operates. Only a new world war or depression can test his claim.

Second, the pre-1965 trough may not have been as deep as the numbers suggest. No numerical restrictions on immigration from the western hemisphere even existed before 1965, and thus any number of Mexicans could enter the United States legally by paying a fee, passing a Spanish literacy test, and obtaining a labor certification. Presumably, many did not bother to do so and instead entered illegally, which could not have been too difficult at a time when the Border Patrol was much smaller and less effective than it is today. Even if many did not enter the United States illegally, they were not counted in the totals contained in the official statistics. It is, therefore, a delicious irony, unremarked by Brimelow, that the same 1965 Act that he so thoroughly deplores also imposed a numerical restriction very much to his liking.

Third, the charts do not really tell us much about whether the causes of immigration fluctuations changed over time. We know that other things did not remain equal; for example, the legal rules governing immigration were in flux. Shortly after numerical limits on immigration were established in the mid-1920s,[65] the Great Depression drove immigration levels down, and World War II kept them low. Thus, the numerical caps could not really have begun to bite until the late 1940s, more than twenty years after their inception, at which point a different, more complex mix of factors (including massive refugee resettlements) [was] shaping immigration flows.

Finally, Brimelow's claim that the welfare state explains immigration's relentless rise during the post-1965 period is hard to square with the fact that this ramping up began in the 1950s, long before the Great Society expansion of the welfare state commenced.

Nevertheless, Brimelow might be correct that the business cycle no longer regulates immigration flows as it once did,[66] and that a legally mandated pause in immigration would enable the United States to better integrate the large post-1965 cohort. Such a new pause might facilitate the successful assimilation of this cohort, much as the pre-1920s cohort benefited from the earlier lull. A new pause might also ease immigration-related social anxieties resulting from the constant addition of newcomers.[67] Group mobility theory, the historical pattern of assimilation, and common sense lend some plausibility to this notion. It is intriguing that immigrants themselves—by a large majority—believe that immigration should either be kept at present levels or reduced, and support for this position increases with their time in the United States.[68] Whether immigrants possess some special insight into how large-scale, continuing immigration retards the assimilation of recent immigrants, or simply wish for selfish reasons to pull up the ladder now that they have climbed aboard, is unclear.

The attractiveness of a pause, however, depends in part on how the pause is defined and on its duration. Brimelow's approach is to permit either no immigration or only skills-based admissions (the reader can't be sure).[69] Others, however, will see no magic, and much mischief, in terminating *all* family-based and humanitarian admissions. For those categories, a more modest reduction in immigration, one that is temporary and whose overall effects can then be gauged, would almost certainly reconcile the competing considerations better than complete cessation.

Brimelow's effort to shift the burden of proof to defenders of immigration by appealing to social risk aversion also relies on a simplistic all-or-nothing approach. On the final page of his book, in a section entitled "What If?," Brimelow argues that immigration's uncertain effects argue for terminating or radically restricting it. If immigration advocates turn out to be wrong, he sug-

gests, we will be left with many disastrous and perhaps irreversible consequences, whereas if the restrictionists are wrong, the worst that will happen is
that the United States must deal with a labor shortage.[70] Risk aversion is a perfectly legitimate policy criterion, and if one shared Brimelow's views of immigration's effects, one might well accept this effort to shift the burden of proof. If
instead one believes, as I do, that legal immigration is on the whole desirable, the
more relevant policy criterion—one that should be particularly congenial to a
conservative like Brimelow—becomes "if it ain't broke, don't fix it"—or, more
precisely, "if it's just partly broke, just fix that part."

    *Racial Composition.* To Brimelow, the most disturbing aspect of the Fall is
the changing racial complexion of the United States. Before 1965, he notes,
immigrants came overwhelmingly from the traditional source countries of northern and western Europe. In those glory days, "not all immigrants were alien to
American eyes," and "native-born Americans were receiving continuous ethnic
reinforcement."[71] But since the abandonment of the national origins quotas in
1965, the vast majority of newcomers have been Hispanic and Asian,[72] with a significant new black inflow from Africa and the non-Spanish Caribbean. In what
he calls the Pincer Chart,[73] he shows (while acknowledging the uncertainties of
long-term demographic projections) that whites, who were 81% of the population in 1790 and 75.7% in 1990, will decline to a bare majority (52.7%) in 2050.[74]
Well before then, moreover, Hispanics will replace blacks as the largest single
minority group. Brimelow then has the immigration liberal pose the key question: *"So what? Why do you care so much about race?"*[75] This is the essential
question, and Brimelow provides several answers. In particular, he points to the
reinforcement and distortion of affirmative action effected by immigration and to
immigration's threat to social cohesion. Because these issues impinge most significantly on cultural assimilation and political power, however, I defer discussion of them to Parts IV and V.

## II. CARRYING CAPACITY

Continued immigration, Brimelow despairs, will be a demographic and environmental disaster for the United States.[76] Nevertheless, although his warnings are
certainly worth attending to, his predictions are highly arbitrary and unrealistic;
he aims more to shock than to persuade. Interestingly, his predictions bear a striking resemblance to certain modes of argument—use of simplistic extrapolations
from present to future, disregard for the complexity and subtlety of social adap-
tations, and presentation of stark doomsday scenarios—that conservatives properly mock when environmentalists and other social reformers advance them.

    The centerpiece of Brimelow's analysis is a chart that he calls "The
Wedge,"[77] which relies on projections developed by Leon Bouvier, a respected
demographer and leading immigration restrictionist.[78] Had we terminated all
immigration in 1970, Brimelow's "Wedge" purports to show, the U.S. population
in 2050 would have been 244 million (i.e., less than the current total). But con-

tinuing immigration at present levels, he predicts, will produce a total in 2050 of 383 million, of which 36% will be post-1970 immigrants and their descendants. The "Wedge" consists of the additional 139 million Americans who will have descended from post-1970 immigrants,[79] unneeded and unwanted bodies that will place an unprecedented strain on the natural and human environments. He also predicts that more immigrants, especially those from the Third World whom the post-1965 rules have brought here, will bring new (and in some cases, old) diseases, high rates of fertility and crime, and low rates of education and skill. They will crowd out the rest of us, swamping our classrooms, extending our slums, polluting our air, and destroying our amenities and communities.[80] These dire consequences, he says, are already occurring.

Straight-line extrapolations from the present could indeed yield 383 million people in fifty-five more years. This is a lot of people, and the prospect of somehow squeezing all of them into our schools, beaches, parking spaces, and housing stock is not a pleasant one. Doing so would surely strain our natural and social environments. But straight-line extrapolations in such matters seldom prove to be correct. For all the scientific gloss of hard numbers, demography is as much art as science. Long-term demographic projections, like economic ones, are necessary and often valuable. Nevertheless, they necessarily assume that human choices are more fixed than they actually are and that the future will therefore be much like the recent past and present (except, of course, for such changes as the demographer can envision and accurately predict). Wise demographers know and say that this assumption is false, but they usually have little choice but to proceed as if it were true.

Demographic projections such as those cited by Brimelow emphasize the population-increasing effects of those immigrant groups whose fertility rates are higher than the fertility rates of natives. These higher rates reflect the greater proportion of immigrants, relative to the general population, who are in their childbearing years, cultural factors, and other causes. When high-fertility groups' share of the immigration stream and of the total U.S. population increases, the projected future population of the United States increases accordingly. This "shifting shares" phenomenon—the larger proportion in the population of high-fertility groups such as Filipinos, southeast Asians, and some Hispanics—drives much of the prediction of future U.S. population growth.[81]

This argument, however, resembles earlier "race suicide" theories that immigration historians and demographers have convincingly debunked by showing that immigrant fertility rates generally converge with those of the native population.[82] The important question, therefore, is how quickly this occurs. It appears that when women from high-fertility countries migrate to the United States, they both reduce and delay their childbearing to the point at which their fertility rates approach the overall U.S. norm. Indeed, compared to demographically similar native women, their rates sometimes are lower.[83] Admittedly, immigrants do accelerate U.S. population growth; since 1980, net immigration has accounted for about 37% of population growth.[84] But the extent and speed of their contribution to that growth in the future are difficult to predict and easy to exaggerate.

Much of Brimelow's concern about carrying capacity seems to relate to the dangers of overcrowding.[85] Even thirty years after the dreaded deluge began, however, the United States remains a country with a relatively low population density.[86] This concern does not simply reflect the vast uninhabited (and perhaps uninhabitable[87]) spaces in the American West. Even America's largest and densest cities are thinly populated relative to other cities in the world, including the most famously attractive ones.[88] Indeed, the population density of New York City is about half what it was in 1910; other major cities are also less densely populated.[89] We have a long way to go before we reach density levels that other Western democracies find perfectly acceptable, even desirable. Our standards of acceptable density may be different from those in Europe, but our standards are not immutable, as the historical urbanization, suburbanization, and "edge city" cycles in the United States attest.

Demographic extrapolations from the present to the future are further confounded by the dynamics of markets, politics, and other powerful social processes that respond to developments that impose widespread social costs. These processes do not sit idly by while change unfolds but instead shape and constrain change, thereby altering its future trajectory. Demographic models cannot readily incorporate this fact, which is nicely captured in "Stein's Law" (stated by economist Herbert Stein): If a trend can't go on like this indefinitely, it won't.[90] Population growth, for example, bids up the prices of housing, education, and other goods; people therefore tend to have fewer children,[91] other things being equal.[92] If increased job competition pushes immigrants' unemployment high enough for long enough, they will tend not to migrate here. If competition for natural resources and other environmental goods becomes more intense, those goods will become more costly, which both rations their use and attracts additional supply; these behavioral responses in turn tend to reduce the price. If policymakers perceive that population growth harms the environment, the economy, and other areas of public concern, they will propose policy changes accordingly.

I am not suggesting that we can blithely count on these responses to eliminate any adverse effects of Population growth—far from it. How well society reacts to these developments depends on the quality of information flows, the nature of politics, the efficiency of markets, and other factors. Even if optimal outcomes are unlikely under these conditions, however, Brimelow's dire predictions should be taken with more than a grain of salt. If our politics and markets are supple and responsive enough to react swiftly and intelligently to population pressures and other strains on carrying capacity, the future need not unduly arouse our fears. Indeed, since 1965, our social institutions have performed reasonably well in this regard, refuting the Chicken Littles of environmental pessimism.[93]

# III. ECONOMIC IMPACTS

Brimelow acknowledges the rich contributions that the pre-1965 immigrants have made to the American economy.[94] He insists, however, that the post-1965 cohort is altogether different. Relying heavily and uncritically on the work of labor economist George Borjas, he argues that "the effect of the 1965 reform has been *to uncouple legal immigration from the needs of the U.S. economy.*"[95] This claim is actually a composite of four separate claims. The first is that labor market skills play a small and shrinking role in admissions policy. Second, the post-1965 cohort is less skilled than earlier cohorts. Third and related, the post-1965 cohort drains the economy more than earlier cohorts because its members, especially illegal aliens, are more likely to demand public assistance and displace native workers. Fourth, this displacement imposes particularly heavy burdens on current and potential African-American workers.

The first claim is correct. A major theme of the debate surrounding the Immigration Act of 1990 was the need to increase the level and relative share of skills-based admissions.[96] In the end, however, the Act only slightly increased the share of these admissions. In 1994, only 15% of admissions were skills-based; moreover, roughly half of these consisted of skilled immigrants' accompanying family members, who may themselves lack skills needed in the United States. Family ties accounted for 62% of the admissions.[97] Because the 1990 Act substantially increased both the total number of immigrants and the numbers authorized for each immigrant category, the absolute number of skills-based immigrants did grow, thus obscuring how minimally the share of skills-based admissions had increased. Family unity, it appears, continues to trump all other immigration policy values.[98] Pending legislation would increase the relative weight of labor market skills, a reform whose advantages are widely appreciated.[99]

The second claim—that the "quality" of immigrants to the United States has declined since the 1965 reforms—is harder to assess. Good data on immigrant labor markets are hard to come by, and analyses are very sensitive to methodology. More to the point, labor economists disagree about the nature and validity of the data, methodology, and conclusions used by Borjas and other immigration analysts. There are several areas of dispute. One concerns the extent to which the "immigrant" category should be disaggregated. Different subcategories of immigrants—family-based admittees, skills-based admittees, refugees/asylees, age groups, source region or country groups, legals versus illegals—in a given cohort exhibit quite different characteristics. Lumping some or all of these subcategories together can significantly affect the outcome of the analysis. Reliance on census data, which employ rather crude, self-reported ethnic categories and almost certainly understate income, is also controversial.

Several generalizations growing out of labor market research do support some of Brimelow's concerns. Many post-1965 immigrants are highly educated, indeed, far more so than the native population. Many others are more skilled in *absolute* terms than the immigrants who preceded them, but because the native population's skills have increased even more in absolute terms and because lower skilled groups comprise a larger share of the total immigration flow, the "quality" gap has widened in *relative* terms.[100] Most of the immigrants who entered illegally—those who qualified for the amnesty under IRCA and those who have entered illegally since then—are low-skilled Mexicans. The education level of Mexican-origin immigrants even among those who are naturalized U.S. citizens, is very low; overall, it averages about seven and a half years of schooling.[101] Other relatively low-skilled immigrant groups are Asian refugees and the elderly.[102] On the other hand, the recent arrivals also include better educated individuals—predominantly nonrefugees from Asia, Africa, and the Middle East— who should help to reduce the gap in the future.[103] This effect, however, will be gradual because their numbers remain relatively low. Again, pending legislation is likely to increase the skill levels of future immigrant cohorts.

Brimelow's third claim is that post-1965 immigrants inflict a net loss on the economy, taking into account the combined effects of their use of public services, their displacement of native workers, their tax payments, and their contribution to productivity. This claim is also difficult to assess precisely, as the existing studies seldom employ comparable definitions, measures, data sets, and methodologies.[104] For example, the outcomes of labor market impact analyses depend on whether the studies assume that particular labor markets (usually metropolitan areas) are closed systems, or whether they instead consider the significant possibility (given the high degree of internal labor mobility in the U.S. economy) that immigrant concentrations in one area induce some native workers to leave that area and discourage other natives who might otherwise migrate there from doing so.

Another controversial question of great political interest concerns immigrants' use of public services and benefits. Immigrant households are somewhat more likely to use welfare (AFDC and SSI) than native ones. Although this differential is small (7.5% of natives, 8.7% of immigrants), it increased during the 1980s as immigrant utilization rates grew and native rates declined. And in a very recent survey, immigrants *self-report* much higher utilization rates.[105] A number of earlier studies had found that if one controls for socioeconomic variables, immigrants were less likely than otherwise demographically similar natives to receive AFDC and SSI.[106] A very recent study using 1990 data indicates that this pattern of lower immigrant welfare utilization continues to be true for AFDC but not for SSI.[107] Immigrants now receive SSI at higher rates than demographically similar natives, a development that has generated strong public and congressional reaction.[108] Like the growing relative quality gap discussed earlier, the higher immigrant utilization of SSI is mostly due to the very large Mexican cohort and to the Asian *refugee* cohort, whose utilization rates more than doubled during the 1980s.[109]

A number of studies have attempted to determine whether immigrants on balance benefit or burden the U.S. economy. Brimelow, citing a highly disputed analysis by Donald Huddle[110] and a puzzling "back-of-the-envelope" estimate by Borjas, obviously thinks that the burdens predominate.[111] Urban Institute researchers Jeffrey Passel and Rebecca Clark recently reviewed the estimates made by Huddle and by state and local governments seeking reimbursement of immigration-related costs from the federal government.[112] Passel and Clark severely criticize these estimates for systematically understating tax collections from immigrants; overstating service costs for immigrants; failing to take account of the economic value generated by immigrant entrepreneurs and immigrant consumer spending; overstating job displacement impacts; overstating the size of the immigrant population, especially illegals; and ignoring the fact that natives also use more in services than they pay in taxes.[113] In particular, they find that Huddle underestimates the taxes paid by immigrants by $50 billion![114] Correcting this error alone, Passel and Clark argue, would defeat the claim that immigrants cost more than they contribute. Indeed, they estimate that the post-1970 immigrants—legal, amnestied, and undocumented—generate a surplus of $27.4 billion a year, not including nontax economic benefits.[115]

The large gap between these estimates reflects some quite technical methodological judgments by researchers. It would be foolish to allow immigration policy to turn on such judgments, especially since neither Huddle's cost estimate nor Passel and Clark's benefit estimate would count for much in a $7 trillion economy. Even so, there is no denying the *political* significance of these numbers: Public attitudes toward immigration are less favorable to the extent that immigrants are perceived to impose even small burdens on the economy and on taxpayers. Recent congressional actions confirm a strong consensus that immigrants (or their sponsors) should at least pay for themselves.[116]

The fourth claim—that post-1965 immigrants may displace many African-American workers[117]—might seem almost self-evidently true. After all, low-skilled immigrants and low-skilled blacks would appear to compete for a shrinking number of low-skill jobs. The terms of this competition, moreover, often favor even non-English speaking immigrants, especially illegals. Immigrants are accustomed to, and may accept, lower wages, and many employers perceive them to be more reliable, hard-working, and docile than native black workers.[118]

Much depends on the extent to which immigrant labor is a substitute for or a complement to native labor. If immigrant labor is a substitute, immigrants would increase unemployment among blacks (who unlike unsuccessful immigrants have no other home to which to return) and would, other things being equal, drive down wage levels for those blacks who are hired. Such effects would be consistent with studies indicating that real wages have declined for low-skill workers during much of the post-1965 period, and especially with studies concluding that recent immigration has contributed to the widening earnings gap between high-skill and low-skill workers.[119] But to the extent that immigrant labor instead complements native labor, immigrant labor would increase job opportunities for natives, including blacks. This increase might occur if immigrants fill labor niches that native workers are abandoning or if immigrants develop new entrepreneurial enclaves. There is evidence that both of these possibilities often occur.[120] Indeed, during the 1980s, immigrant groups seem to have competed more with each other than they did with native workers.[121]

Empirical studies have consistently failed to establish significant immigration-induced harm to native black workers.[122] Nevertheless, various methodological limitations of those studies, as well as subsequent changes in economic and immigration factors, mean that such effects cannot be ruled out.[123] The harmful effects, if any, appear to be much too small to justify a radical change in immigration policy on this ground alone.

# CULTURAL ASSIMILATION

Brimelow suggests that the post-1965 immigrants bear, and presumably transmit to their children, different and less attractive values than did the earlier waves of immigrants.[124] Although he is not clear precisely which values he has in mind, he presumably prefers those that most other people admire—honesty, industry, family stability, morality, education, optimism about the future, and respect for law and legitimate authority.[125] And although he is a bit vague about the indicia of the decline in immigrants' moral values, he does mention three areas of particular concern: crime, limited English proficiency (particularly among Hispanics), and high illegitimacy rates (particularly among Mexican-Americans).[126] Each of these three areas is certainly worth worrying about. Immigrant crime may be even worse than he suggests, and his concern about illegitimacy rates, at least among some immigrant groups, is warranted. On the other hand, his conclusions about limited English proficiency are exaggerated, and he fails to discuss the risk of second-generation attraction to underclass culture, which in the long run may be the most serious cultural problem of all. I discuss each of these areas in turn.

## A. Crime

The incidence of immigrant crime is significant, if only because the number of immigrants is large. Most immigrant crime is drug-related.[127]

Although the number of criminal aliens under law enforcement supervision in the United States is impossible to establish precisely, it has increased approximately ten-fold since 1980, imposing substantial costs of arrest, detention, and deportation. A 1993 congressional study estimated that 450,000 deportable criminal aliens were either incarcerated, on parole, or on probation in federal, state, and local jurisdictions.[128] A more conservative compilation of various federal and state estimates suggests that at least 270,000 deportable aliens are under criminal justice supervision.[129] Newly convicted aliens, of course, constantly replenish and enlarge this population. Illegals account for over half of the deportable aliens in state prisons.[130] Quite apart from other law enforcement costs, the costs of incarcerating alien criminals are high. The operating cost alone of a prisoner-year in federal prisons was estimated in early 1994 to be about $19,000.[131] If this cost were applied to the 100,000 deportable criminal aliens imprisoned in federal, state, and local facilities,[132] it would mean nearly $2 billion in annual incarceration costs.

Although the systematic data on point are somewhat dated, legal immigrants do not appear to commit any more crime than demographically similar Americans; they may even commit less, and that crime may be less serious.[133] Nor does today's immigrant crime appear to be worse than in earlier eras. The immigrants who flooded American cities around the turn of the century (the ancestors of many of today's Americans) were also excoriated as congenitally vicious and unusually crime-prone, not only by the public opinion of the day but also by the Dillingham Commission, which Congress established to report on the need for immigration restrictions.[134] The evidence suggests that those claims were false then, and similar claims appear to be false now.[135]

These historical and demographic points, however, are largely irrelevant to the contemporary political debate, which is concerned with the here and now. Media reports about criminal activity by Asian street gangs,[136] Latin American drug lords,[137] Islamic terrorists,[138] and Russian mafiosi[139] are profoundly disturbing to the American public and surely fuel restrictionist sentiment. In its concern about immigrant crime, as in other respects, the public often fails to differentiate between legal and illegal aliens.

Two abysmal policy lapses of the federal government have aggravated this political response. First, the government has failed to police the border and the interior effectively against illegal aliens, some of whom commit crimes after entry. Second, the government has failed to expel those legal and illegal immigrants who have been convicted of deportable offenses in the United States and who are already in governmental custody. The INS succeeded in deporting 31,000 criminal aliens in 1995,[140] approximately five times as many as it deported in 1989,[141] but this still amounts to just over 10% of the deportable aliens under criminal justice supervision. The federal government is now addressing both of these problems. The Border Patrol has been rapidly expanded[142] and is implementing some new enforcement techniques.[143] The INS, spurred by state and congressional pressures, is finally taking active steps to expedite the removal of criminal aliens; through a combination of new funds and special efforts, the agency hopes to deport 58,000 criminal aliens in 1996.[144] Increased efforts by the Border Patrol, however, have been unsuccessful in the past.[145] The effectiveness of the new campaign, therefore, remains to be seen. Most recently, the Clinton administration proposed to bar companies that violate the immigration laws from receiving federal contracts.[146]

## B. English Language

On the question of immigrants' acquisition of English-language proficiency, however, Brimelow stands on weaker ground. To be sure, he is correct that English proficiency is a precondition to full participation in the economic, political, and cultural aspects of American society. A recent four-country empirical study confirms the conventional wisdom: Dominant-language fluency is highly correlated with labor market returns, especially in the United States.[147] Dominant-language fluency is also important, even if not essential, to immigrants' full participation in the political process, which, despite some legal requirements for minority-language voting materials, is still conducted largely in English.

Brimelow refers to census data indicating that 47% of the U.S. foreign-born population does not speak English "very well" or "at all" and that 71% of foreign-born Mexicans report not speaking it "very well."[148] English fluency is probably the most important step to, and index of, full integration and participation in American society. It would indeed be a disturbing danger signal, and an augury of further linguistic fragmentation, if newcomers were not learning English at an acceptable rate. In any event, the American public is manifestly unwilling to accept this risk.[149]

Brimelow's figures, however, actually tell us little about the prospects for the linguistic assimilation of post-1965 immigrants, much less about how the new immigrants' progress compares to that of their predecessors. The reason is that those figures fail to distinguish between the first and second generations. Yet Americans hold the first generation to a much lower assimilation standard than that to which they hold succeeding ones.[150]

Brimelow overlooks the historical reality that first-generation immigrants have *always* been slow to acquire good English proficiency. This phenomenon is especially common if they arrived as adults, arrived recently, think that they are likely to return, are refugees rather than economic or family migrants, had little earlier exposure to English, had little schooling, or live in a minority-language enclave.[151] The post-1965 immigrants exhibit some of these variables more than earlier ones did, while exhibiting other variables less. Even as to first-generation immigrants, however, English use appears to be quite high.[152]

It is the English fluency of the *second* generation—those born in the United States or brought here as small children by foreign-born parents—that is critical to immigrants' integration and to society's cultural coherence. A recent analysis by Portes and Schauffler summarizes the historical pattern:

> In the past, almost every first generation's loyalty to their ancestral language has given way to an overwhelming preference for English among their children. . . .
> . . . .
> . . . [I]n no other country have foreign languages been extinguished with such speed. In the past, the typical pattern has been for the first generation to learn enough English to survive economically; the second generation continued to speak the parental tongue at home, but English in school, at work and in public life; by the third generation, the home language shifted to English, which effectively became the mother tongue for subsequent generations.
> This pattern has held true for all immigrant groups in the past with the exception of some isolated minorities.[153]

Powerful evidence of the second generation's continued progress in mastering English appears in Portes and Schauffler's recent empirical study of English-language proficiency among eighth- and ninth-grade second-generation students from many Caribbean, Latino, and Asian nationality groups in the Miami area, which has a larger proportion of foreign-born residents than any other American city. According to their data, gathered in 1992, fully 99% of the students reported that they spoke, understood, read, and wrote English "very well" or "well"; only 1% knew little or no English.[154] Time in the United States and ethnic-enclave residency were the most important independent variables; parental education and occupational and class status were unimportant. Moreover, the children's preference for daily communication in English over their parental language was overwhelming—even among recent arrivals, and especially among those living in communities in which the parental language was dominant.[155] The evidence on post-1965 immigrants' English fluency, then, belies Brimelow's animadversions, at least as far as the crucial second generation is concerned.[156]

## C. Illegitimacy

In contrast, his concern about the high illegitimacy rates among some immigrant groups is amply warranted. He approvingly cites Michael Lind to the effect that "Hispanic 'family values' are another immigration enthusiast's myth—Mexican-American out-of-wedlock births, for example, are more than twice the white rate, at 28.9 percent."[157] Other evidence suggests that Mexican, Latin American, and Caribbean immigrant nonmarital fertility rates are much higher than those for immigrants from Asia and Europe.[158]

If such rates accurately indicate the incidence of children growing up in single-parent families, the rates would herald bleak life prospects for those children and hence for the quality of American life more generally. To those who would extenuate high alien illegitimacy on the ground that illegitimacy among black Americans is far higher and illegitimacy among white Americans is rising precipitously, Brimelow offers a compelling rejoinder: "[W]hat's the point of immigrants who are no better than we are?"[159]

Immigrants' cultural impact on American society, however, is a function both of the values that they bring with them to the United States and of those that they *acquire* here as they rub shoulders with Americans. Although Brimelow focuses entirely on the former, the latter are probably more important in the long run. Some evidence on what happens to immigrants' behavior and values as they rub shoulders with Americans is profoundly disturbing. Illegitimacy rates for some immigrant groups—for example, Caribbean immigrants, who tend to live closest to inner-city native minority populations with high illegitimacy rates—seem to *increase* the longer they are in the United States.[160] According to a recent study by demographer Frank Bean,[161] divorce rates, a subject that Brimelow fails to mention, reinforce this pattern. The study indicates that Hispanics, most of whom are Mexicans, exhibit lower divorce rates in their countries of origin than demographically similar U.S. natives do. Divorce rates rise, however, among the second generation here, and by the third generation, divorce rates are equal to those of U.S. natives.[162]

Recent research on second-generation immigrants suggests that these examples may simply illustrate a more general dynamic of cultural transfer. In this pattern, first- and second-generation immigrants, particularly second-generation children, are inducted into American subcultures that transmit some of that subculture's social pathologies to the newcomers. In this way, dysfunctional behavior that is relatively rare in the country of origin may, with exposure to that subculture, become more common among immigrant children to mimic the American norm.

Some sociologists of immigration, notably Alejandro Portes, describe this as a downward or "segmented" assimilation process.[163] Most new immigrants locate in areas that bring their children disproportionately into close contact with native minorities. Many of these natives, who may be the children and grandchildren of immigrants unable to escape from the inner city, suffer from prejudice, disadvantage, joblessness, and a variety of social pathologies that foster a cluster of self-defeating attitudes and behaviors, including negative views of education that contrast sharply with the optimism and socially adaptive strategies that immigrants usually bring with them and seek to transmit to their children. These natives, enraged and defeated by their blocked mobility, can powerfully influence—and contaminate—the values of the new immigrants' children, especially in the shared school environment. Portes starkly depicts the problem:

> The confrontation with the culture of the inner-city places second generation youth in a forced-choice dilemma: to remain loyal to their parents' outlook and mobility aspirations means to face social ostracism and attacks in schools; to become "American" means often to adopt the cultural outlook of the underclass and thus abandon any upward mobility expectations based on individual achievement.[164]

In this context, Portes says, the best option for today's first generation may be to join dense immigrant communities where their children (the second generation) can "capitaliz[e] on the moral and material resources that only these communities can make available."[165] There the children may gain the breathing space and support they need to develop the skills that can move them securely into the American mainstream.[166] But if they fail to develop these skills, the children may succumb to the adversarial culture that surrounds, and insidiously penetrates, the immigrant enclave and may turn for solace to a negatively reconstituted ethnic culture that widens the differences between the second generation and their native counterparts.[167]

For our sake and the sake of the new immigrants, we must pray that they can enable their children to resist these seductions. If the new immigrants succeed in doing so, their children—like most (though not all) second generations have in the past—will in all likelihood enter the mainstream of American society, and Brimelow will have no cause for complaint. If the children fail, however, their future—and ours—may be even bleaker than Brimelow imagines. Although he does not discuss this possibility or the second-generation problem more generally, his argument clearly implies that the risk of failure is one that America can and should avoid either by eliminating immigration altogether or by limiting it to groups that are already so successful when they arrive that their children are relatively invulnerable to the blandishments of underclass culture.

## V. POLITICS

Brimelow believes that the post-1965 immigration is already sapping the strength of the American political system. Some of his fears—for example, irredentist movements by Mexican immigrants to reunite the Southwest with Mexico and Mexican revanchism seeking to manipulate the continuing allegiance of Mexican-Americans[168]—are fatuous and even insulting in their depiction of the latter as pawns whose disloyalty Mexico City could successfully exploit. He warns that neither major party can count on being helped electorally by immigration and that continuing our current pro-immigration policies may spark a voter revolt that could strengthen an already budding third-party movement.[169] The Democrats and Republicans, of course, well understand this: Both the Clinton administration and the Republican majority in Congress are supporting reforms that, while different in some respects, would significantly restrict and restructure legal immigration.[170]

The political specter that haunts him most darkly, however, is balkanization.[171] The fragmentation of nation-states, both real or imagined,[172] into ethnic shards—a process observed in Lebanon, the former Soviet Union and Yugoslavia, many African states, and perhaps even Canada—has become a leitmotif of the post-Cold War world. This unraveling of political authority, often accompanied by massive human rights violations, brutal warfare, economic immiseration, and suppression of political and religious dissent, is an exceedingly dangerous development.

Could it happen here? Brimelow and many other Americans think so, and they believe that post-1965 immigration has increased the odds. Brimelow cites programs or cultural attitude that create incentives for groups to exaggerate their differences, and he denounces the "New Class," which, he claims, wants to devolve the nation-state into ethnic tribes or to transcend the nation-state in the name of universal human rights.[173]

He mentions five specific policies that are effecting "the deconstruction of the American nation as it existed in 1965."[174] The first, of course, is the policy of immigration itself.[175] But how could the mere fact of immigration, even racially heterogeneous immigration, threaten national unity? After all, most of those who have *chosen* America presumably identify at least as strongly with its ideals and institutions as those who just happened to be born here. Especially in the first generation, many might continue to identify strongly with their country or culture of origin, but that was also true of the Germans, the Irish, the Jews, and even Brimelow's own group, the English.[176] Brimelow does not show that the new immigrants are somehow less patriotic than earlier ones or than native-born Americans are today. (Recall that he himself is a recent immigrant swiftly transformed into a flag-waving American). Indeed, new evidence suggests the contrary.[177]

He mentions four other balkanizing policies: bilingualism, multiculturalism, affirmative action, and a "systematic attack on the value of citizenship"[178] Unfortunately, he fails to provide any clear definitions, useful distinctions, or other analysis for the genuinely thoughtful, open-minded reader. Nevertheless, I believe that he is right to worry that these policies are weakening our coherence as a polity.[179] In seeking to use these policies to discredit immigration, however, Brimelow poses a seductive but perniciously false choice. Immigration may have encouraged the adoption of such policies, but it does not require them; we can reject them and still have immigration. If they are misguided policies, as in some respects they are, we can and should reform or repeal them without holding immigration hostage. We must instead evaluate immigration on its own merits. Brimelow might resist such a separation, of course, arguing that immigration by groups other than white "Anglo-Saxons" assures that the United States will maintain such policies, even if they prove to be perverse. I have more confidence, however, in the responsiveness and corrigibility of the American policy-making process. Recent reactions against the more extreme versions of these misguided policies are already taking hold, and I believe that my confidence will ultimately prove justified.

*Bilingualism.* I noted earlier that the crucial second generation of new immigrants seems to be acquiring both competence in and a preference for English, much as their predecessors did.[180] Still, it would be most imprudent to ignore the danger signals raised by evidence suggesting that government-sponsored bilingual education programs have subordinated pedagogical goals, such as improving student performance in school by facilitating rapid English fluency, to the ideological purpose of strengthening the child's identification with her presumed ethnic culture.[181] In my view, ethnic cultural retention is a perfectly appropriate goal when pursued privately by parents and without public aid or interference, but it has no place in the governmental agenda of a society as pluralistic and liberal as ours. Most disturbing of all are recurring indications that this deformation of bilingual education may actually retard the English fluency, the educational progress, and hence the assimilation prospects of already disadvantaged immigrant children.[182] My present point, however, is that we can and should reform bilingual education without abandoning immigration.[183]

*Multiculturalism.* Multiculturalism can take many forms, with vastly different social consequences. A limited multicultural policy affirms the social value of diverse cultural traditions and practices, protects individuals' and groups' freedom to engage in them, and incorporates diversity values into public school curricula, holidays, and national symbols. A more ambitious multiculturalism goes beyond recognition and respect of such traditions to define, preserve, and reinforce group differences through law.

The limited forms of multiculturalism are essential in a pluralistic democracy in which ethnic pride can be personally enriching, group strengthening, and socially integrative.[184] These forms should not weaken newcomers' ability or desire to achieve minimal levels of social assimilation, or exacerbate inter-group conflict.[185] Limited multiculturalism need not degenerate into the intolerance, humorlessness, hypersensitivity, and bogus essentialism that insists that group membership, rather than individual character and personality, is our most defining and precious attribute.[186]

In criticizing more expansive policies of multiculturalism that deploy the law to entrench and even construct group differences, Brimelow parrots an already palpable and increasingly effective public impatience with their excesses.[187] This impatience is salutary so long as it does not in turn breed its own parochialism and intolerance.[188] In a vibrant democracy like ours, policies such as multiculturalism tend to engender their own repudiation and ultimate reversal precisely because enthusiasts push them beyond any sensible limits.

Quite apart from the growing political opposition to perverse versions of multiculturalism, some purely demographic considerations make rigid racial division of the kind that Brimelow predicts most unlikely. First, the racial data that Brimelow cites rely on self-ascriptions that are themselves remarkably changeable over time and on highly arbitrary racial categories that grow less and less meaningful over time.[189] This phenomenon is particularly true of nonblack groups. Most Hispanics, the largest ethnic minority grouping, identify themselves as white.[190] Furthermore, racial and ethnic boundaries blur as people of different groups marry. Exogamy, already high between some groups in the United States, has been increasing for all. Black-white marriage rates (the smallest exogamy category) more than quintupled between 1968 and 1988, rising from only 1.6% of all marriages involving an African-American to 8.9%. Exogamy between blacks and other groups and between whites and other groups has also been increasing.[191] Exogamy between American-born Asian women and non-Asian men is strikingly high, reaching 41.7% in 1990.[192]

The conventional demographic projections that Brimelow uses do not account for these remarkable (and in my view, highly desirable) trends, which seem likely to continue or even accelerate in the future.[193] Such analyses assume that "exogamy is nonexistent by assuming single ancestry offspring, usually taking the father's racial status as the marker."[194] A recent analysis that does seek to take exogamy (but not the other sources of shifting racial identities) into account shows that doing so can make an enormous difference in racial composition projections.[195] The study simulated future racial composition by factoring differential exogamy rates into the analysis and projecting the effect of those rates over multiple generations. If all mixed ancestry persons were classified as single ancestry and self-identified as white, the number of non-Hispanic whites could be 31 million people (nearly 15%) larger than under the conventional census projection by the year 2040.[196]

My point is not that whites therefore have less to fear from demographic change. Rather, the very *meaning* of the traditional racial categories that structure such fears is rapidly becoming obsolete. Social attitudes and choices are evidently catching up to this demographic reality. Static, rigid, self-perpetuating policies of affirmative action and multiculturalism, premised on these obsolete meanings and categories, are already proving to be reactionary, not liberating.

To return to the larger point: Militant, mindless multiculturalism can be a destructive ideology that one should oppose on a variety of empirical and normative grounds. Immigration, even the post-1965 immigration, does not require such folly. Policies calculated to foster, or at least not impede, immigrants' assimilation to the dominant American culture without suppressing their ethnic ties continue to be the best antidote to balkanizing pressures.[197]

*Affirmative Action.* Brimelow complains that, as the demographic pincers close, affirmative action will place Alexander, his white son, at even more of a disadvantage than the poor lad labors under today. But like multiculturalism, race-based affirmative action—at least in its strongest, nonprocessual forms—is a policy with a doubtful political future. The Clinton administration, for example, has not fought very hard for it.[198] But if affirmative action is plainly on the defensive in Congress, the courts, and public opinion, it also enjoys the political advantage of any long-standing, institutionalized program.[199]

Brimelow neither defines affirmative action nor engages in a detailed analysis of it, but he is clear that the post-1965 immigration renders it even more problematic than it would otherwise be. I emphatically agree.[200] Until the recent assault on affirmative action in Congress and the Supreme Court, the policy steadily expanded from the protection of blacks in the employment setting to the protection of new groups in new contexts. The new groups include immigrants who happen to possess the protected demographic characteristics, such as race, even though they did not personally suffer the historical discrimination that prompted affirmative action's solicitude for American blacks or descend from those who did. In my view, this policy is impossible to justify, even if one is not the father of a white child, and especially if one is the father of a black one.

This Review is not the place to analyze the merits and demerits of affirmative action in particular domains or in general.[201] Only affirmative action's connections to the post-1965 immigration concern me here. Affirmative action has benefited the post-1965 immigrants in at least two senses. First, affirmative action programs now confer protected status on the millions of immigrants who happen to be members of currently favored groups. Second, the rhetoric of affirmative action was used to legitimate and augment the power of ethnic interest group politics, spawning a program of so-called diversity admissions—wholly unwarranted, in my view[202]—that adds 55,000 visas each year for immigrants from countries whose nationals supposedly have been disadvantaged by the 1965 law.[203]

In contrast, the racially diverse post-1965 immigration has been decidedly *bad* for affirmative action. I predict that recent immigration, far from serving as a firm buttress for future affirmative action policies as Brimelow believes, will eventually contribute to their demise. Immigration has undermined race-based affirmative action programs by revealing and then magnifying the moral, political, and empirical weaknesses of some of their underpinnings.[204] First, immigration enlarges the beneficiary pool to include immigrants who, unlike American blacks, cannot claim that they themselves have suffered historically rooted discrimination here, but who nevertheless are entitled by affirmative action programs to compete with Americans for program benefits. This phenomenon not only dilutes the programs' benefits (such as they are) but also undermines their moral integrity.

Second, the group-based nature of the claims that affirmative action programs endorse inevitably invites attention to the fact that some immigrant groups, including some that arrived after 1965, endured harsh discrimination based on religion, language, class, and race, yet have managed to achieve greater economic and social progress than have many American blacks.[205]

This record of achievement is bound to weaken the claim of many traditional civil rights activists that policies such as affirmative action are essential to individual and group progress. Third, immigration renders transparent the illogic, even absurdity, of the racial classifications and methodologies on which the integrity of such programs ultimately rests.[206] Finally, as Brimelow points out, the growth of "new minorities, each with their own grievances and attitudes—quite possibly including a lack of guilt about, and even hostility toward, blacks"— casts an ominous shadow over the long-term political prospects of affirmative action and its capacity to promote interracial reconciliation.[207]

Brimelow unaccountably ignores another realm, voting rights, in which immigration erodes the coherence of affirmative action. Under the Voting Rights Act of 1965,[208] the U.S. Department of Justice, with the acquiescence of Congress and the federal courts, has frequently insisted that legislative district boundaries be drawn to maximize the number of seats safely controlled by representatives of racial minorities. Many legal scholars and political scientists question the wisdom, legality, and representational efficacy of this practice,[209] and some political commentators blame it for many of the devastating Democratic losses in the 1994 congressional elections.[210] The Supreme Court recently subjected the Justice Department's policy to heightened constitutional scrutiny.[211]

The post-1965 immigration renders affirmative action districting of this kind even more problematic. By multiplying the number of residentially concentrated ethnic groups that can assert claims to a limited number of safe legislative seats, immigration has intensified intergroup conflict and made negotiated solutions to these inevitably bitter disputes much more difficult. While Asian-origin voters are unlikely in the near future to achieve the numbers and concentrations needed to qualify for this form of relief, Hispanic-Americans, whose numbers are increasing more rapidly than the black population, have already crossed that threshold in a number of jurisdictions and will soon do so in others.[212]

The flaw in Brimelow's logic should now be clear. Whatever one's evaluation of the merits of race-based affirmative action programs and whatever the bearing of immigration on those programs, they can and should be considered separately from the issue of immigration policy. We can choose to have immigration without choosing the kind of affirmative action that discredits immigration by association.

*Citizenship.* Part of "the deconstruction of the American nation" that Brimelow laments results from a "[s]ystematic attack on the value of citizenship, by making it easier for aliens to vote, receive government subsidies, etc."[213] The content of "etc." appears in his call, *inter alia,* for fundamental changes in our approach to citizenship. They include a new Americanization campaign modeled on the programs of the first two decades of this century, an English-language requirement for new immigrants and stricter enforcement of the existing English requirement for naturalized citizens, constitutional amendments eliminating birthright citizenship for the native-born children of illegal aliens and prescribing English as our official language, and possibly the lengthening of the residency period for naturalization to as long as the fourteen years required under the Alien and Sedition Act of 1798 and repealed in 1801.[214]

Brimelow presents these ideas in a manner that treats them more as rallying points and political slogans than as serious, thoughtful proposals for change. He shows no interest in analyzing the evidence bearing on them, the substantial objections that might be made to them, or the features that might be necessary to make them politically palatable or practically implementable. He simply presents items on his laundry list.

Brimelow's *ipse dixit*s will therefore be of little value to policymakers. Nevertheless, some of the items on his list do deserve serious consideration; indeed, some are already receiving it. An example is the issue of birthright citizenship for illegal alien children, which is now under active discussion in Congress.[215] Political scientist Rogers Smith and I coauthored a book analyzing this very question. We argued that the Citizenship Clause of the Fourteenth Amendment,[216] properly interpreted, permits Congress to regulate or even eliminate birthright citizenship for such children if it wishes.[217] We noted that whether Congress *should* prospectively eliminate birthright citizenship, and, if so, *how* to go about it, entail genuinely difficult normative, empirical, and policy questions.[218] We expressed a particular concern (shared by our critics[219]) that such a policy change risks creating a destitute, highly vulnerable, more or less permanent caste of pariah children who, due to ineffective INS border and interior enforcement, might remain in that condition for the rest of their lives in the United States.[220] We proposed strategies to avert this grim possibility, including an amnesty for many then-illegal aliens.[221] Nevertheless, this concern remains deeply troubling, especially today when the number of illegal alien residents in the United States may exceed four million and a new amnesty is politically inconceivable. The ever-insouciant Brimelow, however, appears not to have even considered the extremely difficult problems that this situation creates.

His proposal for an "official English" amendment is an even more telling example of his aversion to analysis. Because a similar policy has already been adopted in twenty-two states,[222] some evidence about how it actually works already exists. Brimelow fails to cite this evidence, which indicates that the policy has had no practical effect—except, perhaps, to convince many Hispanic-Americans, who already have overwhelming incentives to acquire English fluency, that they are unwelcome in their new country.[223]

A new "Americanization" program—if designed to foster immigrants' social and linguistic integration without the paternalism, cultural intolerance, and outright racism that tainted many of the early twentieth century campaigns[224]— might well be desirable. At a minimum, such an effort should significantly augment the woefully inadequate public resources now available for teaching English to adult immigrants.[225] The government should also abandon its traditional passivity with respect to naturalization and instead emphasize its benefits to immigrants.[226] Again, however, Brimelow does not trouble to explore seriously the programmatic content of an Americanization policy.[227]

In truth, his discussion of citizenship is really a diversionary tactic. His political agenda is something he portentously calls "the National Question."[228] He wishes to affirm his belief in a distinctive American nation-state in contrast to the one-worlders who, out of misguided guilt or bland cosmopolitanism, would dismantle our borders and throw open our doors to all comers—the more the merrier, the poorer the better.

This target, of course, is a straw man. There are indeed a smattering of academics, ethnic advocates, immigration lawyers, and militant multiculturalists who, if judged by their rhetoric, seem to fit this description.[229] But, as Brimelow surely knows, they are outliers—no more representative of immigration enthusiasts than Brimelow is of restrictionists. (I know of no restrictionist in Congress, for example, who proposes to go to zero immigration, as Brimelow seems to do.[230]) Americans vigorously disagree about precisely what Americanism consists of. They always have;[231] presumably they always will. Our core political identity is more elusive than that of, say, Japan, Germany, or Sweden—nation-states whose ethnic solidarities have powerfully shaped their self-understandings.[232] But while Americans struggle over the contemporary meaning of Americanism,[233] only a handful would deny that the United States is a distinctive polity that must protect its national sovereignty, nourish its culture, choose among its potential immigrants, and thus turn many away from its shores.

## CONCLUSION

Brimelow claims that American society has fallen into crisis since the new immigrants arrived and that they are responsible for its decline. I have sought to demonstrate that most of his factual claims are either wrong or fail to justify his radical policy prescriptions. For those whom I have not yet convinced, I wish to use this concluding section to test his overarching claim—that the post-1965 immigration flow has been an unequivocal plague on American society. I propose to do so by offering a (necessarily incomplete) answer to the following question: How does the state of American society today compare to its state in 1965, when the new immigrants began coming and when the Fall (according to Brimelow) therefore began? Briefly stated, my answer is that we are in most important respects a far better society than we were before these immigrants arrived. Their contribution to this progress is striking in the growth of the economy, the expansion of civil rights and social tolerance, and the revitalization of many urban neighborhoods. Moreover, these immigrants bear little blame for the great exception to this progress: the increase in the social pathology afflicting some inner-city subcultures.[234] Just as Brimelow cannot prove that the post-1965 immigrants *caused* certain social conditions in America to be worse than they would otherwise have been, it would be impossible for me to show how much of our post-1965 progress they *caused*. The evidence strongly suggests, however, that the post-1965 immigrants contributed to it.

Brimelow's answer to the question, of course, is very different. To him, the America of 1965 was an Edenic paradise compared to today[235]—relatively crime-free, economically prosperous, normatively coherent, politically stable, linguistically unified, demographically stable, and ecologically sustainable. Most important, it was overwhelmingly white. By 1995, the newcomers had changed all that, bringing us a society marked by drugs, violent crime, economic decline, debased family life, a babel of languages, clashing value systems, racial conflict, political divisions, a population bomb, a crowded, degraded environment—and swarthy complexions. No wonder Brimelow anguishes about America's present and about his son Alexander's future![236]

Brimelow's depressing, hand-wringing account of today's America, although common enough among conservatives and liberals alike, is profoundly distorted. It is true that the new immigration coincided with some extremely negative developments in American life. The most important of these is the erosion of family structure, which has blighted the lives of an immense number of children born out-of-wedlock and raised in single- or no-parent households[237] by caretakers who depend on public assistance and who are often only children themselves. Most of what is most pernicious about American society today—its high levels of street crime, drug use, racial fears, domestic violence, welfare dependency, public health menaces such as AIDS, educational failure, and high unemployment among low-skill youth—derives from this fundamental pathology of family structure. There is no gainsaying its deeply corrosive effects on American life.

It is also true, however, that little of this pathology can be attributed to the new immigrants. To be sure, many of them commit drug-related crimes; some sub-groups, mainly Asian refugees, have relatively high welfare rates; and some others, notably Mexican-Americans, have high illegitimacy rates. These behaviors are indeed troubling, as is the fact that they seem to increase the more that the new immigrants interact with Americans.[238] Still, these grim patterns must be kept in perspective: Relatively few of the new immigrants commit crimes, and the vast majority of these are drug-related; we are not *supposed* to select refugees for their skills; and the groups with high illegitimacy rates are comprised disproportionately of illegal aliens, many of whom can be excluded in the future by better border control policies.

What about the other side of the ledger, which Brimelow assiduously ignores? If the post-1965 immigrants have contributed to some of America's failures, have they not also contributed to some of our post-1965 successes? If so, do not these successes contradict Brimelow's alarums about the state of the American polity?

The truth is that the last three decades have witnessed some remarkable advances in American life. While causality in such matters is extremely complex and elusive, the new immigrants can claim some credit for many of these advances. Most plausibly, they have contributed to our continued if slow economic growth,[239] the dramatic rise in the public's tolerance for minorities (including dark-skinned aliens) and its support for racial integration and equality,[240] the renaissance in many previously declining urban neighborhoods,[241] and the diversification and enrichment of many aspects of American culture. Beyond these advances, however, are social improvements that bespeak a robust polity, one that contradicts Brimelow's vision of political dissolution and decline attributable to the new immigrants.[242] I shall mention only three areas of improvement: the environment, politics, and the quality of life.

*Environment.* Brimelow blames the new immigrants for the deterioration of the American environment.[243] In fact, however, the quality of the American environment today is vastly superior to its state in 1965, before these immigrants arrived. Whether the concern is air pollution (indoor or outdoor), water quality, deforestation, pesticides and other chemical risks, radiation hazards, food quality, land preservation, historic preservation, wetlands, farmland, energy efficiency, toxic waste, depletion of raw materials, lead paint, acid rain, or many other conditions, the levels of risk and environmental degradation today are lower, often much lower, than they were in 1965.[244] These improvements rank as one of the greatest triumphs of private mobilization and public policy in our history. Insofar as immigrants contributed to the economic growth that made these policies fiscally and hence politically sustainable, they helped to improve the environment. At the very least, they did not prevent such gains from being realized.

*Politics.* In 1965, blacks and other disadvantaged minorities played at best a marginal role in the American political system. For almost a century, they had been routinely denied the vote guaranteed to them by the Fifteenth Amendment, and there were relatively few racial minority officeholders. There were also few female officeholders, although women had received the franchise almost a half-century earlier. Three decades later, blacks, Asians, Hispanics, women, the disabled, elderly, gays and lesbians, and other minorities are full participants in the political system at all levels of government. Their organizations have led largely successful struggles to enact a plethora of laws—the Voting Rights Act of 1965,[245] the Age Discrimination in Employment Act of 1967,[246] the Age Discrimination Act of 1975,[247] the Education of the Handicapped Act of 1975,[248] the Americans with Disabilities Act of 1990,[249] the Civil Rights Act of 1991,[250] and many others—designed to prevent discrimination and otherwise advance their group interests.

As a result of these developments, the American political system today is for more participatory and responsive to minority interests than it was in 1965.[251] If the level of party discipline in both major parties in Congress is any measure of coherence, American politics today is also more coherent and less fragmented than it has been for decades.[252] This partisanship reflects and enforces a growing ideological polarization between the parties that tends to sharpen policy issues, widen voters' choices, and increase accountability. The bellicosity of partisan politics today is part of the price that we pay for these virtues, and it is well worth it.

Taken together, these changes have transformed the American state into more robust democracy than ever before. They have helped to shape a polity that is far more just and responsive to far more people than it was before the new immigrants came.

*Quality of Life.* I have already noted the enormous economic growth that has occurred since 1965, growth that translates into higher disposable income and living standards for virtually all Americans.[253] It is important to emphasize that even the millions still mired in poverty—a group that, according to the best, consumption-based estimates, is less than half the percentage of the population that it was in 1961—enjoy an improved standard of living.[154] With the enactment and extraordinary expansion of the Food Stamp program, hunger as traditionally understood has been essentially eliminated from American life.[255] The proportion of housing units that are substandard declined from 16% in 1960 and 8.4% in 1970 to practically zero today.[256] Life expectancy for those born in 1992 was nearly five years longer than for those born in 1970.[257] Both the quantity and quality of medical care have improved enormously since 1965, and the rapid growth of the Medicare and Medicaid programs has enabled low-income people to share in those gains.

Infant mortality rates dropped steadily during the post-1965 period; they fell by more than half between 1970 and 1991.[258] The percentage of Americans who completed four or more years of college nearly tripled between 1960 and 1993.[259] The rising quality of many public goods, such as recreational facilities, highways, low-cost entertainment, and (as noted above) the environment, also increased the value of Americans' consumption, albeit in ways not captured by the national income accounts.[260] Finally, the risk of a large-scale war claiming American lives and treasure—a tragic reality in 1965—has diminished almost to the vanishing point today.

These gains in the quality of life since 1965 are remarkable by any standard. All things considered, they may even exceed the gains during the pre-1973 period, when the American economy, as conventionally measured, was expanding at a faster rate. Even when set against the alarming increase in family dissolution and its dire consequences, these gains remain impressive. This dissolution, moreover, principally affects those Americans condemned to live in or in close proximity to the underclass, a group that still constitutes a relatively small share (approximately one to two percent) of the population. The small size of the share, while no consolation to those who comprise it or must reside near it members, nevertheless puts even this great failure into a somewhat broader, more hopeful perspective.

The quality-of-life gains since 1965 for the vast majority of Americans, then, have been enormous, perhaps unparalleled. It is impossible to know, of course, whether those gains would have been even larger or more widespread had we admitted fewer or different immigrants during this period.[261] What we do know is that the post-1965 immigrants, whom Brimelow condemns as afflictions and parasites, did join American society, and that we are now a more just, diverse, and prosperous society today than we were then. We can also be certain that many of the values that immigrants, the new as well as the old, brought with them will be essential to our continued vigor and progress. Today and tomorrow, even more than yesterday, America desperately needs what so many immigrants possess—optimism and energy, orientation to the future, faith in education as the ladder upward, hunger for their own and their children's success, and devotion to a dynamic, hopeful vision of America that has lost focus for many native-born citizens.

We must reform immigration policy to meet our changing needs. In particular, policy should assure that a larger share of the immigration flow consists of individuals who are most likely to succeed in the American economy of the twenty-first century. But it will take much, much more than this book to convince me that we should eliminate or radically reduce that flow. Immigration, including the post-1965 wave, has served America well. If properly regulated, there is every reason to expect that it will continue to do so.

## NOTES

1. Jack Miles aptly refers to it as "bottled brio." Jack Miles, "The Coming Immigration Debate," *Atlantic Monthly,* April 1995, at 130, 131 (reviewing Peter Brimelow, *Alien Nation: Common Sense about America's Immigration Disaster* (1995) [hereinafter *Alien Nation*]).

2. Too personal, in some respects—a point noted by Jack Miles in his largely admiring review. See ibid., p. 140.

3. *Alien Nation*, supra note 1, at 4. On birthright citizenship, see *Hearing Before the Subcommittee on Immigration and Claims and the Subcommittee on the Constitution of the House Committee on the Judiciary,* 104th Cong., 1st Sess. (December 13, 1995) (statement of Peter H. Schuck, Professor, Yale Law School) (hereinafter Schuck Testimony); Letter from Peter H. Schuck, Professor, Yale Law School, and Rogers Smith, Professor, Yale University, to House Subcommittee on Immigration and Claims and House Subcommittee on the Constitution of the House Committee on the Judiciary (February 14, 1996) (supplementing December 1995 testimony) (on file with author) [hereinafter Supplemental Letter].

4. *Alien Nation,* supra note 1, at 263.

5. For example,in his review of the book, Aristide Zolberg expresses surprise and dismay as to "[w]hy this journalistic broadside has received such respectful treatment." Aristide Zolberg, Book Review, 21 *Population and Dev. Review* 659, 659 (1995). A number of other readers have been similarly dismissive.

6. The media and Congress have already given it much prominence, and it is bound to receive more attention as we approach two seismic political events: congressional action on immigration reform legislation and the 1996 election campaign. For a sampling of Brimelow's appearances on national television programs, see "Booknotes" (C-SPAN television broadcast, June 11, 1995), cited in Reuters Daybook, June 11, 1995, available in Lexis, News Library, Curnws File; Charlie Rose (PBS television broadcast. April 20, 1995), transcript reprinted in Lexis, News Library, Curnws File (transcript no. 1360): "Crossfire" (CNN television broadcast, July 4, 1995), available in Lexis, News Library, Curnws File (transcript no. 1398); "Firing Line: Resolved: All Immigration Should Be Drastically Reduced" (PBS television broadcast, June 16, 1995), discussed in Walter Goodman, "Television Review: An Immigration Debate's Real Issue," *New York Times,* June 15, 1995, at C20; "MacNeil/Lehrer NewsHour: *Alien Nation*" (PBS television broadcast, August 16, 1995), available in Lexis, News Library, Curnws File; The McLaughlin Group (television broadcast, August 1995), discussed in Susan Douglas, "Snide Celebrations: Network 7–11 Political Talk Shows and Women's Rights," *Progressive,* October 1995, at 17, 17. Brimelow has also testified before Congress. See *Immigration Issues: Hearing Before the Subcommittee on Immigration and Claims of the House Judiciary Comm.,* 104th Cong., 1st Sess. (May 17, 1995).

7. See *Alien Nation,* supra note 1, at 258. The 1965 amendments, Act of October 3, 1965. Pub. L. No. 89–236, 79 Stat. 911 (codified as amended in scattered sections of 8 U.S.C.), modified the landmark Immigration and Nationality Act of 1952, ch. 477, 66 Stat. 163 (codified as amended at 8 U.S.C. §§ 1101–1523 [1988 and Supp. 1994]).

8. See Immigration Act of 1921, ch. 8, 42 Stat. 5. Congress adopted the national origins quotas in provisional form in 1921, id. 2, 42 Stat. at 5–6, and codified them as a permanent system in 1924, Immigration Act of 1924, ch. 190, 11, 43 Stat. 153, 159–60.

9. Act of October 3, 1965, §§ 1–3, 8, Pub. L. No. 89–236, 79 Stat. at 911–14, 916–17.

10. See Immigration Act of 1978, Pub. L. No. 95–412, 92 Stat. 907; Immigration Reform and Control Act of 1986, Pub. L. No. 99–603, 100 Stat. 3359; Immigration Act of 1990, Pub. L. No. 101–649, 1990 U.S.C.C.A.N. (104 Stat.) 4978.

11. *Alien Nation,* supra note 1, at 262.

12. Id. at 262–63. I say "seems" because he is not altogether clear about how far he is prepared to go in restricting immigration. Brimelow proposes severe cutbacks in each category that would still preserve the category in some form, but he also says that, in the end, complete elimination is the preferred policy. Id. Either Brimelow has not considered the possibility that some of these changes—especially a refusal to allow genuine asylees to enter the United States—would violate human rights conventions to which the United States is a signatory, or he does not care if they do.

13. Brimelow, however, is not as radical as Michael Lind, who, to protect the earnings of native-born Americans, advocates zero net immigration. See Michael Lind, *The Next American Nation: The New Nationalism and the Fourth American Revolution* 321–22 (1995), I should add that Lind's book is both provocative and excellent, although its brief discussion of immigration policy is among its weakest sections.

14. Brimelow's discussion does not distinguish clearly between race, which connotes a close phenotypic affinity among people, and ethnicity, which connotes a cultural affinity, albeit one in which skin color might play an important cohesive role. He uses the terms more or less interchangeably. He assumes that there are well-defined races in the United States today, that they are accurately represented by Census data, and that they bear race-specific cultural values and behavioral propensities of a kind that would or should be relevant to immigration policy. These beliefs are as dangerous as they are false, For a critique of these assumptions, see id. at 118–27.

15. Both the ethnocultural conception of nationhood and the contrasting political conception are traced in Rogers Brubaker, *Citizenship and Nationhood in France and Germany* (1992).

16. See generally *Controlling Immigration: A Global Perspective* (Wayne A. Cornelius et al. eds., 1994) [hereinafter *Controlling Immigration*] (comparing immigration policy and politics of immigration of Western democracies).

17. For recent reviews and analyses of the evidence, See William G. Mayer, *The Changing American Mind: How and Why American Public Opinion Changed between 1960 and 1988,* at 22–28 (1992); Benjamin I. Page and Robert Y. Shapiro, *The Rational Public: Fifty Years of Trends in America's Policy Preferences* 68–81 (1992); Byron M. Roth, *Prescription for Failure: Race Relations in the Age of Social Science* 45–72 (1994). See generally Abigail Thernstrom and Stephan Themstrom, "The Premise of Racial Equality," in *The New Promise of American Life* 88, 88–101 (Lamar Alexander and Chester E. Finn Jr., eds., 1995) (discussing indicia of racism and measures of political and economic progress of African-Americans). Particularly interesting is the increase during the 1980s in the proportion of whites and blacks who said that they had a "fairly close friend" of the other race. In 1989, two-thirds of whites reported having a fairly close black friend, up from 50% in 1981. Similarly, 69% of blacks said that they had a fairly close white friend in 1981; by 1989, this number had increased to 80%. Id. at 95; see also D'Vera Cohn and Ellen Nakashima, "Crossing Racial Lines," *Washington Post,* December 13, 1995, at Al

(discussing newspaper poll that indicates that more than three-quarters of Washington area 12- to 17-year-olds say they have close friend of another race). On the other hand, a recent study finds that at least one aspect of traditional prejudice—the stereotype of blacks as lazy—is still widespread and contributes to whites' opposition to welfare. Martin Gilens, "Racial Attributes and Opposition to Welfare," 57 *J. Pol.* 994 (1995).

18. The most arguable exceptions, such as the contrast between the immigrant friendly Cuban Adjustment Act, Pub. L. No 89–732, 80 Stat. 1161 (1966) (codified as amended at 8 U.S.C. §§ 1101[b][5], 1255 [1988]), and the often harsh treatment of Haitians, are over-determined; they can also be explained on geopolitical and ideological grounds. For opposition to the Cuban emigrées' advantages under the Cuban Adjustment Act, see "The Stick Congress Gave Castro," *New York Times,* August 15, 1991, at A22 (editorial). Haitians have experienced a more hostile reception. See Anthony DePalma, "For Haitians, Voyage to a Land of Inequality," *New York Times,* July 16, 1991, at A1. This differential was much noted—and denied—during the Haitian refugee crisis that followed the Haitian military's overthrow of the government of President Jean-Bertrande Aristide in 1991. See, e.g., Bob Herbeil, "In America: Fasting for Haiti," *New York Times,* May 4, 1994, at A23.

Some observers also attribute much of the support for Proposition 187 in California to racism. See, e.g., Kevin R. Johnson, "An Essay on Immigration Politics, Popular Democracy, and California's Proposition 187. The Political Relevance and Legal Irrelevance of Race," 70 *Washington Law Review* 629, 650–61 (1995); Gerald L. Neuman, "Aliens as Outlaws: Government Services, Proposition 187, and the Structure of Equal Protection Doctrine," 42 *UCLA Law Review* 1425, 1451–52 and n. 125 (1995). There is room, however, for genuine disagreement about the significance of the Latino support for the measure. Compare Peter H. Schuck, "The Message of 187," *American Prospect,* Spring 1995, at 85, 89–90 (viewing support of significant minority of Latinos for Proposition 187 as evidence of nonracist nature of support for measure) with Johnson, supra, at 650–61 (viewing fact that majority of Latinos opposed it as evidence of racism). A federal district court in California has partially enjoined the enforcement of Proposition 187 on constitutional grounds. See *League of United Latin Am. Citizens* v. *Wilson,* 908 F. Supp, 755 (C.D. Cal. 1995).

19. See infra text accompanying notes 76–93 (racial composition); 180–97 (bilingualism and multiculturalism); 198–207 (affirmative action); 208–12 (legislative districting).

20. For a recent review of these eugenic arguments, see Dorothy Nelkin and Mark Michaels, "Biological Categories and Border Controls: The Revival of Eugenics in Anti-Immigration Rhetoric" (September 12, 1995) (Unpublished manuscript, on file with author).

21. The national origins of family-based admissions follow those of the petitioning U.S. citizens or legal resident aliens. For example, the beneficiaries of the massive legalization program, many of whom may now petition on behalf of their family members, were disproportionately from Mexico and other Central American nations. See Frank D. Bean et al., *Opening and Closing the Doors: Evaluating Immigration Reform and Control* fig. 5.1 at 69, fig. 5.2 at 71 (1989).

22. Usually, but not always. Almost half of the immigrants from Africa are white. Telephone Interview with Professor Frank D. Bean, Population Research Center, University of Texas at Austin (November 22, 1995).

23. *Alien Nation,* supra note 1, at 10–11. He immediately adds, "Or, too often, a libertarian. And, on the immigration issue, even some confused conservatives." Id. at 11.

24. Thus, he is both impressed and obviously dismayed by the fact that "when you enter the INS waiting rooms you find yourself in an underworld that is not just teeming but is also almost entirely colored." Id. at 28. He never says why this disturbs him. Similarly, he insists that "[i]t is simply common sense that Americans have a legitimate interest in their country's racial balance." Id. at 264. Frankly, I do not understand why that is so, why race per se should matter.

Unfortunately, his racial awareness does not distinguish him from most Americans today; we seem obsessed with the subject. The difference may be that Brimelow does not simply believe that race does matter. See, e.g., Cornell West, *Race Matters* (1993); see also Peter H. Schuck, "Cornell West's *Race Matters*: A Dissent," *Reconstruction,* 1994 No. 3, at 84 (book review) (praising West's open discussion of controversial race issues but criticizing specifics of West's analysis). He also believes that it should matter—a lot.

25. After making his quip about liberals, Brimelow offers a serious definition. Racism, he writes, is "committing and stubbornly persisting in error about people, regardless of evidence." *Alien Nation,* supra note 1, at 11. He calls this "the only rational definition" of racism. Id. Having noted the question of his own racism and then defined the term, he immediately dismisses the charge on the ground that he is open to evidence. This auto-acquittal, however, is not entirely satisfying. For one thing, his definition of racism as nothing more than an obdurately erroneous methodology of inference is peculiar and evasive. It fails to distinguish racism from many other more morally acceptable, but still regrettable, forms of cognitive error. It also ignores the substantive content of racist views, which of course is their chief point of interest. In common understanding and parlance, racism is a belief in the inherent superiority of one's race, almost invariably accompanied by feelings of animus or contempt toward members of other races. This definition would distinguish racism from what Dinesh D'Souza calls "rational discrimination"—discrimination based not on hostility but on the need to act without full information, which would be costly to acquire, and thus on the basis of generalizations (or stereotypes) that are certain to be wrong in many, perhaps even most, individual cases. See Dinesh D'Souza, *The End of Racism: Principles of a Multiracial Society* (1995).

In this common-sense understanding of racism, it is hard to say whether *Alien Nation* is a racist book. Brimelow's genial discussion reveals an acute sense of racial pride and difference but little outright animus or contempt; his breezy, loose-jointed writing style, which makes no pretense of analytical rigor, leaves it maddeningly unclear precisely what he is claiming. Key concepts such as race and cultural assimilation remain ill- or undefined. His conclusions about group superiority refer to a group's culture, national origin, ethnicity, or class rather than to its race or genetic endowment as such. For example, he notes that street crime is related to "present-orientation," which he says varies among different ethnic groups, and that "[i]nevitably, therefore, certain ethnic cultures are more crime prone than others." *Alien Nation,* supra note 1, at 184. He then refers to the disproportionate arrest rates among blacks. Id. Nowhere, however, does he claim that blacks or other disfavored groups are genetically inferior. See id. Specifically, he disavows any intention to rely on the claims about racial differences in IQ emphasized in Richard J. Herrnstein and Charles Murray, *The Bell Curve: Intelligence and Class Structure in American Life* (1994), although he is careful not to disavow the claims themselves. See *Alien Nation,* supra note 1, at 56 n.*.

On the other hand, the book's central, frequently reiterated claims—that the post-1965 immigrants are diluting the predominantly white "Anglo-Saxon" Protestant stock that made America great and that this gravely threatens American society—certainly resemble claims of racial (or at least national origin) superiority, despite Brimelow's disclaimers. And he seems rather eager to define blacks out of the original American nation (much as Chief Justice Taney infamously and tragically did in the Dred Scott decision, see *Scott v. Sandford,* 60 U.S. [19 How.] 393 [1857]) to support his point that America was essentially while and European until the despised 1965 law was implemented. See *Alien Nation,* supra note 1, at 66–67. For that matter, Brimelow also ignores the presence of substantial numbers of persons of Mexican descent in the Southwest following the U.S. annexation of the region. Nor does Brimelow's lily-white vision of pre–1965 America square with the influx of Chinese and Japanese into California and the West after the Civil War. An interesting contrast is presented by the scrupulously and emphatically nonracist discussion of many of these same points by Michael Lind. See Lind, supra note 13, at 259–98.

26. *Alien Nation,* supra note 1, at 29.

27. See id. at 29–49.

28. Eric Schmitt, "Immigration Bill Advances in the Senate," *New York Times,* March 29, 1996, at A16.

29. See Immigration and Naturalization Service, U.S. Department of Justice, *1994 Statistical Yearbook of the Immigration and Naturalization Service* tbl. 1, tbl. B at 20 (1996) [hereinafter *1994 INS Statistical Yearbook*).

30. See Schmitt. supra note 28, at A16.

31. Immigration and Naturalization Service, U.S. Department of Justice, *Immigration to the United States in Fiscal Year 1994,* at 1–2, tbl. 2 (1995) [hereinafter *1994 Immigration Report*).

32. *1994 INS Statistical Yearbook,* supra note 29, tbl. 1.

33. Id.

34. The figures for these years include IRCA legalizations, of which there were only 6000 in 1994. Id. tbl. 4.

35. Telephone Interview with Michael Hoefer, Chief of Demographic Analysis, Immigration and Naturalization Service (September 20, 1995) [hereinafter Telephone Interview with Hoefer]. The 1994 decline also reflected the termination of certain special programs and other factors. Id. For what it's worth, the INS expects legal immigration to increase in 1996. Telephone Interview with Michael Hoefer, Chief of Demographic Analysis, Immigration and Naturalization Service (April 2, 1996).

36. *1994 INS Statistical Yearbook,* supra note 29, at 19. The legalization program is also contributing to the enormous growth in naturalization petitions that began in 1995, as the program's beneficiaries are now completing the five-year residency period required for naturalization. See Seth Mydans, "The Latest Big Boom: Citizenship," *New York Times,* August 11, 1995, at A12. In contrast, the program for dependent family members of legalized aliens added about 34,000 in 1994, down from 55,000 in 1993. *1994 Immigration Report,* supra note 31, tbl. 2. The program will continue to contribute significantly to the totals for years to come due to the enormous "overhang" of such dependents waiting for visas.

37. See Jeffrey S. Passel, "Commentary: Illegal Migration to the United States— The Demographic Context," in *Controlling Immigration,* supra note 16, at 113, 114–15. Unless otherwise indicated, the discussion of illegal aliens is based on Frank D. Bean et al., Introduction to *Undocumented Migration to the United States: IRCA and the Experience of the 1980s* 1, 1–10 (Frank D. Bean et al. eds., 1990); Thomas J. Espenshade, "Unauthorized Immigration to the United States," 21 *Ann. Rev. Soc.* 195 (1995); and Telephone Interview with Hoefer, supra note 35. The other essays in the Bean volume are quite useful empirical studies of illegal immigration.

38. See Passel, supra note 37, at 114–15.

39. See Wayne A. Cornelius, "From Sojourners to Settlers: The Changing Profile of Mexican Immigration to the United States," in *U.S.-Mexico Relations: Labor Market Interdependence* 155, 155–95 (Jorge A. Bustamante et al. eds., 1992).

40. The number declined to 1.09 million in 1994. Immigration and Naturalization Service, U.S. Department of Justice, *INS Fact Book: Summary of Recent Immigration Data* tbl. 14 (1995).

41. *Alien Nation,* supra note 1, at 33.

42. Id. at 27, 33–34.

43. Robert Warren, Estimates of the Undocumented Immigrant Population Residing in the United States, by Country of Origin and State of Residence: October 1992, at 13 (April 1995) (unpublished paper presented at Population Association of America conference, San Francisco, on file with author); Telephone Interview with Hoefer, supra note 35. A restrictionist group argues for a figure of 400,000 on the basis of a recent Census Bureau report. See John L. Martin, *How Many Illegal Immigrants?* 1 (Center for Immigration Studies Backgrounder No. 4–95, 1995).

44. Telephone Interview with Hoefer, supra note 35.

45. Ashley Dunn, "Skilled Asians Leaving U.S. for High-Tech Jobs at Home," *New York Times,* February 21, 1995, at A1, B5 (reporting that Census Bureau estimates 195,000 foreign-born Americans emigrate each year, highest since World War I).

46. See *Alien Nation,* supra note 1. at 39.

47. See Statistics Div., Immigration and Naturalization Service, U.S. Department of Justice, *Immigration Fact Sheet* 4 (1994) [hereinafter *Immigration Fact Sheet*] ("Emigration"); Telephone Interview with Hoefer, supra note 35.

48. This figure is obtained by subtracting the INS emigration data from the 1950s, see *Immigration Fact Sheet,* supra note 47, from INS immigration data from that decade, see 1994 *INS Statistical Yearbook,* supra note 29 tbl. 1.

49. See Subcommittee on Immigration and Refugee Policy of the Senate Committee on Judiciary and Subcommittees on Immigration, Refugees and International Law of House Committee on the Judiciary, *Final Report of the Select Commission on Immigration and Refugee Policy,* 97th Cong., 1st Sess. 30 (1981) (statement of Rev. Theodore Hesburgh) (recommending cap on legal immigration of 350,000).

50. The impetus for the large increase in illegal migration to the United States is usually attributed to the termination of the Bracero program in 1964. On the Bracero program, see generally Kitty Calavita, *Inside the State: The Bracero Program, Immigration, and the I.N.S.* (1992). There presumably were some illegal aliens early in the century—those who evaded the nonnumerical restrictions imposed by federal law since 1875 and by state law since much earlier. See generally Gerald L. Neuman, "The Lost Century of American Immigration Law (1776–1875)," 93 *Columbia Law Review* 1833 (1993) (explaining pre-1875 immigration laws). As to the latter category, however, see Shuck Testimony, supra note, 3, at 2 n.2.

51. This illegal immigration accounts for at least one-third of all population growth due to immigration. Espenshade, supra note 37, at 200–201.

52. *Alien Nation,* supra note 1. at 35–38, 43–45.

53. For this figure, see the graph entitled "Rate of immigration by decade, 1820–1990" in John J. Miller and Stephen Moore, "The Index of Leading Indicators," in Strangers at Our Gate: Immigration in the 1990s, at 100, 103 (John J. Miller ed., 1994) (citing Bureau of the Census, U.S. Department of Commerce, *Statistical Abstract of the United States 1992* tbl. 5 [1992]). These figures are clearly based only on legal immigration.

54. Bureau of the Census, U.S. Department of Commerce, March 1994 Current Population Survey, cited in Martin, supra note 43, at 1.

55. Bureau of the Census, U.S. Department of Commerce, *Statistical Abstract of the United States 1994* tbl. 54 (1994) (hereinafter *1994 U.S. Statistical Abstract*]. This percentage approximates the foreign-born share of 8.6% in Germany in 1994. Rainer Münz and Rolf Ulrich, "Changing Patterns of Migration: The Case of Germany, 1945–1994," in *Opening the Door: U.S. and German Policies on the Absorption and Integration of Immigration* (Peter H. Schuck et al. eds., forthcoming 1996) [hereinafter *Opening the Door*] (Münz and Ulrich manuscript at 34, on file with author). The foreign-born share in Canada is much higher. See *Controlling Immigration*, supra note 16, tbl. A.9 at 420 (15.4% share in 1986).

56. Brimelow's account of immigration waves appears primarily in *Alien Nation*, supra note 1, at 29–33.

57. *1994 INS Statistical Yearbook*, supra note 29, tbl. 1 at 25.

58. See infra text accompanying notes 62–64.

59. *Alien Nation*, supra note 1, at 38. Unless, of course, Congress enacts pending legislation to restrict legal immigration. See infra note 170 and accompanying text.

60. Id. at 33. Nathan Glazer makes the same claim. See Nathan Glazer, "Immigration and the American Future," *Public Interest,* Winter 1995, at 45, 53 ("The rise and fall of the business cycle and employment still plays some role in immigration, but it is a surprisingly small one.").

61. *Alien Nation*, supra note 1, at 33, 39, 42.

62. See, e.g., id. chart I at 30–31, chart 2 at 32. Brimelow calls chart 2 "a ramp . . . or a springboard." Id. at 33 (ellipsis in original).

63. I mean this literally, as well as figuratively. The charts are scaled in a way that can easily mislead the reader. The scale makes the troughs seem deeper than they were in absolute terms, and the scale exaggerates the significance of the inevitable short-term fluctuations. Brimelow's *trompe l'oeil* is particularly egregious in chart 1, see id. at 30–31, chart 3. see id. at 34, and chart 5, see id. at 42, although this problem plagues many of his diagrams.

64. See 1994 *INS Statistical Yearbook,* supra note 29, tbl. 1.

65. As noted above, nonnumerical restrictions had constrained immigration even before Congress began to regulate immigration in 1875. See supra note 50.

66. For some supporting evidence, which the authors view as "preliminary," see James F. Hollifield and Gary Zuk, "The Political Economy of Immigration: Electoral, Labor, and Business Cycle Effects on Legal Immigration in the United States" 11–16 (September 1995) (unpublished paper presented at migration workshop sponsored by Institute for Migration and Ethnic Studies, University of Amsterdam, on file with author).

67. See *Alien Nation*, supra note 1, at 211–16. For example, he points to historical patterns of increased intermarriage of Chinese immigrants and whites in the South after immigration had been interrupted for a long period of time. Id. at 270.

68. "The Immigrant Experience," *American Enterprise,* November-December 1995, at 102, 103 (relating May-June 1995 survey in which 66% of immigrants here for decade or less expressed this view). The comparable figure for non-immigrant Americans, according to a different survey in June 1995, was 89%. Id.

69. See supra notes 12–13 and accompanying text. Compare *Alien Nation*, supra note 1, at 261 (proposing that only immigrants with skills be admitted) with id. at 261–62 (proposing moratorium on immigration, or a lull at minimum).

70. Id. at 275.

71. Id. at 59. This historical vision of a white brotherhood into which earlier waves of white immigrants from southern and eastern Europe were readily inducted is, of course, a wholly misleading and pernicious account of the undisguised hostility that greeted so many of those who happened to be swarthier, poorer, and religiously different than the Americans of that time and who Brimelow, without recognizing the irony, now includes in the desirable "white" category. See generally Nathan Glazer and Daniel Patrick Moynihan, *Beyond the Melting Pot: The Negroes, Puerto Ricans, Jews, Italians, and Irish of New York City* 137–216 (2d ed. 1970); John Higham, *Strangers in the Land: Patterns of American Nativism, 1860–1925* (Rutgers University Press, 2d ed. 1988) (1955). In contrast to Brimelow, some strident conservatives forthrightly acknowledge this history of discrimination. See, e.g., Thomas Sowell, *Ethnic America: A History* (1981).

72. Immigration analysts commonly speak of "Hispanics" and "Asians." It is exceedingly important. however, to recognize the enormous ethnic, linguistic, religious, national origin, and other diversities within these broad groupings, and even within narrower classifications such as South Asians. Indeed, these diversities are so great as to render such labels virtually meaningless for most purposes, and often misleading. The Census Bureau and other researchers have adopted these rubrics and use them to organize important immigration data. Political actors have also found them quite serviceable. See Yen Le Espiritu, *Asian American Panethnicity: Bridging Institutions and Identities* 112–33 (1992); Peter Skerry, *Mexican-Americans: The Ambivalent Minority* 25–26 (1993); Kevin R. Johnson, "Civil Rights and Immigration: Challenges for the Latino Community in the Twenty-First Century," 8 *La Raza Law Journal* 42, 67–72 (1995). Not surprisingly, the law has fallen into line. In this essay, I reluctantly accede to these most arbitrary and distorting, but largely inescapable, conventional rubrics.

73. The pincer image refers to two arms—one consisting of Hispanics, the other consisting of blacks and Asians—bearing down upon the white population and gradually squeezing it into a minority position.

74. *Alien Nation,* supra note 1, chart 12 at 63. Oddly, he counts Hispanics (21.1% in 2050) as nonwhites in the Pincer Chart, yet only four pages later he notes that almost half of all Hispanics in the 1990 census counted themselves as whites, id. at 67, and he subsequently points out, quite rightly, the larger absurdity of a "Hispanic" category, id. at 218. Although he does not say so, the "Asian" rubric is even more absurd, as it aggregates into one meaningless category groups that do not even share a common language, as do Hispanics.

75. Id. at 66.

76. The demographic parade of horribles that results from immigration is a recurrent theme of Brimelow's book. For his discussion of the environmental consequences in particular, see id. at 187–90.

77. See id. chart 8 at 47.

78. For an example of Bouvier's empirical work, see Leon F. Bouvier and Lindsey Grant, *How Many Americans? Population, Immigration and the Environment* (1994). Other restrictionist writings draw heavily on this work. See, e.g., Roy Beck, *Re-Charting America's Future: Responses to Arguments against Stabilizing U.S. Population and Limiting Immigration* (1994) (citing six Bouvier sources throughout book).

79. See *Alien Nation,* supra note 1, at 47.

80. Id. at 151–55, 186–90.

81. See, e.g., Bouvier and Grant, supra note 78, at 73; Leon Bouvier, *Immigration and Rising U.S. Fertility: A Prospect of Unending Population Growth* 2–11 (Center for Immigration Studies Backgrounder No. 1–91, 1991).

82. See Tamara K. Hareven and John Modell, "Family Patterns," in *Harvard Encyclopedia of American Ethnic Groups* 345, 348–49 (Stephan Thernstrom et al. eds., 1980) (hereinafter *Harvard Encyclopedia*].

83. See, e.g., Francine D. Blau, "The Fertility of Immigrant Women: Evidence from High-Fertility Source Countries, in *Immigration and the Work Force* 93, 126 (George J. Borjas and Richard B. Freeman eds., 1992) [hereinafter *Immigration and the Work Force*]. A recent study claims that the experience of immigrant women in struggling against discrimination significantly reduced their fertility in the United States. See Thomas J. Espenshade and Wenzhen Ye, "Differential Fertility Within an Ethnic Minority: The Effect of 'Trying Harder' Among Chinese-American Women" 41 *Social Problems* 97 (1994).

84. Espenshade, supra note 37, at 201; Passel, supra note 37, at 116. An additional 20% of U.S..population growth resulted from births to immigrants.

85. *Alien Nation,* supra note 1, at 188–89.

86. In 1994, the United States had 74 people per square mile, compared to 623 in the United Kingdom and 275 in France, which are hardly countries that one thinks of as crowded. *1994 U.S. Statistical Abstract,* supra note 55, tbl. 1351.

87. I say "perhaps" because throughout American history, land previously thought to be uninhabitable was successfully developed for residential and other uses. Sections of Washington, D.C., and many other American cities were reclaimed from swampland, and cities such as Los Angeles, Salt Lake City, and Las Vegas were built in the most forbidding desert conditions.

88. In 1992, the population per square mile in New York City, the most densely populated in the United States, was 11,482; the corresponding densities for London and Paris were 10,490 and 19,883, respectively. The figure for Hong Kong, the most densely populated—and one of the richest—in the world, was 250,524. *1994 U.S. Statistical Abstract,* supra note 55, tbl. 1355.

89. Chicago was slightly more densely populated in 1990 than in 1920, but less so than in 1930. I am grateful to Professor Thomas Muller for supplying me with these data, which are based on his research comparing figures from the first few decades of this century as reported in the 1930 U.S. census with population data for 1992.

90. See, e.g., Herbert Stein, "Health Care Basics," *San Diego Union-Tribune,* May 29, 1994, at G1.

91. This has been the pattern in other countries such as Japan, where housing is scarce.

92. This *ceteris paribus* condition, of course, applies to all such predictive statements.

93. See infra notes 243–44 and accompanying text.

94. See *Alien Nation,* supra note 1, at 216 ("[T]he American experience with immigration has been a triumphant success.").

95. Id. at 141.

96. See Peter H. Schuck, "The Politics of Rapid Legal Change: Immigration Policy in the 1980s," 6 *Stud. Am. Pol. Dev.* 37, 86–89 (1992).

97. Telephone Interview with Hoefer, supra note 35.

98. Schuck, supra note 96, at 88.

99. E.g., S. 1394, 104th Cong., 1st Sess. (1995), which passed the Senate Subcommittee on Immigration on November 29, 1995. See 72 *Interpreter Releases* 1605 (December 4, 1995). Senator Simpson's effort to reduce employment-based admissions has failed. See Eric Schmitt, "Author of Immigration Measure in Senate Drops Most Provisions on Foreign Workers," *New York Times*, March 8, 1996, at A20.

100. See George J. Borjas, "National Origin and the Skills of Immigrants in the Postwar Period," in *Immigration and the Work Force*, supra note 83, at 17.

101. Frank D. Bean et al., "Educational and Sociodemographic Incorporation Among Hispanic Immigrants to the United States," in *Immigration and Ethnicity: The Immigration of America's Newest Arrivals* 73, tbls. 3.1, 3.2 at 81–82 (Barry Edmonston and Jeffrey S. Passel eds., 1994) [hereinafter *Immigration and Ethnicity*]. Although this figure is based on census data from 1986 and 1988, the same data indicate that the education level of the Mexican-origin groups declined substantially from that of earlier cohorts of Mexican-origin immigrants, thereby "lend[ing] support to the contention that at least some immigrant groups are less skilled than either other immigrant groups or earlier entrants for the same group." Id. at 86. These data suggest that "immigration no longer selects for relatively better educated Mexicans." Id. at 93. Another disturbing finding is that the educational attainment of third-generation Hispanics, a group dominated by Mexican-Americans, was actually lower than that of their parents, suggesting that the hard-won progress of the second generation does not necessarily continue in the third. Id. at 94; cf infra notes 150–56 and accompanying text (noting need to distinguish among first, second, and third generations of immigrants in evaluating linguistic assimilation).

102. For a comparative study of the skill levels of Asian immigrant national groups that uses years of education as a proxy for skill, see Sharon M. Lee and Barry Edmonston, "The Socioeconomic Status and Integration of Asian Immigrants," in *Immigration and Ethnicity,* supra note 101, at 101, 112–14 and tbl. 4.3 at 113.

103. Alejandro Portes, "Divergent Destinies: Immigration, Poverty, and the Second Generation" 7 (September 1995) (unpublished paper prepared for German-American Project on Immigration and Refugees, on file with author).

104. For a discussion of this problem as it appears in the leading studies, see Georges Vernez and Kevin F. McCarthy, *The Costs of Immigration to Taxpayers: Analytical and Policy Issues* (RAND Center for Research on Immigration Policy, MR–705-Ff/IF, 1996).

105. Eighteen percent of those in the United States for a decade or less have received food stamps, Medicaid, AFDC, and similar aid; 22% of those in United States for 11–20 years have received such aid, and 17% of those in United States for 21 years or more have benefited from such programs. See "The Immigrant Experience," supra note 68, at 103.

106. Of course, even if this pattern of lower incidence of welfare utilization by immigrants were true, it would simply raise anew the question of immigrant "quality." See discussion supra notes 100–103 and accompanying text.

107. See Michael Fix and Jeffrey S. Passel, "Who's on the Dole? It's Not Illegal Immigrants," *Los Angeles Times*, August 3, 1994, at B7 (summarizing results of study based on 1990 census data).

108. See, e.g., *Welfare Revision: Hearing Before Human Resources Subcommittee of House Ways and Means Comm.,* 104th Cong., 1st Sess. (January 27, 1995) (statement of Jane L. Ross, Director, Income Security Issues, General Accounting Office) (detailing dramatic growth in immigrants' claims), available in Lexis, News Library, Curnws File; Ashley Dunn, "For Elderly Immigrants, a Retirement Plan in U.S.," *New York Times*, April 16, 1995, at 1 (same). Pending legislation in both houses of Congress would restrict immigrants' SSI eligibility. See S. 269, 104th Cong., 1st Sess. § 203 (1995); H.R. 4, 104th Cong., 1st Sess. 202 (1995).

109. Frank D. Bean et al., Country-of-Origin, Type of Public Assistance and Patterns of Welfare Recipiency Among U.S. Immigrants and Natives 17–18 and tbl. 4 at 30 (unpublished paper of Population Research Center, University of Texas-Austin, on file

with author). The authors note that the absolute increase in Mexican SSI use reflected the great increase in the number of Mexican immigrants during the decade rather than any increased propensity of the average Mexican immigrant to use it. Id. at 13–14. Indeed, the rate of SSI use among Mexican immigrants actually declined over the decade. Nevertheless, the sheer growth in the Mexican cohort, coupled with its higher-than-immigrant-average utilization rate, drove the overall immigrant rate higher. Id. On the other hand, the number of Asian refugees has already declined and may be even lower in the future. See *1994 INS Statistical Yearbook*, supra note 29, at 75 (supplying statistics for Vietnamese and Laotian refugees, two of largest Asian refugee groups).

110. Donald Huddle, "The Costs of Immigration" (July 1993) (unpublished paper prepared for the Carrying Capacity Network, on file with author). For a sampling of the controversy surrounding Huddle's analysis, see Jane L. Ross, *Illegal Aliens—National Net Cost Estimates Vary Widely, GAO/HEHS–95–133* (July 25, 1995), available in Lexis, News Library, Curnws File.

111. See *Alien Nation,* supra note 1, at 151–53.

112. Jeffrey S. Passel and Rebecca L. Clark. "How Much Do Immigrants Really Cost? A Reappraisal of Huddle's 'The Cost of Immigrants' " (February 1994) (unpublished research report, on file with author).

113. See id.

114. Id. at 3.

115. Id. at 2. In turn, the Center for Immigration Studies, which has worked closely with Huddle, has responded to Passel and Clark with new estimates, focusing on immigrants' future claims against Social Security, that find a net burden of $29.1 billion. Center for Immigration Studies, *The Costs of Immigration: Assessing a Conflicted Issue* 1, 19 (Center for Immigration Studies Backgrounder No. 2–94, 1994). The Center and other restrictionists have often pointed in recent years to the faltering economy in California, where a large percentage of the post–1965 immigrants have settled, as evidence of their negative economic effects. It remains to be seen how the strong resurgence of California's economy, see James Sterngold, "Recovery in California Wears a New Costume," *New York Times,* January 2, 1996, at CIO, will affect these restrictionist arguments.

116. Congress is insisting that sponsors of family-based immigrants be legally responsible in the event that the immigrants become destitute. See S. 269, 104th Cong., 1st Sess. § 204 (1995); H.R. 4, 104th Cong., 1st Sess. 503 (1995).

117. *Alien Nation,* supra note 1, at 174–75.

118. See, e.g., Joleen Kirschenman and Kathryn M. Neckerman, " 'We'd Love to Hire Them, But . . .': The Meaning of Race for Employers," in *The Urban UnderClass* 203, 204 (Christopher Jencks and Paul E. Peterson eds., 1991). For a vivid illustration of this point, see Mary C. Waters, *Black Like Who?* (forthcoming 1996) (finding West Indians preferred to African-Americans as employees).

119. See George J. Borjas, "The Economic Benefits from Immigration," 9 *Journal of Economic Perspectives* 3, 10 (1995) (citing other studies).

120. See Thomas Muller, *Immigrants and the American City* 166–85 (1993).

121. See Elaine Sorensen and Frank D. Bean, "The Immigration Reform and Control Act and the Wages of Mexican Origin Workers: Evidence from Current Population Surveys," 75 *Social Science Quarterly* 1, 16 (1994).

122. After claiming that the post–1965 immigration has contributed to the economic woes of black workers, *Alien Nation,* supra note 1, at 173–75, Brimelow exhibits some caution, saying that it is "at least a possibility," id. at 175. His discussion is entirely one-sided on this point. Reviewing the studies in 1989, Robert Reischauer concluded that

"careful and sophisticated analyses by a number of social scientists provide little evidence that immigrants have had any significant negative impacts on the employment situation of black Americans." Robert D. Reischauer, "Immigration and the Underclass," 501 *Annals of American Academy of Politics and Social Science* 120, 120 (1989) (abstract). A recent study by the U.S. Bureau of Labor Statistics, however, finds that recent high levels of immigration are depressing the wages of low-skilled workers. See "Immigrants Contribute to Rising Gap Between Rich and Poor," *FAIR Immigration Report,* February 1996, at 6 (citing David Jaeger, *Skill Differentials and the Effect of Immigrants on the Wages of Natives* [Bureau of Labor Statistics, U.S. Department of Labor Working Paper No. 273, 1995]). The study does not appear to have examined the effects of immigration specifically on low- and unskilled African-American workers.

123. These possibilities are discussed in Frank D. Bean et al., "Labor Market Dynamics and the Effects of Immigration on African Americans," in *Blacks, Immigration and Race Relations* (Gerald Jaynes ed., forthcoming 1996) (manuscript at 5–18, on file with author), which concludes that immigration into tight labor markets might reduce black unemployment, while immigration into loose ones might increase it.

124. See *Alien Nation,* supra note 1, at 178–90, 211–18.

125. See, e.g., Waters, supra note 118 (finding these values to be preferred by immigrants' employers and co-workers).

126. Id. at 88–89, 145 (English proficiency); id. at 181 (illegitimacy); id. at 182–86 (crime).

127. An estimated 75% of the aliens in federal prisons, compared to 56% of the U.S. citizens there, are incarcerated for drug-related charges. *Criminal Aliens: Hearing Before the Subcommittee on International Law, Immigration and Refugees of the House Comm. on the Judiciary,* 103d Cong., 2d Sess. 165 (1994) [hereinafter 1994 *Criminal Aliens Hearing*) (testimony of Kathleen Hawk, Director, U.S. Bureau of Prisons).

128. *Criminal Aliens in the United States: Hearings Before the Permanent Subcommittee on Investigations of the Senate Comm. on Government Affairs,* 103d Cong., 1st Sess. 12 (1993) [hereinafter *1993 Criminal Aliens Hearing*].

129. See John Williams, *The Criminal Alien Problem* 1 n.2 (October 20, 1995) (memorandum on file with author).

130. A recent statistical study of foreign-born state inmates found that approximately 45% were illegal aliens. See Rebecca L. Clark et al., *Fiscal Impacts of Undocumented Aliens: Selected Estimates for Seven States* tbls. 3.2, 3.4 (1994). The INS estimates that 20% of foreign-born state inmates am not deportable at all. *Removal of Criminal and Illegal Aliens: Hearings before the Subcommittee on Immigration and Claims of the House Judiciary Committee,* 104th Cong., 1st Sess. (War. 23, 1995) (testimony of T. Alexander Aleinikoff, General Counsel, Immigration and Naturalization Service), available in Lexis, News Library, Curnws File [hereinafter Aleinikoff Testimony]. This figure suggests that the remaining 35% of foreign-born inmates are deportable aliens who are not in illegal status.

131. See 1994 *Criminal Aliens Hearing*, supra note 127, at 133 (statement of Rep. Richard H. Lehman).

132. Aleinikoff Testimony, supra note 130.

133. The data, such as they are, appear in Julian L. Simon, *The Economic Consequences of Immigration* 102–103 (1989).

134. On the Dillingham Commission, see Maldwyn Allen Jones, *American Immigration* 152–57 (2d ed. 1992).

135. See Simon, supra note 133, at 102–103.

136. See, e.g., John Kifner, "Immigrant Waves from Asia Bring an Underworld Ashore," *New York Times,* January 6, 1991, at 1.

137. See, e.g., Clifford Krauss, "Drug Arrests in Colombia Lead to Killings in Queens," *New York Times,* November 25, 1995, at 1.

138. See, e.g., Joseph P. Fried, "Sheik and 9 Followers Guilty of a Conspiracy of Terrorism," *New York Times,* October 2, 1995, at A1.

139. See, e.g., Selwyn Raab. "Influx of Russian Gangsters Troubles F.B.I. in Brooklyn," *New York Times*, August 23, 1994, at A1.

140. See Steven A. Holmes, "Large Increase in Deportations Occurred in '95," *New York Times*, December 28, 1995, at A1.

141. See *1993 Criminal Aliens Hearing,* supra note 128, at 77.

142. The Border Patrol now includes 5000 officers, and Congress has instructed the INS to add 1000 more on the Mexican border. *Migration News* (January 1996) (migrant news PLM <migrant@primal.ucdavis.edu>).

143. For example, in the El Paso, Texas, sector of the U-S.-Mexico border, the INS in September 1993 implemented "Operation Hold-the-Line," in which Border Patrol officers were stationed every hundred yards or so along the border. See Joel Brinkley, "A Rare Success at the Border Brought Scant Official Praise," *New York Times*, September 14, 1994, at A1. The deployment reduced apprehensions of illegals from 700 to around 200 per day. Wayne A. Cornelius et al., "Introduction: The Ambivalent Quest for Immigrant Controls," in *Controlling Immigration*, supra note 16, at 3, 35. A 1994 study of "Operation Hold-the-Line," however, determined that the program had not deterred long–distance immigration, diverting such immigration instead to other crossing points along the border. James Bornemeier, "El Paso Plan Deters Illegal Immigrants," *Los Angeles Times*. July 27, 1994, at A3, A 15 (discussing report prepared by Frank Bean and others for U.S. Commission on Immigration Reform).

The INS has also staged simulations at the southern border of an immigration deluge provoked by an internal crisis in Mexico. Sam Dillon, "U.S. Tests Border Patrol in Event of Mexico Crisis," *New York Times*, December 8, 1995, at B16.

144. Aleinikoff Testimony, supra note 130; see also Holmes, supra note 140, at D18 (detailing INS's increased efforts).

145. See Espenshade, supra note 37, at 211–12 (citing data and reasons for failure of enforcement efforts). Espenshade points out that once an illegal immigrant has taken up residence in the interior, "the annual probability of being apprehended is roughly 1–2%." Id. at 212. Immigration control efforts in Europe have also been generally ineffective. See generally *Controlling Immigration*, supra note 16, at 143–97.

146. See Robert Pear, "Clinton to Ban Contracts to Companies that Hire Illegal Aliens," *New York Times,* January 23, 1996, at A12.

147. Barry R. Chiswick and Paul W. Miller, "The Endogeneity Between Language and Earnings: International Analyses," 12 *Journal of Labor Economics* 246, 278–79 (1995).

148. *Alien Nation,* supra note 1, at 88–89.

149. Twenty-two states have already adopted "official English" laws. Joyce Price, "English-Only Advocates Sense Momentum; See Passing Chance for Proposed Bills," *Washington Times*, September 7, 1995, at A2 (listing 22 states). Senator Robert Dole has proposed such a rule at the federal level, id., and other presidential contenders will not be far behind. Indeed, President Clinton signed such a law for Arkansas when he was governor of that state. "Campaign English from Senator Dole," *New York Times*, September 10, 1995, § 4, at 16. While Dole originally pledged, if elected, to seek to eliminate federal

support for bilingual education, see id., he subsequently toned down his rhetoric to permitting bilingual education programs " 'that ensure that people learn English in a timely fashion,' " Margot Hornblower, "Putting Tongues in Cheek: Should Bilingual Education Be Silenced?" *Time,* October 9, 1995, at 40, 42. Congress recently held hearings on English as the common language of the United States. "House Holds Hearing on English as the Common Language," 72 *Interpreter Releases* 1542 (1995).

150. Alejandro Portes puts the point this way:

> [F]irst-generation immigrants are not regarded generally as poor, no matter what their objective situation is, because they are seen as somehow different from domestic minorities. The same is not true of their children who as U.S. citizens and full participants in American society, are unlikely to use a foreign country as a point of reference or as a place to return to. Instead, they will be evaluated and will evaluate themselves by the standards of their new country.

Portes, supra note 103, at 15.

151. Chiswick and Miller, supra note 147, at 278–79. In another paper based on Australian data, Chiswick and Miller show that "ethnic network" variables—particularly the existence of an ethnic press, proximity of relatives, and spouse's origin language—are more important than the mere fact of living in a minority-language enclave in explaining dominant-language fluency. Barry R. Chiswick and Paul W. Miller, "Ethnic Networks and Language Proficiency Among Immigrants" (1995) (unpublished manuscript, on file with author).

152. In a 1995 survey, 81% of immigrants living in the United States for more than 20 years report using "English at home most often"; for those in their first decade, the figure is 49%. See *The Immigrant Experience,* supra note 68, at 103.

153. Alejandro Portes and Richard Schauffler, "Language and the Second Generation: Bilingualism Yesterday and Today," 28 *International Migration Review* 640, 641, 643 (1994) (citing sources).

154. Id. at 647. The authors state that "self-reports of language ability, unlike other individual characteristics, are both reliable and valid." Id. at 646 (citing sources).

155. Id. at 647, 652. Indeed, the authors note that because fluent bilingualism is increasingly an economic asset, the loss of parental-language fluency may pose a greater risk for today's second generation than the nonproblem of inadequate English. Id. at 659. This preference for English was even stronger among Cuban children, who were educated in bilingual schools at the core of an ethnic enclave. Id. at 652.

Brimelow does cite (incorrectly, see *Alien Nation,* supra note 1, at 306 n.4) a study of second-generation schoolchildren in the San Diego and Miami areas that found that Mexican-American children, including those who claimed to be proficient in English, nevertheless retained and preferred to speak the parental language (Spanish) to a much greater degree than children from other nationality groups did. See Rubén G. Rumbaut, "The Crucible Within: Ethnic Identity, Self-Esteem, and Segmented Assimilation Among Children of Immigrants," 28 *International Migration Review* 748, tbl. 3 at 768 (1994).

156. Despite the much higher Spanish preference rate of the Mexican-American children in the Rumbaut study, they are not really an exception. Their English fluency was only slightly lower than some foreign-language groups and was higher than several others, especially some Asian groups. Rumbaut, supra note 155, tbl. 3 at 768. Spanish-language speakers, especially Mexicans, tend to have higher parental-language retention rates, especially if they live near the border, interact with frequent border crossers, live in a community constantly being replenished by first-generation Spanish-speaking immi-

grants, or adopt an adversarial stance toward Anglo society. By the third generation, however, virtually everyone is monolingual. See Alejandro Portes and Rubén G. Rumbaut, *Immigrant America: A Portrait* 183 (1990).

157. *Alien Nation,* supra note 1, at 181.

158. Charles Hirschman, "Problems and Prospects of Studying Immigrant Adaptation from the 1990 Population Census: From Generational Comparisons to the Process of "Becoming American," 28 *International Migration Review* 690, 708–10 (1994). The rates among Asian refugees, however, are much higher than for other Asians. Id. at 710.

159. *Alien Nation,* supra note 1, at 184.

160. Hirschman, supra note 158, at 711.

161. See Frank D. Bean et al., "Socioeconomic and Cultural Incorporation and Marital Disruption Among Mexican Americans" (September 1995) (unpublished paper, on file with author).

162. Id. at 26–27. Frank Bean and his colleagues attribute the rise in divorce rates in the second and third generations to the special uncertainties and vulnerabilities surrounding the immigration experience in the United States that keep families together in the first generation. Id. at 25–26. Even in the third generation, the Hispanic divorce rate does not exceed that of U.S. natives, whereas the black divorce rate is higher than the U.S. average. Nevertheless, this dynamic could have worrisome implications for Mexican-American progress in the United States. As the authors put it, "The greater marital stability of lower socioeconomic status immigrants, when included in average rates of marital disruption, leads to what some might term a falsely rosy picture." id. at 26.

163. See Alejandro Portes and Min Zhou, "The New Second Generation: Segmented Assimilation and Its Variants," 530 *Annals American Academy of Politics and Social Science* 74, 74 (1993).

164. Portes, supra note 103, at 17 (citations omitted).

165. Id. at 23.

166. Portes and Zhou have found empirical evidence for this form of self-consciously delayed assimilation among the Cuban and Punjabi Sikh enclaves in South Florida and California, respectively, contrasting the experiences of these groups to the less protected, downwardly assimilating Haitians in Miami, and Mexicans and Mexican-Americans in central California. See Portes and Zhou, supra note 163, at 87–91.

167. See Bean et al., supra note 101, at 76–77. The Mexican-American experience in educational attainment, furthermore, suggests that continued progress beyond the second generation is by no means assured. See supra note 101 and accompanying text.

168. See *Alien Nation,* supra note 1, at 193–95. For another discussion of this possibility, see Leon Bouvier, *What If . . . ? Immigration Decisions: What Could Have Been, What Could Be* 15 (1994).

169. See *Alien Nation,* supra note 1, at 195–201. As precedent, Brimelow points to the brief rise of the Know-Nothings' American party in the 1850s. He emphasizes that the Know-Nothings, while rabidly anti-Catholic, did not in fact seek to restrict immigration and placed a higher priority on abolition. Id. at 12–13, 200.

170. See Steven A. Holmes, "House Panel Keeps Intact Bill to Restrict Immigration," *New York Times*, October 12, 1995, at A20 (discussing Republican bill to restrict legal immigration), Robert Pear, "Clinton Embraces a Proposal to Cut Immigration by a Third," *New York Times*, June 8, 1995, at B10 (reporting President Clinton's endorsement of proposal by Commission on Immigration Reform to reduce legal immigration by one-third).

171. See *Alien Nation,* supra note 1, at 123–33.

172. The term "imagined" is taken, of course, from Benedict Anderson's coinage. See Benedict Anderson, *Imagined Communities: Reflections on the Origin and Spread of Nationalism* (2d ed. 1991).

173. See *Alien Nation*, supra note 1, at 230–32. Brimelow defines the "New Class" (a term he explicitly borrows from Irving Kristol, see Irving Kristol, *Two Cheers for Capitalism* 26–31 [1978]) as "the professionals who run and benefit from the state . . . and its power to tax." Id. at 230. For an avowedly liberal critique of the balkanizing tendencies of contemporary society that rejects this distinction between the "new class" and other powerful class interests, see Lind, supra note 13, at 327.

174. *Alien Nation*, supra note 1, at 219.

175. Id.

176. Indeed, the fact that many of the new immigrants are refugees fleeing cruel regimes in harsh societies, which Brimelow insists was not true in the good old days, id. at 246, suggests that the newcomers' loyalties are, if anything, less conflicted than those of their predecessors.

177. See *The Immigrant Experience*, supra note 68, at 101 (relating 1995 survey data from June 1995 that indicate that immigrants' belief in American values is as great or greater than that of natives).

178. *Alien Nation*, supra note 1, at 219.

179. Brimelow fails to mention another policy—racially defined and gerrymandered legislative districting—that I believe is perhaps even more dangerous because it reinforces racialist thinking and creates perverse incentives for political behavior, and because it is especially difficult to dislodge once it is in place. See infra notes 208–12 and accompanying text.

180. See supra notes 153–56 and accompanying text.

181. For instances of this ideological subordination, see, for example, Stephanie Gutmann, "The Bilingual Ghetto: Why New York's Schools Won't Teach Immigrants English," *City Journal*, Winter 1992, at 29; Abigail M. Thernstrom, "E Pluribus Plura—Congress and Bilingual Education," *Public Interest*, Summer 1980, at 3. I say "presumed" because of claims that assignment to bilingual classes sometimes reflects nothing more than the school's ascription of ethnicity to the child based on her surname. For an example of this practice, see Gutmann, supra, at 29.

182. See Toby L. Bovitz, "Bilingual Education in New York No Longer Serves Students," *New York Times*, March 23, 1995, at A24 (letter to editor from bilingual psychologist in school system); Sam Dillon, "Report Faults Bilingual Education in New York," *New York Times*, October 20, 1994, at A1; Gutmann, supra note 181, at 29, Jacques Steinberg, "Lawsuit Is Filed Accusing State of Overuse of Bilingual Classes," *New York Times*, September 19, 1995, at B6 (reporting suit by parents' group). But see Maria Newman, "Schools are Likely to Stop Automatic English Testing," *New York Times*. February 27, 1996, at B3 (describing plan to terminate automatic testing of children with Spanish surnames for possible placement in bilingual programs).

183. Legislation pending in Congress would greatly restrict or even eliminate bilingual education. See, e.g., H.R. 1005, 104th Cong., 1st Sess. 3(a) (1995) (repealing former Bilingual Education Act, 20 U.S.C. §§ 3281–3341 (1994)); see also Hornblower, supra note 149, at 42 (detailing congressional and administration positions on bilingual education). To the extent that these changes would eliminate even genuinely transitional, short-term bilingual education entirely, they may go too far.

184. Canada, for example, has made multiculturalism a constitutionally protected value. *Canadian Constitution* (Constitution Act, 1982), Pt. I (Canadian Charter of Rights

and Freedoms), 27 ("This Charter shall be interpreted in a manner consistent with the preservation and enhancement of the multicultural heritage of Canada."). The U.S. Supreme Court has also protected the right of religious and ethnic minorities to preserve their cultural practices. E.g., *Pierce v. Society of Sisters of the Holy Names of Jesus and Mary,* 268 U.S. 510 (1925) (invalidating Oregon law requiring children between ages of eight and sixteen to attend public school); *Meyer v. Nebraska,* 262 U.S. 390 (1923) (striking down Nebraska statute prohibiting teaching of languages other than English and instruction in languages other than English).

185. Glazer, supra note 60, at 46–47.

186. For a spirited attack on this "ideal of authenticity" and on the contrived character of many multiculturalists' symbols, see Lind, supra note 13, at 122–27.

187. For alarming and sometimes tragi-comical examples by insightful observers, see Richard Bernstein, *Dictatorship of Virtue: Multiculturalism and the Battle for America's Future* (1994); Lynne V. Cheney, *Telling the Truth: Why Our Culture and Our Country Have Stopped Making Sense—and What We Can Do about It* (1995).

188. See, e.g., Mary Lefkowitz, *Not Out of Africa: How Afrocentrism Became an Excuse to Teach Myth as History* (1996).

189. See, e.g., Lind, Supra note 13, at 118–37; Mary C. Waters, *Ethnic Options: Choosing Identities in America* 16–51 (1990); Christopher A. Ford, "Administering Identity: The Determination of 'Race' in Race-Conscious Law," 82 *California Law Review* 1231, 1239–40 (1994).

190. The percentage of white-identifying Hispanics depends in part on the structure of the survey instrument and the methodology of the questioner. Bureau of the Census, U.S. Department of Commerce, *Current Population Reports, Series P23–182, Exploring Alternative Race-Ethnic Comparison Groups in Current Population Surveys* 2–3 (1992). For an historical survey of the changing racial and ethnic questions in the census, including the mutability of Hispanic self-identification, see Stephan Thernstrom, "American Ethnic Statistics," in *Immigrants in Two Democracies: French and American Experience* 80, 100 n.5 (Donald L. Horowitz and Gérard Noiriel eds., 1992) (reporting that 21.1% of people who identified with Spanish-origin-group in 1971 gave different origin just one year later; 12% of all those who self-identified as Hispanic had abandoned it).

191. For these exogamy data, see Frank D. Bean et al., "The Changing Demography of U.S. Immigration Flows: Patterns, Projections, and Contexts" 13 (July 1995) (unpublished paper presented at Conference on German-American Migration and Refugee Policies, on file with author).

192. See id. tbl. 4.

193. In a curious, brief discussion of interracial marriage, he acknowledges that it would tend to dissipate the Pincers' pressure and then adds the following "*BUT*" (italics and capitalization in original): "while more Hispanics are intermarrying, the proportion of all Hispanic marriages has fallen, swamped by the sheer growth of the Hispanic population." *Alien Nation,* supra note 1, at 274. The meaning and relevance of this observation escape me.

194. Bean et al., supra note 191, at 14.

195. See Barry Edmonston et al., "Ethnicity, Ancestry, and Exogamy in U.S. Population Projections (April 1994)" (unpublished paper presented before Population Association of America, on file with author).

196. See Bean et al., supra note 191, at 14–15 (summarizing findings in Edmonston et al., supra note 195, at 28). The actual number would depend on how such individuals self-identify in reporting to the census. This in turn may depend on how the Census

Bureau resolves the issue of whether a mixed ancestry category should be established. On the Census Bureau's approach to this question, see Lawrence Wright, "One Drop of Blood," *New Yorker,* July 25, 1994, at 46.

197. For two discussions of this question, see Ford Foundation, *Changing Relations: Newcomers and Established Residents in U.S. Communities* (1993); *Opening the Door,* supra note 55. The first of these would change the focus from immigrants' assimilation to their accommodation, defined as "a process by which all sides in a multifaceted situation, including established residents and groups at different stages of settlement, find ways of adjusting to and supporting one another." Ford Foundation, supra, at 4. To the extent that this change is an exhortation to receiving communities to welcome immigrants, it is benign, but to the extent that it is meant to shift the initiative for, and the principal burdens of, assimilation from immigrants to the established community, it is probably misguided and will engender resistance.

198. See, e.g., Paul M. Barrett, "Pentagon Move to Hurt Minority Builders," *Wall Street Journal,* October 25, 1995, at B2 (reporting that Defense Department, Small Business Administration, and other agencies are curtailing affirmative action programs); Steven A. Holmes, "White House to Suspend a Program for Minorities," *New York Times,* March 8, 1996, at A1 (ordering three-year suspension of minority and female set-aside programs for contracts).

199. The struggle to limit affirmative action will be extended and will proceed differently in different policy domains. See, e.g., B. Drummond Ayres Jr., "Efforts to End Job Preferences Are Faltering," *New York Times,* November 20, 1995, at A1. My criticisms of affirmative action do not refer to policies that require employers, universities, and other entities to engage in more broad-ranging recruitment processes, which I strongly support. These policies are not seriously in question. Rather, I am concerned with policies that either require, or as a practical matter demand, quotas or preferences based on race.

200. See Peter H. Schuck, "The New Immigration and the Old Civil Rights," *American Prospect,* Fall 1993, at 102, 108–11.

201. No one can gauge precisely the overall social effects of race-based affirmative action on its supposed beneficiaries. There are, however, reasons to believe that the net effects are either inconsequential or negative. For example, Thomas Sowell, who has written extensively on affirmative action both in the United States and abroad, has compared the pre- and postaffirmative action periods and found that black employment gains were actually greater during the earlier period. Thomas Sowell, *Preferential Politics: An International Perspective* 113, 115 (1990). In a recent study comparing protected minorities' employment patterns in private firms that adopted either "identity-conscious" (making race relevant) or "identity-blind" (merit-based) personnel decisions, the authors (both strong affirmative action proponents) found that by most measures. improvement in the groups' employment status was not affected by identity-conscious interventions. Alison M. Konrad and Frank Linnehan, "Formalized HRM Structures: Coordinating Equal Employment Opportunity or Concealing Organizational Practices?" 38 *Academic Management Journal* 787 (1995).

On the negative side, members of protected groups whose genuine, hard-won achievements on the job and in universities arc unfairly depreciated because of the supposed favoritism ascribed to affirmative action have suffered much personal indignity, reputational harm, and psychic injury as a result. The social damage to relations between the races has been incalculably great, in my view. According to a recent study, white opposition to affirmative action now encompasses the liberal core of the Democratic party; it is just as strong among those most committed to racial equality as among those least committed to such values. See Martin Gilens et al., "Affirmative Action and the Politics of Realignment" 3–4 (April 1995) (unpublished conference paper prepared for annual meeting of Midwest Political Science Association, on file with author). One fervently hopes that this damage is not irreversible.

202. The beneficiaries of this program, after all, come from countries that were unfairly favored by the pre–1965 immigration policy. For a general critique of diversity programs, including this one, see Stephen H. Legomsky, "Immigration, Equality and Diversity," 31 *Columbia Journal of Transnational Law* 319, 330–35 (1993).

203. Many of these countries, of course, were *advantaged* by the *pre*-1965 law. In fact, the chief beneficiaries of this program, as was intended at the time of enactment, are the Irish, for whom 41% of the diversity visas were reserved during 1992–94. See Schuck, supra note 96, at 71–72.

204. See Schuck, supra note 200, at 108–11 (noting invidious group comparisons invited by race-based affirmative action, and favoring class-based remedies instead); see also Richard D. Kahlenberg, "Equal Opportunity Critics," *New Republic,* July 17 and 24, 1995, at 20 (noting that some opponents of race-based affirmative action are beginning to embrace class-based preferences). Class-based affirmative action also has its critics, see, e.g., Michael Kinsley, "The Spoils of Victimhood," *New Yorker,* March 27, 1995, at 62, 65–66. and would be difficult to implement, see, e.g., Sarah Kershaw, "California's Universities Confront New Diversity Rules," *New York Times*, January 22, 1996, at A10 (discussing problems in applying class-based criteria).

205. See Nathan Glazer, *Affirmative Discrimination: Ethnic Inequality and Public Policy* 168–205 (1975); Nathan Glazer, "Immigrants and Education," in *Clamor at the Gates: The New American Immigration* 213 (Nathan Glazer ed., 1985) [hereinafter *Clamor at the Gates*]; Ivan Light, "Immigrant Entrepreneurs in America: Koreans in Los Angeles," in *Clamor at the Gates* supra, at 16 1; Peter 1. Rose, "Asian Americans: From Pariahs to Paragons," in *Clamor at the Gates* supra, at 181; Schuck, supra note 200, at 107. For a microscopic view of these invidious comparisons as they operate in the workplace, see generally Waters, supra note 118.

206. See, e.g., Ford, supra note 189, at 1234 ("However analytically 'soft' a particular classification may be, making it a centerpiece of government resource-allocation will require that it be 'hardened' dramatically."); Wright, supra note 196, at 46.

207. *Alien Nation,* supra note 1, at 65 (emphasis omitted). This possibility seems especially great among Asian-Americans, who tend to be more conservative politically than African-Americans.

208. 42 U.S.C. §§ 1971–1973p (1988 and Supp. 1993).

209. See, e.g., Lani Guinier, *The Tyranny of the Majority: Fundamental Fairness in Representative Democracy* 41–70 (1994); Carol M. Swain, *Black Faces, Black Interests: The Representation of African Americans in Congress,* at vii–ix, 193–225 (1993); Abigail Thernstrom, *Whose Votes Count?: Affirmative Action and Minority Voting Rights* (1987); James F. Blumstein, "Racial Gerrymandering and Vote Dilution: *Shaw* v. *Reno* in Doctrinal Context" 26 *Rutgers Law Journal* 517 (1995); Schuck, supra note 200, at 105–11; Peter H. Schuck, "What Went Wrong with the Voting Rights Act," *Washington Monthly,* November 1987, at 51. Other scholars have enthusiastically endorsed it. See, e.g., Bernard Grofman et al., *Minority Representation and the Quest for Voting Equality* 131–37 (1992). Luis R. Fraga, "Latino Political Incorporation and the Voting Rights Act," in *Controversies in Minority Voting: The Voting Rights Act in Perspective* 278 (Bernard Grofman and Chandler Davidson eds., 1992) [hereinafter *Controversies in Minority Voting*]; Pamela S. Karlan, "The Rights to Vote: Some Pessimism About Formalism," 71 *Texas Law Review*

1705, 1737–40 (1993); Allan J. Lichtman, "Redistricting, in Black and White," *New York Times*, December 7, 1994, at A23.

210. See, e.g., Juan Williams, "Blacked Out in the Newt Congress: The Black Caucus Regroups as Jesse Mulls a Third Party Bid," *Washington Post*, November 20, 1994, at C1.

211. The leading cases are *Shaw* v. *Reno*, 113 S. Ct. 2816 (1993). and *Miller* v. *Johnson*, 115 S. Ct. 2475 (1995).

212. See Hugh Davis Graham, "Voting Rights and the American Regulatory State," in *Controversies in Minority Voting*, supra note 209, at 177, 195–96. On growing Asian-American political activism, see Steven A. Holmes, "Anti-Immigrant Mood Moves Asians to Organize," *New York Times*, January 3, 1996, at A1.

213. *Alien Nation*, supra note 1, at 219 (emphasis omitted). The key, he writes, is "[a]voiding the Romans' mistake of diluting their citizenship into insignificance." Id. at 267.

214. Id. at 264–67.

215. See Schuck Testimony, supra note 3; Supplemental Letter, supra note 3; see also Neil A. Lewis, "Bill Seeks to End Automatic Citizenship for All Born in the U.S.," *New York Times*, December 14, 1995, at A26.

216. U.S. Constitution amend. XIV, 1.

217. Peter H. Schuck and Rogers M. Smith, *Citizenship without Consent: Illegal Aliens in the American Polity* 5, 72–89 (1985); see also Peter H. Schuck, "Membership in the Liberal Polity: The Devaluation of American Citizenship," 3 *Geo. Immigration Law Journal* 1 (arguing that birthright citizenship and minimal incentives for aliens to naturalize have lowered value of U.S. citizenship).

218. Schuck and Smith, supra note 217, at 90–115.

219. The most probing criticisms—although not persuasive in our view—are found in Gerald L. Neuman, *Strangers to the Constitution: Immigrants, Borders and Fundamental Law* (forthcoming 1996) (manuscript at 473–535, on file with author); David A. Martin, "Membership and Consent: Abstract or Organic?" 1 *Yale Journal of International Law* 278 (1985). But see Peter H. Schuck and Rogers M. Smith, "Membership and Consent: Actual or Mythic? A Reply to David A. Martin," 11 *Yale Journal of International Law* 545 (1986).

220. See Schuck and Smith, supra note 217, at 97–100, 136–37.

221. Id. at 99, 135. Our book was published well before Congress enacted such an amnesty in the 1986 IRCA legislation. We recommended such a measure in the book.

222. See discussion supra note 149 and accompanying text; see also "Montana Law on English," *New York Times*, April 3, 1995, at B8 (describing law that makes English official language of state government). But see "Court Strikes Language Law," *New York Times*, December 9, 1994, at A18 (relating decision of Ninth Circuit that invalidated on First Amendment grounds amendment to Arizona Constitution requiring state employees to speak only English on job).

223. See Jack Citrin, "Language Politics and American Identity," *Public Interest*, Spring 1990, at 96, 108 ("The instrumental consequences of state and local 'official English' legislation are virtually nil, and in the absence of a genuine threat to the status of English, the formal subordination of other languages is mainly divisive.").

224. For a description of the Americanization movements of the first two decades of the twentieth century, see Philip Gleason, "American Identity and Americanization," in *Harvard Encyclopedia*, supra note 82, at 31, 39–41. 57–58 (entry and bibliographic sources).

225. Such classes are chronically over-subscribed, and the waiting lists are long. David Leanhardt, "Immigrants' Hopes Converge on English Class: Eager to Break Language Barrier Would-Be Students Overwhelm Programs for Adults," *Washington Post,* July 25, 1994, at B1; Deborah Sontag, "English as Precious Language: Immigrants Hungry for Literacy Find That Classes Are Few," *New York Times,* August 29, 1993, at 29.

226. The current INS administration is already instituting such a change, with some success. Its timing could hardly be better. For reasons having little to do with the INS's new effort and much to do with the threat to legal immigrants' public benefits posed by pending legislation and an imminent change in Mexico's own citizenship law, see Sam Dillon, "Mexico Woos U.S. Mexicans, Proposing Dual Nationality," *New York Times,* December 10, 1995, § 1, at 16 (discussing proposed Mexican constitutional amendment that would permit Mexicans living in United States to retain Mexican nationality upon becoming U.S. citizens), a stunning increase in the number of naturalization petitions is now occurring. See, e.g., Louis Freedberg, "Citizenship Wave Surprises INS: Applications Pour in as Immigrants Act to Protect Benefits," *San Francisco Chronicle,* April 13, 1995, at A1, A23 (detailing increase in naturalization petitions in INS's San Francisco district and the United States). The total for 1995 will probably exceed one million.

One presumes that Brimelow opposes this development, since he thinks that naturalization should be a far more protracted process and therefore applauds the Know-Nothings' battle cry: "Nationalize, then Naturalize." *Alien Nation,* supra note 1, at 12–13, 265. I believe that the current five-year minimum period, which is already longer than those in a number of immigrant nations, has served us well. In any event, most naturalizing immigrants take longer than five years. See *1994 INS Statistical Yearbook,* supra note 29, tbl. K at 128.

227. For a recent, thoughtful exploration of some normative issues concerning citizenship, see the papers on that subject in "Symposium, Immigration Law and the New Century: The Developing Regime," 35 *Va. Journal of International Law* 1 (1994).

228. See *Alien Nation,* supra note 1, at 232, 264–67.

229. For scholars advocating open borders, or at least a strong presumption in favor of them, see, for example, Bruce A. Ackerman, *Social Justice in the Liberal State* 89–95 (1980); Joseph H. Carens, "Aliens and Citizens: The Case for Open Borders," 49 *Review Policies* 251 (1987); R. George Wright, "Federal Immigration Law and the Case for Open Entry," 27 *Loy. L.A. Law Review* 1265 (1994).

230. Even the group Negative Population Growth, which is radical enough to want to reduce the U.S. population to 125–150 million (about half its present size), proposes legal immigration of up to 100,000 per year. See advertisement in *New Republic,* October 23, 1995, after 37. But see Lind, supra note 13, at 206–207 (discussing proposals for increased immigration).

231. See Gleason, supra note 224, at 39–41.

232. For an interesting effort by one immigrant to define Americanism, See Ted Morgan, *On Becoming American* (1978).

233. For one such effort that strongly eschews "Anglo-centric" conceptions of the American nation (such as Brimelow's), see Lind, supra note 13, at 352–88.

234. I say "little," not none. Aliens' drug-related crime, see supra notes 127–46 and accompanying text, is the principal exception.

235. He tells us that he and his brother "gave it an A+." *Alien Nation,* supra note 1, at 221.

236. He says that "we still give it an A+" but then adds "what's left of it." Id. By this qualification he presumably means the part that the new immigrants have not yet destroyed.

237. A March 1995 Census Bureau report indicates that 30.8% of families with children were headed by a single parent in 1994; the corresponding rate was 13% in 1970. Of the 11.5 million such families, the vast majority—9.9 million—were headed by women. "2-Parent Families Increasing in U.S.," *New York Times*, October 17, 1995, at A17.

238. See supra notes 160–67 and accompanying text. Other American (mis)behaviors also seem to rub off on immigrants. For example, the prostate cancer rate among Japanese men increases markedly when they immigrate to the United States, apparently because of their change to a high-fat diet here. The prostate cancer rate per 100,000 increased from eight for men in Japan to 30 for first-generation Japanese immigrants in Los Angeles and to 34 for second-generation immigrants; among white men in Los Angeles it is 66. Jane Brody, "Low-Fat Diet in Mice Slows Prostate Cancer," *New York Times*, October 18, 1995, at C13.

239. The per capita gross national product increased almost 60% in constant dollars between 1965 and 1993; per capita disposable income increased almost 75% during the same period. 1994 *U.S. Statistical Abstract*, supra note 55, tbl. 691.

240. See sources cited supra note 17.

241. See, e.g., Muller, supra note 120, at 151–60; Louis Winnick, *New People in Old Neighborhoods: The Role of New Immigrants in Rejuvenating New York's Communities* (1990).

242. Brimelow's narrative of decline is commonplace today. It is also told by some who would probably agree with him on little else. See, e.g., Charles A. Reich, *Opposing the System* (1995).

243. *Alien Nation*, supra note 1, at 187–90.

244. For a detailed discussion of these changes, see generally Gregg Easterbrook, *A Moment on the Earth: The Coming of Age of Environmental Optimism* (1995); Aaron Wildavsky, *But Is It True?: A Citizen's Guide to Environmental Health and Safety Issues* (1995); *The True State of the Planet: Ten of the World's Premier Environmental Researchers in a Major Challenge to the Environmental Movement* (Ronald Bailey ed., 1995).

245. 42 U.S.C. §§ 1971–1973p (1988 and Supp. 1993).

246. 29 U.S.C. §§ 621–634 (1988 and Supp. 1993).

247. 42 U.S.C. §§ 6101–6107 (1988).

248. 20 U.S.C. §§ 1400–1485 (1994).

249. 42 U.S.C. §§ 12101–12213 (Supp- 1993).

250. Civil Rights Act of 1991, Pub. L 102–166, 105 Stat. 107 (codified at scattered sections of 42 U.S.C.).

251. Indeed, one can argue that it is too responsive to special interests of all kinds and insufficiently deliberative.

252. See Adam Clymer, "With Political Discipline, It Works Like Parliament," *New York Times*, August 6, 1995, §4, at 6 (analyzing high level of party discipline among congressional Republicans and resulting improvement in discipline among congressional Democrats).

253. See supra note 239.

254. See Daniel T. Slesnick, "Gaining Ground: Poverty in the Postwar United States," 101 *Journal of Political Economics*, tbl. 3 at 16 (1993). As the share of the poor has diminished, moreover, the ranks of the wealthy have swelled. According to one estimate, the number of families with earnings of over $100,000 in constant dollars has increased from slightly more than I million in 1967 to 5.6 million in 1993. David Frum, "Welcome, Nouveaux Riches," *New York Times*, August 14, 1995, at A15. For a recent account of the improved living conditions of the rural South Carolina poor between the

1960s and today, see Dana Milbank, "Up from Hunger: War on Poverty Won Some Battles as Return to Poor Region Shows," *Wall Street Journal,* October 30, 1995, at A1.

255. For an account of this development, see R. Shep Melnick, *Between the Lines: Interpreting Welfare Rights* 183–232 (1994). The quality of life for the most destitute Americans, including the homeless and panhandlers, has improved dramatically as well. See Robert C. Ellickson, "Controlling Chronic Misconduct in City Spaces: Of Panhandlers, Skid Rows, and Public-Space Zoning," 105 *Yale Law Journal* 1165, 1190–91, 1203–1204 (1996).

256. John C. Weicher, "Private Production: Has the Rising Tide Lifted All Boats?" in *Housing America's Poor* 45, 46 (Peter D. Salins ed., 1987). The data also indicate that blacks have shared in these improvements:

> the percentage of black households lacking complete plumbing plunged . . . and the percentage living with more than one person per room dropped from 28.3% in 1960 to 9.1% in 1980. . . . The available data indicate that these auspicious trends have continued since 1980. The residential situation of the institutionalized poor has also improved as prisons, mental hospitals, and similar accommodations have become much more livable.

Robert C. Ellickson, "The Untenable Case for an Unconditional Right to Shelter," 15 *Harvard Law Journal* and *Public Policy* 17, 27 (1992) (footnotes omitted).

257. *1994 U.S. Statistical Abstract,* supra note 55, tbl. 114.

258. Id. tbl. 120. The decline was almost as rapid for blacks and other nonwhites. Id.

259. Steven A. Holmes, "A Generally Healthy America Emerges in a Census Report," *New York Times,* October 13, 1994, at B13.

260. The inadequacy of many of the dominant measures of public and private wealth, income, and consumption is an old complaint. See, e.g., Peter Passell, "Economic Scene," *New York Times,* October 12, 1995, at D2 (reviewing previous and current criticisms of national income accounting).

261. The difficulty of this question is not eased much by *A Tale of Ten Cities: Immigration's Effect on the Family Environment in American Cities,* a report coauthored by demographer Leon Bouvier and Scipio Garling and published by the Federation for American Immigration Reform in November 1995. Federation for American Immigration Reform, *A Tale of Ten Cities: Immigration's Effect on the Family Environment in American Cities* (1995). This report compares the quality of life in five pairs of matched cities, each pair of which includes a high- and a low-immigration city. The report finds in the low-immigration cities a much better quality of life, as measured by nine categories of variables: education, income, occupation, home life, housing, cultural adaptation, crime, community, and health. Comparisons of this kind, however, usually suffer from methodological weaknesses that make causal inferences highly problematic, especially the inability to control for the many variables that make the paired cities different for nonimmigration reasons. For a critique of the methodology of this report, see John E. Berthoud, "FAIR's 'A Tale of Ten Cities': A Fair Analysis?" (November 1995) (unpublished report by Vice-President of Alexis de Tocqueville Institution, on file with author). In addition to this serious problem, *A Tale of Ten Cities* selected high-immigration cities with large concentrations of illegal aliens, which inevitably distort the data. It also ignored the fact that, while most immigration-related costs are borne locally, most immigration-generated benefits (e.g., increased tax revenues and economic efficiency) are realized at higher levels.

# PART II

# HISTORICAL AND LEGAL BACKGROUND

# 3.

# National Origins Quotas Should Be Retained (1964)

## Marion Moncure Duncan

### STATEMENT OF MRS. ROBERT V. H. DUNCAN, PRESIDENT GENERAL, NATIONAL SOCIETY, DAUGHTERS OF THE AMERICAN REVOLUTION . . .

M r. Chairman and members of the committee, thank you for your courtesy and indulgence in permitting me the opportunity to speak today. As president general, I officially represent the National Society, Daughters of the American Revolution, a nonpolitical organization dedicated to historic, educational, and patriotic objectives, whose membership runs approximately 185,000 in the 50 States, the District of Columbia, and some oversea units, comprising nearly 3,000 local chapter groups.

I speak in support of maintaining the existing provisions of the Immigration and Nationality Act of 1952, especially the national origins quota system, and against proposed liberalizing amendments thereto, particularly, the deletion of the aforesaid national quota system and/or the establishment of a 5-year staggered accumulated immigration pool reserve.

Since you have already heard considerable testimony in past weeks, my remarks will be kept as brief as possible, stressing only the most pertinent points on which DAR membership has concern. In so doing, I speak not as a specialist or authority in a particular field. Rather, the focus is that of attempting to present to you and ask your consideration of the conscientious convictions of an organization keenly and, more importantly, actively interested in this subject almost since its own inception nearly three-quarters of a century ago. Such interest actually dates back prior to the time any immigration statutes were of record. To substantiate this statement, lest there be any misconception such as was remarked to

Marion Moncure Duncan, statement before the U.S. House of Representatives Committee on the Judiciary, August 10, 1964.

me in ignorance a year ago that "the DAR is against immigrants," with pride I point out as follows:

It was in 1913 the first—and for a number of years the only—naturalization school in this country was founded, operated, and financed by the DAR here in Washington, D.C., and continued so until the school was later incorporated—and still operates—in the District of Columbia school system.

Another tangible and definite example of this organization's interest in immigrants coming to America seeking citizenship has been the consistent and continuous printing over the years, since 1920 (oftimes in many languages) of the "DAR Manual for Citizenship." I have provided a copy for you gentlemen. In years past this has been sent abroad through an international committee to interest folks in coming to America.

Over 9 million copies of this volume have been donated free in an effort to aid and abet an adequate understanding and full appreciation of good citizenship among immigrants. Aside from the quantity supplied, many heartwarming letters attest the value and benefit of this endeavor.

DAR chapters and individuals regularly, year in and year out, sponsor programs and/or participate in connection with naturalization courts.

Further, there is an intangible factor having bearing on the matter at hand. It is the "personal followthrough" which has ever been an integral part of DAR interest in and service to worthy would-be Americans. Sometimes this means a dinner in the home, or a dentist or doctor referral for a sick family member. It can also culminate in a presentation ceremony where a prized DAR Americanism Award is given to a naturalized American in recognition of outstanding service to his new homeland. (NOTE.—Native-born citizens are ineligible for this honor.)

Over 40 years ago, the well-known and outstanding DAR constructive social service assistance program for guidance to aliens at Ellis and Angel Islands was initiated. Thereafter, upon Government change at these two ports of entry, the present DAR physical therapy scholarship program emerged which is continued today.

Gentlemen, the purpose in reciting the foregoing points was twofold: First, to establish the fact that the National Society, Daughters of the American Revolution, has been and continues interested in this minority group of our population and that interest is based upon firsthand knowledge, personal and direct; further, and secondly, the effort is to assure you that in appearing here today against the proposed bill to drastically change Public Law 414, the DAR is not taking a stand against immigration per se. Any inference in that direction is in error and completely false. DAR, as a national organization, is among the foremost "to extend a helping hand" to immigrants admitted on an intelligent, orderly, equitable basis such as is allowed under the current Immigration and Nationality Act of 1952. If, from time to time, there be need for change or adjustment, it should be provided through logical, deliberate amendment, still retaining the national origins quota system and other vitally basic, protective features of the law. These constitute a first line of defense in perpetuating and maintaining our institutions of freedom and the American way of life. To discard them would endanger both.

From [the] point that immigration is definitely a matter of national welfare and security, it is imperative that a logical and rational method of governing and administering same be maintained. The [1952] Walter-McCarran Act has done and will continue equitably to accomplish just this. It denies no nation a quota, but it does provide a reasonable, orderly, mathematical formula (based, of course, upon the 1920 census figures) which is devoid of the political pressures which could inevitably be expected to beset any commission authorized to reapportion unused quotas as proposed in the legislation before you.

By way of background: What prompted passage of the Immigration-Nationality Act of 1952? It will be recalled that this was the product of a tedious, comprehensive study of nearly 5 years' duration, covering some 200 laws on selective immigration, special orders and exclusions, and spanned the period from passage of the first quota law by Congress in 1924. This law codified and coordinated all existing immigration, nationality, and deportation laws.

Despite repeated efforts to weaken, circumvent and bypass this protective legislation, its soundness has been demonstrated over the period it has been in operation.

It embodies the following important features—all in the best interest of our constitutional republic:

(a) Recognizing the cultural identity and historic population basis of this Nation, it officially preserved the national origin quota system as the basis for immigration, wisely giving preference to those nations whose composite culture—Anglo-Saxon from northern and western European countries—has been responsible for and actually produced the American heritage as we know it today.

(b) It abolished certain discriminatory provisions in our immigration laws—those against sexes and persons of Asiatic origin.

(c) "Quality versus quantity" preference for skilled aliens was provided, as well as broadened classifications for nonquota immigrants. No nation or race is listed ineligible for immigration and naturalization, although the acknowledged purpose is to preserve this country's culture, free institutions, free enterprise economy and racial complex, yes, and likely even language. Ready assimilability of the majority of immigrants is a prime factor.

(d) It provides the U.S. Immigration Department with needed authority to cope with subversive aliens by strengthening security provisions.

## Why DAR Is for Retention of the Immigration and Nationality Act of 1952

Perhaps the sentiment and deep concern of the DAR relative to the matter of immigration and its appeal for retention of the present law is best expressed by excerpting salient points from recent resolutions on the subject:

(1) For building unity and cohesiveness among American citizens, whose social, economic and spiritual mind has been and is under increasing pressures and conflicts, wise and comprehensive steps must be taken.

(2) For the protection and interest of all citizens from foreign elements

imbued with ideologies wholly at variance with our republican form of government should be excluded.

On basis of FBI [Federal Bureau of Investigation] analysis statistics and information available through investigation by the House Un-American Activities Committee, loopholes through which thousands of criminal aliens may enter this country constitute a continuing threat for the safety of American institutions.

(3) Since it is a recognized fact that free migration allowing unhampered movement of agents is necessary for triumph of either a world socialist state or international communism as a world conspiracy, this would explain the motivation on the part of enemies of this country for concentrated effort to undermine the existing immigration law.

(4) Admittedly, major problems confronting the Nation and threatening its national economy are unemployment, housing, education, security, population explosion, and other domestic problems such as juvenile delinquency, crime, and racial tensions. This is borne out by numerous statistics and the current Federal war on poverty effort. In view of this, revisions as per proposed new quotas to greatly increase the number of immigrants would be a threat to the security and well-being of this Nation, especially in face of the cold war inasmuch as it would be impossible to obtain adequate security checks on immigrants from satellite Communist-controlled countries.

In summation: A comparative study would indicate increased aggravation of existing problems and unfavorable repercussions on all facets of our economy such as employment, housing, education, welfare, health, and national security, offering additional threat to the American heritage—cultural, social, and ethnic traditions.

DAR is against H.R. 7700 and similar weakening bills because while DAR would be the first to admit the importance of immigrants to America, its membership ties linking directly with the first waves of immigrants to these shores, it would seem well, however, to point out a "then and now" difference factor currently exists attributable to time and circumstance—no uncomplimentary inference therein. A common desire shared by immigrants of all time to America has been the seeking of freedom or the escape from tyranny. But in the early days, say the first 150 years, it is noteworthy that those who came shared common Anglo-Saxon bonds and arrived with the full knowledge and intent of founders or pioneers who knew there was a wilderness to conquer and a nation to build. Their coming indicated a willingness to make a contribution and assume such a role. In the intervening years, many fine, high-caliber immigrants, and I know some at personal sacrifice, following ideals in which they believed, have likewise come to America imbued with a constructive desire to produce and add to the glory of their new homeland. They, however, have come to a nation already established with cultural patterns set and traditions already rooted.

Further, in recent years, en masse refugee movements, though responding to the very same ideal which is America, have been motivated primarily by escape. This has had a tendency possibly to dim individual purpose and dedication and possibly project beyond other considerations, the available benefits to be secured as an American citizen.

Abandonment of the national origins system would drastically alter the source of our immigration. Any change would not take into consideration that those whose background and heritage most closely resemble our own are most readily assimilable.

In recent testimony before you, this point was touched upon by a high official (reference Congressional Record, July 21, 1964, p. 16939) when he said, "To apply the new principle rigidly would result, after a few years, in eliminating immigration from these countries almost entirely." Admittedly such a situation would be undesirable. A strict first-come, first-served basis of allocating visa quotas as proposed would create certain problems in countries of northern and western Europe, and could ultimately dry up influx from that area.

Going a step further, would not the abolishment of the national origin quota system work a hardship and possibly result in actual discrimination against the very nations who supplied the people who now comprise the majority of our historic population mixture? Further, such a change in our existing laws would appear to be an outright accommodation to the heaviest population explosions throughout the world—India, Asia, and Africa. Certainly these countries could naturally be expected to take full advantage of such an increased quota opportunity.

Is it, therefore, desirable or in the best interest to assign possible 10-percent quotas to say proliferating African nations to the end that our own internal problems become manifold? America, as all other nations, is concerned over rapid population growth of this era. Staggering statistics are readily available on every hand.

Attention is called to the fact that immigration is not an alien's right; it is a privilege. With privilege comes its handmaiden responsibility. Before tampering with the present immigration law, much less destroying its basic principles, due regard must also be given to our own unemployment situation. No less an authority than the late President John F. Kennedy, who was for this bill, stated on March 3, 1963, that we had 5 million unemployed and 2 million people displaced each year by advancing technology and automation.

Irrespective of recent and recurring reports on unemployment showing temporary increases or decreases, the fact is, it remains a matter of economic concern. Latest figures available as of June 1964 indicate 4.7 million or 5.3 percent.

In view of this, it would seem highly incongruent if not outright incredible to find ourselves in a situation, on the one hand, waging war on poverty and unemployment at home, while on the other hand, simultaneously and indiscriminately letting down immigration bars to those abroad. Not only employment alone but mental health and retardation problems could greatly increase. Another source of concern to the heavy laden taxpayer to whom already the national debt figure is astronomical.

It is asserted that our economy will get three consumers for every worker admitted and that our economy generates jobs at a rate better than one for every three consumers. Why, then, are we presently plagued with unemployment? And how is it possible to guarantee that these new immigrants will "fill jobs that are going begging because there are not enough skilled workers in our economy who have the needed skills?" Are there enough such jobs going begging to justify destroying an immigration law which has been described as our first line of defense?

Rightly, it would seem U.S. citizens should have first claim on jobs and housing in this country. With manpower available and the recent emphasis on expanded educational facilities, why is not definite concentrated effort made to provide and accelerate vocational and special skill training for the many who either through disinclination, native inability or otherwise are not qualified potentials for schooling in the field of science, medicine, law, or other such professions?

## Unused Quota Allocation

Without the quota system, it is doubtful whether or not America could indefinitely maintain its traditional heritage: Economic, cultural, social, ethnic, or even language.

Free institutions as we have known them would stand to undergo radical change if the proposal to permit reapportionment of unused quotas is also adopted. It is felt reassignment of unused quotas would be as damaging to the basic principles of the Immigration and Nationality Act as repeal of the national origins system itself. The proviso that the President reserve a portion of the pool for allocation to qualified immigrants further extends the power of the executive branch of the Government.

## Infiltration-Security Clearance

No less important is the fact that it is almost impossible to adequately screen persons coming from satellite countries.

It may well be embarrassing to proponents of liberalizing amendments to find that some of the most active opposition against the Walter-McCarran Act is provided by the Communists. According to the House Committee on Un-American Activities, the Communist Party has created, and now controls, in 15 key States, 180 "front" organizations dedicated exclusively to the purpose of creating grassroots pressure in the Congress to destroy the act—which is what most of the proposed amendments would do.

In this connection, I am reminded of the expressive words of the late beloved poet, Robert Frost, who, in "A Poet's Reflections on America and the World," put it this way: "Sizing up America: You ask me if America is still a great country. Well, it's easy to see that, if we don't know how great America is, Russia does."

## Summary

The National Society, Daughters of the American Revolution, which initially supported the Walter-McCarran bill when it was introduced and has continuously done so since, wishes again to officially reaffirm its support of the existing law, firmly believing that the present Immigration and Nationality Act of 1952 not only safeguards our constitutional Republic and perpetuates our American heritage, but by maintaining its established standards, that it actually protects the naturalized American on a par with the native born, and as well offers encouragement to desirable immigrants to become future American citizens. Any breakdown in this system would be an open invitation to Communist infiltration. Likewise, a poor law, newly enacted, and improperly administered, could provide the same opportunity to the detriment, if not the actual downfall, of our country.

The well-intentioned, humanitarian plea that America's unrestricted assumption of the overpopulous, troubled, ailing people of the world within our own borders is unrealistic, impractical, and if done in excess could spell economic bankruptcy for our people from point of both employment and overladen taxes to say nothing of a collapse of morale and spiritual values if nonassimilable aliens of dissimilar ethnic background and culture by wholesale and indiscriminate transporting en masse overturn the balance of our national character.

In connection with the liberalization proposals, it would seem timely to refer to the words of Senator [Patrick] McCarran, who, when he presented the bill, warned:

> If the enemies of this legislation succeed in riddling it to pieces, or in amending it beyond recognition, they will have contributed more to promote this Nation's downfall than any other group since we achieved our independence as a nation.

Somewhat the same sentiment was expressed by Abraham Lincoln, who admonished:

> You cannot strengthen the weak by weakening the strong; and you cannot help men permanently by doing for them what they could and should do for themselves.

Many inspiring words have been written of America. I would conclude with those of the late historian, James Truslow Adams:

> America's greatest contribution to the world has been that of the American dream, the dream of a land where life shall be richer, fuller, and better, with opportunity for every person according to his ability and achievement.

The question is: Can it continue so if, through reckless abandon, the United States becomes mired, causing the country to lose its image as the land of opportunity, the home of the free? Ours is the responsibility to maintain and preserve it for the future. . . .

# 4.

# A Nation of Immigrants

## John F. Kennedy

The Immigration and Nationality Act of 1952 undertook to codify all our national laws on immigration. This was a proper and long overdue task. But it was not just a housekeeping chore. In the course of the deliberation over the Act, many basic decisions about our immigration policy were made. The total racial bar against the naturalization of Japanese, Koreans and other East Asians was removed, and a minimum annual quota of one hundred was provided for each of these countries. Provision was also made to make it easier to reunite husbands and wives. Most important of all was the decision to do nothing about the national origins system.

The famous words of Emma Lazarus on the pedestal of the Statue of Liberty read: "Give me your tired, your poor, your huddled masses yearning to breathe free." Until 1921 this was an accurate picture of our society. Under present law it would be appropriate to add: "as long as they come from Northern Europe, are not too tired or too poor or slightly ill, never stole a loaf of bread, never joined any questionable organization, and can document their activities for the past two years."

Furthermore, the national origins quota system has strong overtones of an indefensible racial preference. It is strongly weighted toward so-called Anglo-Saxons, a phrase which one writer calls "a term of art" encompassing almost anyone from Northern and Western Europe. Sinclair Lewis described his hero, Martin Arrowsmith, this way: "a typical pure-bred-Anglo-Saxon American—which means that be was a union of German, French, Scotch-Irish, perhaps a little Spanish, conceivably of the strains lumped together as 'Jewish,' and a great deal of English, which is itself a combination of primitive Britain, Celt, Phoenician, Roman, German, Dane and Swede."

Yet, however much our present policy may be deplored, it still remains our

From *A Nation of Immigrants* by John F. Kennedy. Copyright © 1964 by Anti-Defamation League of B'nai B'rith. Reprinted by permission of HarperCollins Publishers, Inc.

national policy. As President Truman said when he vetoed the Immigration and Nationality Act (only to have that veto overridden): "The idea behind this discriminatory policy was, to put it boldly, that Americans with English or Irish names were better people and better citizens than Americans with Italian or Greek or Polish names. . . . Such a concept is utterly unworthy of our traditions and our ideals."

Partly as a result of the inflexibility of the national origins quota system, the government has had to resort to temporary expedients to meet emergency situations. The 1957 Kennedy amendment, which permitted alien spouses, parents and children with inconsequential disqualifications to enter the United States, was responsive to this need. In 1948 Congress passed the Displaced Persons Act allowing more than 400,000 people made homeless by the war to come to this country. In 1953 Congress passed the Refugee Relief Act to admit about 200,000 people, most of whom had fled from behind the Iron Curtain. Under this Act and under a clause of the Immigration and Nationality Act of 1952, not originally intended for use in such situations, some thirty thousand Freedom Fighters from Hungary were admitted in 1957. As a result it became necessary to pass a special law in 1958 to regularize the status of many of these immigrants.

Following the 1958 earthquakes in the Azores which left so many Portuguese homeless, none of these people could enter the United States as quota immigrants. Persons of Dutch origin in the Netherlands who were displaced from Indonesia were also ineligible to enter the United States as quota immigrants. Both needs were met by the Pastore-Kennedy-Walter Act of 1958 admitting a number of them on a nonquota basis into the United States. In 1962 a special law had to be passed to permit the immigration of several thousand Chinese refugees who had escaped from Communist China to Hong Kong. The same legislative procedure was used as in the 1957 Hungarian program. Each world crisis is met by a new exception to the Immigration and Nationality Act of 1952. Each exception reflects the natural humanitarian impulses of the American people, which is in keeping with our traditions of shelter to the homeless and refuge for the oppressed.

While none of these measures are, of themselves, especially generous responses to the tremendous problems to which they are addressed, they all have a great impact on our foreign policy. They demonstrate that there is still a place in America for people fleeing from tyranny or natural calamity. Nevertheless, the effect of these actions is diluted by the very fact that they are viewed as exceptions to our national policy rather than as a part of that policy.

Another measure of the inadequacy of the Immigration and Nationality Act bas been the huge volume of private immigration bills introduced in Congress. These are bills to deal with individual hardship cases for which the general law fails to provide. In the Eighty-seventh Congress over 3,500 such bills were introduced. Private immigration bills make up about half of our legislation today.

It is not hard to see why. A poor European college girl was convicted three times for putting slugs in a pay telephone, and fifteen years later, married to an American teacher abroad, she was denied entrance to our country because of three separate convictions for a crime involving moral turpitude. Or another case:

An Italian immigrant living in Massachusetts with his small children could not bring his wife to the United States because she had been convicted on two counts involving moral turpitude. Her crimes? In 1913 and 1939 she had stolen bundles of sticks to build a fire. It took acts of Congress to reunite both these families.

These are examples of the inadequacies of the present law. They are important of themselves because people's lives are affected by them. But they are more important for what they represent of the way America looks at the world and the way America looks at itself.

There is, of course, a legitimate argument for some limitation upon immigration. We no longer need settlers for virgin lands, and our economy is expanding more slowly than in the nineteenth and early twentieth centuries. A superficial analysis of the heated arguments over immigration policy which have taken place since 1952 might give the impression that there was an irreconcilable conflict, as if one side wanted to go back to the policy of our founding fathers, of unrestricted immigration, and the other side wanted to stop all further immigration. In fact, there are only a few basic differences between the most liberal bill offered in recent years, sponsored by former Senator Herbert H. Lehman, and the supporters of the status quo. The present law admits 156,700 quota immigrants annually. The Lehman bill (like a bill introduced by Senator Philip A. Hart and cosponsored by over one-third of the members of the Senate) would admit 250,000.

The clash of opinion arises not over the number of immigrants to be admitted, but over the test for admission—the national origins quota system. Instead of using the discriminatory test of where the immigrant was born, the reform proposals would base admission on the immigrant's possession of skills our country needs and on the humanitarian ground of reuniting families. Such legislation does not seek to make over the face of America. Immigrants would still be given tests for health, intelligence, morality and security.

The force of this argument is recognized by the special measures enacted since 1952 which have ignored the established pattern of favoring Northern and Western Europe immigration over Southern and Eastern European countries. These statutes have resulted in the admission of a great many more persons from Southern European countries than would have been possible under the McCarran-Walter Act.

But more than a decade has elapsed since the last substantial amendment to these laws. There is a compelling need for Congress to re-examine and make changes in them.

Religious and civic organizations, ethnic associations and newspaper editorials, citizens from every walk of life and groups of every description have expressed their support for a more rational and less prejudiced immigration law. Congressional leaders of both parties have urged the adoption of new legislation that would eliminate the most objectionable features of the McCarran-Walter Act and the nationalities quota system.

It is not only the initial assignment of quota numbers which is arbitrary and unjust; additional inequity results from the failure of the law to permit full utilization of the authorized quota numbers. The tiny principality of Andorra in the

Pyrenees Mountains, with 6,500 Spanish-speaking inhabitants, has an American immigration quota of 100, while Spain, with 30 million people, has a quota of only 250. While American citizens wait for years for their relatives to receive a quota, approximately sixty thousand numbers are wasted each year because the countries to which they are assigned have far more numbers allocated to them than they have emigrants seeking to move to the United States. There is no way at present in which these numbers can be reassigned to nations where immense backlogs of applicants for admission to the United States have accumulated. This deficiency in the law should be corrected.

A special discriminatory formula is now applied to the immigration of persons who are attributable by their ancestry to an area called the Asia-Pacific triangle. This area embraces all countries from Pakistan to Japan and the Pacific islands north of Australia and New Zealand. Usually, the quota under which a prospective immigrant must enter is determined by his place of birth. However, if as much as one-half of an immigrant's ancestors came from nations in the Asia-Pacific triangle, he must rely upon the small quota assigned to the country of his ancestry, regardless of where he was born. This provision of the law should be repealed.

The Presidential message to Congress of July 23, 1963, recommended that the national origins system be replaced by a formula governing immigration to the United States which takes into account: (1) the skills of the immigrant and their relationships to our needs; (2) the family relationship between immigrants and persons already here, so that the reuniting of families is encouraged; and (3) the priority of registration. Present law grants a preference to immigrants with special skills, education or training. It also grants a preference to various relatives of the United States citizens and lawfully resident aliens. But it does so only within a national origins quota. It should be modified so that those with the greatest ability to add to the national welfare, no matter where they are born, are granted the highest priority. The next priority should go to those who seek to be reunited with their relatives. For applicants with equal claims, the earliest registrant should be the first admitted.

In order to remove other existing barriers to the reuniting of families, two additional improvements in the law are needed.

First, parents of American citizens, who now have a preferred quota status, should be accorded nonquota status.

Second, parents of aliens resident in the United States, who now have no preference, should be accorded a preference, after skilled specialists and other relatives of citizens and alien residents.

These changes will have little effect on the number of immigrants admitted. They will have a major effect insofar as they relieve the hardship many of our citizens and residents now face in being separated from their parents.

These changes will not solve all the problems of immigration. But they will insure that progress will continue to be made toward our ideals and toward the realization of humanitarian objectives.

We must avoid what the Irish poet John Boyle O'Reilly once called

> Organized charity, scrimped and iced,
> In the name of a cautious, statistical Christ.

Immigration policy should be generous; it should be fair; it should be flexible. With such a policy we can turn to the world, and to our own past, with clean hands and a clear conscience. Such a policy would be but a reaffirmation of old principles. It would be an expression of our agreement with George Washington that "The bosom of America is open to receive not only the opulent and respectable stranger, but the oppressed and persecuted of all nations and religions; whom we shall welcome to a participation of all our rights and privileges, if by decency and propriety of conduct they appear to merit the enjoyment."

# 5.

# Immigration Law: A Bird's-Eye View

## Nadia Nedzel

Immigration law is solely concerned with the acceptance or rejection of citizens and nationals of other nations; it traditionally does not deal with how such aliens must be treated once they are here. However, what makes an already complicated field more complicated is that the two areas of law (which I will call immigration law and alienage law, respectively[1]) are becoming more and more intertwined. Traditionally, immigration law was concerned with controlling the influx of those that brought crime, disease, or poverty with them. Increasingly, in the United States, an additional aim has been to limit the immigration of those whose willingness to work for low pay is likely to have an adverse effect on wages and working conditions. But, when the influx of undocumented aliens continues despite attempts at border intervention, state and federal governments consider how to make illegal entrance less attractive by sanctioning employers of illegal aliens and by limiting benefits available to those who are not here legally. This article is intended to give an overview of the landscape of immigration and alienage law. It will begin with a discussion of the history of immigration legislation in the United States and will sketch out the organization and structure of Congress's Immigration and Nationality Act (INA) and some of the problems that have developed in the course of its implementation by the executive branch of the government. The article will conclude with a discussion of some of the major judicial doctrines that have shaded interpretation of the act, as well as some of the legal theories, issues, and controversies that make this a complicated field of law.

This article was written expressly for this volume.

The author would like to thank Professors James É. Viator and David W. Gruning for their continuing advice and encouragement, the Hon. Carl E. Stewart for encouraging me to develop an interest in immigration law, and Clinical Professor Evangeline G. Abriel for her invaluable guidance and comments on a previous draft of this article. Mistakes remain mine alone.

# THE HISTORY AND DEVELOPMENT OF IMMIGRATION LEGISLATION IN THE UNITED STATES

While the phrases inscribed on the Statue of Liberty are prosaic and dear to many of us who are descendants of immigrants, those phrases are not "black letter" law—or any other kind of law. Discussion of immigration regulation in the United States typically begins with the myth that the borders of the United States were open until the enactment of federal legislation in the 1870s and 1880s.[2] It has been persuasively argued that this myth that United States law encouraged immigration in the first decades of this country distorts discussion of key issues of immigration law.[3] In fact, movement into and between states was regulated by both state and federal legislation. The borders were not legally open—though as a practical matter these laws could not be effectively implemented and there was very little to impede people from coming and going.[4]

The federal government was concerned with immigration issues even prior to the passage of the Constitution in 1789, though there was very little federal legislation passed under the Articles of Confederation. The primary reason why the federal government did not pass more immigration law was that the United States was as much an alliance of sovereign states as it was a sovereign entity in and of itself.[5] Regulation of immigration was left to the several states. Nevertheless, under the authority of the Continental Congress, British convicts were refused entry, and Congress specifically called for states to pass additional laws preventing the immigration of convicts.[6] Furthermore, Article IV of the Articles of Confederation excepted "paupers, vagabonds and fugitives from justice" from the equal enjoyment of the privileges and immunities of citizenship." There was no particular exclusion under federal law for health questions because it was standard practice for states to impose a quarantine on ships bearing passengers with infectious diseases.[7]

As is to be expected, at that early stage in the country's history, state legislation controlling immigration was much more detailed than federal legislation. States were concerned with regulating the movement of criminals in an effort to protect citizens from crime,[8] regulating the entrance of persons with diseases in a concern for the public health,[9] regulating the movement of those likely to become public charges,[10] and regulating slavery.[11] Regulating the importation of slaves was of concern to all states—free and slave alike. Some slave states acted to prohibit the international slave trade, and some free states provided that slaves entering the state would be free.[12] Additionally, some slave states insisted that regulating the movement of free blacks was essential to the preservation of the institution of slavery, and some free states also erected barriers to the entry of free blacks.[13]

Even after the passage of the Constitution, it was unclear whether the federal government had much power to regulate immigration, and the divisiveness of the issue of slavery was reflected in the Constitution's only provision concerned with immigration. The Constitution provides that "The Migration or Importation of Such Persons as any of the States Now existing shall think proper to admit, shall not be prohibited by the Congress prior to the Year one thousand eight hundred and eight, but a Tax or duty may be imposed on such Importation, not exceeding ten dollars for each Person."[14] This clause was intended to initially disable Congress from regulating the importation of slaves from abroad, but it also made it unclear whether Congress had any power whatsoever to regulate immigration.

Despite this lack of clarity, in 1798, in response to perceived dangers from French revolutionaries, Congress passed two acts concerned with immigration. The Alien Act granted the president unfettered discretion to arrest and deport any alien he regarded as dangerous.[15] This act was vehemently condemned and later abandoned on the ground that Congress had been delegated no power to control the admission of aliens. Conversely, the other act passed at the same time—the Alien Enemies Act granting the president the power to remove alien enemies during hostilities—was viewed as an exercise of the war power and remains on the books.[16]

Thus, early immigration law was a mixture of state and federal legislation and policy, with more state than federal legislation. It has been proposed that once slavery ceased to divide the nation, it became possible to regulate immigration on a national level, and it was in response to the nineteenth century's waves of immigration that national regulation was increasingly perceived as desirable.[17] Traditionally, the issues of crime, poverty, and disease among immigrants were considered to be matters of legitimate local (as opposed to federal) concern. As originally conceived, regulation of immigration was not equated with foreign policy but rather with preserving and protecting the health and welfare of those who were already citizens of the United States and of the several states.

The first post–Civil War federal acts restricting immigration reflect traditional concerns with crime, poverty, and disease. In 1875, Congress passed statutes excluding convicts and prostitutes; in 1882 it excluded "idiots, lunatics, convicts and persons likely to become public charges"; and in 1891 it added exclusions based on contagious diseases, polygamy, and criminal offenses involving moral turpitude.[18] Amendments in 1903 expanded the classes of excludable aliens along the same three lines.

Another concern also came to be reflected in exclusion law. With the discovery of gold in California, large numbers of Chinese laborers were attracted to the West Coast. Moreover, relevant treaty provisions encouraged the immigration. As the Supreme Court described it:

> The competition steadily increased as the laborers came in crowds on each steamer that arrived from China, or Hong Kong, an adjacent English port. They were generally industrious and frugal. Not being accompanied by families, except in rare instances, their expenses were small; and they were content with the simplest fare, such as would not suffice for our laborers and artisans. The competition between them and our people was for this reason altogether in their favor, and the consequent irritation, proportionately deep and bitter, was followed, in many cases, by open conflicts, to the great disturbance of the public peace.
>
> The differences of race added greatly to the difficulties of the situation. Notwithstanding the favorable provisions of the new articles of the Treaty of 1868 [between the U.S. and China], by which all the privileges, immunities, and

exemptions were extended to subjects of China in the United States which were accorded to citizens or subjects of the most favored nation, they remained strangers in the land, residing apart by themselves, and adhering to the customs and usages of their own country. It seems impossible for them to assimilate with our people or to make any change in their habits or modes of living. As they grew in numbers each year the people of the coast saw, or believed they saw, in the facility of immigration, and in the crowded millions of China, where population presses upon the means of subsistence, great danger that at no distant day that portion of our country would be overrun by them unless prompt action was taken to restrict their immigration. The people there accordingly petitioned earnestly for protective legislation.[19]

In 1882 Congress passed the nation's first immigration law targeting a specific ethnic or racial group.[20] This law was quickly strengthened into the Chinese Exclusion Act, which suspended immigration of Chinese laborers and forbade any court from admitting Chinese to citizenship. Labor and wage concerns were not assuaged, and, later in the same decade, Congress passed the Contract Labor Laws addressing the same employment concerns underlying the previous bill. These later laws excluded cheap foreign labor that would depress the labor market and provided for deportation of aliens brought in violation of contract labor laws. A head tax was used to further discourage immigration of those aliens likely to price their labor more cheaply than the existent work force.

In the first decade of the twentieth century, almost 8.8 million immigrants were admitted by the Bureau of Immigration and Naturalization. The majority of these immigrants were from southern or eastern Europe and were slow to assimilate. As with the Chinese, in response to pressure from those who felt threatened by this new group of immigrants, Congress passed restrictive measures to discourage immigration. The addition of a literacy requirement to this 1917 act effectively barred numbers of illiterate southern and eastern Europeans, and an eight-dollar head tax further discouraged their immigration. Though these measures made it more difficult to immigrate, Europeans were not barred as were Asians.

After World War I, in response to further fears that southern and eastern Europeans would inundate the United States, Congress set quotas for each nationality as a percentage of the number of foreign nationals represented in the 1910 census. In other words, Congress's goal in designing the quota system was to standardize the 1910 cultural background stew recipe in the melting pot of the United States. Naturally, the resulting system favored Anglo-Saxon and other immigrants from northern and western Europe.

The situation changed after World War II. With the postwar economic upswing, the United States once again needed labor from abroad and consequently changed the law. It negotiated a temporary worker program with Mexico, repealed the ban on Chinese immigration, and made provisions to admit a number of war refugees. Because spouses of United States citizens were exempted, marriage to a U.S. citizen became a well-known way of circumventing the quotas.

Despite the relaxation of some quotas to allow immigration of refugees flee-ing eastern Europe, systems favoring Anglo-Saxon and other western and north-ern European groups continued until the McCarran-Walter Act of 1952. This act retained a national origin quota system favoring immigrants from northern and western Europe, established racial quotas for Asians, and established preferences within quotas for aliens with special skills. It also established the basic structure of present immigration law by detailing exclusion and deportation grounds, establishing procedures for deportation and provisions for relief from deporta-tion, and it established exclusions on political grounds (by excluding anyone "likely to" engage in "subversive [Communist] activity").

Equally important, however, the 1952 act established four types of entrance preferences. First preference was given to those with high education, technical training, specialized experience, or exceptional ability needed by the U.S. econ-omy, and their spouses and children. The next preference was allotted to parents and children of citizens, then parents and children of permanent residents, and the final preference was given to the immediate families (spouses, children, and siblings) of those admitted under the quotas.

In the Civil Rights era, the 1952 act was heavily criticized because of the racial and ethnic discrimination inherent in its quota systems.[21] In response to this criticism, the 1965 act eliminated quotas and instead put caps on immigration from the Eastern and Western hemispheres. The act also switched around the order of preferences. Immediate relatives (spouses and unmarried children) of citizens and permanent resident aliens were put in the highest category, while those of "exceptional ability" or in the professions were relegated to the third ranking, followed by more distant relatives, needed workers, and refugees.

By 1986, the Immigration and Nationalization Service (hereinafter the "INS") was unable to keep up with the number of deportable aliens. In order to discourage the hiring of aliens not authorized to work in the United States, Con-gress established sanctions against employers of illegal aliens in the Immigration Reform and Control Act (IRCA). At the same time as it was attempting to bol-ster methods of keeping certain aliens out, Congress recognized the difficulty inherent in trying to deport large numbers of aliens whose presence had been tol-erated for a certain number of years, and so granted amnesty to certain groups in exchange for establishing sanctions and penalties for employers of undocu-mented aliens. Congress also implemented measures to prevent aliens from mar-rying U.S. citizens solely in an effort to obtain citizenship (known as "marriage fraud"), and it established expedited deportations for aggravated felons.

In the last five years, Congress has further tinkered with immigration law. Recent acts have placed an overall cap on immigration, expanded antidiscrimi-nation programs, and attempted to encourage diversity immigration by using a lottery from countries that are underrepresented. Congress has also established temporary protected status programs to enable nationals of areas suffering polit-ical upheaval (refugees) to remain in the United States up to eighteen months, asylum for those who reasonably fear persecution in their homelands, and has encouraged immigration of scientists and engineers from the former Soviet

Union. In response to terrorist attacks and increasing numbers of illegal aliens who commit criminal acts, Congress has passed legislation intended to make it more difficult for terrorists to gain access to the United States, and to make it increasingly easy to deport criminal aliens.

Most recently, in the Personal Responsibility and Work Opportunity Reconciliation Act (hereafter the Personal Responsibility Act)[22] and the Illegal Immigration Reform and Immigrant Responsibility Act (IIRIRA),[23] Congress passed legislation intended to discourage poverty-stricken aliens from coming into the country illegally by further restricting noncitizens' eligibility for a number of public benefit programs. The Personal Responsibility Act emphasizes that self-sufficiency has been a basic principle of U.S. immigration law since the earliest immigration statutes, and it continues to be the policy that "aliens within the Nation's borders not depend on public resources to meet their needs, but rather rely on their own capabilities and the resources of their families, their sponsors, and private organizations."[24] In addition to the limitations on public benefits, IIRIRA added provisions for expedited deportation of criminal or otherwise inadmissible aliens, and a requirement that immigrant applicants give proof of vaccination against vaccine-preventable diseases. More Border Patrol agents are to be hired and a preinspection program at foreign airports is to be developed to gain more control over the borders. A new division of investigators is to be created to detect those who overstay their visas. Thus, the most recent federal legislation reflects the original concerns of the earliest state and federal acts, as well as the earliest problems in enforcing those laws: protecting against an influx of criminal aliens, protecting against an influx of aliens likely to become public charges, protecting against the spread of disease, and protecting labor concerns. The provision for more agents is a direct acknowledgment of this country's continued inability to prevent illegal entry.

## THE STRUCTURE OF THE CURRENT IMMIGRATION AND NATIONALITY ACT

While the preceding chronology illuminates the immigration concerns that continue to generate congressional legislation, a close overview of that legislation will facilitate an understanding of some of the controversies concerning the application and constitutionality of current immigration laws. The Immigration and Nationality Act of 1952 begins by granting administrative power to the attorney general and the secretary of state, and it provides that aliens may appeal to federal courts for review of final deportation orders only after they have followed the administrative review process dictated by the act.[25] Next, the act describes the selection system used in deciding which aliens shall be admitted, starting with the method of calculating the yearly limits.[26] With typical congressional obfuscation, this section provides that "[A]liens born in a foreign state or dependent area who may be issued immigrant visas or who may otherwise acquire the status of an alien lawfully admitted to the United States for permanent residence" are limited to (1) family-sponsored immigrants "in a number not to exceed in any fiscal year the number specified in subsection C for that year, and not to exceed in any of the first 3 quarters of any year 27 percent of the worldwide level under such subsection for all of such fiscal year"; (2) employment-based immigrants (another calculation); and (3) diversity immigrants (55,000 each fiscal year). Translated into English, this means that Congress has set ceilings for each of three categories of admissible immigrants: those whose immigration is based on family already in the United States, those whose admissibility is based on their employment, and those who are being admitted because they won the low-admission country lottery. The 1990 revision of the ceilings and calculation methods substantially increased immigration to levels higher than ever before. Certain aliens such as the immediate relatives (children, spouses, and parents) of U.S. citizens are not subject to numerical limitation. In addition to describing how many aliens may be admitted, this section of the act details out preference priorities,[27] the procedure for granting immigrant status,[28] admission of refugees and emergency situation refugees,[29] asylum procedure,[30] and the admission of special (seasonal) agricultural workers.[31]

## Family-Sponsored Immigration[32]

The three categories of preferences are very detailed and specific. Family-based preference requires sponsorship by close relatives who are themselves citizens or lawful permanent residents of the United States. The first of the four subpreferences provides for admission of unmarried sons and daughters of U.S. citizens. The second allows for admission of spouses and unmarried children of lawful permanent residents, the third provides for admission of married children of U.S. citizens, and the fourth provides for admission of siblings of U.S. citizens. In the past, the provision for siblings of citizens has caused controversy because it potentially provides for admissibility of a vastly greater web of family relations than do the qualifications based on marriage and parentage, but Congress has declined to change it.[33] Sponsorship means that the relatives in the United States must provide an affidavit promising to support the immigrant, or that the immigrant will be able to provide for himself. IIRIRA raises the requirement by adding that the affidavit must promise that the immigrant will be supported either by himself or by his family to 125 percent of the federal poverty line. The act also requires that the affidavit be executed as a contract and legally enforceable in the United States, and the sponsor must agree to reimburse the cost of any benefit if the sponsored alien receives any kind of federal public aid described in the act.[34]

## Employment-Based Immigration[35]

The 1990 act provided for a 160-percent increase of admissions for employment-based immigration. Employment-based immigration is divided into five subpreferences.[36] The first preference is for those with "extraordinary ability, outstanding professors and researchers, and certain multinational executives and managers."

(The Nobel Prize would suffice as proof of "extraordinary ability."[37]) The second preference is for professionals holding advanced degrees or who because of "exceptional" ability will substantially benefit the economy, culture, education, or welfare of the United States (licensed nurses and physical therapists go to the head of the line because of chronic shortages in those fields[38]). The third preference is for those with baccalaureate degrees, or skilled and unskilled workers in fields in which there is a shortage of American workers. Certification by the Department of Labor is required for admission of those in the second and third categories,[39] and all but those of "exceptional ability" must have a U.S. employer petition for them. The fourth preference is for "special immigrants"—religious workers, former long-time employees of the U.S. government, and other miscellaneous provisions. The fifth preference provides for immigration of investors whose investments will create a minimum of ten jobs in the United States.

Sometimes it is easier to visualize the effect of a change in legislation with a specific example. My paternal grandfather, a pathologist, and his family were held at Ellis Island for three months in the 1920s. While my grandparents would have been allowed in immediately under the Russian quota, my uncle, who was an infant at the time, was born in Turkey. My grandparents had to wait until there was a slot in the Turkish quota in order to bring in their baby. Under the present-day preference scheme, if my grandfather was admitted under either the family-sponsored or employment-based preferences, then his family would be allowed in as well. (My mother's parents, in the same situation, learned enough about the quotas to lie and claimed that their infant daughter [my aunt] was born in Russia, not Turkey.)

## Diversity Immigration[40]

The third and smallest category of preferences is that described as "diversity immigration." Diversity immigration is for those from specific "underrepresented countries" determined by an "extraordinarily intricate formula" that rules out those from high-admission countries.[41] In 1995, the formula ruled out nationals from Canada, the Dominican Republic, El Salvador, India, Jamaica, Mexico, the People's Republic of China, the Philippines, South Korea, Taiwan, the United Kingdom, and Vietnam. Additionally, there are certain threshold requirements for those who want to be included in the diversity allotment: they must have a high school education or its equivalent, or a minimum of two years' experience in an occupation requiring two years of training, and they may file only one application per year. Selection is done by lottery and while immediate families may accompany those immigrants selected by the lottery, they will count against the diversity ceiling.

After discussing how many may be admitted for immigration status, the act describes the admission qualifications for aliens and what documents they need. It also delineates conditional permanent resident status: the alien spouse of an American citizen may be granted permanent status on a conditional basis if the situation is such that it is possible the marriage is fraudulent. After two years of residency, if the alien spouse can establish the authenticity of the marriage, then the condition will be removed.

## Inadmissibility

A lengthy provision of this section of the act is that listing classes of aliens who are ineligible to receive visas and ineligible for admission.[42] In contrast, a deportable alien is someone who has already been admitted to the United States when the INS determines that he is not qualified to remain.[43] An alien is deportable for the very reasons he would have been inadmissible in the first place,[44] and a few more.

Previously, the terms "excludable" (inadmissible) and "deportable" had different procedural effects: the government owed a higher duty and a more extensive removal procedure to a "deportable" alien than it did to someone it regarded as not yet having entered the United States. The new IIRIRA provisions are an attempt to do away with some of the arbitrary effects of this jurisprudentially created distinction while at the same time providing for expedited inspection and removal of those adjudged clearly inadmissible. Under the new provisions, if an alien has not gone through the admissions process, regardless of whether he is first presenting himself for admission or whether he was found here, he must first prove his admissibility to an INS inspecting official in an abbreviated inspection or else the INS is required to return him from whence he came within ninety days.[45]

As the reader should expect, an alien may be found to be inadmissible on health-related grounds due to a physical or mental disorder that may pose a threat to the property, safety, or welfare of himself or others.[46] If the Secretary of Health and Human Services determines that an alien has a "communicable disease of public health significance, including "infection with the etiologic agent for acquired immune deficiency syndrome" (in other words, if he is HIV positive), then that alien is inadmissible on health-related grounds. An alien is also inadmissible if he has been convicted of a crime of moral turpitude; has multiple criminal convictions; is a known trafficker in controlled substances, prostitution, or commercialized vice; or if the INS reasonably believes he is involved in terrorism. Moreover, as mentioned above, inadmissibility may be predicated on political grounds: an alien may be inadmissible if his entry would have potentially serious adverse foreign policy consequences, if the alien is voluntarily a member of a totalitarian party, or if he participated in Nazi persecutions. An alien is ineligible if he is likely at any time to become a public charge, or if he has been arrested and deported within the previous five years. As a counterbalance to the potential harsh results of some of these provisions, the attorney general (i.e., the INS) is given the discretion to waive inadmissibility in certain limited instances for humanitarian purposes, to assure family unity, or where it is otherwise in the public interest to do so.

After prescribing the conditions for the issuance of visas, and giving the secretary of state the power to further regulate visas,[47] the act discusses provisions relating to entry and exclusion. An alien must submit to inspection and may be detained as he attempts to enter the United States.[48] Previously, if an alien did not submit to inspection and was later found in the United States, he would be regarded as never having entered, and would then be due only the due process of an exclusionary proceeding, rather than the more substantial protections of a deportation proceeding.

As mentioned above, under the new procedure, aliens present in the United States who have not submitted to inspection are regarded as applicants for admission. If determined inadmissible, then an INS officer "shall" order them removed without further hearing or review unless the alien indicates an intention to apply for asylum.[49] If the alien indicates an intention to apply for asylum, or if he has papers showing he is here with INS permission, or if he can prove he has been here for the past two years, then he may be accorded a more substantial removal proceeding.

Judicial review of the summary deportation proceeding is extremely limited. Review can be given in a habeas corpus proceeding but is limited to determining whether the plaintiff is an alien, whether she was ordered removed, and whether she can prove by a preponderance of the evidence that she has been lawfully permitted for permanent residence or granted refugee or asylum status.[50] The alien may not argue that she was not inadmissible, nor may she argue that she is entitled to any relief from removal.[51] Challenges to the constitutionality of this summary removal process are limited to the United States District Court for the District of Columbia, and such challenges are limited in scope to the issue of whether these INA sections and regulations implementing them are constitutional.[52] Such challenges are being anticipated by lawyers in the field.[53]

## Deportation[54]

As mentioned earlier, deportability and inadmissibility are different. The section of the Immigration and Nationality Act discussing deportation delineates who is deportable, the procedures followed, when deportation may be suspended or status adjusted, and how departure is to be effectuated. An alien already in the United States is deportable if he would have been inadmissible at the time of entry.[55] He is also deportable if he is present in the United States unlawfully, if he violated the nonimmigrant status granted by his visa, if he committed marital fraud, or if he was involved in smuggling aliens into the United States. Furthermore, he may be deported for falsification of documents, for failing to register a change of address, or for committing crimes, especially if he is convicted of an offense involving controlled substances or firearms or domestic violence. As with excludability, the attorney general may waive deportation for fraudulent entry on certain delineated grounds.

As mentioned above, the new IIRIRA statutes provide an alien with a more extensive removal proceeding before an immigration judge:[56] (1) if it is not clear that the alien is admissible even though he has papers showing he is here with the permission of the INS; (2) if he can prove that he has been in the United States for the past two years; or (3) if he asks for political asylum and though the asylum officer finds that the alien has a credible fear of persecution and is eligible for asylum,[57] that decision is challenged by another immigration officer. The proceeding before the immigration judge (the "IJ"), like the deportation proceedings under previous law, is somewhat like a trial. The alien must be given notice reasonable under the circumstances, and he has the privilege of being represented by counsel (at his own or nongovernmental expense).[58] He must have a reasonable opportunity to examine the evidence against him, to present evidence on his own behalf, and to cross-examine the government's witnesses. All testimony and evidence will be recorded.

Unlike common law trials, however, the immigration judge has very broad authority more in keeping with procedure in a civil law trial. He administers oaths, receives evidence, interrogates, examines, and cross-examines the alien and any witnesses. Moreover, if the alien is appearing as an applicant for admission, then the alien herself has the high burden of establishing clearly and beyond doubt that she is entitled to be admitted and is not inadmissible.[59] If the alien facing the removal proceeding was previously admitted, then she must prove that she was previously admitted under the somewhat easier standard of "clear and convincing evidence." Once she does so, the burden reverts to the INS to prove that she is deportable.

Judicial review of a proceeding before an immigration judge is limited.[60] An alien may file one motion to reconsider a decision that he is removable. He can be ordered removed even if he fails to appear at the removal proceeding if the INS establishes that he was notified and that he is removable. An alien may appeal to a court for review of a determination of deportability only after he has exhausted all administrative remedies, and a court has no jurisdiction to review any discretionary judgments of the INS (except asylum), and no jurisdiction to review an order of removal against an alien who was convicted of certain criminal offenses. Moreover, a decision that an alien is not eligible for admission is conclusive unless manifestly contrary to law, and a denial of asylum by the INS is conclusive unless manifestly contrary to law and an abuse of discretion.

## Alienage Law: Employment of Unauthorized Aliens

In the Immigration Reform and Control Act (IRCA), Congress passed measures to sanction employers of unauthorized aliens. IRCA provisions make it unlawful to employ an alien knowing that he is unauthorized to work in the United States, and unlawful to employ an "individual" (whether or not that person is an alien) without having verified that he is so authorized.[61] In order to verify authorization, an employer is required to examine the individual's documents. Those documents may include a U.S. passport, a resident alien card (the proverbial "green card"), or another authorized document bearing a photograph and security features. Furthermore, the employer must determine whether or not the document presented reasonably appears to be genuine, and then must fill out and retain a verification form documenting that he checked the individual's documentation. An employer may be subject to a cease and desist order as well as a stiff civil money penalty for hiring, recruiting, or referring violations. A pattern of IRCA violations may mean a criminal penalty of up to $3000 for each unauthorized alien, imprisonment for up to six months, or both.

In addition to penalizing employers who hire unauthorized aliens, IRCA also provides for a Special Counsel to investigate allegations that an employer has discriminated against individuals on the basis of national origin or citizenship status.[62] If a complaint is made that an employer is engaging in an unfair immigration-related employment practice, a hearing will be conducted by an administrative law judge, who may require the hiring of the individual as an employee or the payment of back pay, and who may award attorney's fees to the prevailing party. Thus, Congress has attempted to balance its bulwark against employment of unauthorized aliens with measures to prevent any resulting employment discrimination made by employers fearful of civil and criminal penalties for accidentally hiring unauthorized aliens.

## Naturalization

The Constitution specifically mandates that Congress has the power "to establish an uniform Rule of Naturalization . . . throughout the United States,"[63] and the next major section of the INA deals with nationality and naturalization. It begins by defining those considered citizens of the United States at birth,[64] and then discusses naturalization.[65] In order to be eligible for naturalization, one must understand the English language and have a knowledge and understanding of the fundamentals of "the history, and of the principles and form of government of the United States"—though those requirements are modified for those over fifty-five years old or those who are mentally or physically impaired.[66] Additionally, in order to be naturalized, one must demonstrate a continuous residence in the United States for at least five years as "a person of good moral character, attached to the principles of the Constitution of the United States, and well disposed to the good order and happiness of the United States."[67] For those who make extraordinary contributions to national security (i.e., those who have been informants or spies for the CIA), the residency requirement may be reduced to one year, while those who support totalitarian forms of government or who are members of the Communist Party are barred from naturalization.

To apply for naturalization, an applicant must file a signed, sworn application that he fulfills the requirements for naturalization.[68] An INS officer then conducts a personal investigation, authenticating that the applicant lives where he says he does and has engaged in business or work for at least five years prior to the filing of the application. A standardized citizenship test is administered to determine that a petitioner for naturalization fulfills the English language, literacy, and knowledge of U.S. government requirements. The applicant must further demonstrate that he is of good moral character and must show that he is attached to the principles of the Constitution by renouncing any allegiance he may have to a foreign sovereignty, and by giving an oath that he will be willing to bear arms on behalf of the United States. If he can demonstrate that religious beliefs prevent him from bearing arms, the immigrant may be allowed to give a modified oath promising to perform service or work of national importance when legally required to do so.[69]

Though the judiciary originally had the responsibility of administering the naturalization process, the act of 1990 made naturalization almost entirely an administrative procedure because of an increasing volume of citizenship applicants and the heavy dockets of the federal courts.[70] The attorney general has sole authority to naturalize persons as citizens of the United States, but the oath of allegiance may be administered by a state or federal court. If an application for naturalization is denied, the applicant may request a hearing before a higher-ranking INS officer. Upon further denial, the applicant may seek *de novo* (full) review before a federal district court. Thus, the process due someone who is being denied naturalization is greater than that due someone who is being deported. Naturalization can be revoked for a number of reasons, including unlawful procurement of citizenship in the first place.[71] In addition to prescribing rules, procedures, and penalties (where appropriate) for immigration, exclusion, deportation, and naturalization, the INA contains a section establishing aid for resettlement of refugees.

# ADMINISTRATION AND ENFORCEMENT OF THE IMMIGRATION AND NATIONALITY ACT

The INA and its interpretation generates a myriad of practice and policy issues incurred by the administration and enforcement of this large and complex piece of legislation. An increasing number of federal agencies become involved in dealing with various provisions. Thus, a person who wants to immigrate to the United States may deal with several federal agencies, including the Department of State if she is applying for a visa from abroad, the Immigration and Naturalization Service (INS) with which she files her visa petition, the Department of Labor if her petition is employment-based, the Public Health Service to determine if she is excludable for health reasons, and the Board of Immigration Appeals if she decides to appeal a deportation or exclusion order.

## Administrative and Managerial Problems

The attorney general has the principal authority for the administration and enforcement of the act and is required to delegate responsibility to the Immigration and Naturalization Service.[72] It has been pointed out that administering and enforcing can be quite different undertakings:

> [a]dministering any complex statute . . . often requires the administrators to counsel affected individuals regarding their possible rights, liabilities and future actions . . . and help guide them through the process. In large measure, these functions involve service to the public. Enforcement of a statute, however, particularly one that is frequently violated, might properly call forth an attitude of tough-mindedness and suspicion on the part of the officials involved. The two

functions can coexist if the agency is carefully organized and the administrators are sensitive, skillful and well-trained, but there is inevitably tension between the tasks. Because the INA is both highly complex and notoriously violated on a broad scale, the tension here becomes particularly acute.[73]

Moreover, the INS has not been respected as either well run or efficient in a very long time, and even with the 1990 expansion of the ceilings on immigration, there are long waiting lists for those who want to immigrate. It is chronically underbudgeted and understaffed, and immigration lawyers have been known to become skilled at buttonholing officials in corridors and waiting rooms. They also acknowledge that in the past sometimes their skill lay in winning delays and relying on INS inefficiency rather than winning cases for their clients, and that they hoped that in the interim, "something good would happen": the deportable alien would apply for amnesty, obtain asylum, secure an employment-based or family-based visa, arrange for voluntary departure, qualify for waiver or suspension of deportation, return to his country of origin, or otherwise delay the proceeding.[74] While the expectation is that this will change as a result of IIRIRA's streamlined procedures and its expansion of the INS, the consequences of the statutory changes remain to be seen.

## Controversies in Implementing Employment-based Preferences

In the three largest employment-based preference categories, the Department of Labor (DOL) must certify that there is a shortage of available and qualified workers in the alien's field at the place of employment and that the alien's hiring will not adversely affect local wages or working conditions. The burden of proving the dearth of American workers and the need to hire a particular alien is placed on the prospective employer (and his immigration attorney).[75] The certification process has generated a whole body of highly technical and complicated law. Additionally, the labor department's regulations require that employers must pay the certified alien at least the prevailing wage, even if he would be willing to work for less.[76] This regulation, designed to ensure that the immigrant's hire will not erode local wages, has led to controversies in determining the prevailing wage when the DOL and the prospective employer disagree about what types of jobs are "substantially comparable" to the one being offered. Typically, the DOL argues that the offered wage is low as compared to similar jobs in the area, and the employer argues that the DOL's comparisons are arbitrary and inaccurate. Policy issues surrounding the regulation bring into play the same low-wages-versus-loss-of-jobs economic questions that surround the minimum wage law.

## Controversies involving Deportation and Exclusion

Controversies surrounding deportation and exclusion often involved how aliens were treated while they awaited deportation. In a very famous case, the Supreme

Court held that "Whatever the procedure authorized by Congress is, it is due process as far as an alien denied entry is concerned" (*United States ex rel Knauff* v. *Shaughnessy,* 338 U.S. 537, 544, 70 S. CT. 309, 94 L. Ed. 317 [1950]). This plenary power "entry" doctrine was further developed in *Shaughnessy* v. *United States ex rel. Mezei,* 345 U.S. 206, 73 S. Ct. 625, 97 L. Ed. 956 (1953). Mezei was born in Hungary or Rumania, and lived in the United States for twenty-five years. In 1948 he sailed to Europe to visit his dying mother in Rumania. He was denied entry to Rumania, and remained in Hungary for close to two years because he had trouble securing an exit permit. Finally, armed with a quota immigration visa issued by the American Consul in Budapest, he returned to New York. Upon arrival in the United States, he was excluded for security reasons and held at Ellis Island. Twice he shipped out to return to Europe, but France and Great Britain refused him permission to land. The State Department was unable to get him readmitted to Hungary, and close to a dozen Latin American countries also turned him down. He finally told the INS that he was not going to make any more efforts to leave. Stuck on Ellis Island for two years, he finally brought suit pursuant to a writ of habeas corpus. The Supreme Court held that in view of the exclusion on the basis of security reasons, his continued detention at Ellis Island did not deprive him of any statutory or constitutional rights. Thus, like the Flying Dutchman, he was doomed to sail at Ellis Island indefinitely until the INS finally relented and paroled him into the United States after a total of four years detention.[77]

The principles stated in *Mezei* and *Knauff* had developed into the concept of "entry": an alien who "entered" the United States was entitled to a deportation hearing, while one who had not "entered" got only an exclusion hearing. Mere physical presence in the United States was not enough to establish entry.[78] Though excludable aliens were usually summarily returned to their homeland, there were occasions where, like Mezei, that was not possible, and the effect of the entry doctrine had been to authorize the INS to detain aliens for long periods of time. Most recently, suits have been brought on behalf of detained Haitians and on behalf of Mariel refugees released from Cuba's prisons. In 1994, the Ninth Circuit ordered the release of a Mariel refugee who had been held in detention for eight years, but then vacated and reversed its opinion en banc in agreement with almost every other circuit that had considered the detention of Marielitos.[79] The entry doctrine and the plenary power doctrine it is associated with severely limited judicial review of INS treatment of excludable and deportable aliens, and have been subjected to an endless stream of scholarly criticism.

Under IIRIRA, those who are present in the United States without admission or those who, like many Haitians, are interdicted on the high seas, are deemed applicants for admission.[80] Thus, the "entry" doctrine is replaced by the "admissions" doctrine. Under the admissions doctrine, whether an alien arrived yesterday for inspection at the border, or whether she has been here for under two years without admission, she will receive the same preliminary inspection interview by an INS officer.

As was noted above, while the INS fails to separate administrative and en-

forcement functions in most areas, the INA does provide for special inquiry officers (immigration judges) in deportation proceedings. The creation of the Executive Office of Immigration Review, by whom the IJs are employed,[81] separates
immigration judges from the INS and is intended to insure that they adjudicate
impartially. However, critics have charged that an "enforcement mentality" per-
vades immigration-related agencies so that they habitually lean toward exclusion
and deportation even when a neutral interpretation of the INA would dictate otherwise, and that the EOIR's structural independence is therefore inadequate.[82]

A formal deportation leads to severe limitations on an alien who may later
want to reenter the United States. Under new IIRIRA provisions, being found
here unlawfully may also lead to similar consequences. An alien who departs
voluntarily even before the commencement of removal proceedings will be
barred from admission for three years if he was present in the United States for
more than 180 days unlawfully.[83] If he was here more than a year, or if he waited
until he received final determination of removability, he may be inadmissible for
up to ten years. An alien who was deported because he was convicted of an
aggravated crime is barred for twenty years.

In the past, almost all undocumented aliens arranged for voluntary departure. The new laws are apparently designed to encourage them to make their
stays less than 180 days, and to encourage them to leave before proceedings are
commenced—not to wait until the INS finds out about them. On the other hand,
possibly because a number of commentators have expressed concern that it is
unfair to summarily deport those who have been in the United States long enough
to develop strong ties, the new laws allow an undocumented alien who has been
here more than two years a greater chance of proving admissibility by allowing
him access to the IJ procedure, rather than summary removal.[84]

## Alienage Law

While there are a number of policy and administrative issues surrounding the
legal admission of immigrants, what has generated the most controversy lately is
how best to prevent and discourage illegal (undocumented) immigration. There
are only two possible ways to discourage illegal immigration: (1) prevent ingress
( through the use of fences, checkpoints, and patrols), and (2) enforce egress by
detecting, deporting, and discouraging undocumented aliens already in the
United States. Alienage provisions are intended to encourage present EWIs to
leave, and discourage potential EWIs from coming.[85] While aliens enter the
United States unlawfully for a number of reasons—to join family already here, to
flee persecution in their homeland, or to go to school—the vast majority come to
look for better paying work and a higher standard of living.[86] Their impact is
highly concentrated in a few states: California, Florida, Texas, New York, Illinois,
Arizona, and New Jersey have 86 percent of the nation's undocumented aliens.[87]
The act passed late in 1996 addresses ingress concerns by doubling the number
of border guards and providing for new methods of detecting fraudulent entries.[88]
With regard to the alienage-law provisions, two types of legislation have devel-

oped: legislation to discourage employment of undocumented aliens (IRCA), and legislation to minimize undocumented aliens' access to public benefits.

## IRCA

IRCA has been criticized as ineffective. Early on, there had been some evidence that habitual employers of illegal immigrants ignored the substance of the legislation—accepting documents even though they had reason to believe that they were fraudulent.[89] The INS has since taken steps to discourage this practice, but it is not clear that it does not still occur.[90] On the flip side, there is also evidence that employers have become so afraid of the sanctions that they discriminate against those who appear to be of other than U.S. origin.[91] This ineffectiveness of the provisions against discrimination has been blamed on INS shortcomings:

> Poor management, lack of control over its information gathering systems, fiscal ineptitude, and lack of consistent national policy have created a regulatory disaster in the workplace on the part of the INS. The INS does not currently have, nor has it ever had the skills, resources, or background to fulfill IRCA's aims. In short, the INS is ill-equipped to fulfill IRCA's ambitious agenda of reducing illegal immigration. Instead, the INS's inadequate management has led in turn to increased document fraud, increased employer discrimination, and employer misunderstanding over IRCA's requirements within workplaces nation-wide.[92]

In response to criticism such as this, IIRIRA created a task force to develop changes in employer sanctions and develop a new employment verification program.

## Access to Public Benefits

On another front, while they may benefit temporarily from the odd federally funded emergency program, most federally funded public benefits programs have been off-limits to EWIs even prior to the Personal Responsibility Act, including Aid to Families with Dependent Children (welfare), Supplemental Security Income (SSI), nonemergency Medicaid and Medicare, food stamps, and public housing.[93] Undocumented aliens have been eligible for WIC (Supplemental Food Program for Women, Infants, and Children), emergency medical services, some social service programs under the Social Security Act, and the school lunch program.[94] With regard to aliens in general, the new act states that changes are being implemented because "current eligibility rules for public assistance and unenforceable financial support agreements have proved wholly incapable of assuring that individual aliens not burden the public benefits system."[95] The act provides that undocumented aliens are ineligible for all federal public benefits except treatment of an emergency medical condition; noncash, in-kind emergency disaster relief; public health assistance for immunizations; testing and treatment of symptoms of communicable diseases ("whether or not such symptoms are caused by a communicable disease"); services such as soup kitchens, crisis counseling, and intervention under the sole discretion of the attorney general, and any housing they have already received through HUD and other such programs.[96] Documented aliens remain ineligible for federal means-tested public benefits for five years from entry, and will no longer be eligible for SSI or food stamps in that time period—except for those who are refugees, asylees, veterans, and those aliens who have been battered by their spouses.[97] Additionally, Congress is giving states the authority to prohibit aliens from programs of general cash public assistance (welfare), and is providing that states' have the authority to make determinations concerning the eligibility of documented aliens for public benefits—if a state chooses to follow the federal classifications, then it cannot be attacked for unconstitutional discrimination.[98]

According to a study done by the Urban Institute in 1994, the greatest impact of the presence of undocumented immigrants is on the states' public education systems, not the federal benefit programs that were always off-limits to them: "it is estimated that current expenditures for providing public education to undocumented aliens across the seven states for fiscal year 1993 was $3.1 billion" (as compared with $1.9 billion estimated to have been collected in taxes from these same immigrants).

Early in the last decade, Texas attempted to discourage illegal immigration (and protect its budget) by denying access to public elementary and secondary education to children of undocumented aliens. In a famous case, *Plyler v. Doe,* 457 U.S. 202, 102 S. Ct. 2382, 72 L. Ed. 2s 786 (1982), the Supreme Court held that the Texas law violated the children's right to equal protection under the Fifth and Fourteenth Amendments. Using a strict scrutiny approach, the Court found that Texas had failed to demonstrate that the classification based on lack of documentation was precisely tailored to serve a compelling governmental interest. The Court reasoned that while public education is not a "right" granted to individuals by the Constitution, education has a fundamental role in maintaining the fabric of our society. The children, though subject to deportation, had no ability to affect their parents' conduct or their own status as illegal aliens. Given the reality that many such children would remain in this country indefinitely due to the lack of an effective bar to the employment of their parents, and given that Texas had not shown that undocumented aliens imposed any significant burden on the state's economy, the Court found that the Texas law would impose a lifetime hardship on a discrete class of children not accountable for their disabling status and that denying them a basic education would foreclose any realistic possibility that they will contribute in even the smallest way to the progress of the nation.

In *Plyler,* the Supreme Court was struck by the children's powerlessness. Many legal scholars are also struck by the powerlessness of undocumented aliens in general, and at least one prominent legal scholar has written extensively on this topic, stressing that many undocumented persons are in this country for lengthy periods, and that they, like lawful permanent residents, do not have the right to vote and are thus legally very vulnerable.[99] Though advocacy groups may be able to exert some political pressure on their behalf, noncitizens cannot directly participate in the electoral process. Moreover, they are politically unpopular and are subject to the marginalizing effects of ethnicity, class, and gender.

Their fear of the government further compounds illegal immigrants' powerlessness and makes them vulnerable to various types of human predators.

Last year, California passed Proposition 187, aimed at denying public services and benefits to illegal aliens—including denying public elementary and secondary education and public postsecondary education, as well as publicly funded nonemergency health care and other public social services. While the imposition of Proposition 187 has been held up by a flurry of lawsuits, it and IIRIRA have engendered a flurry of commentary. In fact, UCLA devoted one whole issue of its law review to a symposium on Proposition 187, publishing articles by a number of scholars.[100]

The reason such legislation draws so much legal controversy—besides the human issues—is because it pulls into play a number of important legal premises involving the structure of our government. In *Chae Chin Ping,* the Supreme Court said that immigration is a national rather than local concern because the highest duty of every nation is to preserve its independence and give security against foreign aggression, and therefore, if the legislature considered the presence of foreigners of a different race to be dangerous to peace and security, it has the power to exclude them.[101] In another Chinese Exclusion case, the Court said that where Congress has decided that the officers of the executive department have the final determination of exclusion, the Court will not reverse that judgment.[102] Close to ninety years later, the court said, in affirming a denial of Medicare benefits to lawful permanent resident aliens who were also Cuban refugees, that

> There are literally millions of aliens within the jurisdiction of the United States. The Fifth Amendment, as well as the Fourteenth Amendment, protects every one of these persons from deprivation of life, liberty, or property without due process of law. Even one whose presence in this country is unlawful, involuntary, or transitory is entitled to that Constitutional protection.[103]

The Court continued on to state that while the Due Process Clause protects all persons regardless of whether they are aliens or citizens, that does not mean that aliens are entitled to enjoy all the advantages of citizenship. A vast number of constitutional and statutory provisions are based on the premise that a legitimate distinction between the two groups justifies the granting of benefits to one class not accorded to the other. Additionally, aliens need not be considered as a single legal class for due process and equal protection purposes because the members of this group are not necessarily similarly situated, and in fact the group contains people with a wide variety of ties to this country.[104]

Moreover,

> [f]or reasons long recognized as valid, the responsibility for regulating the relationship between the United States and our alien visitors has been committed to the political branches of the Federal Government. Since decisions in these matters may implicate our relations with foreign powers, and since a wide variety of classifications must be defined in the light of changing political and economic circumstances, such decisions are frequently of a character more appro-

priate to either the Legislature or the Executive than to the Judiciary. The appellees are two of the 440,000 Cuban refugees arrived in the U.S. between 1961 and 1972 admitted in order to make a humane response to a natural catastrophe or an international political situation. Any rule of constitutional law that would inhibit the flexibility of the political branches of government to respond to changing world conditions should be adopted only with the greatest caution. The reasons that preclude judicial review of political questions also dictate a narrow standard of review of decisions made by the Congress or the President in the area of immigration and naturalization.[105]

These excerpts delineate three intertwined and judicially created doctrines of immigration law: (1) Congress and the executive department have plenary power when it comes to deciding how issues involving immigration are to be handled, and nearly plenary power when it comes to issues of alienage; (2) states are preempted when it comes to immigration law, and may also be to some extent preempted when it comes to alienage law; and (3) judicial review is to be applied sparingly to federal immigration and alienage law.

The general principle that state powers are completely preempted is being modified. As we have seen, in the early decades of the republic it was assumed that immigration was primarily a concern of the states. The premise that regulation of immigration is an exclusive power of the federal government has developed slowly over time.[106] While Proposition 187 includes the same kind of restrictions on primary education that were found to be unconstitutional in *Plyler,* the state-power provisions of IIRIRA and the Personal Responsibility Act indicate that states may not be powerless to regulate alienage issues. The language of the Personal Responsibility Act even seems to preclude judicial review of the exercise of this power: "a State that chooses to follow the Federal classification in determining the eligibility of such aliens for public assistance shall be considered to have chosen the least restrictive means available for achieving the compelling governmental interest of assuring that aliens be self-reliant in accordance with national immigration policy."[107] Note that this indicates that states may have some say-so over alienage issues, but it nowhere indicates that states will be given any power in immigration matters.

The doctrine of judicial review was established in *Marbury* v. *Madison,* where the Supreme Court asserted its power to review the constitutionality of the actions of both the executive and legislative branches of the federal court.[108] Nowhere does the Constitution state whether the judiciary or Congress or the president has the final determination of when a law is made in pursuance of the Constitution, but it has been asserted that the concept of judicial review really rests upon three separate bases: (1) that the Constitution binds all parts of the federal government, (2) that it is enforceable by the Court in actions before it, and (3) that the judiciary is charged with interpreting the Constitution in a unique manner so that its rulings are binding on all other departments of the government.[109] If one grants the basic concept of judicial review of federal statutes, then one can justify the theory that the federal judiciary has the power to review the acts of state governments under the Supremacy clause of Article VI of the Constitution which makes state law subordinate to the federal treaties and laws, as well as the Constitution.[110]

With regard to immigration and alienage law, the Supreme Court has often refused to assert judicial review, finding that the legislative and executive departments have plenary power because of an interface with foreign policy, or because of its duty to safeguard the national population; however, the precise degree of deference has varied with both the context and the era. In fact, the Supreme Court's review ranges from the strict scrutiny normally associated with suspect classifications to a near abdication of any judicial review responsibilities, and making alienage jurisprudence nearly incoherent.[111] Generally, the Court subjects state alienage cases to heightened review, while granting extreme deference to federal cases—compare *Plyler* v. *Doe* with *Mathews* v. *Diaz* or *Mezei*.[112] It has also been argued that, in the Court's eyes, the unfettered process of ensuring the existence and growth of a national community reigns paramount over the concerns of individual noncitizens and their claims to substantive constitutional protection.[113] In the early years, the belief was that the courts had literally no power to review the constitutionality of Congress's actions, but more recently the Court has held that there may be some judicial role especially where a specific deportation or exclusion provision calls into question an immigrant's right to procedural due process.[114] Several commentators have noted that this exception has expanded over time, but recognize that the doctrine of plenary power is not likely to be overthrown."[115] Some hope that this expansion will lead to a restricted plenary power doctrine—a "PPD-lite."[116] Others argue that the doctrine should be completely overthrown.[117]

## CONCLUSION

The concerns of immigration law have remained the same since the earliest days of the republic: the protection of the health, safety, and welfare of the citizenry by regulating or preventing the immigration of those who carry disease, those who bring crime, or those whose presence is perceived as a threat to the economy either because they do not bring marketable skills and enterprising vigor or because they will compete with those who are already here for a limited number of jobs. Legislation passed by Congress in 1995 and 1996 is aimed at increasing the efficiency of the Immigration and Naturalization Service as well as rectifying some of the inequities that resulted from previous legislation and its interpretation by the judiciary as well as by the INS itself.

In keeping with these aims, IIRIRA seems to have done away with the entry doctrine that led to Flying Dutchman cases such as *Mezei,* but the extent and effect of this change remains to be seen. Likewise, Congress has granted the states some leeway in deciding how to limit the availability of public assistance to aliens, but, again, the effects both anticipated and unanticipated of this change also remain to be seen. Already the INS has given notice that it is having difficulty implementing some of the provisions intended to increase its efficiency in detaining and deporting those clearly inadmissible. In October 1996, the INS notified the Committee on the Judiciary that it has insufficient detention space and personnel to carry out the 1995 Antiterrorism and Effective Death Penalty Act's mandate that it detain all aliens who are inadmissible or deportable for having committed crimes.[118]

Generally speaking, immigration remains "radically insulated and divergent" from other areas of public law because of the restrictions on judicial review.[119] As a practical matter, judicial intervention would not be likely to affect outcomes because of the broad discretion given to the attorney general by the Immigration and Nationality Act itself and because much of the criticism aimed at the INS is based on administrative problems, as well as policy and constitutional issues. Be that as it may, the Supreme Court is not likely to be able to effectuate major policy changes, and, thus, the difficulties inherent in balancing the country's humanitarian desires against its need to protect those already part of the constitutional community may remain in the realm of politics.[120]

## NOTES

1. See Stephen H. Legomsky, "Ten More Years of Plenary Power: Immigration, Congress, and the Courts," 22 *Hastings Constitutional Law Quarterly* 925 n. 2 (1995) (indicating a distinction between law that governs the admission and expulsion of aliens, termed "immigration law," and the more general law of aliens' rights and obligations).

2. Gerald L. Neuman, "The Lost Century of American Immigration Law (1776–1875)," 93 *Columbia Law Review* 1833, 1833–34 (1993). For legal literature reflecting the myth that the borders of the United States were legally open until 1875, see, e.g., David Weissbrodt, *Immigration Law and Procedure in a Nutshell* § 1–2 (3d. ed., 1992), " [t]he United States officially favored unrestricted immigration for [almost a hundred years] after the nation's birth"; Ira J. Kurzban, *Immigration Law Sourcebook* 1 (5th ed., 1995), "First 100 Years—1776–1875: Open Door; Unimpeded Immigration."

3. Neuman, supra note 2 at 1834.

4. See id. at 1884.

5. Merrill Jensen, *The Articles of the Confederation* (1939); Peter S. Onuf, "The First Federal Constitution: The Articles of Confederation," in *The Framing and Ratification of the Constitution* 82–97 (Leonard W. Levy and Dennis J. Mahoney, eds., 1987).

6. 13 *Journal of Congress* 105–106 (September 16, 1788) (quoted in Neuman, supra note 2, p. 1842).

7. See Neuman, supra note 2, p. 1860.

8. Neuman, supra note 2, pp. 1841–46.

9. Id., at 1859–65.

10. Id., at 1846–59.

11. Id., at 1865–80.

12. Id., at 1878–79.

13. Id.

14. U.S. Const. art. 1, § 9, cl. 1.

15. Act of June 25, 1798, ch. 58, 1 Stat. 570.

16. See 50 U.S.C. §§ 21–24.

17. Neuman, supra note 2, at 1897.

18. Any number of time lines on this subject are available. See, e.g., Kurzban, supra note 2; Weissbrodt, supra note 2.

19. *Chae Chan Ping* v. *U.S.,* 130 U.S. 581 (1889).

20. The Chinese Exclusion Act.

21. See Chilton Williamson Jr., *The Immigration Mystique: America's False Conscience* (1996) for an interesting and controversial consideration of the 1965 revisions to the INA.

22. H.R. 3734, 104th Cong., 2d sess., pl 104–193 (August 22, 1996).

23. H.R., 104th Cong., 2d sess., pl 104–208 (September 30, 1996).

24. 8 U.S.C. 1601.

25. 8 U.S.C. 1103, 1104, 1105a; INA 103, 104, 106. (The exclusive review provision is a standard where Congress creates an agency to conduct the major part of the administration of an act—as with Social Security.)

26. 8 U.S.C. § 1151; INA § 201.

27. 8 U.S.C. § 1153; INA § 203.

28. 8 U.S.C. § 1154; INA § 204.

29. 8 U.S.C. § 1157; INA § 207.

30. 8 U.S.C. § 1158; INA § 208.

31. 8 U.S.C. §§ 1160, 1161; INA § 210.

32. 8 U.S.C. § 1153(a); INA § 203(a).

33. *The Preference System: Hearings Before the Subcommittee on Immigration and Refugee Policy of the Senate Committee on the Judiciary,* 97th Cong., 1st sess. 213 (1981) (testimony of Professor Mark R. Rosenzweig) (quoted in Thomas Alexander Aleinikoff, David A. Martin, Hiroshi Motomura, *Immigration Process and Policy* 190 [3d ed., 1995], hereinafter *Immigration Process and Policy*). While the Senate has considered eliminating or limiting this category, the 1990 act made no changes other than slightly expanding the ceiling limit. The slight expansion only minimally effects a substantial backlog of admissions requests in this category. See *Immigration Process and Policy,* pp. 190–91.

34. INA § 213A.

35. 8 U.S.C. § 1153(b); INA § 203(b).

36. 8 U.S.C. § 1153, INA § 203(b), as discussed in *Immigration Process and Policy,* pp. 128–29.

37. H.R. Rep. No. 101–723, pt. 1, at 59 (1990).

38. 20 C.F.R. § 656.10. See also INA § 212(m).

39. 8 U.S.C. § 1154(b), INA § 204(b); 8 U.S.C. § 1182(a)(5)(A), INA § 212(a)(5)(A).

40. 8 U.S.C. § 1153(c); INA § 203(c).

41. 8 U.S.C. § 1153(c), INA § 203(c). See *Immigration Process and Policy,* p. 130.

42. 8 U.S.C. § 1182; INA § 212.

43. 8 U.S.C. § 1227(a); INA § 237(a).

44. 8 U.S.C. § 1227(a)(1)(A); INA § 237(a)(1)(A).

45. 8 U.S.C. § 1182(a)(7); INA § 212(a)(7). Also INA §241.

46. 8 U.S.C. § 1182(a)(1); § INA 212.

47. 8 U.S.C. § 1201–1204; § INA 221.

48. 8 U.S.C. § 1222; § INA 232.

49. INA § 235(b)(2)(a).

50. INA § 242(e).

51. INA § 242(e).

52. INA § 242(e).

53. *Advisory for Immigration Advocates: Changes in Immigration Law Affecting Noncitizens* by the National Immigration Project of the National Lawyers Guild, reprinted in materials for its skills seminar on Strategy and Practice under the New Immigration Laws, October 23, 1996.

54. INA Chapter 5—Adjustment of Status, 8 U.S.C. § 1227; INA § 237.

55. 8 U.S.C. §1227; INA § 237.

56. INA § 240.

57. INA §§ 235(b)(1)(B)(v), 208.

58. INA § 240(b)(4).

59. INA § 240(c)(2).

60. INA § 242(b)(4)(d).

61. 8 U.S.C. § 1324a; INA § 274A.

62. 8 U.S.C. § 1324b; INA § 274B.

63. U.S. Const. art. 1, § 8, cl. 4.

64. 8 U.S.C. § 1401; INA § 301.

65. 8 U.S.C. § 1421; INA § 310.

66. 8 U.S.C. § 1423; INA § 312.

67. 8 U.S.C. § 1427; INA § 316.

68. 8 U.S.C. §§ 1444, 1445; INA §§ 333, 334.

69. 8 U.S.C. § 1448; INA § 337.

70. H.R. Rep. No. 101–187, at 8–10 (1989), quoted in *Immigration Process and Policy*, p. 101.

71. 8 U.S.C. § 1451; INA § 340.

72. 8 U.S.C. § 1103, INA § 103.

73. *Immigration Process and Policy,* pp. 100–101. See also Peter H. Schuck and Theodore Hsien Wang, *Continuity and Change: Patterns of Immigration Litigation in the Courts, 1979–1990,* 45 *Stanford Law Review* 115, 177 (1992) ("[T]he INS' enforcement orientation has often hindered its ability to provide effective services and fair adjudication. The many successful challenges to the INS' asylum and legalization programs suggest that the problem of integrating enforcement, service, and adjudication functions to produce consistent, judicially-approved standards may be an endemic one.").

74. Calvin Trillin, "Making Adjustments," *New Yorker,* May 28, 1984, pp. 50–52, 56–57, reprinted in part in *Immigration Process and Policy*, pp. 105–107; see also Peter H. Schuck and Theodore Hsien Wang, "Continuity and Change: Patterns of Immigration Litigation in the Courts, 1979–1990," 45 *Stanford Law Review* 115, 174 (1992).

75. See generally *Immigration Process and Policy,* pp. 192–220.

76. 20 C.F.R. § 656.40.

77. *Immigration Process and Policy,* p. 402. Immigration officers sometimes elect to release an alien on parole pending further investigation. While parole releases an alien from detention facilities and allows him to travel away from the border, he is still subject to exclusion proceedings. A parolee still has not satisfied the criteria for "entry"—freedom from official restraint, *Leng May Ma* v. *Barber,* 357 U.S. 185, 78 S. Ct. 1072, 2 L. Ed. 2d 1246 (1958). See discussion of parole, Weissbrot, DT, supra note 1, at 230–31, *Immigration Process and Policy*, pp. 379–84. "Parole may be used for a variety of purposes, either before or after an administrative finding of excludability: to permit medical treatment, to allow appearance in litigation or a criminal prosecution to prevent inhumane separation of

families or for other humanitarian reasons, or to permit release pending adjudication of an exclusion case." *Immigration Process and Policy,* p. 383.

78. *Leng May Ma* v. *Barber,* 357 U.S. 185, 78 S. Ct. 1072, 2 L. Ed. 2d 1246 (1958). See discussion in *Immigration Process and Policy,* p. 472; *Immigration Law and Procedure in a Nutshell* 229–30 (3d ed., 1992).

79. *Barrera-Echavarria* v. *Rison,* 21 F.3d 314 (9th Cir. 1994), vacated, 44 F.3d 1441 (9th Cir. 1995), cert. denied _ U.S., _, 13 3 L. Ed. 2d 407, 116 S. Ct. 479 (1995). For discussion of this case, see *Immigration Process and Policy,* pp. 472–73; Wendy R. St. Charles, "Recognizing Constitutional Rights of Excludable Aliens: The Ninth Circuit Goes Out on a Limb to Free the 'Flying Dutchman'—Dispensing with a Legal Fiction Creates an Opportunity for Reform," 4 *Journal of Transnational Law & Policy* 145 (1995).

80. INA § 235.

81. INA § 101(b)(4).

82. See *Immigration Process and Policy,* pp. 101–11.

83. INA § 212(a)(9)(B).

84. INA § 235(b)(1)(A)iii(II).

85. See S. Rep. No. 62, 98th Cong., 1st sess. 7–8 (1983), excerpted in *Immigration Process and Policy,* pp. 297–98.

86. See *Immigration Process and Policy,* pp. 275–83.

87. R. Clark, J. Passel, W. Zimmermann, and M. Fix, *Fiscal Impacts of Undocumented Aliens: Selected Estimates for Seven States* 6 (1994) quoted in *Immigration Process and Policy,* pp. 283–85.

88. Illegal Immigration Reform and Immigrant Responsibility Act of 1996 §§ 101–125.

89. See *Immigration Process and Policy,* p. 304 (citing Cornelius, "The U.S. Demand for Mexican Labor," in *Mexican Migration to the United States: Origins, Consequences, and Policy Options* 25, 43–44 (W. Cornelius and J. Bustamante, eds., 1989).

90. See *Immigration Process and Policy,* p. 315. See, e.g., *Collins Foods International, Inc.* v. *U.S. INS,* 948 F.2d 549 (1991) (excerpted in *Immigration Process and Policy,* pp. 300–303).

91. Sarah M. Kendall, "Comment: America's Minorities are Shown the 'Back Door'. . . Again: The Discriminatory Impact of the Immigration Reform and Control Act," 18 *Houston Journal of International Law* 899 (1996).

92. Kendall, supra note 55 at 932.

93. *Immigration Process and Policy,* pp. 283–84. For discussion of what federal benefits are available to aliens both before and after see also Evangeline G. Abriel, "Rethinking Preemption for Purposes of Aliens and Public Benefits," 42 *UCLA Law Review* 1597, 1600–1605.

94. *Immigration Process and Policy,* pp. 283–84.

95. 8 U.S.C. § 1601(4).

96. 8 U.S.C. § 1611(b)(1); 501.

97. 8 U.S.C. §§ 1612, 1613.

98. IIRIRA § 553, 8 U.S.C. 1601 (7).

99. Kevin R. Johnson, "Los Olvidados: Images of the Immigrant, Political Power of Noncitizens, and Immigration Law and Enforcement," 1993 *BYU Law Review* 1139, 1144 (1993); Kevin R. Johnson, "Public Benefits and Immigration: The Intersection of Immigration Status, Ethnicity, Gender, and Class," 42 *UCLA Law Review* 1509, 1574 (1995). See also Lucy Salyer, *Laws as Harsh as Tigers* 93 (arguing that the combination of societal pressure, ineffective administration, and constrained judicial review have led

Congress to create an administrative system expressly designed to limit the avenues of recourse available to all aliens) (1995).

100.  See, e.g., Gerald L. Neuman, "Aliens as Outlaws: Government Services, Proposition 187, and the Structure of Equal Protection Doctrine," 42 *UCLA Law Review* 1425 (1995); Stephen H. Legomsky, "Immigration, Federalism, and the Welfare State," 42 *UCLA Law Review* 1453 (1995); Kevin R. Johnson, "Public Benefits and Immigration: the Intersection of Immigration Status, Ethnicity, Gender, and Class," 42 *UCLA Law Review* 1509 (1995); Abriel, supra note 80.

101.  *Chae Chin Ping,* 130 U.S. 581, 609–11 (1989).

102.  *Lem Moon Sing* v. *United States,* 158 U.S. 538, 550, 15 S. Ct. 967, 39 L. Ed. 1082 (1895).

103.  *Mathews* v. *Diaz,* 426 U.S. 67, 77 (1976).

104.  Id.

105.  *Mathews* v. *Diaz,* 426 U.S. at 81–82.

106.  Neuman, supra note 2, at 1885–96.

107.  Personal Responsibility and Work Opportunity Reconciliation Act of 1996 § 400(7), 142 Cong. R. H8871 (daily ed., July 30, 1996). § 553 IIRIRA.

108.  John E. Nowak and Ronald D. Rotunda, *Constitutional Law* 2 (4th ed., 1991) (discussing *Marbury* v. *Madison,* 5 U.S. [1 Cranch] 137, 2 L. Ed. 60 [1803]).

109.  Nowak and Rotunda, supra note 93 at 9 (citing Corwin, "*Marbury* v. *Madison* and the Doctrine of Judicial Review, 12 *Michigan Law Review* 538 (1914).

110.  Id., at 17.

111.  Michael Scaperlanda, "Partial Membership: Aliens and the Constitutional Community," 81 *Iowa Law Review* 707, 707 (1996).

112.  Id., at 723.

113.  Id., at 770.

114.  Stephen H. Legomsky, "Ten More Years of Plenary Power: Immigration, Congress, and the Courts," *Hastings Constitutional Law Quarterly* 925, 926 (1995). See, e.g., *Landon* v. *Plasencia,* 459 U.S. 21, 32–37 (1982); *Yamataya* v. *Fisher* [the Japanese Immigrant Case], 189 U.S. 86, 100 (1903); *Wong Yang Sung* v. *McGrath,* 339 U.S. 33 (1950).

115.  Legomsky, *Ten More Years,* supra note 75 at 936–37. See also Peter H. Schuck, "The Transformation of Immigration Law," 84 *Columbia Law Review* 1, 84–89 (1984).

116.  Id., see also T. Alexander Aleinikoff, "The United States Constitution in its Third Century: Foreign Affairs: Rights—Here and There: Federal Regulation of Aliens and the Constitution," 83 *American Journal of International Law* 862, 869–70 (1989).

117.  Hiroshi Motomura, "The Curious Evolution of Immigration Law: Procedural Surrogates for Substantive Constitutional Rights," 92 *Columbia Law Review* 1625 (1992).

118.  Letter from Commissioner Doris Meissner to Hon. Henry J. Hyde, Chairman, Committee on the Judiciary (October 9, 1996) (reprinted in *Seminar Materials for the National Immigration Project of the National Lawyers Guild: Strategy & Practice under the New Immigration Laws 114* [October 23, 1996]).

119.  Peter H. Schuck, "The Transformation of Immigration Law," 84 *Columbia Law Review* 1, 1 (1984).

120.  See Michael Scaperlanda, "Partial Membership: Aliens and the Constitutional Community," 81 *Iowa Law Review* 707, 773 (1996). See also Linda S. Bosniak, "Membership, Equality, and the Difference that Alienage Makes," 69 *NYU Law Review* 1047 (1994) (Examining alien status relative to constitutional standards on the basis of community membership).

# 6.

# "The Worst Job in the World?"

## An Interview with Doris Meissner
## by Claudia Dreifus

Q: The Senate's retiring immigration expert, Alan Simpson, says you have the worst job in the world.

Meissner: I read where he said that. Well, I think the Immigration Service is a *fascinating* place. I don't think that in my lifetime the immigration issue has ever had the saliency and the resonance that it has at this moment. This is the second-largest immigration period in our country's history. Only a few years ago, we had about 300,000 naturalizations a year. In 1994 that jumped to about 500,000 and in 1995 to 1,000,000. And with the new welfare reform legislation that Congress has just passed [which prevents most noncitizens from getting public assistance], I suspect the numbers will go up.

Q: To curb illegal immigration from Mexico, Pat Buchanan has suggested a fence along the Southwest border.

A: How are we going to do that? What Buchanan is missing is that "the border" is a lot bigger than our 2,000-mile frontier with Mexico. Our borders are also the beaches of Florida, the airports and overseas consulates where visas are issued. About 40 percent of the illegal immigrants in this country are people who have overstayed legally issued documents.

Now, there's a 14-mile stretch of San Diego that has traditionally accounted for 50 percent of the people illegally crossing into the United States, and that is an area where we're gaining control. We're fortifying the border, infusing people, technology and equipment. We're doing fencing where it makes sense.

---

From *New York Times Magazine* (October 27, 1996): 52–54. Reprinted by permission of Ellen Levine Literary Agency. Copyright © 1996 by Claudia Dreifus. First published in the *New York Times Magazine*.

Q: Congress has just passed a comprehensive immigration bill. Give us your assessment of the good, the bad and the ugly.

A: The good is what *didn't* happen with this bill. The Gallegly amendment [which would have thrown the children of illegal immigrants out of public schools] was defeated. A back-door set of changes [aimed at curbing] legal immigration was dropped. Fundamentally, the new law helps by maintaining a distinction between legal and illegal immigration.

On the other side, the new law has deportation provisions that are mandatory and retroactive and that will affect a lot of people who've been here for a long time. I can see a great deal of pressure coming down on the agency—a lot of telephone calls to me and private legislation on behalf of individuals—and the I.N.S. will be viewed as the bad guy, as harsh and unrelenting, when in fact we're just carrying out the will of Congress.

Q: Congress also grafted substantial revisions in immigration law onto several pieces of unrelated legislation. The welfare reform law, for instance, has a section barring *legal* immigrants from receiving most benefits. How will these changes affect the I.N.S.?

A: Nobody disputes that illegal immigrants should be denied benefits. But they are *already* ineligible for all the major cash-assistance programs. This welfare bill said that those who've come in legally, who've played by the rules and are paying taxes will, should they fall on hard times, not be treated the way citizens are. That's a major change in the social contract.

There is a right way and a wrong way to deal with illegal immigration. The right way is to prevent and deter illegal entry at the borders, and also at the workplace. Most people who come into the country illegally come for jobs. So being effective means making it hard for an illegal immigrant to get employment. Yet with this Congress, it's been an uphill battle to get resources for employer enforcement.

Q: George Soros, the financier and philanthropist, read about the new immigration law and said, "I am appalled by Congress's recent action to deny vital public assistance to noncitizens who are lawfully resident in this country," and he set up a $50 million fund to help counter it. Do you find it embarrassing that a private figure felt compelled to do this?

A: Why should I find it embarrassing? It's a fabulous and noble thing he has done. I'm distressed and sorry that the circumstances are such that there's a need for such a step.

Q: In the book *Alien Nation,* Peter Brimelow argued that high immigration levels—particularly from underdeveloped countries—were going to wreck this country. How do you feel about his point, that race and ethnicity should be factors in determining immigration policy?

A. I didn't read his book, but I do know this: We are a society committed to equal opportunity, and in 1965 we rejected national origins as a basis of immigration. But race and ethnicity are not the dispositive factors here. The crucial issue is the strength of our civil society. We have to be absolutely certain that new people learn that we live in a democratic society where there are certain things we do—vote, send the kids to school, pick up the trash, join the P.T.A. Speaking English is the single most important factor in immigrants' making a success of it.

Q: So you oppose the idea of national origins being a factor in immigration policy. But the new bill requires that any American wishing to sponsor immigrants must have an income 125 percent above the poverty level. Previously, a sponsor needed only an income at poverty level. Doesn't this discriminate against immigrants from poor countries?

A: This was something we opposed. At first, Congress had this at 200 percent, then 140 percent; 125 percent was the compromise.

Q: A lot of proposals floating around state legislatures are aimed at throwing the children of illegal immigrants out of public schools. Do you find such ideas helpful?

A: No. I also disagree with the similar notion of barring the U.S.-born children of illegals from citizenship. Now, it used to be that a child born in the United States would create the basis for the parents getting legal status. That has been changed—the parents cannot get legal status until the child is 21. It's hard to imagine that people come and have a baby for the sake of waiting 21 years in order to get legal status.

Q: Alan Simpson insists they do.

A: Well, the evidence does not show that. I mean, this is an area in immigration where the cure is worse than the disease. If you were to have this provision where children born of illegals would not become citizens, you would build into the society a class that would never have any rights. That's not healthy for the rest of us.

Q: New Americans almost always describe their experiences with the immigration service as Orwellian nightmares. Are they exaggerating?

A: Well, this has not been an agency known for its customer friendliness. And I don't know if it can become that. Our people are often in a position of being surly because they haven't been equipped to do their jobs properly. They work in terrible and demoralizing settings; they lack the modern information systems they need to give reliable information; they rely on byzantine forms and too many forms.

Q: One of the agency's more customer-friendly innovations has been a program called Citizenship U.S.A., which speeds up the processing of naturalization applications and often has mass swearing-in ceremonies, at which you occasionally preside. Why has this program made some Republicans in Congress so angry?

A. Citizenship is one of those issues that's very easy to support until it seems that you're doing it in a serious fashion. And we are. And we've done it in the face of extraordinary numbers of applications. If we had kept doing business as usual, we would now be hearing an unbelievable cacophony of criticism about our inefficiency, our ineffectiveness.

# PART III

# THE ECONOMICS AND POLITICS OF IMMIGRATION

# 7.

# Still an Open Door?: U.S. Immigration Policy and the American Economy

## Vernon M. Briggs Jr. and Stephen Moore

## INTRODUCTION

Many decades ago, prize-winning author Oscar Handlin wrote that he "once thought to write a history of immigration. Then I discovered that immigrants *are* American history" (Handlin 1951). That the United States today is a nation of immigrants is not just a tired and worn-out cliché. No other country on earth has brought together so many people from so many diverse nations and then successfully integrated them into one society.

The statistics on immigration to the United States are awe-inspiring. In this century, some fifty million immigrants have come—one of the largest migrations of people ever. In the 1980s alone, nearly eight million newcomers arrived to these shores, some as skill-based and family-based legal immigrants, some as refugees fleeing persecution from abroad, and some as illegal aliens—almost all of them in a quest to find freedom and economic opportunity. According to the 1990 census, roughly one in twelve residents of the United States was born abroad. In some states, such as California, Florida, and Texas, nearly one in four residents is an immigrant. It is estimated that there are more people of Polish descent living in the United States than in Poland.

Few Americans would dispute that this large migration of freedom-seekers has been a net asset to the United States economy in this century. What is disputed is whether continuing immigration at current or even expanded levels is in the national interest. Many of today's economic ills are said to be intensified by the new immigrants, especially those from less developed countries (Lamm and Imhoff 1986). Some opponents of immigration have suggested that although immigrants served a vital purpose in helping build the United States in its early stages of economic development, more people are neither necessary nor desirable as America enters a stage of economic maturity (Briggs 1992).

Immigrants are certainly not an unmixed blessing. When the newcomers first arrive, they impose short-term costs on the citizenry. Because immigration means more people, they cause more congestion on our highways, a more crowded housing market, and longer waiting lines in stores and hospitals. In states such as California, immigrants' children are heavy users of an already overburdened public school system, and so on. Some immigrants abuse the welfare system, which means that tax dollars from Americans are transferred to immigrant populations. Los Angeles County officials estimate that immigrants' use of county services costs the local government hundreds of millions of dollars each year. It is also true that in many occupations and local labor markets, newly arriving immigrants intensify competition for jobs. And the very fact that large immigration brings about economic and social change—even when that change might be economically constructive—is often unwelcome for many U.S.-born citizens who are nostalgic for "the good old days."

The benefits of immigration, however, are manifold. Perhaps the most important benefit is that immigrants come to the United States with critically needed talents, energies, and ambitions that serve as an engine for economic progress and help the United States retain economic and geopolitical leadership. Because for most of the world's immigrants, America is their first choice, the United States is in a unique position within the industrialized world to select the most brilliant and inventive minds from the United Kingdom, Canada, China, Korea, India, Ireland, Mexico, Philippines, Russia, Taiwan, and other nations. Because most immigrants are not poor, tired, huddled masses, but rather are above the average of their compatriots in skill and education levels, the immigration process has a highly beneficial self-selection component, a skimming of the cream of the best workers and top brainpower from the rest of the world (Gibney 1990). In short, the importation of human capital through immigration is perhaps America's premier comparative advantage in a global economy today.

Immigrants are not just additional people; they are people with uniquely developed skills, talents, and cultural backgrounds. Their diversity is an unqualified benefit to the United States: it helps cultivate new knowledge-creation and technological innovation. Their unique skills allow America to fill those niches in the labor market that cannot be filled by U.S.-born citizens. Immigrants are not just productive themselves, they also make U.S.-born citizens more productive.

An equally critical advantage of immigration to the United States is that it is a continuous process of national rebirth and rejuvenation of the American spirit of enterprise. This is no small advantage. More than perhaps any other single national policy, the continued admission of enterprising new immigrants safeguards the United States from economic and geopolitical decline—the kind of evolutionary decline that has been the fate of so many other powerful and prosperous empires of the past. "What gives resonance to our republic," noted former UN Ambassador Jeane Kirkpatrick at the hundredth anniversary of the Statue of

Liberty, "is its continual renewal by new citizens who bring to us a special sense of the importance of freedom and liberty" (Kirkpatrick 1986).

Specifically, the most critical economic benefits from immigration are:

- Immigrants are highly entrepreneurial. Their rate of business start-ups and self-employment tend[s] to be higher than that of U.S.-born citizens. Most immigrant enterprises are small and not unusually profitable. But others, such as Wang Computers, founded in Seattle by an Asian immigrant, are Fortune 500 firms employing thousands of U.S. workers.

- Immigrants contribute to the global competitiveness of U.S. corporations, particularly in high-technology industries. Tens of thousands of exceptionally talented scientists and engineers are preserving the global leadership of U.S. firms in frontier industries such as biotechnology, robotics, computers, electronics, semiconductors, and pharmaceuticals. Silicon Valley is the modern-day American melting pot.

- Many U.S. industries are highly dependent on the flow of hard-working, low-skilled immigrant labor. These include the fruit and vegetable, apparel and garment, poultry, and restaurant industries, among others. Without an influx of immigrant labor, many of these industries would close down or move their operations overseas—meaning fewer jobs for American workers and a weakening of our international trade balances. Indeed, the *Wall Street Journal* has described low-skilled immigrants as "the backbone of the California economy."

- The children of immigrants tend to be highly successful professionals with very high education levels and earnings. A very high percentage of high-school valedictorians, Westinghouse Science Contest award winners, Spelling Bee champions, and National Merit Scholars are immigrants or the children of immigrants. Immigrant children tend to have higher earnings than U.S.-born workers, and they tend to be highly represented in professional occupations. America's corporate and political leaders of tomorrow are the children of today's immigrants.

- Most important, immigrants increase the aggregate income of U.S.-born citizens and thereby increase U.S. economic growth. Studies show that the net effect of immigrants—even low-skilled immigrants—is to raise the overall productivity level of U.S. citizens. The long-term impact of immigration is higher economic growth and higher living standards for U.S. citizens.

Opponents of immigration maintain that the economic costs of a generous immigration policy outweigh these benefits. However, research shows that almost all of the major objections to continued immigration are exaggerated. In fact, a careful review of the evidence on the economic impact of immigration leads to the following conclusions:

1. Immigrants use welfare and other social services at about the same rate that U.S.-born citizens do. The taxes paid by immigrants typically cover the cost of public services they use.

2. The newest immigrants—particularly Asians—are not less skilled or less educated than previous waves of immigrants, and they may be even more skilled and entrepreneurial than immigrants of the past. There is no evidence to suggest that we are at a historic turning point with respect to the benefits of immigration.

3. There is no evidence to support the claim that over the long term immigrants cause unemployment or depress wages of U.S. citizens. Immigrants create at least as many jobs as they take by expanding the size of the economy.

4. The United States is not being overpopulated by immigrants, and immigration is not at a historically unprecedented level today. The United States is capable of absorbing well over a million immigrants per year without overwhelming our physical and social infrastructure.

5. The impact of immigrants on heavily impacted cites is almost uniformly positive. Immigrants have prevented a catastrophic decline in the population and thus the tax base of large cites; they have revived declining inner city areas; and have started tens of thousands of new business enterprises in urban America.

Let us review each of these claims individually, then discuss in detail how immigrants benefit the U.S. economy, and finally, suggest reforms to the immigration laws that may multiply these benefits.

## THE DEMOGRAPHIC IMPACT OF IMMIGRANTS

There is an apocryphal story of a German immigrant who, after taking the oath of United States citizenship, was asked how it felt to be an American. Without skipping a beat, the man responded with his thick German accent, "I suddenly feel a rising tide of resentment against all these foreigners coming to these shores."

Most Americans have come to believe that the United States is accepting unprecedented numbers of immigrants—that the nation is virtually "under siege" from foreigners. Many of our politicians have tried to reinforce this sense of an out-of-control border by resorting in some cases to frightening rhetoric. Former presidential candidate Patrick Buchanan (1990) spoke of the need to "build a sea wall around the United States" to keep out "the rising masses of foreigners." Former Colorado Governor Richard Lamm (1986) warns that the millions of legal and illegal immigrants coming to these shores are causing a "cultural contamination."

The truth is that there is very little validity to such hysteria. It is indeed true that immigration reached very high levels in the 1980s: nearly eight million legal

## Figure 1. Population Growth by Decade

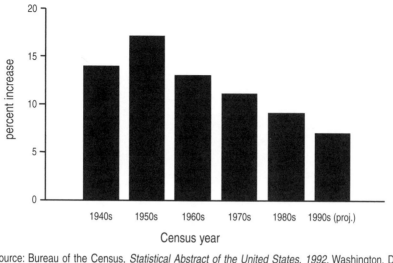

Source: Bureau of the Census, *Statistical Abstract of the United States, 1992*. Washington, D.C.: U.S. Department of Commerce, p. 8; projections by author.

immigrants arrived from 1980 to 1990, roughly one million as refugees, one million as job-related immigrants, and six million family-based immigrants. This is the highest number of immigrants to come to the United States in any decade except the great wave that arrived through Ellis Island between 1900 and 1910. For selected regions of the country, this represented a substantial flow of new people to be integrated into the economy. Roughly half of all immigrants settled in just four states: California, Florida, Texas, and Illinois.

Opponents of immigration often charge that immigrants are causing an over-population problem in the United States. Some environmental groups maintain that America's policy should be population stabilization and that immigration impedes this goal. However, if overpopulation is measured by the number of people per square mile, then the United States is one of the most underpopulated industrial nations in the world. Moreover, there is no economic or environmental rationale why population stabilization is preferable to a growth rate of 1, 2, or 3 percent. Most of the recent economic research has come to dismiss the argument that population growth is in any way inimical to economic growth or sound environmental policy (J. Simon 1981; J. Simon and Moore 1989). In fact, there is substantial evidence that moderate positive population expansion is more consistent with economic growth than zero growth or negative growth (J. Simon 1981).

But let us accept for a moment the proposition that rapid population growth is harmful, and that this is a worry for America. The anti-population groups frequently back their assertion that immigration is causing too-rapid growth with statistics that show that over the past decade immigrants have accounted for a

### Table 1. Growth of U.S. Labor Force by Decade, 1940–2000*

|  | Labor Force at End of Decade (Millions) | Increase in Labor Force (Millions) | Percentage Increase in Labor Force |
|---|---|---|---|
| 1940–1950 | 62.2 | 9.5 | 18 |
| 1950–1960 | 69.6 | 7.4 | 12 |
| 1960–1970 | 82.8 | 13.2 | 19 |
| 1970–1980 | 106.9 | 24.1 | 29 |
| 1980–1990 | 124.9 | 18.0 | 17 |
| 1990–2000 | 143.5 | 18.6 | 15 |

*Assumes ten million immigrants (one million per year) between 1991 and 2000, and a labor-force participation rate for immigrants of 70 percent.

Source: William B. Johnston and Arnold Packer, *Workforce 2000.* Indianapolis: Hudson Institute, 1987, and calculations by author.

much larger share of U.S. population growth than ever before. Yet this is an extremely slippery, if not deceptive, statistic. For example, if a nation had zero population growth among its native-born population over a given period and then allowed the admission of even one immigrant, immigration would account for 100 percent of population growth. But that would prove little about the real impact of immigration.

In fact, the reason immigration accounts for a high rate of population growth is precisely because the U.S. birth rate declined in the 1970s and 1980s and now remains very near the replacement rate (Wattenberg 1985). If our concern is overpopulation, the fact that U.S.-born citizens are having fewer children is not an argument for less immigration; if anything, it is an argument that America can easily absorb *more* immigrants without risking a population explosion.

One thing is certain: even with substantially higher immigration than today, America is not on the brink of a population explosion. In the 1980s, despite eight million new immigrants, population growth was lower than during any decade since the wartime 1940s. Two years ago, I examined the demographic impact of various levels of immigration over the decade of the 1990s (Moore 1990c). The upper-bound estimate of immigration levels analyzed was ten million over the decade. Would such an immigrant flow contribute to a skyrocketing population in the United States? The answer, as shown in figure 1, is clearly no. Even assuming this unlikely upper limit of immigration, the population growth rate in the 1990s would be only about half the level of the 1950s. Most demographers predict that population growth will remain low during the first few decades of the next century, because of lower birth rates and the aging of the baby boom generation (Wattenberg 1985). Hence, there is little reason to restrain immigration to the United States because of population worries.

## Figure 2. Immigrant Arrivals as a Proportion of U.S. Population, 1850–2000

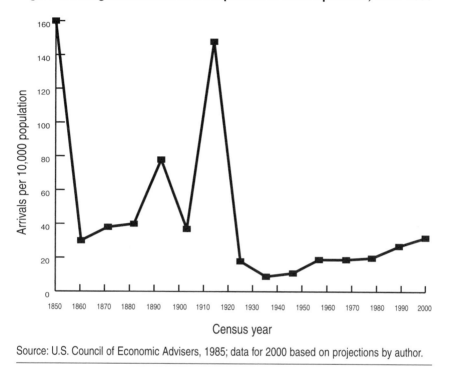

Source: U.S. Council of Economic Advisers, 1985; data for 2000 based on projections by author.

Another demographic factor that will mitigate the burden of absorbing immigrants in the 1990s is the very slow growth expected in the labor force. Table 1 shows that even if immigration were to increase to about one million entrants per year for the rest of the decade, the U.S. labor force would increase at half the pace of the 1970s. This does not appear to be a great cause for worry.

Perhaps the best measure of America's ability to absorb immigrants into the social and physical infrastructure is the number of immigrants admitted as a share of the total population. To see why, consider two cities, one of 1,000 people and one of 100,000 people. Now assume that 1,000 immigrants enter each city. In the city of 1,000, the immigrants will double the population, causing all sorts of short-term problems—shortages of housing, office space, parking, and maybe even food; a burden on schools; long lines at stores; intense competition for jobs; and an immense impact on the culture of the city, among others. But in the city of 100,000 people, an increase of 1,000 immigrants would be virtually unnoticed. The immigrants would be absorbed very quickly into the job market and the existing social institutions. This is why it is important to know how many immigrants enter the United States relative to the number of people already here, which is the immigration rate.

## Figure 3. Foreign-Born Population of the United States, 1850–1990

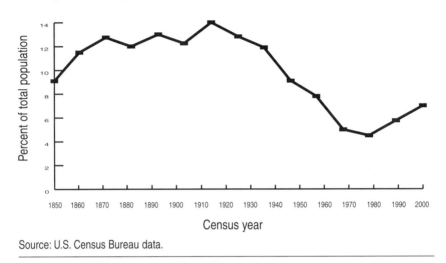

Census year

Source: U.S. Census Bureau data.

The U.S. immigration rate has risen from about 2.0 per 1,000 residents in the 1950s and 1960s to about 3.2 per 1,000 residents in the 1980s. This is not cause for great concern, however. As figure 2 illustrates, in earlier periods of our history, the immigration rate has been as high as 16 per 1,000—five times higher than today. The average immigration rate over the past 150 years has been about 5 per 1,000 residents. To reach this rate, the United States would have to open its doors to about 1.3 million immigrants per year; as figure 2 shows, the immigration rate in this decade will be less than 3.5 per 1,000. This is not a terribly troubling prospect.

Today, more than twenty million Americans—or more than one in twelve U.S. residents—is foreign-born. This is a fairly large increase from the 1950s and 1960s, when one in twenty Americans was foreign-born. In early periods, as many as one in six Americans was foreign-born: we were much more a nation of immigrants a century ago than we are today (see figure 3). The argument is made by immigration critics that at the turn of the century, America was a young, underdeveloped nation that needed strong bodies; in the 1990s we need strong minds. But as I will document below, we need strong minds *and* strong bodies today, and immigration is continuously providing us with both.

Immigration critics often suggest that American immigration policy is overly generous by arguing that the United States has opened its doors to more immigrants and refugees than the rest of the world combined. But comparing the number of immigrants entering each industrialized country relative to its overall population, we see that the United States no longer appears overly generous in distributing visas. Of the three major immigrant-receiving countries—Australia, Canada, and the United States—the United States has the lowest immigration rate. In 1985, the United States allowed entry to 3 immigrants per 1,000 population,

## Figure 4. Immigrants Admitted by Region and Period

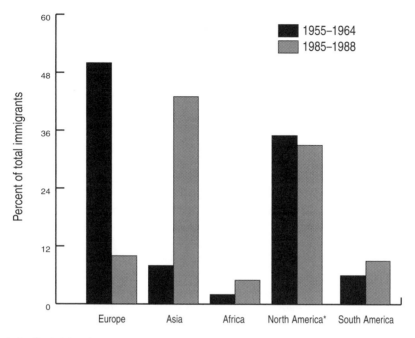

*Includes Central America

Source: *Statistical Yearbook of the Immigration and Naturalization Service, 1990.* Washington, D.C.:
INS, 1990, p. 39.

Australia 12, and Canada 3.5. Even Denmark (6 per 1,000), Germany (7 per 1,000), Switzerland (15 per 1,000), and the United Kingdom (4 per 1,000) had more immigrants as a share of resident population than the United States (Council of Europe 1986). The economic evidence for Australia, Canada, and the United Kingdom indicates that immigration to these countries has had a mostly positive impact on growth rates (J. Simon 1990).

An issue of mounting concern for many Americans and some policymakers is the ethnic composition of the "new immigrants." Nineteen-ninety-two presidential candidate Patrick Buchanan (1990) has insisted that America is losing its "white European culture." In a highly publicized cover story of the *National Review,* Peter Brimelow (1992) voices concern over the growing tide of non-European immigration. A prediction by demographers that by 2050 whites in Texas would be a minority received front-page billing in many newspapers. This is not just a cultural issue. Some economists maintain that the Europeans of earlier periods brought to the United States much higher skill levels than the Asian and Hispanic immigrants of today (Borjas 1990).

Even with changes made in the Immigration Act of 1990, most immigrants today gain entry through the family-reunification system. This policy of giving first preference to immigrants who wish to come to the United States to reunite with family members was instituted in 1965. Today, about 80 percent of immigrants are family-sponsored, about 15 percent are political refugees, and about 5 percent are skill-based immigrants. Since enactment of the Immigration Act of 1965, the ethnic composition of immigration has changed markedly—but not in ways that most people suspect.

According to the 1981 Select Commission on Immigration, from 1800 through 1920, between 80 and 90 percent of immigrants were of European ancestry. Since then, European immigration has continually declined to comprise between 10 and 15 percent of the total immigrant flow in the mid-1980s (Moore 1989). (In very recent years, however, evidence suggests that immigration from Europe is rising sharply.) Many Americans think that the big shift in the 1970s and 1980s was to allow entry of more Hispanics from Central America. In fact, since the 1920s immigration from the rest of North America has remained steady at between 35 and 45 percent of the total. Hispanics have been coming to the United States in large numbers for seventy years. A U.S. General Accounting Office report (1988a) concludes that the number of immigrants from Mexico has been "quite stable in this century."

What is different today from 1965 is that European immigration has been supplanted by *Asian* immigration. Figure 4 shows that in 1965 almost half of all immigrants came from Europe and 10 percent from Asia, but that by 1990, those percentages had essentially reversed (Moore 1989). In the 1980s, the number of Asians grew by 80 percent to seven million (Dunn 1990).

The key issue then, with respect to the changing ethnic composition of America's "newest immigrants," is whether immigration from Asia has had a favorable or unfavorable impact on the U.S. economy. This subject will be discussed in greater detail below, but for now it is worth noting that most research indicates a very high return from Cambodian, Chinese, Indian, Japanese, Pakistani, Taiwanese, and Vietnamese immigrants. The 1990 census reveals that the earnings of Asians are higher than those of any other ethnic group, including whites (Dunn 1990). The average Asian family income is $36,000, versus $29,000 for all U.S. households.

One major reason why there has been a decline in European immigration has little to do with U.S. immigration policy, but is because until recently, immigrants (except for a handful of refugees) from Poland, Russia, Hungary, Rumania, and other former Soviet-bloc totalitarian regimes have been unable to emigrate. In the 1980s, only about 3 percent of America's immigrants came from the Eastern bloc—roughly the same number that arrived from the small island of Jamaica.

All of the above analysis shows that immigration is not at troublingly high rates today. But what about during the next century? The answer is that coming demographic changes through at least 2040 will make increased immigration more vital to the U.S. national interest than at any time in recent history. The demographic change to which I refer is the aging of the "baby boom" generation.

In a *Wall Street Journal* editorial, Peter Francese (1990), president of American Demographics, explains the urgency of an immigration policy attuned to this impending demographic crisis:

There are powerful demographic forces at work in the U.S. that virtually mandate federal policy be changed to permit more immigration than we have now.
The rapid increase in the number of very elderly people, combined with declining numbers of young adults and a record low population growth rate, will put
this nation in a demographic vise.

Paying for the income security and medical needs of the elderly while at
the same time improving the educational opportunities and well-being of children will squeeze future U.S. workers in the grip of higher federal payroll taxes,
state taxes and local property taxes. . . .

We cannot wait 20 years to see what will happen when the baby boomers
retire and ask what happened to their Social Security trust fund.

The U.S. needs to admit more immigrants now to get us out of the demographic bind.

Statistics confirm this gloomy assessment. Over the next twenty years, the
number of Americans over age eighty-five and highly dependent on government
programs such as Social Security and Medicare will increase from less than four
million to more than six million. New entrants to the workforce (those between
ages twenty and twenty-nine) will drop by about 10 percent.

A study I conducted for the California-based Alexis de Tocqueville Institute
(Moore 1990b) shows that this "demographic bind" described by Francese can in
part be solved through increased immigration. First, it is critical to realize that
without increase immigration the "graying of the workforce," a natural consequence of the aging of the baby boom generation, will impose significant costs
on future workers when the baby boomers actually retire. In 1970, there were
four workers for every retired person; by 1990, there were three workers for
every retired person; by 2030, there will be less than two workers for every
retiree. To provide promised health care and Social Security benefits to these
baby boomers would require nearly a 40 percent increase in payroll taxes. This
is a huge cost to impose on the next generation of workers.

Social Security Administration data (1989) suggests that because increased
immigration provides more workers immediately, the impending fiscal time
bomb can be defused by immigration. The reason for this is that every permanent
increase of 100,000 in the number of legal immigrant admissions increases payroll receipts by roughly 0.10 percent of taxable payroll—or about $2.4 billion
each year (in 1990 dollars) (Social Security Administration 1989). If immigration
levels were increased by roughly 400,000 per year, the present-value benefit to
the Social Security Trust Fund over the period 1991–2015 would be $72.2 billion.
The present-value benefit to the trust fund over the next fifty years (1991–2040)
would be $292 billion (see table 2). Of course, these immigrants will collect
Social Security benefits when they retire, but they will have their own children
paying into the trust fund. Hence, increased immigration in the next century
would substantially alleviate the fiscal crisis in the Social Security and Medicare
systems without relying on raising taxes or substantially reducing benefits.

## Policy Recommendation

Historical experience shows that the United States can easily sustain an immigration level of one million new entrants per year for the rest of this century. In the next century, because of America's changing demographic profile, particularly the aging of the baby boom generation, more workers will be needed to sustain the U.S. economy and pay the retirement costs of current workers. This can be achieved in part by continuing to raise immigration levels to about 1.5 million admissions per year.

America's immigration policy should encourage ethnic diversity to the extent possible. A special immigrant visa, "freedom visas," should be established for the people of Eastern Europe, who for the past forty years have not been permitted to immigrate to the United States. A total of 50,000 freedom visas should be issued each year to the people of Poland, Hungary, Russia, the Czech Republic, Slovakia, and other former Soviet-bloc countries.

# IMMIGRATION, THE WELFARE STATE, AND TAXES

The development of a modern-day welfare state in the United States and other industrialized nations has become a popular argument for substantially limiting immigration. Governor Pete Wilson of California says that his state's chronic multi-billion budget deficits are a result of social services used by low-income immigrants. Similarly, Nobel-prize winning economist Gary Becker (1992) of the University of Chicago has expressed misgivings recently about an open-door immigration policy because he fears that America's modern-day welfare system may act as a magnet to immigrants from poor countries, therefore substantially raising government outlays.

The prospect that the availability of welfare benefits would attract immigrants is a valid concern. The United States offers a substantial number of social safety-net programs to low-income Americans, most of which were not available thirty years ago. In addition to cash subsidies, such as AFDC (Aid for Families with Dependent Children, or welfare), these benefits include Food Stamps, public housing, child nutrition programs, Medicaid, unemployment insurance, and others. In some states, such as California and New York, the cash value of these benefits can exceed $14,000 a year for nonworking parents—far more than the average family income in most nations.

Are immigrants especially heavy users of the U.S. welfare programs? Some recent studies would seem to suggest that the answer is yes. An influential and widely cited study by the Los Angeles County Board of Supervisors (1992), for example, examines the tax payments and service usage of "recent legal immigrants," "undocumented aliens," and "children of undocumented aliens" in 1991. It finds that immigrants use hundreds of millions of dollars of county services each year, including the hospital, school, and welfare systems. These immigrants make up 25 percent of all county residents, but collect 31 percent of all county services, including, dramatically, 68 percent of all county health services. Meanwhile, they pay only 10 percent of county taxes. The net result from this disproportionately high use of services, alleges the Los Angeles County Board of Supervisors, is that it cost the county $947 million in 1991 to provide government services to the immigrants, while these immigrants paid only $139 million in taxes. The immigrants also cost the school districts an estimated $1.5 billion. In short, immigrants apparently are a large drain on California's taxpayers.

It is worth describing the methodological errors of the Los Angeles County study because these same problems plague much of the research on the use of social services by immigrants. The report focuses almost exclusively on local services and taxes, ignoring state and federal taxes paid by immigrants. When state and federal taxes are included in the picture, the tax payments by immigrants rise to $4.3 billion per year. Since immigrants use few state services, and even fewer federal services, the surpluses supplied to federal and state coffers may very well offset the deficit to local governments. The Los Angeles County study did not address this critical question.

More important, the Los Angeles County Board of Supervisors study only examines the impact of "recent immigrants"; immigrants who arrived before 1980 are treated as U.S.-born. But immigrants earn higher incomes, contribute more in taxes, and use less of many services the longer they have been in the United States. To exclude from a cost-benefit calculation the immigrants' impact once they have been in the United States more than ten years—that is, precisely when they start to have a high economic return—would be equivalent to assessing the cost-benefit of a child from birth until age twenty. Children would appear to be a terrible investment for the first twenty years, because they produce very little and consume very much. Like children, immigrants' short-term costs must be balanced against increasing payoffs, through higher tax payments and earnings, in the future.

When the use of public services, especially welfare, by *all immigrants* is compared with that of use of all U.S.-born citizens, the rates are remarkably similar. A study by economist Ellen Seghal (1985) of the U.S. Bureau of Labor Statistics examines welfare usage in 1984 of several major federal programs of immigrants who entered the United States before 1982. She finds that the share of foreign-born collecting public assistance—including unemployment compensation, Food Stamps, Supplemental Security Income (SSI), and AFDC—was 12.8 percent. The percentage for U.S.-born was 13.9 percent. She concludes that the widespread perception of immigrants as welfare abusers is wrong: "The foreign born do not seem more likely than the U.S.-born to be recipients of government services" (p. 24).

Most research on immigrant use of welfare confirms the conclusion that immigrants are not much different in the use of social services than U.S.-born citizens. A study by the City of New York's Office of City Planning (cited in Bogen 1986) examines the use of public assistance by a sample of the two million foreign-born in the metropolitan area in 1980. It finds that the public assistance rate was 7.7 percent for immigrants and 13.3 percent for the population as a whole.

George Borjas (1990) of the University of California examines 1970 and 1980 census data with respect to welfare (AFDC and SSI) and other economic variables. He finds that in 1970, immigrants were slightly less likely to be on welfare than native-born citizens (5.9 percent for immigrants, 6.1 percent for U.S.-born), and that in 1980 the percentage of U.S.-born residents on welfare was 8.0 percent, while the percentage for immigrants was 9.1 percent. This is not much of a difference. The newly released U.S. census data for 1990 show the same result: immigrants are just slightly more dependent on welfare than U.S.-born citizens (6 percent versus 7 percent).

Hispanic immigrants are alleged to be especially heavy users of welfare services, but the research generally does not verify this stereotype. One of the most comprehensive studies on Hispanic immigration in California was published by the Urban Institute (Muller and Espenshade 1985). The authors find that annual welfare benefits averaged $575 per California household, but less than half this amount, or $251, per Mexican immigrant household. The one public service that is used inordinately by the Mexican immigrants is education: it costs the state $1,966 for each Mexican family in public education expenditures, compared to only $872 for the average family.

A RAND Corporation analysis (McCarthy and Valdez 1985) of Mexican immigrants in California comes to much the same conclusion. The study finds that Mexican immigrants' use of schools and medical services is very high, but only because of their age profile—immigrants come when they are young. As for social services, the researchers indicate that "common perceptions that the immigrants draw heavily on welfare are not supported by either survey data or by service providers' reports." Only 5 percent of Mexicans (citizens, legal immigrants, and illegal immigrants) are found to be receiving cash assistance in 1980.

One reason immigrants do not use the welfare system excessively is that immigration involves a natural selection process of individuals who are highly motivated and energized. Immigrants come to work, not to go on welfare. The evidence supports this contention. Immigrants tend to have high labor-force participation rates and tend to work longer hours than U.S.-born residents. Borjas (1990) found that in 1980 immigrant men were slightly more likely than U.S.-born men to be in the labor force: 90 percent versus 89 percent (pp. 134–49). This characteristic of immigrants appears to cross ethnic groupings. For example, a study by David Hayes Bautista of the University of California at Los Angeles on the social impact of various ethnic groups in California finds that 81 percent of Latino men were in the labor force in 1990, compared to 76 percent of white men and 67 percent of black men (cited in Myer 1992, 32). Bautista concludes: "When we look at the data, we get a very different picture of Latino immigration. Rather than being viewed as a threat, it should be seen as strengthening our economy" (Myer 1992, 32).

Still, for many financially strapped cities the issue of funding services to immigrants is of growing concern. The problem for localities is that at least half of the government services used by immigrants are provided by localities, but according to the RAND Corporation, an estimated two-thirds of the tax payments by immigrants are paid to the federal government, primarily in the form of income and Social Security taxes, and less than 15 percent are paid to local governments (McCarthy and Valdez 1985). The Urban Institute study on immigration in California in the 1970s thoroughly documents this financing mismatch problem (Muller and Espenshade 1985). It finds that in 1980 the fiscal deficit at the state level was $1,779 per Mexican household, and Los Angeles County lost $466 per immigrant household. But the federal government enjoyed a healthy fiscal windfall from each Mexican household in Los Angeles County. It is important to note that the Urban Institute researchers find that even though the value of the local services California immigrants use is greater than the amount they pay in local taxes, they are still a significant economic asset to the California communities in which they reside. Muller and Espenshade (1985) conclude: "The over-all economic benefits accruing to the average Los Angeles household from the presence of Mexican immigrants probably outweigh the economic costs of fiscal deficits."

Researchers have begun to examine the issue of whether the total taxes paid by the immigrants at all levels of government cover the total costs of public services they use at all levels of government. The most comprehensive study on this topic was conducted by economist Julian Simon (1984) at the University of Maryland. Simon uses Census Bureau data from 1975 to calculate the total cost of public services used by immigrants at various lengths of stay in the United States to build a lifetime benefit profile for immigrants. He assumes, for instance, that immigrants who entered in 1972 are typical of immigrants after three years in the United States, immigrants who entered in 1971 were typical of immigrants after four years, and so on. The services examined include health care, Social Security, unemployment insurance, education, welfare, and an allowance for other government programs such as infrastructure. Simon then uses the same procedure to build a lifetime profile of taxes paid by immigrants. He does this by examining the earnings of immigrants over their working years and deducing their tax payments, which are assumed to be roughly proportional to income.

Simon finds that in their early years in the United States, immigrants use less public services than U.S.-born citizens, but that in their later years, they begin to use roughly the same amount of services. This is partly because newly arriving immigrants collect almost no benefits from the largest public assistance program, Social Security, and because newly arriving immigrants are not eligible for many welfare programs, such as unemployment insurance. For example, for their first fifteen years in the United States, immigrants use roughly $1,500 of services (in 1975 dollars) each year, whereas after fifteen years, immigrants use almost $2,300 of services. The average for U.S.-born citizens was also about $2,300. As for earnings and taxes, for the first five to ten years, immigrant earnings are below those of U.S.-born workers; after ten to fifteen years, the earnings match those of natives; and after fifteen years, the immigrants' earnings rise permanently above U.S.-born earnings. Several independent studies, including Chiswick (1978) verify this lifetime earning pattern.

Simon then creates an immigrant balance sheet by placing the taxes paid and public services used side by side to assess the value of immigrant as one would a physical investment:

**Table 2. Impact of Immigrants on the Social Security Trust Fund, 1991–2065**

| | Increase in Social Security Revenues with 1 Million Immigrants per Year* for | | |
|---|---|---|---|
| | 25 Years (1991–2015) | 50 Years (1991–2040) | 75 Years (1991–2065) |
| Annual increase (percent) | 0.12 | 0.26 | 0.28 |
| Average annual increase in Trust Fund (billions) | $ 3.1 | $ 6.7 | $ 7.2 |
| Present value in 1991 of total increase (billions) | $72.2 | $292.0 | $435.8 |

*Assumes that the increase in net immigration is 300,000 per year (400,000 immigrating, less 100,000 emigrating).

Source: Social Security Administration, "Federal Old-Age and Survivors Insurance and Disability Insurance Trust Funds," Board of Trustees Report. Washington, D.C.: U.S. Government Printing Office, April 1989; Stephen Moore, *People and American Competitiveness: Estimating the Economic Impact of Legal Immigration Reform,* Stanford, CA: Alexis de Tocqueville Institute, 1990.

In every year following entry (until the immigrants themselves retire, at which time their children are supporting them through the Social Security and Medicare system) immigrants benefit natives through the public coffers. And a calculation of the net present value of the stream of difference shows that immigrants are a remarkably good investment at any conceivable rate of discount.

At a 3 percent rate of discount (the riskless rate of real return on a government security), the lifetime benefit of immigrants to U.S. citizens via the tax code is roughly $20,000. "One may conclude," states Simon, "that the average immigrant is an excellent investment on almost any reasonable set of parameter estimates" (Simon 1984).

In sum, legal immigrants do pay their own way. This conclusion raises a critical government financing issue: If immigrants contribute positively to the overall fiscal balance of federal coffers, but are a fiscal drain on the local level, steps could be taken to reduce the disparity and at the same time leave all levels of government with a more improved fiscal position than if the immigrants did not come at all. One potential solution would be for the federal government to reimburse local governments for a portion of the costs of providing services to immigrants.

Finally, we need to make a special examination of the fiscal impact of refugees. Refugees have some very different characteristics than economic immigrants. Refugees generally use substantially more services than immigrants; they are more likely to be unemployed or outside the workforce; and they have much lower earnings than immigrants. One of the most comprehensive studies to date of refugees' economic performance is by Susan Forbes (1985) of the Refugee Policy Group. Forbes reviews most of the research on refugees and uncovers several troubling findings for the newest arrivals. In 1984, 64 percent of the U.S. population was in the labor force, but only 55 percent of refugees were. Seven percent of Americans were unemployed, compared to 15 percent of refugees.

Unlike economic immigrants, who are ineligible for many public assistance programs, newly arriving refugees are immediately eligible for special resettlement and adjustment assistance (a package that can be worth up to $5,000), in addition to all normal public assistance benefits—and large numbers take advantage of this eligibility. During the first year of admission, about 75 percent of refugees are on public assistance; after their second year in the United States, more than half are on public assistance; and even after their third year, roughly a third collect some form of cash assistance from the government (Forbes 1985).

The good news is, however, that refugees do climb the ladder of economic progress in much the same manner, albeit at a slower rate, as immigrants (see Moore 1990a). For example, according to the Office of Refugee Resettlement (1989), of the Southeast Asian refugees who arrived in the United States in 1985, half were unemployed at the end of 1985, but only 20 percent were unemployed in 1986, 9 percent in 1987, and 5 percent in 1988. That is, after four years, the 1985 refugees' unemployment rate matched the national rate. Labor-force participation also rises steadily over time for males. Rita J. Simon and Julian L. Simon (1984) find that in 1981, 42 percent of Soviet Jewish male refugees worked at least thirty-five hours a week, whereas 91 percent who had arrived before 1973 did. Finally, Barry Chiswick (1978) finds that, as with immigrants, refugees' incomes rise steadily over time, but that it takes much longer for refugees to "catch up" to the national average than for legal immigrants.

Still, the very high rates of dependency among refugees during their first three years in the United States is disturbing. Immediate access to welfare is a policy that is bad for refugees and U.S. taxpayers. There is substantial evidence that the availability of welfare deters and delays the entry of refugees into the labor force. In California, the state with the highest welfare benefits, 85 percent of refugees who had been in the United States three years or less in 1984 were on public assistance; in Texas, where welfare benefits are less than half the level in California, less than 20 percent of similar refugees were on welfare, (Forbes 1985). The availability of generous welfare benefits "appears to sap refugees' economic energies," conclude economists Reginald Baker and David North (1994) in their study of the 1975 Southeast Asian refugees. U.S. welfare policies designed to provide a compassionate safety-net for refugees, may be doing the newcomers more harm than good (Moore 1990a).

On balance, however, immigrants and refugees appear to be a good deal for the United States: their taxes cover the costs of their public services. So concludes the 1985 *Economic Report of the President,* which includes an exhaustive investigation into the economic effects of immigrants. Its findings on the fiscal impact of immigrants summarizes well the fiscal impact of immigrants:

> On the whole, international migrants appear to pay their own way from a public finance standpoint. Most come to the United States to work, and government benefits do not appear to be a major attraction. Some immigrants arrive with fairly high educational levels, and their training imposes no substantial costs on the public. Their rising levels of income produce a rising stream of tax payments

to all levels of government. Their initial dependence on welfare benefits is usually limited, and they finance their participation in Social Security retirement benefits with years of contributions. (Council of Economic Advisers 1986)

## Policy Recommendation

Immigrants as a group do not abuse the welfare system. Some do, however. One of the long-standing conditions of entry for immigrants is that they not become a public charge. This policy should be more strictly enforced. For their first five years in the United States, immigrants should be ineligible for most cash and non-cash welfare benefits, with emergency medical care being a notable exception. Immigrants who go on welfare during their first five years in the United States should be denied continued residency.

The explicit purpose of refugee assistance programs is to "help refugees achieve economic self-sufficiency within the shortest time possible following their arrival in the United States." In practice, these programs have had precisely the opposite effect, contributing to a culture of dependency within refugee communities. Most special refugee assistance programs should be eliminated. Refugee assistance should be privately provided by nonprofit resettlement agencies and ethnic associations.

# WHY AMERICA STILL NEEDS IMMIGRANTS

> The empires of the future, are the empires of the mind.
> —Winston Churchill

Each of the preceding sections has been primarily a refutation of common myths about the economic costs of immigration to the United States. The evidence is compelling that immigrants are not a drain on the American economy. But this does not answer the question of why the United States should continue to accept immigration at all? In this section, I make an affirmative case for a liberal immigration policy by highlighting the economic benefits of immigrants.

## Immigration and the High-Technology Frontier

In the 1980s, the United States assumed world leadership in many high-technology industries, including computer design and software, pharmaceuticals, health care technology, electronics, robotics, and aerospace engineering, among others. This leadership position has been significantly enhanced by the presence in the United States of foreign-born talent. It is not uncommon to find highly profitable firms in the nation's high-tech corridors, from Route 128 in Massachusetts to Silicon Valley in California, that employ more immigrants than U.S.-born workers. British, Taiwanese, Korean, Indian, Filipino, and Cuban scientists are the lifeblood of some of America's most successful high-tech firms (Moore 1991).

No company illustrates this point better than Intel Corporation, which recorded more than $1.1 billion in profits in 1992. Three members of its top management are immigrants, including founder and CEO Andrew S. Grove. Some its most successful and revolutionary computer technologies were pioneered by immigrants, such as the 8080 microprocessor (an expanded-power computer chip), which was invented by a Japanese; and polysilicon FET gates (the basic unit of memory storage on modern computer chips), invented by an Italian. Dick Ward, manager of Intel's training program, says:

> Our whole business is predicated on inventing the next generation of computer technologies. The engine that drives that quest is brain-power. And here at Intel, much of that brainpower comes from immigrants. (Interview with author, October 1990)

At Du Pont Merck Pharmaceutical Co., an $800 million a year health-care products firm based in Wilmington, Delaware, immigrants are responsible for many of the company's most promising new product innovations. For example, Losartan, an anti-hypertensive drug, was developed by a team of scientists that included two Chinese immigrants and a Lithuanian (Mandell and Farrell 1992, 117). Joseph Mollica, president of Du Pont Merck, says that bringing together talent from different cultures and backgrounds means diversity of insight that "lets you look at problems and opportunities from a slightly different point of view" (Mandel and Farrell 1992, 117).

At the high-growth International Paper Company in Hawthorne, New York, 60 percent of the Operations Analysis and Engineering Department are immigrants (Moore 1991, 47). One of the firm's most productive research teams consists of immigrants from Turkey, Israel, Philippines, Egypt, India, Taiwan, and Uruguay.

A final example is Cypress Semiconductor Corporation in San Jose, California, the thirteenth-largest semiconductor company in the United States, with sales of $250 million in 1992. The firm's vice-president for research is a refugee from Cuba. Its two most outstanding technicians, responsible for new product development, are from India and Mexico. The firm's president and founder, T. J. Rodgers, says that Cypress is "critically dependent on immigrants ranging from semi-skilled assembly line workers to top technical people" (interview with author, March 1993).

Intel, Du Pont Merck, International Paper, and Cypress Semiconductor are not unique in their reliance on immigration. Robert Kelley Jr., president of SO/CAL/TEN, an association of nearly 200 California high-tech firms, insists that "Without the influx of Asians in the 1980s, we would not have had the entrepreneurial explosion we've seen in California" (quoted in Kotkin 1989, 24). David N. K. Wang, vice-president of Applied Materials Inc., a California-based computer-technology firm, adds, "Silicon Valley is one of the most international business centers in the world" (Hof 1992, 120). The numbers confirm this assessment. There are currently well over 15,000 Asian immigrants employed in Silicon Valley alone (*Economist,* 27 January 1990). This is roughly one-fourth of the workforce in that high-tech capital (Barkan 1989, 55). More than 10,000 of these Asians are Chinese or Indian. At IBM's facility in Yorktown Heights, NY, one-fourth of the researchers are Asian. At AT&T's world-renowned Bell Labs, 40 percent of the scientists are first- or second-generation Asian immigrants (Kotkin 1992, 108).

An even more heartening success story is that of Phoenix Laser Systems, in San Jose, California. The founder and director of research for this cutting-edge medical laser firm is Alfred Sklar, a Cuban immigrant who escaped Castro in the 1960s. Sklar is recognized as the central brain of a pioneering effort to perfect laser and surgical technologies that could cure several forms of blindness and could eventually revolutionize optical surgery in the United States and throughout the world. Sklar has been touted by the *Wall Street Journal* as one of America's "brilliant scientists . . . challenging the laser industry with radically new machines that could prove cheaper, safer, and more accurate than more common laser approaches" (1990).

New research is beginning to quantify the contributions of immigrants to America's leading technology-driven industries. One of the most comprehensive studies on the impact of the foreign-born on America's scientific industries was conducted by the National Research Council (1988), which finds:

> A survey of the R&D directors of 20 firms that account for a large fraction of the technological output of the United States indicated that their particular industries are, in fact, dependent upon foreign talent and that such dependency is growing. Several respondents stated that "foreign talent was a critical element of the firm's operations."
>
> Thus, it is clear . . . that these foreign-born engineers enrich our culture and make substantial contributions to the U.S. economic well-being and competitiveness and that without the use of noncitizen and foreign-born engineers, universities and industries would experience difficulty in staffing current educational, research, development, and technological programs.

Few would dispute that America's international competitiveness in the next century will be closely tied to the nation's ability to retain its world leadership in high-growth, capital-intensive industries. The U.S. ability to do so is linked closely to its continued ability to attract and retain highly talented workers from abroad.

## Immigrant Scientists, Engineers, and Scholars

International leadership in science, technology, and basic R&D is not dictated by the quantity of scientists and researchers as much as by their quality. A few highly creative innovators can create and capture entire new industries.

Immigrants to the United States are a source of large quantities of high-quality scientists, engineers, mathematicians, computer specialists, and medical specialists. For example, a 1990 *New York Times Magazine* article, entitled "In the Trenches of Science," discusses the discovery of superconductivity: a technology that is expected to spawn hundreds of vital new commercial applications in the next century (cited in Wattenberg 1991, 55–56). The scientist who discovered superconductivity is a physicist at the University of Houston, Ching-Wu Chu, who was born in China and came to the United States in 1972. He is a top contender for a Nobel prize.

American scientific and engineering prowess in the world today is in large part attributable to the influx of highly talented immigrants over the past three decades. In 1980, one of three engineers working in the United States was an immigrant (National Science Foundation 1986). Fifty-five percent of the doctoral degrees awarded in engineering at American universities in 1985 went to foreign-born students (National Science Foundation 1986). Throughout the 1980s, two out of five mathematics and computer science doctorates went to immigrant students, and according to the National Science Foundation, more than 80 percent of these students will stay and work for U.S. firms.

The impact of these foreign scholars has been uniformly positive. According to the National Research Council (1988):

> Very significant, positive aspects arise from the presence of foreign-born engineers in our society. It must be recognized that with these foreign engineers the United States is attracting an unusually gifted group of individuals with high intellectual competence and diligence. The diversity of intellectual backgrounds and experience that other foreign born engineers have brought in the past greatly contributed to U.S. engineering competence, and there are no reasons to believe that new immigrants will not contribute similarly. (p. 3)

The study examined the issue of whether foreign-born engineers depress the wage rates of U.S.-born engineers, and concludes that such a claim "is not supported by the evidence" (p. 3). It also finds that foreign-born graduates create a windfall for the U.S. economy because "the dollar cost to the country for acquiring the services of these unusually gifted individuals is relatively low, substantially less than the real cost of bringing a U.S. citizen to the same level of training and performance."

Brookings Institution scholars J. Lemer and R. Roy (1984) have examined the quality of these immigrant scientists and engineers. They uncover solid evidence that a large number of the most outstanding scientific scholars in the world are immigrants living in the United States. For example, they find that immigrants are overrepresented among the memberships of the National Academy of Engineering and the National Academy of Sciences. They also find that between 1901 and 1982, "immigrant engineers/scientists constitute between 20 and 50 percent of the Nobel prize winners, depending on the discipline involved." In sum, if Ching-Wu Chu does win a Nobel prize for superconductivity he will join a long list of U.S. winners who are immigrants.

Lerner and Roy (1984) attempt to quantify the value of the education transferred to the United States through the immigration of scientists and engineers. They find that the total value to the United States of these immigrants from 1950 to 1975 is roughly equivalent to an annual net flow of capital to the United States of as much as $8. 6 billion (p. 250). This was more than the total amount of U.S. foreign aid to the Third World over this period. Lerner and Roy summarize their findings:

> From the very visible presence of foreign physicians in all major city hospital staffs to the Nobel prize winners imported to these shores, this unplanned—yet enormously significant—immigration strategy has played a significant role in building the technical personnel base of the U.S.

Many of these scholars also contribute significantly to the cultivation of U.S.-born talent. It is almost certain that U.S.-born engineering and science students benefit from competing against the top analytical minds from around the world. Moreover, the recruitment and retention of foreign faculty is essential to maintaining the high standards of U.S. institutions of higher education. William Kirwan (1990), president of the University of Maryland, College Park, explains:

> In order to prepare the currant generation of college students for leadership roles in private industry and government, academic institutions must have access to the very best faculty members from this nation and across the world. American universities have traditionally recruited a small but critical number of world-class teaching faculty from abroad.

Our children's economic future will be richer if the gates are kept wide open to such scholars.

## Immigrants as Entrepreneurs

One of the most favorable characteristics of immigrants is their high propensity to start new businesses. Table [3] shows the rate of new business start-ups and the gross sales of such firms by ethnic groups in 1982, and indicates that some immigrant groups are much more likely to start new businesses than are natives. For example, according to Portes and Rumbaut (1990), "In Los Angeles, the propensity for self-employment is three times greater for Koreans than among the population as a whole. Grocery stores, restaurants, gas stations, liquor stores, and real estate offices are typical Korean businesses. "Cubans also are prodigious creators of new businesses. The number of Cuban-owned firms in Miami has expanded from 919 in 1967, to 8,000 in 1976, to 28,000 in 1990 (*Economist,* 11 May 1991, 20). A final example: on Jefferson Boulevard in Dallas there are over 800 businesses operating today, three-quarters of which are owned and operated by first- and second-generation Hispanic immigrants (Mandel and Farrell 1992, 118). Just ten years ago, before the influx of Mexicans and other Central Americans, this neighborhood was in decay, with vacant stores and "for sale" signs; today, it is a thriving ethnic neighborhood.

It is undeniably true that, as with all new business start-ups, most immigrant establishments are small and marginally profitable. The average immigrant firm employs about four workers and records roughly $200,000 in annual sales

(Portes and Rumbaut 1990, 76). However, such small businesses are a significant source of jobs: from 1975 to 1985, more than one-quarter of all new jobs were created by firms with less than twenty workers.

The stereotype of immigrants running small neighborhood shops, corner groceries, and dry cleaning establishments obscures the vital fact that some immigrant firms, particularly in the scientific and high-technology industries, are extraordinarily successful and vital to U.S. global competitiveness. A 1990 study by the Alexis de Tocqueville Institute surveys high-technology firms in Silicon Valley and finds that roughly one in four had been founded by immigrants—some 270 of them formed by Hong Kong and Mainland Chinese immigrants (cited in Fossedal 1990b). Many of them are highly profitable:

- Solectron, a San Jose circuit-board assembly company, is owned and operated by a Taiwanese immigrant. Sales have grown by an average of 50 percent each year over the past twelve years, totalling $180 million in 1991. It is one of the leading U.S. companies successfully breaking the decade-long domination of Japanese and Korean companies in the area of computer design. In 1991, Solectron won the prestigious Malcolm Baldrige National Quality Award (Mandel and Farrell 1992).

- AST Research is a computer company in Irvine that was founded in 1972 by a Pakistani and two Chinese immigrants. Its first-year sales were barely $500,000; in 1992, sales were $500 million (Mandel and Farrell 1992).

- In 1983, two Vietnamese electronics technicians and a Chinese engineer launched Integrated Circuits, Inc., a computer-assembly firm in Los Angeles. By 1986, its sales exceeded $25 million, and it employed some 300 U.S. workers (Mandel and Farrell 1992).

- American Megatrends, Inc., a designer of highly sophisticated computer software in Norcross, Georgia, was co-founded in 1985 by Subramonian Shankar, an immigrant computer engineer from India. In 1991, AMI boasted sales of $70 million. The company now employs 130 workers. "That is one good thing about America," observes Shankar. "If you are determined to succeed, there are ways to get it done" (quoted in Mandel and Farrell 1992).

One of the engines of entrepreneurial capitalism is risk-taking. The act of leaving one's homeland and immigrating to a new country and a different culture involves substantial risk. Indeed, this is part of the self-selection process that makes immigrants desirable. But immigrants also share other specific traits that contribute to their enterprising nature and their success in business. One is their tight community bonds. Within Asian communities, for example, various forms of highly efficient but informal community-based revolving credit arrangements have evolved, which allow immigrants to finance new enterprises (U.S. Department of Labor 1989, 173). This is an Oriental custom that goes back many centuries. In Korea it is called "kye," in Vietnamese, "hui," and in Japanese, "tanamoshi" (Dunn 1990). This practice for financing small ethnic businesses is especially important because new immigrants typically lack access to conventional lenders. These kinds of neighborhood-based business-financing arrangements are now being duplicated within black communities in New York, Washington, D.C., and other cities.

## Immigrants: The Best and the Brightest

It was said about the great wave of immigrants who came to America on steamships at the turn of the century that the cowardly stayed home and the weak died on the way. This meant that America was attracting a group of new citizens who tended to be highly motivated, resourceful, and enterprising. As James Fallows (1983) writes: "Looked at from the economic point of view, the immigrant's grit and courage, and even his anxieties, impart productive energy to the society he joins."

It is a romantic myth about the United States that the immigrants who come are, as Emma Lazarus put it in her famous poem, "poor, tired, and huddled masses." In fact, for more than a century, immigration has been a process by which America skims the cream of other nation's human capital.

Several studies have documented that the immigrants who come to the United States tend to be more skilled, more highly educated, wealthier, and generally more economically successful than the average citizen in their home countries. This is true of immigrants from both developed and Third World nations. A study by Ugalde, Bean, and Cardenas (1979) finds that Dominicans who immigrate to the United States are more likely to be literate, have higher skills, and be from the city—and for those who do come from rural areas, to be predominantly from large and medium-sized farms rather than from among the landless peasantry. Thomas Sower (1981) of the Hoover Institute reports that black immigrants from the West Indies have far higher skill levels than their fellow countrymen who did not migrate (pp. 216–20). He also finds that the income levels of West Indian immigrants are higher than West Indian natives, higher than American blacks, and even higher than native-born white Americans. West Indian immigrants have been so successful that they have become known as "black Jews" (Sowell 1981, 219).

Among Iranians who came to the United States in 1979, 57 percent were professional, technical, or managerial workers. In Iran, only 6 percent of the workforce falls into those high-skill categories (Gibney 1990, 372). In that same year, 68 percent of the immigrants from India fell into these high-skill categories, compared to less than 5 percent among the entire Indian workforce (Gibney 1990, 372). Finally, 15 percent of the 6,000 Haitians who entered the United States in 1979 through normal immigration channels (as opposed to being refugees) were professionals, administrators, or managers, compared to 1 percent for the Haitian workforce (Gibney 1990, 372).

Even among refugees, however, there is evidence that skill and education levels are above the average of their compatriots. For example, Rita Simon (1984b) shows that 48 percent of male Soviet Jewish refugees entering the

United States in the 1960s and 1970s had been engineers in the Soviet Union. Of the first wave of late-1970s Vietnamese refugees—admittedly the most skilled and "easiest to settle" of the groups from that war-torn country—56 percent were in white-collar jobs in the United States by 1984, compared with less than 20 for all of Vietnam (Loescher and Scanlon 1986).

There is even evidence that illegal immigrants are not the poverty-stricken and least-skilled of their native countries. Surveys of undocumented immigrants to the United States from Mexico document that only about 5 percent of them were unemployed in Mexico, whereas the average Mexican unemployment rate was about three times that level. A much higher percentage of Mexican undocumented immigrants worked in white-collar occupations in Mexico than the average among Mexican citizens. And illiteracy among the undocumented Mexicans is about 10 percent, compared to about 22 percent for the Mexican population as a whole (Portes and Rumbaut 1990).

## The Children of Immigrants

Perhaps the greatest and most overlooked contribution of immigrants to the economy is their progeny—including both those who come to the United States with their parents and those who are born in the United States of immigrant parents. The *Washington Post* (23 June 1990) highlighted the remarkable level of achievement of the children of immigrants:

> Thirteen of the 17 valedictorians in Boston public high schools this year are foreign-born, the highest number officials can remember.
>
> They come from around the world, including from China, Vietnam, Portugal, El Salvador, France, Italy, Jamaica, and Czechoslovakia. Some arrived only in the last five years, most could not speak English when they arrived. School officials attributed the high percentage to an influx of immigrants and the motivation of children who had to overcome tremendous obstacles just to get into the United States.

Public high schools in Washington, D.C., Chicago, and Los Angeles also report remarkably disproportionate numbers of immigrant children as valedictorians. Another measure of the high level of achievement of immigrants is the number of Westinghouse Science Awards they win:

> In 1988 the two highest honors in the national Westinghouse Science Talent Search went to immigrant students in New York public schools: Chetan Nayak from India and Janet Tseng from Taiwan. Since 1981 almost one-third of the scholarship winners in this high school competition, the oldest and most prestigious in the United States, have been Asian-Americans. (*Time,* 4 December 1988, 134)

The children of immigrants also tend to reach exceptionally high levels of achievement as adults, in terms of earnings and professional skills. The normal pattern has been that immigrants who enter as adults are often entrepreneurs or

**Table 3. Immigrant and Minority Firm Ownership and Performance, 1982**

|  | Firms per 100,000 Population | Employees per Firm | Gross Receipts per Firm (thousands) |
|---|---|---|---|
| Mexican | 275.9 | 4.4 | $201.1 |
| Cuban | 638.2 | 4.3 | $267.6 |
| Central and South American | 455.8 | 3.3 | $181.7 |
| Chinese | 1,750.6 | 6.5 | $351.7 |
| Japanese | 968.8 | 4.7 | $293.0 |
| Korean | 2,223.4 | 3.1 | $216.0 |
| Filipino | 391.7 | 2.7 | $133.7 |
| Indian | 1,764.4 | 3.2 | $176.2 |
| Vietnamese | 366.4 | 2.4 | $131.8 |
| American Black | 145.8 | 4.3 | $220.8 |

Sources: Bureau of the Census, *Survey of Minority-Owned Business Enterprises, 1982—Blacks, Hispanics, and Asian Americans,* Release MB82-1/3. Washington, D.C.: U.S. Department of Commerce, 1985, table 1; Alejandro Portes and Ruben G. Rumbaut, *Immigrant America.* Berkeley: University of California Press, 1990, 76.

wage-earners who scrimp and save and work long hours to make a better life for their children; and they are successful at this. The children of immigrants tend to be overrepresented in highly paid professions, including medicine, law, and business management. Among almost all ethnic groups, earnings are higher among the children of immigrants than of the immigrants themselves (Chiswick 1979). Moreover, second-generation immigrants have more economic success than third- and fourth-generation Americans. Economist Barry Chiswick has calculated that throughout this century, the children of immigrants have had earnings that are on average 10 percent above those of comparably educated U.S.-born children (cited in McConnell 1988, 101). This means that one cost of limiting immigrant admissions would be the loss of immigrants' talented and motivated children.

## Immigration and U.S. Economic Growth: Past and Future

By the middle of the twentieth century, America surpassed all other nations in living standards and output. This economic growth coincided with several periods of very heavy immigration to the United States. Several studies have found that immigrants contributed directly to this economic expansion. The last stage of a study by Richard Vedder, Lowell Galloway, and myself investigated the impact of immigration on annual U.S. economic growth rates from 1926 to 1987. Economic growth was measured as the amount of capital available to workers, or the capital-labor ratio, which is a critical determinant of wages and per capita output. The study (Vedder, Galloway, and Moore 1990) finds that the capital-labor ratio is positively associated with the percentage of foreign-born at any given time in a statistically significant sense.

Other studies on the overall economic impact of immigrants have come to similar conclusions. A comprehensive analysis of the effect of immigration on the nation's economic well-being by the President's Council of Economic Advisers (1986) concludes that "the net effect of an increase in the labor supply due to immigration is to increase the aggregate income of the native born population."

Interestingly, the positive impact of immigrants on the aggregate incomes of natives is true even of the lowest-skilled immigrants, despite the fact that they may lower wages for some workers. For example, the U.S. Department of Labor (1989) finds: "Low skilled immigrants usually increase the average earnings of higher-skilled workers and the profits returned to capital. In fact, immigration increases aggregate income by more than the immigrant's wages—regardless of his or her skill level" (p. 18; see also Chiswick 1979, 357–99).

The vast majority of economists agree with this benign assessment. In 1989 I surveyed the past presidents of the American Economic Association, the U.S. winners of the Nobel prize in economics, and the past members of the President's Council of Economic Advisers for a study sponsored by the Hudson Institute and the Alexis De Tocqueville Institute (Moore 1990b). Of the forty respondents, 80 percent believed that immigration has had a "very positive impact" on U.S. economic growth in the twentieth century. None of the respondents believed that the impact has been negative. Roughly two-thirds of these top economists believed that increased immigration would have a "favorable impact on the U.S. standard of living."

There is near-universal agreement that immigration has had a positive economic impact in this century, but what about the next? How would we go about predicting which nations will grow rich and prosperous in the twenty-first century? And what factors will be most critical to a nation's economic growth?

In the past, scholars and political leaders have believed that those nations richest in natural resources, or which had the mightiest militaries, the strongest bodies, or the widest empires would prosper. In the next century, however, the comparative advantage will almost certainly belong to those nations with the most inventive minds and with economic systems that reward talented people to generate new products and new technologies that lead to the creation of new wealth. That is, in the next century, the scarcest natural resource will be talent and brainpower.

To retain its economic primacy in the world, the United States unquestionably must improve its education system and its training system for native-born Americans. But this should not, as some scholars suggest, preclude the adoption of a strategic immigration policy that exploits America's almost unique ability among nations to import needed human capital through the immigration process, which can be done at virtually no cost to American citizens. Indeed, the United States is already doing this today to a significant—though underappreciated—extent.

A liberal immigration policy is a critical step to ensuring that the twenty-first century, like the twentieth, is an American century.

# 8.

# Know the Flow

## George J. Borjas

The flow of legal immigrants has increased steadily since the 1930s, when only 500,000 immigrants were admitted during the entire decade. In the 1950s, 250,000 legal immigrants entered the United States each year. By the 1990s, nearly 900,000 legal immigrants were being admitted every year. A large number of people also enter the country illegally, despite the enactment of the Immigration Reform and Control Act of 1986. Last year the Border Patrol apprehended 1.1 million illegal aliens, more than two per minute. We have also witnessed a radical change in the national-origin mix of immigrants. Over two-thirds of immigrants during the 1950s originated in Europe or Canada. By the 1980s, only about 12 percent originated in Europe or Canada, as against 37 percent who originated in Asia and almost 50 percent who originated in Latin America.

In view of these historic changes, it is not surprising that immigration has resurfaced as a pivotal issue. The debate has blurred the traditional lines between the Left and the Right, leading to odd political alliances: Bill Bennett siding with Fidel Castro and the California Teachers Association in proclaiming the evils of Proposition 187, Pat Buchanan siding with environmentalist groups to argue that the flow of legal immigrants must be reduced.

For the most part, the immigration debate focuses on economic issues. The stakes are high, and so it is not surprising that the participants use facts, factoids, and outright distortions to champion their point of view. For instance, depending on whose numbers we believe, immigrants either pay $27 billion more in taxes than they take out of the welfare system or take out $42 billion more than they pay. A number of myths permeate the field. Before we can engage in a serious debate, it is worth contemplating a simple question: What do we know about the economic impact of immigrants on the United States?

*Myth: By historical standards, immigration today is not all that high.*

In 1910, 14 percent of the American population was foreign-born; by 1990, only 8 percent was. This trend causes some observers to argue that immigration fears are blown out of proportion because, by historical standards, immigrants now make up a small proportion of the population. Yet by several measures immigration today is at or near record levels. Between 1901 and 1910, at the height of the Great Migration, 8.8 million legal immigrants entered the United States. If present trends continue, as many as 10 million legal immigrants, and perhaps another 3 million illegals, will have entered the country in the 1990s. The United States, therefore, will probably have admitted more immigrants in this decade than in any other decade in its history.

Moreover, because of the decline in the number of children borne by American women, immigration now accounts for nearly 40 percent of the growth in population, compared to about 50 percent at the beginning of the century. At least one of every three new workers who enters the U.S. labor market during the 1990s will be an immigrant. By this yardstick, immigrants play a crucial role in determining demographic and economic trends in the United States.

*Myth: Immigrants do well in the labor market.*

If the typical new immigrant were a highly skilled worker, we would be engaged in a very different discussion over immigration policy. Imagine the nature of the debate about Proposition 187 if the flow of illegal aliens was composed mainly of teachers, academics, and journalists. The country's intellectual elite would probably be manning the barricades to prevent the illegal entry of competing workers.

Most of the immigrants now entering the United States, however, are less skilled workers who have little hope of reaching economic parity with native workers during their lifetimes. Recent immigrants are not as skilled, in comparison to the native-born population, as earlier waves.

The typical immigrant who had just arrived in the U.S. in 1970 had 11.1 years of schooling, compared to 11.5 years for the typical native worker at that time. By 1990, the typical new arrival had 11.9 years of schooling, compared to 13.2 years for natives. In view of the widening gap in educational attainment, it is not surprising that the wage differential between immigrants and natives rose dramatically. The most recent arrivals enumerated in the 1970 census earned 16.6 percent less than natives. By 1990, the wage disadvantage was 31.7 percent.

The poor economic performance of recent immigrants at the time of entry would not be a cause for concern if the economic disadvantage diminished over time, as immigrants assimilated. The available evidence, however, suggests that the gap will not narrow substantially during the immigrants' working lives. The process of economic assimilation takes place mainly in the first two decades after arrival and narrows the wage gap by about 10 percentage points. This rate of assimilation allowed earlier immigrants, for whom the initial gap was less than 20 percent, to almost catch up with natives, but it is not sufficient to permit recent immigrants, for whom the gap starts at more than 30 percent, to reach economic parity.

*Myth: Immigrants use welfare less than natives do.*

Less skilled workers, whether immigrants or natives, are more likely to qualify for and participate in welfare programs. There is little doubt that immigrant use of welfare programs is on the rise. In 1970, immigrants were slightly less likely to receive cash benefits (such as Aid to Families with Dependent Children and Supplemental Security Income) than natives. In 1970, 5.5 percent of newly arrived immigrant households received welfare, compared to 6 percent of native households. By 1990, 8.3 percent of newly arrived immigrant households received public assistance, compared to 7.4 percent of native households.

Moreover, the welfare-participation rate of a given immigrant wave increases over time. The wave that arrived between 1965 and 1969 had a welfare participation rate of 5.5 percent in 1970. By 1990, the participation rate of this cohort had risen to 9.8 percent. It seems that assimilation involves not only learning about labor-market opportunities but also learning about the income opportunities provided by the welfare state.

The dollar benefits received by immigrant households that are on welfare have also increased rapidly. The typical native household on welfare received roughly $4,000 in cash benefits each year (in 1989 dollars) throughout the 1970–1990 period. In contrast, the typical immigrant household on welfare received about $3,800 in 1970 and about $5,400 in 1990.

As a result of the increasing participation of immigrants in welfare programs and the larger benefits they are collecting, immigrants now receive a disproportionate share of cash benefits. In 1970, 6.8 percent of U.S. households were headed by an immigrant, and these immigrant households received 6.7 percent of all cash benefits, so that immigrants were slightly under-represented in the distribution of these welfare benefits. By 1990, the situation had changed drastically: 8.4 percent of households were headed by an immigrant, and these households received 13.1 percent of all cash benefits. Put differently, the cash benefits received by immigrant households in 1990 were 56 percent higher than they would have been if immigrants had used the welfare system to the same extent as natives.

By contrast, immigrants do not receive a disproportionately high share of non-welfare income. In 1970, they received approximately 6.3 percent of all non-welfare income, slightly less than their proportion of the population. By 1990, they received 8.3 percent of all non-welfare income, about the same as their proportion of the population. Because immigrants do not get a disproportionately high share of income, they also do not pay a disproportionately high share of taxes.

*Myth: Immigrants pay their way in the welfare state.*

A widely publicized 1994 study by the Urban Institute concluded that immigrants pay over $27 billion more in taxes than it costs to provide them with schooling and welfare services. On the other hand, Donald Huddle (in a study conducted for the Carrying Capacity Network, an anti-population-growth group) concluded that the net costs of immigration exceeded $40 billion. These accounting exercises inevitably incorporate many hidden and questionable assumptions.

To illustrate, let's conduct a simple, back-of-the-envelope calculation of the costs and benefits of immigration. As noted above, the 1990 census indicated that immigrants received about 13.1 percent of all cash benefits distributed in the United

States. At that time, roughly $181.3 billion was spent on all means-tested entitlement programs (including Food Stamps, Medicaid, etc.). If we assume that immigrants received 13.1 percent of these expenditures, they accounted for $23.8 billion.

How much do immigrants pay in taxes? According to the census, the total non-welfare income of immigrant households was $284.7 billion. If the total tax rate (including federal, state, and local taxes) was 30 percent, immigrant households paid about $85.4 billion in taxes. The calculation thus indicates that immigrants pay more in taxes ($85.4 billion) than they take out of the welfare system ($23.8 billion).

## CHANGING THE ASSUMPTIONS

But this comparison assumes that immigrant taxes are used only to fund their use of entitlement programs. One can justify this assumption by arguing that all other government programs provide pure "public goods," so that spending on these programs is the same regardless of immigration. Immigrants, however, increase the congestion of amenities provided by government (e.g., parks, freeways, schools, jails). The cost of providing these public goods to the immigrant population is not zero.

Obviously, different assumptions about the cost of providing these goods will lead to different conclusions about whether immigrants pay their way in the welfare state. If the cost is zero, immigrants make a substantial contribution to the treasury. If, on the other hand, the average cost of providing services to immigrants equals the average cost of providing services to natives, immigrants should be charged for the various government programs as if they were natives. In 1990, 91.1 percent of taxes were used to pay for programs other than means-tested entitlement programs. If we charge immigrants 91.1 percent of their tax payments for using these other programs, then only 8.9 percent of immigrants' taxes are left to fund their use of means-tested entitlement programs. Immigrants would then contribute only $7.6 billion (or 8.9 percent of the $85.4 billion they pay) to the funding of these programs. The tax burden resulting from immigration would be on the order of $16 billion.

The Urban Institute's claim that immigrants create a $27-billion "net surplus" for the United States assumes that immigrants do not increase the cost of any programs other than the ones included in the Institute's calculations (mainly welfare and education). Because we do not know by how much immigrants raise the cost of freeways, national parks, and even defense, accounting exercises that claim to estimate the fiscal impact of immigration should be viewed suspiciously.

Furthermore, the typical accounting exercise does not consider the long-run impact of immigration on government expenditures. For instance, some argue that immigrants make a net contribution to the Social Security system because they are paying into the system now and are not collecting benefits. But immigrants are on average about 30 years old when they enter the United States. As a result, many immigrants pay into the Social Security system for a much shorter time than natives, yet collect roughly the same benefits. In other words, a sizable bill will come due some day, and our children (as well as the immigrants' children) will have to pay it.

The accounting exercises also take a myopic view of expenditures on education. In California alone, it is estimated that roughly $1.7 billion was spent on educating the children of illegal aliens in 1993. These costs, however, must be weighed against the benefits of having a more educated work force later on. Moreover, immigrants who enter the United States after they have completed their education import "free" human capital, from which substantial benefits might accrue.

*Myth: Refugees and illegal aliens are the source of the immigration problem.*

There are huge differences in educational attainment, earnings, and welfare propensities among groups of different national origins. In 1990, immigrants from France and Germany earned about 25 percent more than natives, those from China and Peru earned 21 percent less than natives, and those from El Salvador and Mexico earned 40 percent less than natives. Similarly, only about 2 to 4 percent of the households originating in South Africa, Taiwan, or the United Kingdom received public assistance, as opposed to 11 to 12 percent of the households originating in Ecuador or Mexico and nearly 50 percent of the households originating in Laos or Cambodia. In view of these differences, it is tempting to blame a relatively small number of groups for the disturbing trends in the economic impact of immigration.

The Urban Institute's study offers a typical example of this blame game. The data presented by the Institute's researchers indicate that 41 percent of recent immigrants were high-school dropouts, compared to only 23 percent of natives. Nevertheless, they conclude that the "low educational attainment or poor 'quality' of recent immigrants . . . is directly attributable to illegal immigrants and refugees, not to legal immigrants."

The researchers reach this conclusion by manipulating the data. In defining "legal immigrants," the study omits refugees, presumably because they are admitted under a different set of rules. The researchers also want to omit illegal aliens. The census, however, does not provide any information on who is legal and who is not, so they simply omit immigrants from Mexico (and several Central American countries). The rationale is that a large number of illegal aliens are Mexicans. It is also true, however, that a very large number of legal immigrants are Mexicans. In fact, Mexicans are the largest group in the legal immigrant flow, accounting for almost a quarter of the immigrants admitted legally in the 1980s. By excluding Mexicans from the calculation, the Urban Institute can conclude that "legal" (read: non-Mexican, non-refugee) immigrants don't look quite so bad. In other words, there is no immigration problem once we get rid of the "problem" immigrants.

The blame game also shows up in the Manhattan Institute's recent "Index of Leading Immigration Indicators," which dismisses the high propensity of "immigrants to receive public assistance by noting that "immigrants are more likely than natives to receive welfare, but that is due mainly to very high rates of welfare use among refugees and the elderly." How we define both the native and the immigrant populations influences what we conclude about the economic and social benefits from immigration. The bar graph reports the welfare-participation rates for various groups of native and immigrant households in 1990. Overall, immigrants are more likely to be on welfare than natives. If one looks only at the non-refugee population, however, the welfare gap between immigrants and natives essentially disappears. If we also omit the elderly, we find that non-refugee, non-Mexican immigrants are less likely to be on welfare than natives.

But before we conclude that we have found the source of the immigration problem (that is, the refugees, the presumed illegals, and the elderly), there are two points that are worth remembering. Just as we can minimize the immigration problem by getting rid of the problem immigrants, we can play a similar game with the native population. As the graph also illustrates, even highly "select" groups of immigrants are more likely to be on welfare than non-Hispanic white natives. More important, even if we were to find that these select groups of legal immigrants have the same propensity to be on welfare as a similarly select group of natives, we would still have a problem. After all, shouldn't our immigration policy strive to admit workers who do more than just replicate the social and economic problems of our native population? Yet, instead of considering the economic potential of applicants when handing out entry visas, our current policy awards entry visas mainly to applicants who have relatives already residing here.

*Myth: Immigrants do not hurt the earnings of native workers.*

Another reason to be concerned about the impact of unskilled immigrants is that they probably reduce the economic opportunities of unskilled natives. Economists have typically estimated the impact of immigration on native earnings by comparing the earnings of natives who reside in "immigrant" cities (such as Los Angeles and San Diego) with the earnings of natives who reside in cities where few immigrants live (such as Atlanta and Pittsburgh). These cross-city comparisons suggest that the average native wage is lower, but only slightly, in labor markets where immigrants tend to cluster. If one city has 10 percent more immigrants than another, the native wage in the city with more immigrants is only about 0.2 percent lower.

But this correlation does not necessarily indicate that immigrants have a negligible impact on native workers. Suppose immigration into Los Angeles lowers the earnings of natives in L.A. substantially. Native workers are not likely to stand idly by and watch their economic opportunities evaporate. Many will move out of the Los Angeles basin into other cities, and people who were considering moving to L.A. will now move elsewhere instead. As natives respond to immigration by voting with their feet (creating "the new white flight"), the adverse impact of immigration on the L.A. labor market is transmitted to the entire economy. In the end, all competing native workers are worse off from immigration, not simply those residing in cities where immigrants cluster.

There is some evidence that this "macro" effect of immigration on native earning opportunities is significant. The 1980s witnessed a substantial increase in the wage gap between workers who did not have a high-school diploma and workers with more education. The decade also witnessed the entry of large numbers of less skilled immigrants. Recent evidence suggests that perhaps a third of the 10-percentage-point decline in the relative wage of high-school dropouts between 1980 and 1988 can be attributed to the flow of less skilled immigrants.

*Myth: Americans gain a lot from immigration.*

A number of observers claim that immigration is very beneficial for natives. It is typically argued that immigrants spur economic growth, lower prices for American consumers, and increase the demand for goods and services produced by native-owned firms. It is telling that these claims are seldom, if ever, backed up by numbers. It is simply taken as a tenet of faith that Americans gain from immigration and that these benefits are substantial.

The belief that immigration spurs economic growth arises from the fact that there is a positive correlation between the number of immigrants in a particular city and the rate of economic growth in that city. This correlation is interpreted to mean that when immigrants enter a locality, economic growth follows. This interpretation, however, assumes that immigrants are not very smart. Why would anyone migrate to a city with a stagnant economy? Immigrants (like natives) look at economic conditions before deciding where to settle. The positive correlation between economic growth and immigration, therefore, might simply indicate that immigrants are smart in choosing where to live.

# REDISTRIBUTION OF WEALTH

In any case, the numbers do suggest that natives, as a group, gain from immigration. Immigration, however, does more than just raise the national income that accrues to natives; it also induces a substantial redistribution of wealth. In particular, wealth is redistributed from native workers who compete with immigrant workers to those who employ immigrants and use immigrants' services. I have recently estimated that native workers, on the whole, lose about $133 billion a year, or 1.9 percent of GDP in a $7-trillion economy, mainly because immigrants drive down the wages of competing workers. At the same time, employers and other users of immigrants' services, such as owners of large farms and the Zoë Bairds of the world, gain substantially. These gains are on the order of $140 billion, or 2 percent of GDP. The net gain, therefore, is only on the order of 0. 1 percent of GDP, or about $7 billion. But although the net gain is small, some Americans gain very much. This simple fact explains why a small, well-financed, and powerful segment of the population finds it difficult to understand why most other Americans are so concerned about immigration.

*Myth: Immigrants are more likely to be entrepreneurs, and these entrepreneurs are very successful.*

It is often claimed that immigrants create more jobs than they take because a large number of them become successful entrepreneurs. Asserting that "immigrant companies have generated hundreds of thousands of good jobs in California," Ron Unz uses Silicon Valley and the computer industry to illustrate how immigrant entrepreneurship benefits our country ["Value Added," *New Republic,* November 7, 1995].

Sentimentality aside, it simply is not true that the entrepreneurial spirit burns more brightly among immigrants than among natives. The Census Bureau's statistics indicate that only 6.8 percent of immigrant workers in 1990 were self-employed, compared to 7 percent of native workers. Although entrepreneurship is an important economic activity among some immigrant groups (15 percent of Greek and 18 percent of Korean immigrants were self-employed), it does not characterize the bulk of the immigrant population. Only 6 percent of Vietnamese immigrants, 5 percent of Mexican immigrants, and 3 percent of Filipino immigrants were self-employed.

We should not use these statistics to denigrate the significant entrepreneurial contribution made by some immigrants. For instance, it might be that even though most immigrants do not become entrepreneurs, those who do are wildly successful and contribute significantly to the American economy. The proponents of this argument typically do not back up their assertion with data (since none exist) but instead rely on anecdotes. However, for every Philippe Kahn (an illegal alien who founded Borland International), there is a Bill Gates. Moreover, on average, the self-employed do not do very well in the labor market, regardless of whether they are immigrants or natives. Small firms have very high failure rates, and self-employed workers often earn less than wage-and-salary workers who have comparable skills.

*Myth: The melting pot works fast.*

In 1990, 10 percent of the people living in America were "second generation" (that is, were born here but had at least one parent born elsewhere). By 2050, if current trends continue, the share of second-generation Americans will increase to about 14 percent, and an additional 9 percent of the population will be the grandchildren of current immigrants. The impact of immigration depends not only on how immigrants perform in the U.S. economy but also on the economic performance of their offspring. Despite this, the current debate almost completely ignores the implications of immigration policy for the economic and social well-being of this country in the twenty-first century.

We ignore these implications at our peril. The experience of the children of earlier immigrant waves suggests that, although second-generation workers earn more than their immigrant parents, on average the intergenerational improvement is not that large. At best, the children of immigrants earn about 10 percent more than their parents. Because recent immigrant waves are relatively unskilled and earn about 20 percent less than natives throughout much of their fives, this pattern would imply that second-generation workers in the next century may also have a substantial economic disadvantage.

There is also evidence that the huge wage differentials among different national-origin groups in a given generation are transmitted to their children. For example, in 1940 immigrants from the Philippines earned about 41 percent less than immigrants from Italy. In 1970, second-generation Filipino-Americans earned 17 percent less than second-generation Italian-Americans. Today's skill differentials among foreign-born groups become tomorrow's skill differentials among American-born ethnic groups. It might take up to four generations for the ethnic differences in economic status introduced by current immigration to disappear.

## THE NEED FOR ACTION

We do not yet know how the welfare state and the multicultural agenda favored by many segments of the intellectual elite will alter the speed at which the melting pot does its job. A prudent observer can only conclude that these misguided policies will retard the forging of Americans. This factor, combined with the relatively low skills of recent immigrant waves and their high rates of welfare reciprocy, might mean we are already witnessing the creation of a large new underclass. As other countries have learned at a very high cost, ethnicity matters, and it matters for a long time.

The debate over immigration policy is much too important to be guided by ignorance or by a distortion of the facts. The available evidence suggests reasons for conservatives, and even for open-border libertarians, to be worried about immigration. Perhaps if we can agree on the essence of the problem, we can proceed to a more rational discussion of the policy solutions.

Time is running out, however. The failure of the political system to address the problems caused by illegal aliens led to the enactment of Proposition 187, a proposition that many of us (even if we believe that illegal aliens create problems) view as ill-advised and ill-crafted. The longer the politicians bury their heads in the sand, the more likely that the Proposition 187 movement will spawn a "Proposition 188" to control legal immigration.

This resolution to the debate would be unfortunate, because it would probably lead to far more draconian measures than are justified. If we wish to pursue a more rational policy that nourishes some forms of legal immigration, that upholds the traditions that made America an "immigrant nation," and that takes advantage of the many economic, social, and cultural contributions that a well-chosen immigrant flow can confer upon the U.S., we will have to act soon and decisively.

# 9.

# Peaceful Invasions: Immigration and Changing America

## Leon F. Bouvier

## IMMIGRATION, POPULATION GROWTH, AND THE ENVIRONMENT

Virtually all discussions in Congress about legal immigration center on questions of *who* this nation should permit to immigrate so as to benefit the nation's labor force. The 1990 legislation, for example, concerned itself with the occupational characteristics as well as the country of origin of potential immigrants. The larger question, of *how many* immigrants are appropriate, was not discussed. Yet, as a result of this legislation, the United States population in 2050 will be about 35 million larger than it would be if such legislation were not passed. This failure to take population growth into account is unfortunate, because the number of immigrants the United States admits is not only a major determinant of future United States population size, but also has significant ramifications for environmental protection.

If current demographic trends are maintained, there will be 388 million Americans in the year 2050. With slight increases in fertility and immigration, there could be 454 million Americans in the year 2050. Looking farther into the future, the range of possibilities becomes even more dramatic: the same scenario that produces 454 million Americans in 2050 leads to 900 million Americans by 2120. Demographers Ahlburg and Vaupel foresee a possible population of 811 million by 2080.

A U.S. population of 800 million may seem incredible, but the annual average growth rate that produces it runs at only 1.3 percent per year. This is the same

From *Peaceful Invasions: Immigration and Changing America* by Leon F. Bouvier (Lanham, Md.: University Press of America, 1992), 127–39. Copyright © 1992. Reprinted by permission of the publisher.

as the average annual growth rate that has prevailed in the United States over the last half-century and not too much above the 1 percent average annual growth rate of the last decade.[1]

In other words, the United States could have more people in 100 years than India has today. This is not a welcome prospect.

## PUBLIC POLICY AND POPULATION GROWTH

Public policy in the United States influences fertility in subtle and not-so-subtle ways. State and federal governments fund (or don't fund) family planning clinics; restrict (or don't restrict) the availability of abortion; provide (or don't provide) sex education and population education. In many diverse ways, our national and state governments and the culture in general influence family size decisions. But these decisions remain—and should remain—those of individuals alone. Changes in life expectancy also affect the size of the population. But all agree that life expectancy should be increased for all Americans. Immigration remains the one aspect of domestic population growth that is—in theory at least—regulated by the federal government in the national interest.

With fertility at late 1980 levels (1.8) and net immigration reduced to 350,000, stabilization could be achieved by the middle of the next century at about 316 million; or, with increased fertility and immigration, the United States could be on a course toward a virtually unimaginable one billion Americans.

Thus, immigration policy is a far-reaching means to influence population growth. Goals for U.S. population size should be an essential part of every discussion of immigration policy.

## U.S. POPULATION GROWTH AND THE ENVIRONMENT

Environmental protection is a matter of widespread concern in the United States and throughout the world. Millions of Americans participated in Earth Day celebrations in spring of 1990. Some three-quarters of Americans consider themselves environmentalists as measured by polls, and membership in environmental groups has been rising dramatically. The political importance of environmental issues can be seen in the extent to which elected officials (and those campaigning for public office) make the claim to be solidly for the environment. Even President Bush proclaims himself to be the "environment president."

Although *domestic* population growth has been far from the public eye since the early 1970s, environmental groups (including the Sierra Club and Population-Environment-Balance for example) have long believed that human population growth is harmful to the environment, and that population stabilization is essential in the long run if environmental goals are to be achieved and maintained.

# GLOBAL CLIMATE CHANGE

The drought of 1988, together with the unseasonably warm winter of 1989 made all Americans aware that this warming trend was a possible harbinger of the dreaded "greenhouse effect." Many respected scientists are warning that the greenhouse effect could cause unprecedented disruption to the global environment.

Many gases emitted into the earth's atmosphere (including carbon dioxide, methane, chlorofluorocarbons, and nitrous oxide) are known to trap heat. The concentration of these "greenhouse gases" will continue to increase until significant changes are made in energy use. It is estimated that the earth is already committed to an average temperature increase of 3.5–9 degrees Fahrenheit (2–5 degrees Centigrade) before a new equilibrium is achieved. This is an increase without precedent in recorded history.

In order to slow the rate of build-up of greenhouse gases, far-reaching measures must be adopted. Those recommended by the Sierra Club include: (1) a ban on the production and releases of chlorofluorocarbons, which not only contribute to the greenhouse effect but are also the chief culprits in the destruction of the stratospheric ozone layer; (2) a decrease in the use of coal and increase in the energy conservation and the use of renewable energy sources; (3) a halt to the destruction of forest ecosystems and a major program of reforestation; (4) a greatly increased effort to reduce the rate of population growth in each country of the world, with the eventual goal of a stabilized world population size.

Although population growth is more rapid in developing nations, per capita energy use in the United States is so large that even a small rate increase of population growth in the United States results in large increases in energy use—and hence, production of greenhouse gases.

Not only would the United States benefit directly from a stabilization of its own population, but people throughout the world would benefit through reduced United States production of greenhouse gases.

# FOOD PRODUCTION

The United States has long been a food exporting nation. Given the demands of many rapidly growing nations of the Third World and parts of Eastern Europe, this is very fortunate. However, with increasing population and growing individual consumption by Americans, surpluses in food production are dwindling rapidly.

In 1972, USDA experts concluded that:

> American agriculture appears capable . . . of meeting the challenges of the year 2000. Even under the most demanding assumptions about food and constraints on technology, food and fiber needs could be met without great difficulty, but would require some increase in prices. . . . If this analysis were continued out to the year 2020, the cost of bringing additional farmland into production could possibly increase food prices substantially.[2]

More recently entomologist David Pimentel testified before the Select Commission an Immigration and Refugee Policy that if soil erosion can be stopped and if the availability of energy at today's relative prices is unchanged, the United States could increase productivity (and thus production) by 25 to 30 percent over the next 50 years.[3]

The United States population will grow by over 35 percent between 1990 and 2040. If this rate is not reduced, either Americans will be eating less well or American farmers will be exporting far fewer food products. To be sure, new agronomy methods may be discovered which will increase productivity beyond Pimentel's estimates. However, this only postpones the inevitable. If the United States population keeps growing, sooner or later food production will be insufficient for export.

Not only will this be harmful for the countries in dire need of food imports, it will also pose problems for the United States trade deficit where food exports help keep that deficit lower than it otherwise would be.

## WATER SUPPLY

Water shortage is a large and growing problem in some parts of the nation. This is not a new problem. In 1972, in a report prepared for the Commission on Population Growth and the American Future, Ronald Ridker concluded,

> Growth in population and economic activities during the next half century will force upon us significant expenditures for treatment and storage facilities [of water]; moreover, for a growing number of regions, such investments will eventually prove inadequate. When one takes a region-by-region look at the situation, it becomes clear that the scope for redistribution of water, activities, and people is more limited and difficult to achieve than it might appear at first glance.[4]

Some eighteen years later the problem of adequate water supply remains.[5] Average per capita withdrawal in the United States increased 22 percent between 1970 and 1980. This was less than the 37 percent increase of the previous ten years, but still roughly twice the rate of population growth. In 1985, average water withdrawal by Americans amounted to 1,950 gallons per person, of which 450 gallons were consumed. Americans use about three times as much water per capita as do the Japanese.[6]

Furthermore, water supply is not evenly distributed with the west receiving 30 percent of the fresh water runoff but accounting for 80 percent of the consumption. In California, these problems are compounded by rapid population growth. A report by the National Academy of Sciences says that in order to accommodate the needs of the burgeoning population in California more water will have to be shipped in from someplace else. And that someplace else will be harder, if not impossible, to find.[7]

Regarding water quality, the 1987 Council of State Governments report concludes:

For the first time we are confronted with water quality problems everywhere. Every state is experiencing contaminated groundwater supplies, unsafe drinking water, and higher costs for maintaining a supply of water to meet growing demand. These problems are a result of modern society and will become more severe with the *growth of population* and the expansion of the man-made environment.[8] (emphasis added)

## AIR QUALITY

There is sufficient air for all of us to breathe. However, it does not take a doomsayer to be alarmed at the quality of that air that all of us breathe. About 90 percent of the air pollutants in the United States can be attributed to the burning of fossil fuels. Half of all the air pollutants come from motor vehicles and another 28 percent come from power and industrial plants. Air quality improved during the 1970s in large part due to the passage of the Clean Air Acts of 1970 and 1977. Between 1982 and 1985, however, ambient levels of major pollutants other than lead either remained the same or climbed slightly. These increases are the result of Reagan administration cutbacks in enforcement of air pollution control regulations.

They are also the result of growth. Clearly, clean air cannot be achieved without strong pollution controls on individual automobiles and on emissions from factories. Yet, as many metropolitan areas have discovered, the sheer amount of growth, by putting more automobiles on the road, can erode gains achieved at great cost through emission controls. Fortunately, a new Clean Air Act was passed in late 1990. However, in order to be successful, a Clean Air Act must also incorporate a plan for population stabilization, not only for the nation as a whole, but also for specific areas with severe air quality problems.

## WASTE DISPOSAL

Landfills everywhere are nearing capacity and public opinion opposes "imported waste." All Americans remember the 1988 two-month odyssey of the infamous Islip, Long Island, garbage barge. During that barge's travel it was refused permission to unload its cargo by six states and three countries. Ultimately that cargo was burned in a Brooklyn incinerator. In 1990, Indiana objected strenuously to continued garbage disposal in that state by New Jersey. These episodes illustrate the enormous sewage and waste disposal problems Americans are facing. The United States produces 160 million tons of municipal solid waste per year, nearly 3.5 pounds per day for every man, woman, and child in the nation. With expected increases in population as well as in consumption, the 200 million ton per year mark will be soon be reached. Even without any increases in consumption, that mark will be reached within 20 years.

Problems are greater in large metropolitan areas. Southern California, for example, has already reached its limits for burying garbage: the landfills are full. Sewage problems are equally severe.

> Spills of raw sewage into the ocean off Southern California are becoming commonplace. Fish found in the Santa Monica Bay are not edible due to diseases and contamination. The city of Los Angeles processes most of its sewage at the Hyperion Sewage Treatment plant which is unable to keep up with demands caused by increased population. Because of this, 800 million gallons of only minimally treated sewage spews into the ocean every day.[9]

On the Atlantic, similar problems are emerging as noted by the garbage found on New Jersey shores and elsewhere in recent summers.

The proportion of materials recycled can certainly be greatly improved and waste production can be reduced. Yet even if per capita production of wastes is halved, should the population double, the nation will be even worse off than when it started, because waste production will be back at the same level, with the easy waste-reduction steps already having been taken.

## WETLANDS

Far too little attention is being paid to the staggering loss of inland wetlands throughout the United States. "Located away from ocean tides, these are the bogs and swamps that act as nature's sponges. They soak up pollutants, provide breeding grounds and habitat for wildlife including migratory fowl. Without these humble swamps, floods become a far greater menace."[10]

Because choice lands are already developed, draining the nation's inland wetlands to make way for development is increasing despite federal and state laws designed to protect these diminishing wetlands. Over half of the nation's wetlands have been destroyed and at least an additional 300,000 acres are destroyed every year—all for housing and commercial development. Unfortunately, the Bush administration's recent redefinition of "wetlands" will exacerbate the problem.

## INFRASTRUCTURE

The infrastructure problems facing the United States are growing. Roads, bridges, water systems, railroads and mass transit are all deteriorating. According to the Report of the National Governors' Association 1989 meeting, the price to bring America's transportation infrastructure into reasonable condition within the next 20 years is estimated to range from $1 trillion to $3 trillion, requiring annual outlays in the range of $50 billion to $150 billion.[11] Roads and bridges are the biggest problems. Over 200,000 miles of the nation's roads are in "poor" or "very poor" shape, and another million miles are rated only "fair." Of the nation's

575,000 highway bridges, 42 percent are structurally deficient or functionally obsolete. In some regions of the country, many bridges have already deteriorated to the point of being safety hazards for the public.

Over the last two decades, traffic has grown five times faster than highway capacity. In the next two decades, congestion is projected to become five times worse. In California, transportation officials fear that it will be virtually impossible for enough new highway miles to be constructed to keep pace with population growth. Similar problems are noted in most of the nation's metropolitan areas as suburbs are extended farther and farther away from the central cities to accommodate the burgeoning population. The result is sprawl development, choked highways and massive traffic congestion. The average speed on Los Angeles freeways, already a very low 37 miles per hour, is projected to drop to 17 miles per hour by the year 2000.

The list of population-related infrastructure problems is almost endless. Consider the nation's crowded beaches and National Parks; consider its deteriorating water and sewage systems; consider its transit system, whether bus, plane or train. "Airports anticipate a 72 percent increase in passenger volume in this decade; by 1997, 33 major airports are expected to experience, cumulatively, 20,000 hours of delays annually."[12]

Population growth worsens each of these problems. All levels of government are struggling to catch up with the needs of growing numbers, and all too often fail to maintain the systems built in the past or to improve them for the future.

Consider too that the added 100 or 200 million Americans will not be equally distributed among the 50 states. Visualize more than 50 million people living in California, at least 25 million in Southern California, compared to 15 million today. Visualize 30 million people living in Texas; another 30 million in Florida, and yet another 25 million in New York, with more than half of them in the New York City metropolitan area. Without any movement to such underpopulated places as the Dakotas and Montana, such regional population concentrations are a distinct possibility if the United States population increases by 100 million or more over the next 60 years.

## WORLD POPULATION GROWTH

*World* population increase is widely recognized as one of the most serious problems facing humankind. Scientist Norman Myers has called the 1990s "the most decisive decade in humankind's history," the "final window of opportunity" to come to grips with the world's population and environmental problems, and protect the habitability of the planet. Myers, in considering how much environmental destruction has already been made inevitable, examines an unusual hypothesis:

> Suppose that in the year 2000, humanity were to be eliminated from the face of the Earth. The in-built inertia of [biological] decline would by then be so great that species would continue to disappear in ever larger numbers, due to "delayed

fall-out processes." The ecological injury already done would have triggered the irreversible unravelling of food webs, leading to domino-effect extinctions for many decades, even for a whole century.[13]

Imagine the environmental destruction associated with a world population of 10 or 15 billion!

The root of all these problems can be traced at least in part to the incredible rate of population growth on the planet. Just 150 years ago, world population reached one billion. Recently, the 5 billion mark was passed. In the hour or so it many have taken the reader to reach this chapter, 16,000 babies were born while about 6 thousand people died. The world's population increased by 10,000 people.

In 1980, in his farewell message to the nation, President Jimmy Carter addressed the problems of population and the environment:

> There are real and growing dangers to our simple and most precious possessions; the air we breathe; the water we drink; and the land which sustains us. The rapid depletion of irreplaceable minerals, the erosion of topsoil, the destruction of beauty, the blight of pollution, the demand of increasing billions of people, all combine to create problems which are easy to observe and predict, but difficult to resolve. If we do not act, the world of the year 2000 will be much less able to sustain life than it is now. But there is no reason for despair. Acknowledging these realities is the first step in dealing with them. We can meet the resource problems of the world—water, food, minerals, farmlands, forests, overpopulation, pollution—if we tackle them with courage and foresight.

Unfortunately, President Carter's successors have not heeded his warnings.

## PROPONENTS OF UNITED STATES POPULATION GROWTH

Concern about *world* population growth is widespread and not seriously questioned. However, a few widely quoted individuals have argued that, in effect, the United States is exempt from the principle that population stabilization is beneficial. They claim that growth is beneficial for the United States.

This is simply wrong. The United States does not need population increase beyond the 60 million increase that is virtually inevitable. Rather, every expansion of the number of Americans hurts the nation's ability to solve its environmental and other problems. Indeed, environmental scientists David and Marcia Pimentel argue that: "For the United States to be self-sustaining in solar energy, given our land, water, and biological resources, our population should be less than 100 million. . . . However, with a drastic reduction in standard of living, the current population level might be sustained."[14]

Because the average consumption of Americans far exceeds that of any other country, any increase in the number of Americans has a disproportionate negative effect. According to Norman Myers:

The one billion people at the top of the pile generally do not feature high population rates, but such are their materialist lifestyles—many of them, for instance, consume 100 times as much commercial energy as do most Bangladeshis, Ethiopians, and Bolivians—that in certain respects the additional 1.75 million Americans each year may well do as much damage to the biosphere as the 85 million additional Third Worlders.[15]

Large-scale immigration to the United States helps the few who migrate, but harms the billions who do not. In terms of global warming, waste production, energy use, and many other environmental concerns, citizens of the world can breathe easier when United States population stops increasing. It does not matter whether United States population increase comes from fertility or immigration—ending it helps protect both the world environment and the environment of the United States.

Furthermore it is quite possible that a portion of the very recent increase in fertility may reflect the changing ethnic proportions of the population. As long as these ethnic shares continue to grow, overall fertility will rise. As long as the fertility of minority groups surpasses that of the current majority population, the growing numbers in the minorities will raise the nation's overall fertility.

Let us assume that the current total fertility rates for the four principal ethnic groups in the United States are as follows: Anglo 1.8; Black 2.3; Hispanic 3.0; Asian and Others 2.3. While we cannot vouch for the accuracy of these figures, they are undoubtedly close to the eventual figures for 1990. Let us further assume that shifts in the ethnic composition of the population will be as described in the basic scenario. The Anglo share will fall from 76 percent in 1990 to 65 in 2020 and 54 in 2050 while that for Hispanics will rise from 9 percent to 15 and 22 percent, and others accordingly.

Given these assumptions, the total fertility rate would rise from 2.0 in 1990 to 2.1 in 2020 and 2.2 in 2050—without any actual increases in the fertility of any one ethnic group, but rather as a result of "shifting shares" in the overall population. Such "small" increases of .01 every thirty years may seem inconsequential. They are not. According to recent Census Bureau projections, the difference between fertility remaining constant at 1.8 and fertility gradually rising to 2.2 by 2050 (while holding mortality and migration constant) amounts to over 63 million by that year![16] A very slight increase in fertility yields massive increases in population size decades later. Given these numbers, it would appear that any end to population growth in the United States is nowhere in sight so long as immigration levels remain high.

## CONCLUSION

This brief discussion of the environmental and population problems facing the nation makes it clear that these problems will not be easy to solve. Population growth is a major factor in making solutions to these problems more difficult, and population stabilization would go a long way toward making such solutions easier.

Every scenario for America's population future shows substantial population increases. Even our "Low" scenario of low fertility (1.8) and net immigration of 350,000 results in a 60 million increase in the number of Americans before stabilization at 316 million in 2050. So the United States will need to find ways to resolve its energy, air quality, water supply, and infrastructure problems with *at least* 60 million more people driving cars, heating their homes, visiting in parks.

But the real question for Americans is *how many more* Americans are desirable beyond the virtually unavoidable 60 million increase. The environmental arguments for "limits to growth" are overwhelming in theory. The rationale for rapid population stabilization in the United States is also borne out by the work of those actively trying to solve environmental problems and by the experience of average Americans in their everyday lives.

A population of 900 million Americans is too disturbing to even contemplate. That is also the case for 454 million Americans, or even 388 million. The nation's goal should be the attainment of population stabilization as soon as reasonably possible.

# THE POLITICS OF POPULATION

Despite all the evidence of the need for population stabilization, and despite the fact that many nations in the world have adopted explicit population policies supporting slower growth, American policy-makers have been reluctant to address population issues directly.

In 1970, in the shadow of the 1968 publication of Paul Ehrlich's *The Population Bomb,* the federal government established the first national program to fund family planning clinics.[17] In 1973, the United States Supreme Court legalized abortion throughout the nation.

A Presidential Commission on Population and the American Future concluded in 1972 that "in the long run, no substantial benefits will result from further growth of the Nation's population, rather that the gradual stabilization of our population through voluntary means would contribute significantly to the Nation's ability to solve its problems."[18] The Commission came down squarely in favor of the two-child family. Immigration was then about 400,000 per year, and the Commission recommended "that immigration levels reflect increased and that immigration policy be reviewed periodically to reflect demographic conditions [i.e., population growth] and considerations."[19]

In 1972, United States fertility fell below the "replacement level" of 2100 children per 1000 women and has stayed below until today. As the 1970s progressed, it became clear that immigration policy offered the greatest opportunity for public policy action towards a national population policy, and that large increases in immigration posed the greatest challenge to population stabilization. To whatever concerns policy-makers may have had about the political consequences of the fertility implications of a population policy were added concerns about tackling the issue of "how many immigrants."

Federal legislation declaring a policy of population stabilization has been introduced into every Congress for the past decade, but has never garnered much attention. Now may be the most opportune time for the discussion of population policy, in the context of development of overall immigration goals.

# TOWARD A NATIONAL POPULATION POLICY

Developing a national population policy means adopting an explicit goal for population size. The most reasonable population policy—and in fact the only inevitable one—would be the adoption of a year and a population level as a target for population stabilization; i.e., an end to population increase.

Now is the time for a broad national discussion of such a population goal. With population stabilization, one of the major components of the nation's environmental problems would be resolved. In addition, as discussed earlier, the rest of the world could breathe easier, knowing that rampant United States consumption of resources and creation of pollution would be more easily abated.

# NOTES

1. Ahlburg and Vaupel, "Alternative Projections," 645.

2. A. Barry Carr and David W. Culver, "Agriculture, Population and the Environment," in R. Ridker, ed., *Population, Resources and the Environment* (Commission on American Growth and the American Future, Washington, D.C.: Government Printing Office, 1972), 193–94.

3. David Pimentel, testimony before the Select Commission on Immigration and Refugee Policy, 1980.

4. Ronald Ridker, *Resource and Environmental Consequences of Population Growth in the United States: A Summary* (Commission on American Growth and the American Future, Washington, D.C.: Government Printing Office, 1972), 221.

5. Water withdrawn must be distinguished from water consumption. Withdrawal involves taking water from a groundwater or surface water source and transporting it to a place of use. Consumption occurs when water that has been withdrawn is not available for reuse in the area from which it is withdrawn. (G. Tyler Miller, *Resource Conservation and Management* [Belmont: Wadsworth Publishing Co., 1990], 195.)

6. Kenneth R. Sheets, "War Over Water: Crisis of the Eighties," *U.S. News and World Report,* 31 October 1993, 7.

7. As cited by Dawn Glesser Moore, testimony before the Subcommittee on Census and Population of the Committee on Post Office and Civil Service, U.S. House of Representatives, 12 April 1988, 3.

8. Kenneth Cole, "Clean Water: National Issue, Regional Concern," in *States' Summit '87: Issues and Choices for the 1990s,* Council of State Governments Annual Meeting, Boston, December 1987, 8.

9. Moore, testimony, 19.

10. Neal Peirce, "Breakthrough for Wetlands: EPA's Reilly Lobbies a Maryland Law," *The Virginian-Pilot,* 22 May 1989, A-7.

11. As cited in David Broder, "On the Roads Again: Governors in the Lead," *Washington Post,* 8 August 1989, 12.

12. George Will, "Congealed in Traffic," *Washington Post,* 11 March 1990, B7.

13. Norman Myers, "People and Environment: The Watershed Decade," *People* (London) 17, no. 1 (1990): 17.

14. David Pimentel and Marcia Pimentel, "Land, Energy and Water: The Constraints Governing Ideal U.S. Population Size," *The NPG Forum* (1990): 5.

15. Myers, "People and Environment," 19.

16. U.S. Bureau of the Census, Projections of the Population of the United States, by Age, Sex, and Race: 1988 to 2080, 16.

17. The co-sponsors of this legislation in the House of Representatives were long-time population activist James H. Scheuer (D-NY) and a little-known relatively new Congressman from Texas, George Herbert Walker Bush.

18. Commission on Population Growth and the American Future, *Population and the American Future* (Washington, D.C.: Government Printing Office, 1972), 50.

19. Ibid., 40.

# 10.

# New Americans by Choice: Political Perspectives of Latino Immigrants

## Harry Pachon and Louis DeSipio

## LATINO IMMIGRANT POLITICAL ACCESS, VALUES, AND PARTICIPATION

Despite the fact that approximately two-thirds of Latino immigrants eligible for U.S. citizenship had not yet naturalized, they did report being engaged in U.S. politics. This evidence of engagement came despite a perception among a majority of Latino immigrants that U.S. society and, to a lesser degree, the Immigration and Naturalization Service, discriminated against Latinos. The engagement took several forms. Latino immigrants reported participating in various forms of political activity, particularly following politics in the news. Among the naturalized, a high percentage was registered to vote.

The fact that Latinos who are naturalized are engaged and interested in politics reveals the political potential that Latinos might have if more were naturalized. Not only did the naturalized have high voter registration rates—higher on average than the population as a whole—their voter turnout rates were also quite high. Latino immigrants followed the pattern of the population as a whole, turning out in lower numbers for local and school board elections than for state and national races. Of particular note in these data are the rates for Mexican-origin U.S. citizens. In state and local elections, they showed the highest rates of voter turnout. In sum, these indicators of political interest and political activity among Latinos demonstrate just how meaningful a Latino electoral empowerment strategy based on mass naturalization could be. . . .

---

*From *New Americans by Choice: Political Perspectives of Latino Immigrants* by Harry Pachon and Louis DeSipio (Boulder, Colo.: Westview Press, 1994). Copyright © 1994. Reprinted by permission of Harry Pachon.

## Perceptions of Discrimination

With the exception of Cubans, the majority of each of the Latino national origin groups perceived that U.S. society discriminates against Latinos (Table 1). Central Americans were the most likely to perceive this.

Despite the general perception among all but Cuban immigrants of societal discrimination, few reported that they or their families had experienced discrimination (Table 2). South Americans were the most likely to report having been the target of discrimination; slightly more than one-quarter reported this experience. Dominicans were the least likely to report discrimination, with slightly more than 10 percent having experienced it.

Among those who experienced discrimination, the frequencies varied by national origin (Table 3). More than two-thirds of Cubans and Dominicans who had encountered discrimination reported that this experience was rare. Mexicans were also more likely than other Latino immigrants to report that their experience with discrimination was rare. Central Americans and South Americans were more likely to report that their or their families' experiences with discrimination were occasional rather than rare or frequent.

Few respondents reported that they or their families experienced frequent discrimination. Just 3 percent of Dominicans who had experienced discrimination reported that their experience was frequent. At the other extreme, nearly 30 percent of South Americans reported experiencing frequent discrimination.

Fewer respondents reported that INS discriminated against Latinos than reported that U.S. society as a whole discriminated (Table 4). Many, however, were not sure if INS discriminated. Approximately one-quarter of Mexicans, Cubans, Central Americans, and South Americans and 40 percent of Dominicans reported that they were not sure if INS discriminated. INS scored much higher rates of doubt than did the society as a whole (Table 1).

#### Table 1. Perception of Discrimination Against Latinos, by National Origin

| Does U.S. Society Discriminate Against Latinos? | Mexico | Cuba | Dominican Republic | Central America | South America |
|---|---|---|---|---|---|
| Yes | 352 | 170 | 61 | 119 | 120 |
|  | 52.6% | 42.5% | 56.1% | 71.1% | 60.3% |
| No | 289 | 222 | 42 | 44 | 76 |
|  | 43.2% | 55.6% | 38.5% | 26.3% | 38.4% |
| Unsure | 28 | 8 | 6 | 4 | 3 |
|  | 4.3% | 1.9% | 5.5% | 2.6% | 1.3% |
| Total | 670 | 399 | 109 | 168 | 199 |
|  | 100.0% | 100.0% | 100.0% | 100.0% | 100.0% |

**Table 2. Personal or Familial Experience of Discrimination, by National Origin**

| Has Respondent's Family Experienced Discrimination? | Mexico | Cuba | Dominican Republic | Central America | South America |
|---|---|---|---|---|---|
| Yes | 152 | 74 | 12 | 37 | 59 |
| | 21.7% | 17.2% | 11.2% | 21.6% | 27.5% |
| No | 550 | 354 | 97 | 134 | 155 |
| | 78.3% | 82.8% | 88.8% | 78.4% | 72.5% |
| Total | 703 | 428 | 109 | 171 | 214 |
| | 100.0% | 100.0% | 100.0% | 100.0% | 100.0% |

**Table 3. Frequency of Familial Discrimination, by National Origin**

| Frequency of Familial Discrimination | Mexico | Cuba | Dominican Republic | Central America | South America |
|---|---|---|---|---|---|
| Rarely | 75 | 48 | 9 | 13 | 18 |
| | 49.5% | 68.7% | 74.3% | 34.4% | 33.7% |
| Occasionally | 53 | 16 | 3 | 16 | 20 |
| | 34.6% | 22.8% | 22.6% | 45.0% | 37.0% |
| Frequently | 24 | 6 | 0 | 8 | 16 |
| | 15.9% | 8.5% | 3.1% | 20.6% | 29.3% |
| Total | 152 | 70 | 12 | 36 | 53 |
| | 100.0% | 100.0% | 100.0% | 100.0% | 100.0% |

**Table 4. Perception of INS Discrimination Against Latinos, by National Origin**

| Does INS Discriminate Against Latinos More Than Other Immigrant Ethnic Groups? | Mexico | Cuba | Dominican Republic | Central America | South America |
|---|---|---|---|---|---|
| Yes | 187 | 72 | 22 | 59 | 74 |
| | 26.8% | 17.0% | 21.3% | 35.0% | 34.5% |
| No | 329 | 247 | 41 | 68 | 86 |
| | 47.2% | 57.9% | 39.1% | 40.0% | 39.7% |
| Unsure | 182 | 107 | 41 | 42 | 56 |
| | 26.1% | 25.1% | 39.7% | 25.0% | 25.8% |
| Total | 697 | 426 | 105 | 169 | 216 |
| | 100.0% | 100.0% | 100.0% | 100.0% | 100.0% |

# POLITICAL KNOWLEDGE AND PARTISAN LEANINGS

## Findings

Among those Latino immigrants who tried to name the vice president, most answered correctly (Table 5). The rates of those who did not attempt to answer varied by national origin, with Mexican immigrants the most likely not to try.

Even fewer respondents were able to name the governor of their state (Table 6). Again, however, among those who tried most answered correctly.

With the two exceptions of Cubans and Central Americans, most of the non-U.S. citizens had not yet identified themselves with one of the political parties (Table 7). Among those respondents who expressed partisanship, not surprisingly Cubans were strongly Republican and Mexicans almost as strongly Democratic. Dominican and South American non-U.S. citizens with partisan attachments followed the Mexican model of two-to-one or greater support for the Democrats. Central Americans were more evenly divided, with a slight Republican bias.

Naturalized Cubans overwhelmingly reported Republican party adherence (Table 8). Naturalized Dominicans, and Mexicans to a slightly lesser degree, reported overwhelming support for the Democrats. Naturalized South Americans were slightly more likely to support the Republicans than they were to support the Democrats. Central Americans were split down the middle with a slight bias toward the Democrats.

Naturalized Latino citizens retained higher-than-average rates of lack of partisan affiliation. These rates ranged from 16 percent among Cubans to 33 percent among Mexicans.

Prior to the NLIS, little was known about the partisan leanings of Dominicans, Central Americans, and South Americans. These findings indicate that Dominicans follow the model of Mexicans, with strong Democratic partisanship. Central Americans and South Americans, on the other hand, reported more evenly divided levels of partisanship with strong levels of support for both parties. Yet, data from the NLIS demonstrate that for most Latino immigrants the process of partisan affiliation was not complete. Many Latino immigrants reported that they were unaffiliated.

**Table 5. Ability to Name the Vice President, by National Origin**

| Ability to Name Vice President | Mexico | Cuba | Dominican Republic | Central America | South America |
|---|---|---|---|---|---|
| Did not attempt | 216 | 43 | 23 | 28 | 32 |
|  | 30.5% | 9.9% | 21.2% | 16.5% | 14.6% |
| Tried, but named incorrectly | 31 | 4 | 3 | 2 | 3 |
|  | 4.4% | 1.0% | 2.3% | 1.2% | 1.3% |
| Named correctly | 462 | 382 | 85 | 142 | 181 |
|  | 65.1% | 89.1% | 76.5% | 82.3% | 84.0% |
| Total | 709 | 429 | 110 | 172 | 216 |
|  | 100.0% | 100.0% | 100.0% | 100.0% | 100.0% |

**Table 6. Ability to Name the Respondent's State Governor, by National Origin**

| Ability to Name Governor | Mexico | Cuba | Dominican Republic | Central America | South America |
|---|---|---|---|---|---|
| Did not attempt | 373 | 136 | 52 | 70 | 56 |
| | 52.6% | 31.8% | 47.5% | 40.5% | 25.9% |
| Tried, but named incorrectly | 69 | 11 | 3 | 10 | 19 |
| | 9.7% | 2.6% | 2.8% | 5.6% | 8.8% |
| Named correctly | 267 | 281 | 55 | 93 | 141 |
| | 37.7% | 65.6% | 49.7% | 53.9% | 65.3% |
| Total | 709 | 429 | 110 | 172 | 216 |
| | 100.0% | 100.0% | 100.0% | 100.0% | 100.0% |

**Table 7. Non-U.S.-Citizen Partisan Leanings, by National Origin**

| Partisan Leaning | Mexico | Cuba | Dominican Republic | Central America | South America |
|---|---|---|---|---|---|
| Republican | 33 | 98 | 6 | 27 | 9 |
| | 6.4% | 50.1% | 7.8% | 27.1% | 7.2% |
| Democrat | 80 | 14 | 14 | 22 | 31 |
| | 15.4% | 7.1% | 18.7% | 22.0% | 23.7% |
| Independent | 35 | 3 | 2 | 2 | 20 |
| | 6.8% | 1.6% | 2.2% | 2.4% | 15.2% |
| Other party | 3 | 0 | 4 | 0 | 0 |
| | 0.6% | 0.2% | 5.9% | 0.0% | 0.0% |
| Unaffiliated | 366 | 80 | 50 | 48 | 71 |
| | 70.8% | 40.9% | 65.4% | 48.5% | 53.9% |
| Total | 517 | 195 | 76 | 99 | 132 |
| | 100.0% | 100.0% | 100.0% | 100.0% | 100.0% |

**Table 8. U.S. Citizen Partisanship, by National Origin**

| Partisan Identification | Mexico | Cuba | Dominican Republic | Central America | South America |
|---|---|---|---|---|---|
| Republican | 24 | 144 | 2 | 20 | 20 |
| | 15.7% | 63.0% | 7.3% | 33.4% | 33.8% |
| Democrat | 64 | 19 | 18 | 22 | 14 |
| | 41.6% | 8.5% | 53.4% | 35.2% | 22.9% |
| Independent | 15 | 29 | 2 | 1 | 13 |
| | 10.1% | 12.8% | 5.1% | 1.3% | 21.2% |
| Other party | 0 | 0 | 1 | 0 | 0 |
| | 0.0% | 0.0% | 4.3% | 0.0% | 0.0% |
| Unaffiliated | 50 | 36 | 10 | 18 | 13 |
| | 32.7% | 15.7% | 29.9% | 30.1% | 22.1% |
| Total | 153 | 228 | 33 | 61 | 61 |
| | 100.0% | 100.0% | 100.0% | 100.0% | 100.0% |

# POLITICAL PARTICIPATION

## Findings

Among Latino immigrants who resided in their country of origin as adults, many participated in political activities (Table 9). While few voted, majorities of Dominicans, Central Americans, and South Americans participated in marches in their country of origin. A bare majority of Dominicans also followed home-country political news.

Across all measures of home-country political activities, Mexican immigrants were the least likely to be politically active and Dominicans the most likely.

The majority of each of the Latino national origin groups reported that they followed U.S. politics in the news (Table 10). With one exception, all other U.S. political activities saw few participants. The exception was contributing money or attending political fundraisers. The majority of Cubans and between 20 and 30 percent of Dominicans, Central Americans, and South Americans contributed money or attended fundraisers.

Among naturalized Latinos, the overwhelming majority of each of the national origin groups was registered to vote (Table 11). These registration rates exceeded 80 percent for all groups except for Mexicans, who had a 69 percent voter registration rate.

Among the registered voters, majorities of Mexicans, Cubans, and Central Americans voted in the most recent state election (Table 12). Mexicans had the highest voter turnout rate in the most recent state election.

Voter turnout in the most recent local election was not as high among naturalized Latino immigrants as it was for the most recent state election (Table 13). Mexicans were the only national origin group to have a majority that reported turning out. Dominicans and South Americans reported the lowest turnout rates.

School board elections saw even lower turnout rates (Table 14). Central Americans and Mexicans had the highest turnout rates and Dominicans the lowest for these elections.

Among those who had naturalized by 1984, a majority of each group but Mexicans voted in the presidential race (Table 15). Seventy-one percent of registered Cubans turned out in this race. The NLIS was conducted just prior to the 1988 campaign, so it is not possible to report voter turnout among the naturalized for the 1988 race.

**Table 9. Participation in Home-Country Political Activity,
Among Respondents Who Migrated as Adults, by National Origin**

| Type of Home-Country Political Activity | Mexico | Cuba | Dominican Republic | Central America | South America |
|---|---|---|---|---|---|
| Followed political news | 105 | 122 | 47 | 41 | 73 |
| | 25.4% | 40.9% | 50.4% | 34.9% | 44.0% |
| | (n=413) | (n=298) | (n=93) | (n=119) | (n=167) |
| Marched | 157 | 95 | 65 | 66 | 92 |
| | 37.3% | 32.0% | 70.0% | 55.7% | 55.4% |
| | (n=413) | (n=298) | (n=93) | (n=119) | (n=167) |
| Voted | 16 | 38 | 8 | 5 | 11 |
| | 3.9% | 12.8% | 8.8% | 4.3% | 6.5% |
| | (n=413) | (n=298) | (n=93) | (n=119) | (n=167) |

**Table 10. Participation in U.S. Political Activity, by National Origin**

| Type of U.S. Political Activity | Mexico | Cuba | Dominican Republic | Central America | South America |
|---|---|---|---|---|---|
| Followed political news | 383 | 265 | 61 | 95 | 133 |
| | 54.1% | 61.9% | 55.9% | 58.2% | 61.7% |
| | (n=708) | (n=428) | (n=109) | (n=164) | (n=216) |
| Wrote letters about U.S. political issues | 51 | 53 | 6 | 11 | 20 |
| | 7.3% | 12.3% | 5.3% | 6.6% | 9.4% |
| | (n=707) | (n=428) | (n=109) | (n=167) | (n=216) |
| Distributed leaflets about political issues | 32 | 40 | 3 | 12 | 3 |
| | 4.5% | 9.5% | 2.7% | 6.9% | 1.6% |
| | (n=704) | (n=427) | (n=109) | (n=167) | (n=216) |
| Marched | 40 | 65 | 6 | 15 | 13 |
| | 5.7% | 15.2% | 5.3% | 9.3% | 5.8% |
| | (n=705) | (n=428) | (n=109) | (n=163) | (n=216) |
| Contributed money or attended fundraisers | 99 | 221 | 31 | 47 | 46 |
| | 15.3% | 52.4% | 28.5% | 28.7% | 21.7% |
| | (n=651) | (n=422) | (n=108) | (n=163) | (n=212) |
| Voted | 55 | 71 | 9 | 11 | 20 |
| | 7.9% | 16.5% | 8.2% | 6.2% | 9.1% |
| | (n=692) | (n=428) | (n=110) | (n=170) | (n=216) |
| Helped people register to vote | 19 | 25 | 10 | 1 | 4 |
| | 2.7% | 5.8% | 8.8% | 0.8% | 1.7% |
| | (n=700) | (n=428) | (n=110) | (n=167) | (n=216) |

**Table 11. Voter Registration Among U.S. Citizens, by National Origin**

| Registered to Vote in the United States | Mexico | Cuba | Dominican Republic | Central America | South America |
|---|---|---|---|---|---|
| Yes | 110 | 205 | 28 | 49 | 53 |
|  | 69.3% | 88.0% | 86.2% | 81.3% | 82.7% |
| No | 49 | 28 | 5 | 11 | 11 |
|  | 30.7% | 12.0% | 13.8% | 18.7% | 17.3% |
| Total | 159 | 232 | 33 | 60 | 64 |
|  | 100.0% | 100.0% | 100.0% | 100.0% | 100.0% |

**Table 12. Voter Turnout Among Registered Voters in Most Recent State Election, by National Origin**

| Voted in the Last State Election | Mexico | Cuba | Dominican Republic | Central America | South America |
|---|---|---|---|---|---|
| Yes | 69 | 129 | 13 | 28 | 25 |
|  | 63.3% | 63.1% | 44.9% | 56.3% | 47.5% |
| No | 40 | 75 | 16 | 21 | 28 |
|  | 36.7% | 36.9% | 55.1% | 43.7% | 52.5% |
| Total | 109 | 205 | 28 | 49 | 53 |
|  | 100.0% | 100.0% | 100.0% | 100.0% | 100.0% |

**Table 13. Voter Turnout Among Registered Voters in the Most Recent Local Election, by National Origin**

| Voted in the Last Local Election | Mexico | Cuba | Dominican Republic | Central America | South America |
|---|---|---|---|---|---|
| Yes | 61 | 96 | 9 | 21 | 20 |
|  | 56.4% | 46.9% | 31.9% | 43.1% | 37.6% |
| No | 47 | 109 | 19 | 28 | 33 |
|  | 43.6% | 53.1% | 68.1% | 56.9% | 62.4% |
| Total | 109 | 205 | 28 | 49 | 53 |
|  | 100.0% | 100.0% | 100.0% | 100.0% | 100.0% |

**Table 14. Voter Turnout Among Registered Voters in the
Most Recent School Board Election, by National Origin**

| *Voted in the Last School Board Election* | *Mexico* | *Cuba* | *Dominican Republic* | *Central America* | *South America* |
|---|---|---|---|---|---|
| Yes | 40 | 39 | 1 | 21 | 14 |
| | 36.9% | 19.3% | 5.0% | 42.0% | 25.5% |
| No | 68 | 165 | 27 | 28 | 40 |
| | 63.1% | 80.7% | 95.0% | 58.0% | 74.5% |
| Total | 109 | 205 | 28 | 49 | 53 |
| | 100.0% | 100.0% | 100.0% | 100.0% | 100.0% |

**Table 15. Voter Turnout in the 1984 Presidential Election Among Registered
Voters Who Had Naturalized by 1984, by National Origin**

| *Voted in the 1984 Presidential Election* | *Mexico* | *Cuba* | *Dominican Republic* | *Central America* | *South America* |
|---|---|---|---|---|---|
| Yes | 58 | 135 | 16 | 22 | 29 |
| | 37.6% | 70.7% | 56.5% | 52.9% | 52.0% |
| No | 96 | 56 | 12 | 20 | 27 |
| | 62.4% | 29.3% | 43.5% | 47.1% | 48.0% |
| Total | 153 | 191 | 29 | 42 | 57 |
| | 100.0% | 100.0% | 100.0% | 100.0% | 100.0% |

# PART IV

# CULTURAL CHALLENGE OF IMMIGRATION

# 11.

# The Disuniting of America

## Arthur M. Schlesinger Jr.

## E PLURIBUS UNUM?

The attack on the common American identity is the culmination of the cult of ethnicity. That attack was mounted in the first instance by European Americans of non-British origin ("unmeltable ethnics") against the British foundations of American culture; then, latterly and massively, by Americans of non-European origin against the European foundations of that culture. As Theodore Roosevelt's foreboding suggests, the European immigration itself palpitated with internal hostilities, everyone at everybody else's throats—hardly the "monocultural" crowd portrayed by ethnocentric separatists. After all, the two great "world" wars of the twentieth century began as fights among European states. Making a single society out of this diversity of antagonistic European people is a hard enough job. The new salience of non-European, nonwhite stocks compounds the challenge. And the non-Europeans, or at least their self-appointed spokesmen, bring with them a resentment, in some cases a hatred, of Europe and the West provoked by generations of Western colonialism, racism, condescension, contempt, and cruel exploitation.

## I

Will not this rising flow of non-European immigrants create a "minority majority" that will make Eurocentrism obsolete by the twenty-first century? This is the fear of some white Americans and the hope (and sometimes the threat) of some nonwhites.

From *The Disuniting of America: Reflections on a Multicultural Society* by Arthur M. Schlesinger Jr. Copyright © 1992, 1991 by Arthur M. Schlesinger Jr. Reprinted by permission of W. W. Norton & Company, Inc.

Immigrants were responsible for a third of population growth during the 1980s. More arrived than in any decade since the second of the century. And the composition of the newcomers changed dramatically. In 1910 nearly 90 percent of immigrants came from Europe. In the 1980s more than 80 percent came from Asia and Latin America.

Still, foreign-born residents constitute only about 7 percent of the population today as against nearly 15 percent when the first Roosevelt and Wilson were worrying about hyphenated Americans. Stephan Thernstrom doubts that the minority majority will ever arrive. The black share in the population has grown rather slowly—9.9 percent in 1920, 10 percent in 1950, 11.1 percent in 1970, 12.1 percent in 1990. Neither Asian-Americans nor Hispanic-Americans go in for especially large families; and family size in any case tends to decline as income and intermarriage increase. "If today's immigrants assimilate to American ways as readily as their predecessors at the turn of the century—as seems to be happening," Thernstrom concludes, "there won't be a minority majority issue anyway."

America has so long seen itself as the asylum for the oppressed and persecuted—and has done itself and the world so much good thereby—that any curtailment of immigration offends something in the American soul. No one wants to be a Know-Nothing. Yet uncontrolled immigration is an impossibility; so the criteria of control are questions the American democracy must confront. We have shifted the basis of admission three times this century—from national origins in 1924 to family reunification in 1965 to needed skills in 1990. The future of immigration policy depends on the capacity of the assimilation process to continue to do what it has done so well in the past: to lead newcomers to an acceptance of the language, the institutions, and the political ideals that hold the nation together.

# II

Is Europe really the root of all evil? The crimes of Europe against lesser breeds without the law (not to mention even worse crimes—Hitlerism and Stalinism—against other Europeans) are famous. But these crimes do not alter other facts of history: that Europe was the birthplace of the United States of America, that European ideas and culture formed the republic, that the United States is an extension of European civilization, and that nearly 80 percent of Americans are of European descent.

When Irving Howe, hardly a notorious conservative, dared write, "The Bible, Homer, Plato, Sophocles, Shakespeare are central to our culture," an outraged reader ("having graduated this past year from Amherst") wrote, "Where on Howe's list is the Quran, the Gita, Confucius, and other central cultural artifacts of the peoples of our nation?" No one can doubt the importance of these works nor the influence they have had on other societies. But on American society? It may be too bad that dead white European males have played so large a role in shaping our culture. But that's the way it is. One cannot erase history.

These humdrum historical facts, and not some dastardly imperialist conspiracy, explain the Eurocentric slant in American schools. Would anyone seriously argue that teachers should conceal the European origins of American civilization? or that schools should cater to the 20 percent and ignore the 80 percent? Of course the 20 percent and their contributions should be integrated into the curriculum too, which is the point of cultural pluralism.

But self-styled "multiculturalists" are very often ethnocentric separatists who see little in the Western heritage beyond Western crimes. The Western tradition, in this view, is inherently racist, sexist, "classist," hegemonic; irredeemably repressive, irredeemably oppressive. The spread of Western culture is due not to any innate quality but simply to the spread of Western power. Thus the popularity of European classical music around the world—and, one supposes, of American jazz and rock too—is evidence not of wide appeal but of "the pattern of imperialism, in which the conquered culture adopts that of the conqueror."

Such animus toward Europe lay behind the well-known crusade against the Western-civilization course at Stanford ("Hey-hey, ho-ho, Western culture's got to go!"). According to the National Endowment for the Humanities, students can graduate from 78 percent of American colleges and universities without taking a course in the history of Western civilization. A number of institutions—among them Dartmouth, Wisconsin, Mt. Holyoke—require courses in third-world or ethnic studies but not in Western civilization. The mood is one of divesting Americans of the sinful European inheritance and seeking redemptive infusions from non-Western cultures.

## III

One of the oddities of the situation is that the assault on the Western tradition is conducted very largely with analytical weapons forged in the West. What are the names invoked by the coalition of latter-day Marxists, deconstructionists, post-structuralists, radical feminists, Afrocentrists? Marx, Nietzsche, Gramsci, Derrida, Foucault, Lacan, Sartre, de Beauvoir, Habermas, the Frankfurt "critical theory" school—Europeans all. The "unmasking," "demythologizing," "decanonizing," "dehegemonizing" blitz against Western culture depends on methods of critical analysis unique to the West—which surely testifies to the internally redemptive potentialities of the Western tradition.

Even Afrocentrists seem to accept subliminally the very Eurocentric standards they think they are rejecting. "Black intellectuals condemn Western civilization," Professor Pearce Williams says, "yet ardently wish to prove it was founded by their ancestors." And, like Frantz Fanon and Leopold Senghor, whose books figure prominently on their reading lists, Afrocentric ideologues are intellectual children of the West they repudiate. Fanon, the eloquent spokesman of the African wretched of the earth, had French as his native tongue and based his analyses on Freud, Marx, and Sartre. Senghor, the prophet of Negritude, wrote in French, established the Senegalese educational system on the French model and, when he left the presidency of Senegal, retired to France.

Western hegemony, it would seem, can be the source of protest as well as of power. Indeed, the invasion of American schools by the Afrocentric curriculum, not to mention the conquest of university departments of English and comparative literature by deconstructionists, poststructuralists, etc., are developments that by themselves refute the extreme theory of "cultural hegemony." Of course, Gramsci had a point. Ruling values do dominate and permeate any society; but they do not have the rigid and monolithic grip on American democracy that academic leftists claim.

Radical academics denounce the "canon" as an instrument of European oppression enforcing the hegemony of the white race, the male sex, and the capitalist class, designed, in the words of one professor, "to rewrite the past and construct the present from the perspective of the privileged and the powerful." Or in the elegant words of another—and a professor of theological ethics at that: "The canon of great literature was created by high Anglican assholes to underwrite their social class."

The poor old canon is seen not only as conspiratorial but as static. Yet nothing changes more regularly and reliably than the canon: compare, for example, the canon in American poetry as defined by Edmund Clarence Stedman in his *Poets of America* (1885) with the canon of 1935 or of 1985 (whatever happened to Longfellow and Whittier?); or recall the changes that have overtaken the canonical literature of American history in the last half-century (who reads Beard and Parrington now?). And the critics clearly have no principled objection to the idea of the canon. They simply wish to replace an old gang by a new gang. After all, a canon means only that because you can't read everything, you give some books priority over others.

Oddly enough, serious Marxists—Marx and Engels, Lukacs, Trotsky, Gramsci—had the greatest respect for what Lukacs called "the classical heritage of mankind." Well they should have, for most great literature and much good history are deeply subversive in their impact on orthodoxies. Consider the present-day American literary canon: Emerson, Jefferson, Melville, Whitman, Hawthorne, Thoreau, Lincoln, Twain, Dickinson, William and Henry James, Henry Adams, Holmes, Dreiser, Faulkner, O'Neill. Lackeys of the ruling class? Apologists for the privileged and the powerful? Agents of American imperialism? Come on!

It is time to adjourn the chat about hegemony. If hegemony were as real as the cultural radicals pretend, Afrocentrism would never have got anywhere, and the heirs of William Lyon Phelps would still be running the Modern Language Association.

# IV

Is the Western tradition a bar to progress and a curse on humanity? Would it really do America and the world good to get rid of the European legacy?

No doubt Europe has done terrible things not least to itself. But what culture has not? History, said Edward Gibbon, is little more than the register of the crimes, follies, and misfortunes of mankind. The sins of the West are no worse than the sins of Asia or of the Middle East or of Africa.

There remains, however, a crucial difference between the Western tradition and the others. The crimes of the West have produced their own antidotes. They have provoked great movements to end slavery, to raise the status of women, to abolish torture, to combat racism, to defend freedom of inquiry and expression, to advance personal liberty and human rights.

Whatever the particular crimes of Europe, that continent is also the source—the *unique* source—of those liberating ideas of individual liberty, political democracy, the rule of law, human rights, and cultural freedom that constitute our most precious legacy and to which most of the world today aspires. These are *European* ideas, not Asian, nor African, nor Middle Eastern ideas, except by adoption.

The freedoms of inquiry and of artistic creation, for example, are Western values. Consider the differing reactions to the case of Salman Rushdie: what the West saw as an intolerable attack on individual freedom the Middle East saw as a proper punishment for an evildoer who had violated the mores of his group. Individualism itself is looked on with abhorrence and dread by collectivist cultures in which loyalty to the group overrides personal goals—cultures that, social scientists say, comprise about 70 percent of the world's population.

There is surely no reason for Western civilization to have guilt trips laid on it by champions of cultures based on despotism, superstition, tribalism, and fanaticism. In this regard the Afrocentrists are especially absurd. The West needs no lectures on the superior virtue of those "sun people" who sustained slavery until Western imperialism abolished it (and, it is reported, sustain it to this day in Mauritania and the Sudan), who still keep women in subjection and cut off their clitorises, who carry out racial persecutions not only against Indians and other Asians but against fellow Africans from the wrong tribes, who show themselves either incapable of operating a democracy or ideologically hostile to the democratic idea, and who in their tyrannies and massacres, their Idi Amins and Boukassas, have stamped with utmost brutality on human rights.

Certainly the European overlords did little enough to prepare Africa for self-government. But democracy would find it hard in any case to put down roots in a tribalist and patrimonial culture that, long before the West invaded Africa, had sacralized the personal authority of chieftains and ordained the submission of the rest. What the West would call corruption is regarded through much of Africa as no more than the prerogative of power. Competitive political parties, an independent judiciary, a free press, the rule of law are alien to African traditions.

It was the French, not the Algerians, who freed Algerian women from the veil (much to the irritation of Frantz Fanon, who regarded deveiling as symbolic rape); as in India it was the British, not the Indians, who ended (or did their best to end) the horrible custom of *suttee*—widows burning themselves alive on their husbands' funeral pyres. And it was the West, not the non-Western cultures, that launched the crusade to abolish slavery—and in doing so encountered mighty resistance, especially in the Islamic world (where Moslems, with fine impartiality, enslaved whites as well as blacks). Those many brave and humane Africans who are struggling these days for decent societies are animated by Western, not by African, ideals. White guilt can be pushed too far.

The Western commitment to human rights has unquestionably been intermittent and imperfect. Yet the ideal remains—and movement toward it has been real, if sporadic. Today it is the *Western* democratic tradition that attracts and empowers people of all continents, creeds, and colors. When the Chinese students cried and died for democracy in Tiananmen Square, they brought with them not representations of Confucius or Buddha but a model of the Statue of Liberty.

## V

The great American asylum, as Crèvecoeur called it, open, as Washington said, to the oppressed and persecuted of all nations, has been from the start an experiment in a multiethnic society. This is a bolder experiment than we sometimes remember. History is littered with the wreck of states that tried to combine diverse ethnic or linguistic or religious groups within a single sovereignty. Today's headlines tell of imminent crisis or impending dissolution in one or another multiethnic polity—the Soviet Union, India, Yugoslavia, Czechoslovakia, Ireland, Belgium, Canada, Lebanon, Cyprus, Israel, Ceylon, Spain, Nigeria, Kenya, Angola, Trinidad, Guyana. . . . The list is almost endless. The luck so far of the American experiment has been due in large part to the vision of the melting pot. "No other nation," Margaret Thatcher has said, "has so successfully combined people of different races and nations within a single culture."

But even in the United States, ethnic ideologues have not been without effect. They have set themselves against the old American ideal of assimilation. They call on the republic to think in terms not of individual but of group identity and to move the polity from individual rights to group rights. They have made a certain progress in transforming the United States into a more segregated society. They have done their best to turn a college generation against Europe and the Western tradition. They have imposed ethnocentric, Afrocentric, and bilingual curricula on public schools, well designed to hold minority children out of American society. They have told young people from minority groups that the Western democratic tradition is not for them. They have encouraged minorities to see themselves as victims and to live by alibis rather than to claim the opportunities opened for them by the potent combination of black protest and white guilt. They have filled the air with recrimination and rancor and have remarkably advanced the fragmentation of American life.

Yet I believe the campaign against the idea of common ideals and a single society will fall. Gunnar Myrdal was surely right: for all the damage it has done, the upsurge of ethnicity is a superficial enthusiasm stirred by romantic ideologues and unscrupulous hucksters whose claim to speak for their minorities is thoughtlessly accepted by the media. I doubt that the ethnic vogue expresses a reversal of direction from assimilation to apartheid among the minorities themselves. Indeed, the more the ideologues press the case for ethnic separatism, the less they appeal to the mass of their own groups. They have thus far done better in intimidating the white majority than in converting their own constituencies.

"No nation in history," writes Lawrence Fuchs, the political scientist and immigration expert in his fine book *The American Kaleidoscope,* "had proved as successful as the United States in managing ethnic diversity. No nation before had ever made diversity itself a source of national identity and unity." The second sentence explains the success described in the first, and the mechanism for translating diversity into unity has been the American Creed, the civic culture— the very assimilating, unifying culture that is today challenged, and not seldom rejected, by the ideologues of ethnicity.

A historian's guess is that the resources of the Creed have not been exhausted. Americanization has not lost its charms. Many sons and daughters of ethnic neighborhoods still want to shed their ethnicity and move to the suburbs as fast as they can—where they will be received with far more tolerance than they would have been 70 years ago. The desire for achievement and success in American society remains a potent force for assimilation. Ethnic subcultures, Stephen Steinberg, author of *The Ethnic Myth,* points out, fade away "because circumstances forced them to make choices that undermined the basis for cultural survival."

Others may enjoy their ethnic neighborhoods but see no conflict between foreign descent and American loyalty. Unlike the multiculturalists, they celebrate not only what is distinctive in their own backgrounds but what they hold in common with the rest of the population.

The ethnic identification often tends toward superficiality. The sociologist Richard Alba's study of children and grandchildren of immigrants in the Albany, New York, area shows the most popular "ethnic experience" to be sampling the ancestral cuisine. Still, less than half the respondents picked that, and only 1 percent ate ethnic food every day. Only one-fifth acknowledged a sense of special relationship to people of their own ethnic background; less than one-sixth taught their children about their ethnic origins; almost none was fluent in the language of the old country. "It is hard to avoid the conclusion," Alba writes, "that ethnic experience is shallow for the great majority of whites."

If ethnic experience is a good deal less shallow for blacks, it is because of their bitter experience in America, not because of their memories of Africa. Nonetheless most blacks prefer "black" to "African-Americans," fight bravely and patriotically for their country, and would move to the suburbs too if income and racism would permit.

As for Hispanic-Americans, first-generation Hispanics born in the United States speak English fluently, according to a Rand Corporation study; more than half of second-generation Hispanics give up Spanish altogether. When *Vista,* an English-language monthly for Hispanics, asked its readers what historical figures they most admired, Washington, Lincoln, and Theodore Roosevelt led the list, with Benito Juarez trailing behind as fourth, and Eleanor Roosevelt and Martin Luther King Jr. tied for fifth. So much for ethnic role models.

Nor, despite the effort of ethnic ideologues, are minority groups all that hermetically sealed off from each other, except in special situations, like colleges, where ideologues are authority figures. The wedding notices in any newspaper testify to increased equanimity with with which people these days marry across ethnic lines, across religious lines, even, though to a smaller degree, across racial lines. Around half of Asian-American marriages are with non-Orientals, and the Census Bureau estimates one million interracial—mostly black-white—marriages in 1990 as against 310,000 in 1970.

## VI

The ethnic revolt against the melting pot has reached the point, in rhetoric at least, though not I think in reality, of a denial of the idea of a common culture and a single society. If large numbers of people really accept this, the republic would be in serious trouble. The question poses itself: how to restore the balance between *unum* and *pluribus*?

The old American homogeneity disappeared well over a century ago, never to return. Ever since, we have been preoccupied in one way or another with the problem, as Herbert Croly phrased [it] 80 years back in *The Promise of American Life,* "of preventing such divisions from dissolving the society into which they enter—of keeping such a highly differentiated society fundamentally sound and whole." This required, Croly believed, an "ultimate bond of union." There was only one way by which solidarity could be restored, "and that is by means of a democratic social ideal. . . ."

The genius of America lies in its capacity to forge a single nation from peoples of remarkably diverse racial, religious, and ethnic origin. It has done so because democratic principles provide both the philosophical bond of union and practical experience in civic participation. The American Creed envisages a nation composed of individuals making their own choices and accountable to themselves, not a nation based on inviolable ethnic communities. The Constitution turns on individual rights, not on group rights. Law, in order to rectify past wrongs, has from time to time (and in my view often properly so) acknowledged the claims of groups; but this is the exception, not the rule.

Our democratic principles contemplate an open society founded on tolerance of differences and on mutual respect. In practice, America has been more open to some than to others. But it is more open to all today than it was yesterday and is likely to be even more open tomorrow than today. The steady movement of American life has been from exclusion to inclusion.

Historically and culturally this republic has an Anglo-Saxon base; but from the start the base has been modified, enriched, and reconstituted by transfusions from other continents and civilizations. The movement from exclusion to inclusion causes a constant revision in the texture of our culture. The ethnic transfusions affect all aspects of American life—our politics, our literature, our music, our painting, our movies, our cuisine, our customs, our dreams.

Black Americans in particular have influenced the ever-changing national culture in many ways. They have lived here for centuries, and, unless one believes in racist mysticism, they belong far more to American culture than to the culture of Africa. Their history is part of the Western democratic tradition, not an alternative to it. Henry Louis Gates Jr. reminds us of James Baldwin's remark about coming to Europe to find out that he was "as American as any Texas G.I." No one does black Americans more disservice than those Afrocentric ideologues who would define them out of the West.

The interplay of diverse traditions produces the America we know. "Paradoxical though it may seem," Diane Ravitch has well said, "the United States has a common culture that is multicultural." That is why unifying political ideals coexist so easily and cheerfully with diversity in social and cultural values. Within the overarching political commitment, people are free to live as they choose, ethnically and otherwise. Differences will remain; some are reinvented; some are used to drive us apart. But as we renew our allegiance to the unifying ideals, we provide the solvent that will prevent differences from escalating into antagonism and hatred.

One powerful reason for the movement from exclusion to inclusion is that the American Creed facilitates the appeal from the actual to the ideal. When we talk of the American democratic faith, we must understand it in its true dimensions. It is not an impervious, final, and complacent orthodoxy, intolerant of deviation and dissent, fulfilled in flag salutes, oaths of allegiance, and hands over the heart. It is an ever-evolving philosophy, fulfilling its ideals through debate, self-criticism, protest, disrespect, and irreverence; a tradition in which all have rights of heterodoxy and opportunities for self-assertion. The Creed has been the means by which Americans have haltingly but persistently narrowed the gap between performance and principle. It is what all Americans should learn, because it is what binds all Americans together.

Let us by all means in this increasingly mixed-up world learn about those other continents and civilizations. But let us master our own history first. Lamentable as some may think it, we inherit an American experience, as America inherits a European experience. To deny the essentially European origins of American culture is to falsify history.

Americans of whatever origin should take pride in the distinctive inheritance to which they have all contributed, as other nations take pride in their distinctive inheritances. Belief in one's own culture does not require disdain for other cultures. But one step at a time: no culture can hope to ingest other cultures all at once, certainly not before it ingests its own. As we begin to master our own culture, then we can explore the world.

Our schools and colleges have a responsibility to teach history for its own sake—as part of the intellectual equipment of civilized persons—and not to degrade history by allowing its contents to be dictated by pressure groups, whether political, economic, religious, or ethnic. The past may sometimes give offense to one or another minority; that is no reason for rewriting history. Giving pressure groups vetoes over textbooks and courses betrays both history and education. Properly taught, history will convey a sense of the variety, continuity, and adaptability of cultures, of the need for understanding other cultures, of the ability of individuals and peoples to overcome obstacles, of the importance of critical analysis and dispassionate judgment in every area of life.

Above all, history can give a sense of national identity. We don't have to believe that our values are absolutely better than the next fellow's or the next country's, but we have no doubt that they are better *for us,* reared as we are—and are worth living by and worth dying for. For our values are not matters of whim and happenstance. History has given them to us. They are anchored in our national experience, in our great national documents, in our national heroes, in our folkways, traditions, and standards. People with a different history will have differing values. But we believe that our own are better for us. They work for us; and, for that reason, we live and die by them.

It has taken time to make the values real for all our citizens, and we still have a good distance to go, but we have made progress. If we now repudiate the quite marvelous inheritance that history bestows on us, we invite the fragmentation of the national community into a quarrelsome spatter of enclaves, ghettos, tribes. The bonds of cohesion in our society are sufficiently fragile, or so it seems to me, that it makes no sense to strain them by encouraging and exalting cultural and linguistic apartheid.

The American identity will never be fixed and final; it will always be in the making. Changes in the population have always brought changes in the national ethos and will continue to do so; but not, one must hope, at the expense of national integration. The question America confronts as a pluralistic society is how to vindicate cherished cultures and traditions without breaking the bonds of cohesion—common ideals, common political institutions, common language, common culture, common fate—that hold the republic together.

Our task is to combine due appreciation of the splendid diversity of the nation with due emphasis on the great unifying Western ideas of individual freedom, political democracy, and human rights. These are the ideas that define the American nationality—and that today empower people of all continents, races, and creeds.

"What then is the American, this new man? . . . Here individuals of all nations are melted into a new race of men." Still a good answer—still the best hope.

## NOTES

Stephan Thernstrom's quotation on p. 222 is from his article "The Minority Majority Will Never Come," *The Wall Street Journal,* July 26, 1990.

For a historian's cogent discussion about the last paragraph in section I, p. 222, see Otis Graham Jr.'s article "Immigration and the National Interest" in *U.S. Immigration in the 1980s: Reappraisal and Reform,* ed. David Simcox (Westview Press, 1988), pp. 124–36.

The quotation on p. 222 is from Nathan Newman to the editors of *Dissent,* summer 1989, p. 413.

The quotation on p. 223 concerning European classical music is from Clyde Money-hun's letter "Culture Schlock," *The New Republic,* March 4, 1991; see also Edward Roth-stein's article "Roll Over Beethoven," *The New Republic,* February 4, 1991.

The passage attributed to the National Endowment for the Humanities on p. 223 is from Lynne V. Cheney's book *Fifty Hours: A Core Curriculum for College Students* (Washington, D.C., 1989), p. 7.

The passage on p. 223 concerning required courses in third-world or ethnic studies is from Dinesh D'Souza's "Illiberal Education," p. 53.

Pearce Williams's quotation on p. 223 is from his article "Did Egypt Originate Geometry Theorem?"

Henry A. Giroux is the first professor quoted on p. 224. His quotation is from John Searle's article "The Storm Over the University," *The New York Review of Books,* December 6, 1990.

Stanley Hauerwas of the Duke Divinity School is the second professor quoted on p. 224. His quotation is from Pam Kelley's article "For Duke Profs, The Hot Debate Is What to Teach," *The Charlotte Observer,* September 28, 1990. I have supplied the full word that the *Observer* primly rendered as "—holes."

The passage about Marxists on p. 224 is from Irving Howe's admirable essay "The Value of the Canon," *The New Republic,* February 18, 1991.

For more information about the collectivist cultures on p. 225, see the research described by Daniel Goleman, "The Group and the Self: New Focus on a Cultural Rift," *The New York Times,* December 25, 1990.

The passage on p. 225 concerning Algerian women is from Frantz Fanon's book *A Dying Colonialism* (London, 1965), pp. 37, 46.

Margaret Thatcher's quotation on p. 226 is from David S. Broder's article "Her View of the U.S. Had a Euro-Cynical Bent," *International Herald Tribune,* March 13, 1991.

Lawrence Fuchs's quotation on p. 227 is from *The American Kaleidoscope,* p. 492.

Stephen Steinberg's quotation on p. 227 is from his book *The Ethnic Myth,* p. 257.

Richard Alba's quotation on p. 227 is from his book *Ethnic Identity: The Transformation of White America.* See the discussion in Andrew Hacker's article "Trans-National America," *The New York Review of Books,* November 22, 1990.

The passages on p. 227 concerning Hispanic-Americans and historical leaders are from Lawrence Fuchs's *The American Kaleidoscope.*

The statistics concerning Asian-American marriages on p. 228 are from Stephan Thernstrom's article "Is America's Ethnic Revival a Fad Like Jogging?" *U.S. News & World Report,* November 17, 1980.

The statistics from the Census Bureau on p. 228 are from Gregory Stephens's letter "Interracial Marriage," *San Francisco Chronicle,* December 24, 1990.

Herbert Croly's quotations on p. 228 are from his book *The Promise of American Life* (New York, 1909), pp. 139, 194. Croly was talking about class, not ethnic, divisions—indeed, he rather believed in the inferiority of blacks—but his general point remains sound.

The James Baldwin quotation on p. 229 is from his essay "The Discovery of What It Means to Be an American," quoted by Henry Louis Gates Jr., *Nation,* July 15/22, 1991.

Diane Ravitch's quotation on p. 229 is from her article "Multiculturalism," p. 339.

# 12.

# Along the Tortilla Curtain

## Pete Hamill

You move through the hot, polluted Tijuana morning, past shops and gas stations and cantinas, past the tourist traps of the Avenida Revolución, past the egg-shaped Cultural Center and the new shopping malls and the government housing with bright patches of laundry hanging on balconies; then it's through streets of painted adobe peeling in the sun, ball fields where kids play without gloves, and you see ahead and above you ten-thousand-odd shacks perched uneasily upon the Tijuana hills, and you glimpse the green road signs for the beaches as the immense luminous light of the Pacific brightens the sky. You turn, and alongside the road there's a chain link fence. It's ten feet high.

On the other side of the fence is the United States.

There are wide gashes in the fence, which was once called the Tortilla Curtain. You could drive three wide loads, side by side, through the tears in this pathetic curtain. On this morning, on both sides of the fence (more often called *la línea* by the locals), there are small groups of young Mexican men dressed in polyester shirts and worn shoes and faded jeans, and holding small bags. These are a few of the people who are changing the United States, members of a huge army of irregulars engaged in the largest, most successful invasion ever made of North America.

On this day, they smoke cigarettes. They make small jokes. They munch on tacos prepared by a flat-faced, pig-tailed Indian woman whose stand is parked by the roadside. They sip soda. And some of them gaze across the arid scrub and sandy chaparral at the blurred white buildings of the U.S. town of San Ysidro. They wait patiently and do not hide. And if you pull over, and buy a soda from the woman, and speak some Spanish, they will talk.

"I tried last night," says the young man named Jeronimo Vasquez, who wears

From *Esquire* (February 1990): 39–41. Reprinted by permission of International Creative Management, Inc. Copyright © 1990 by Pete Hamill. Originally published in *Esquire*.

a Chicago Bears T-shirt under a denim jacket. "But it was too dangerous, too many helicopters last night, too much light. . . ." He looks out at the open stretch of gnarled land, past the light towers, at the distant white buildings. "Maybe tonight we will go to Zapata Canyon. . . ." He is from Oaxaca, he says, deep in the hungry Mexican south. He has been to the United States three times, working in the fields; it is now Tuesday, and he starts a job near Stockton on the following Monday, picker's work arranged by his cousin. "I have much time. . . ."

Abruptly, he turns away to watch some action. Two young men are running across the dried scrub on the U.S. side, kicking up little clouds of white dust, while a Border Patrol car goes after them. The young men dodge, circle, running the broken field, and suddenly stand very still as the car draws close. They are immediately added to the cold statistics of border apprehensions. But they are really mere sacrifices; over on the left, three other men run low and hunched, like infantrymen in a fire fight. "*Corre, corre,*" Jeronimo Vasquez whispers. "Run run. . . ." They do. And when they vanish into some distant scrub, he clenches a fist like a triumphant fan. He is not alone. All the others cheer, as does the woman selling tacos, and on the steep hill above the road, a man stands before a tar-paper shack, waves a Mexican flag, and shouts: "*Gol!*" And everyone laughs.

We've all read articles about the 1,950-mile-long border between the United States and Mexico, seen documentaries, heard the bellowing rhetoric of the C-Span politicians enraged at the border's weakness; but until you stand beside it, the border is an abstraction. Up close, you see immediately that the border is at once a concrete place with holes in the fence, and a game, a joke, an affront, a wish, a mere line etched by a draftsman on a map. No wonder George Bush gave up on interdiction as a tactic in the War on Drugs; there are literally hundreds of Ho Chi Minh trails leading into the United States from the south (and others from Canada, of course, and the sea). On some parts of the Mexican border there is one border patrolman for every twenty-six miles; it doesn't require a smuggling genius to figure out how to get twenty tons of cocaine to a Los Angeles warehouse. To fill in the gaps, to guard all the other U.S. borders, would require millions of armed guards, many billions of dollars. And somehow, Jeronimo Vasquez would still appear on a Monday morning in Stockton.

Those young men beside the ruined fence—not the *narcotraficantes*—are the most typical members of the peaceful invasion. Nobody knows how many come across each year, although in 1988 920,000 were stopped, arrested, and sent back to Mexico by the border wardens. Thousands more make it. Some are described by the outnumbered and overwhelmed immigration police as OTMs (Other Than Mexican, which is to say, Salvadorans, Guatemalans, Nicaraguans, Costa Ricans fleeing the war zones, and South Americans and Asians fleeing poverty). Some, like Jeronimo Vasquez, come for a few months, earn money, and return to families in Mexico; others come to stay.

"When you see a woman crossing," says Jeronimo Vasquez, "you know she's going to stay. It means she has a husband on the other side, maybe even children. She's not going back. Most of the women are from Salvador, not so many Mexicans. . . ."

Tijuana is one of their major staging grounds. In 1940 it was a town of seventeen thousand citizens, many of whom were employed in providing pleasure for visiting Americans. The clenched, blue-nosed forces of American puritanism gave the town its function. In 1915 California banned horse racing; dance halls and prostitution were made illegal in 1917; and in 1920 Prohibition became the law of the land. So thousands of Americans began crossing the border to do what they could not do at home: shoot crap, bet on horses, get drunk, and get laid.

Movie stars came down from Hollywood with people to whom they weren't married. Gangsters traveled from as far away as Chicago and New York. Women with money had abortions at the Paris Clinic. Sailors arrived from San Diego to lose their virgin status, get their first doses of the clap, and too often to spend nights in the Tijuana jail. The Casino of Agua Caliente was erected in 1928, a glorious architectural mixture of the Alhambra and a Florentine villa, complete with gambling, drinking, a nightclub, big bands, tennis, golf, a swimming pool, and fancy restaurants. Babe Ruth and Jack Dempsey were among the clients, and a young dancer named Margarita Cansino did a nightclub act with her father before changing her name to Rita Hayworth. The casino was closed in 1935 by the Mexican president, and only one of its old towers still remains. But sin did not depart with the gamblers or the end of Prohibition. The town boomed during the war, and thousands of Americans still remember the bizarre sex shows and rampant prostitution of the era and the availability of something called marijuana. Today the run-down cantinas and whorehouses of the Zona Norte are like a living museum of Tijuana's gaudy past.

"It's very dangerous here for women," Jeronimo Vasquez said. "The coyotes tell them they will take them across, for money. If they don't have enough money, they talk them into becoming *putas* for a week or a month. And they never get out. . . ."

Although commercial sex and good marijuana are still available in Tijuana, sin, alas, is no longer the city's major industry. Today the population is more than one million. City and suburbs are crowded with *maquiladora* plants, assembling foreign goods for export to the United States. These factories pay the highest wages in Mexico (although still quite low by U.S. standards) and attract workers from all over the republic. Among permanent residents, unemployment is very low.

But it's said that at any given time, one third of the people in Tijuana are transients, waiting to cross to *el otro lado*. A whole subculture that feeds off this traffic can be seen around the Tijuana bus station: coyotes (guides) who for a fee will bring them across; *enganchadores* (labor contractors) who promise jobs; roominghouse operators; hustlers; crooked cops prepared to extort money from the non-Mexicans. The prospective migrants are not simply field hands, making the hazardous passage to the valleys of California to do work that even the most poverty-ravaged Americans will not do. Mexico is also experiencing a "skill drain." As soon as a young Mexican acquires a skill or craft—carpentry, wood finishing, auto repair—he has the option of departing for the north. The bags held by some of the young men with Jeronimo Vasquez contained tools. And since the economic collapse of 1982 hammered every citizen of Mexico, millions have exercised the option. The destinations of these young skilled Mexicans aren't limited to the sweatshops of Los Angeles or the broiling fields of the Imperial Valley; increasingly the migrants settle in the cities of the North and East. In New York, I've met Mexicans from as far away as Chiapas, the impoverished state that borders Guatemala.

Such men are more likely to stay permanently in the United States than are the migrant agricultural laborers like Jeronimo Vasquez. The skilled workers and craftsmen buy documents that make them seem legal. They establish families. They learn English. They pay taxes and use services. Many of them applied for amnesty under the terms of the Simpson-Rodino Act; the new arrivals are not eligible, but they are still coming.

I'm one of those who believe this is a good thing. The energy of the Mexican immigrant, his capacity for work, has become essential to this country. While Mexicans, legal and illegal, work in fields, wash dishes, grind away in sweatshops, clean bedpans, and mow lawns (and fix transmissions, polish wood, build bookcases), millions of American citizens would rather sit on stoops and wait for welfare checks. If every Mexican in this country went home next week, Americans would starve. The lettuce on your plate in that restaurant got there because a Mexican bent low in the sun and pulled it from the earth. Nothing, in fact, is more bizarre than the stereotype of the "lazy" Mexican, leaning against the wall with his sombrero pulled over his face. I've been traveling to Mexico for more than thirty years; the only such Mexicans I've ever seen turned out to be suffering from malnutrition.

But the great migration from Mexico is certainly altering the United States, just as the migration of Eastern European Jews and southern Italians changed the nation at the beginning of the century and the arrival of Irish Catholics changed it a half century earlier. Every immigrant brings with him an entire culture, a dense mixture of beliefs, assumptions, and nostalgias about family, manhood, sex, laughter, music, food, religion. His myths are not American myths. In this respect, the Mexican immigrant is no different from the Irish, Germans, Italians, and Jews. The ideological descendants of the Know-Nothings and other "nativist" types are, or course, alarmed. They worry about the Browning of America. They talk about the high birthrate of the Latino arrivals, their supposed refusal to learn English, their divided loyalties.

Much of this is racist nonsense, based on the assumption that Mexicans are inherently "inferior" to people who look like Michael J. Fox. But it also ignores the wider context. The Mexican migration to the United States is another part of the vast demographic ride that has swept most of the world in this century: the journey from the countryside to the city, from field to factory, from south to north—and from illiteracy to the book. But there is one huge irony attached to the Mexican migration. These people are moving in the largest numbers into precisely those states that the United States took at gunpoint in the Mexican War or 1846–48: California, Arizona, New Mexico, Texas, Nevada, and Utah, along with parts of Wyoming, Colorado, and Oklahoma. In a way, those young men crossing into San Ysidro and Chula Vista each night are entering the lost provinces of Old Mexico, and some Mexican intellectuals even refer sardonically to this great movement as *La Reconquista*—the Reconquest. It certainly is a wonderful turn on the old doctrine of manifest destiny, which John L. O'Sullivan, the New York journalist who coined the phrase in 1845, said was our right "to overspread the continent allotted by Providence for the free development of our yearly multiplying millions."

The yearly multiplying millions of Mexico will continue moving north unless one of two things happens: the U.S. economy totally collapses, or the Mexican economy expands dramatically. Since neither is likely to happen, the United States of the twenty-first century is certain to be browner, and speak more Spanish, and continue to see its own culture transformed. The Know-Nothings are, of course, enraged at this great demographic shift and are demanding that Washington seal the borders. As always with fanatics and paranoids, they have no sense of irony. They were probably among those flag-waving patriots who were filled with a sense of triumph when free men danced on the moral ruins of the Berlin Wall last November; they see no inconsistency in the demand for a new Great Wall, between us and Mexico.

The addled talk goes on, and in the hills of Tijuana, young men like Jeronimo Vasquez continue to wait for the chance to sprint across the midnight scrub in pursuit of the golden promise of the other side. *Corre,* hombre, *corre.* . . .

# 13.

# Scapegoating Immigrants

## Elizabeth Martinez

Time to face some troublesome facts. In Los Angeles during the 1992 uprisings many long-time Mexican-American residents said "We're not the ones rioting, it's those immigrants"—meaning Mexicans and Central Americans. At a San Francisco rally marking the 30th anniversary of the March on Washington last August, Dolores Huerta was speaking. A middle-aged African American woman stood and screamed angrily at Huerta, "Go back to Mexico! We need our jobs!"

Incidents like these—and there are many more—leave us with certain questions: will African Americans be made the shock troops of an ugly campaign by racist whites to scapegoat immigrants for the social ills devastating Black and other poor communities? Will established Latino residents forget where they came from and fail to see the racist, classist divisiveness in today's immigrant-bashing? Shall we all remain blind to the need for solidarity among African Americans and Caribbean Blacks, Arab Americans, Asian Pacific Americans, and Latinos—not to mention progressive whites—in combating today's international attack on immigrants?

Imperatively the times call for understanding what the hell is going on and why. Three questions confront us, as formulated by a homeboy friend the other night: "Who is the gun pointed at? Why is the gun being pointed? What is the gun?"

## WHO IS THE GUN POINTED AT?

From the U.S. to Germany to Australia, anti-immigrant actions and policies have escalated in often deadly fashion during recent years. In the United States, President Bill Clinton wasted little time breaking his campaign promise to end Bush's inhuman policy toward Haitian refugees. Under Bush and Clinton some 40,000 Haitians have been summarily returned to a military-police dictatorship of unbridled brutality where they would be lucky to escape immediate death. Surely this year's award for racist immigration policy should go to the U.S., whose officials were sending unarmed Haitian refugees back to Haiti last October even as other officials pulled armed U.S. forces out, saying Haiti was just too dangerous.

Clinton's action also gave the green light to the right wing's anti-immigrant agenda. His own proposals (see "An Activist's Guide") are aimed at tighter Border Patrol control and a speedup in reviewing asylum requests that could send people to their deaths faster.

In California, government officials have generated a tidal wave of anti-immigrant laws or programs. Gov. Pete Wilson led the way with a stream of outrageous proposals, among them denying citizenship to children born in the U.S. of undocumented parents. He got four passed in October which include a ban on giving driver's licenses to the undocumented, requiring state and local agencies providing job training or placement to verify a person being a legal resident, and increasing penalties against getting Medi-Cal benefits "fraudulently" or helping others to do so.

Not to be outshone by a Republican, California's two new Democratic women Senators offered their own measures. Even the erstwhile liberal Sen. Barbara Boxer urged sending the National Guard to defend the U.S.-Mexico border against my relatives. Some "reformist" politicians like Rep. Romano Mazzoli advocate stricter enforcement of employer sanctions. At the heart of the 1986 Immigration Reform and Control Act, these sanctions provided for penalties against those who knowingly hire the undocumented; the sanctions haven't worked but they have encouraged discrimination against anyone who looks or sounds "foreign." As for the Hispanic Congressional Caucus, it has taken a mix of positions.

The North American Free Trade Agreement (NAFTA) also sparks anti-foreign, anti-immigrant sentiment. NAFTA negotiations never address the civil and labor rights of immigrants—only Mexico's responsibilities to stop northbound traffic. An anti-immigrant attitude prevails in the debate over NAFTA, the main issue being whether NAFTA will increase or diminish immigration from Mexico.

California, where 40 percent of those who immigrate to the U.S. settle, has repeatedly seen bombings and other violent attacks on Asian and Latino immigrants or their advocates by ultra-rightists. One image speaks to all these actions. Irma Muñoz, a 20-year old woman who immigrated from Mexico recently, became a successful engineering student at the University of California, Davis, and began working publicly as an intern for a state legislator advocating less reactionary immigration policies. Last April two white male students at UC Davis punched her, cut her hair, and scrawled on her arms and her back with a black magic marker: "Wetback" and "Go home you illegal." If she told anyone about the attack, they warned, she would be killed along with "your wetback friends" like the legislator.

In Texas, where the second largest immigration occurs, the spectacular

"Operation Blockade" went up last September. A Border Patrol inspiration, it put 650 armed agents in a 20-mile long line facing the Juarez-El Paso border for 24 hours a day, supposedly to prevent "illegals" entering from Mexico—but of course they harassed those with papers too. Overtime costs quickly ran up to $300,000 and anybody could walk around either end of the 20-mile line, but no matter; at this writing the operation continues and will also be replicated in the San Diego area. Somebody fretted that the word "blockade" implies an act of war so the San Diego operation is called "Enhanced Enforcement Strategy." That does sound nicer.

New York, the third main destination of immigrants, saw a tidal wave of anti-immigrant (particularly anti-Arab and anti-Muslim) hatred after the World Trade Center bombing. A September 1993 poll of 1,203 New Yorkers reported "startlingly negative attitudes on recent immigration in a city renowned for its international character." More than 63 percent said the number of recent immigrants was too high and more than two-thirds said immigrants had made New York a worse place to live. As for "illegal" immigrants, 55 percent saw them as a serious terrorist threat and 82 percent of the U.S.-born said they believed tighter controls over immigration could have prevented the World Trade Center bombing.

Add to such hysteria the racist depiction of U.S. shores being assaulted by boatloads of Chinese refugees. Incidents also occur in scattered locales like Fall River, Massachusetts, where 12 white men murdered a Cambodian American and severely beat his friend last August 14 while racially taunting both. Or the University of Nevada in Las Vegas, where an India-American student died after being set on fire by two men—one white, one African-American—who said they didn't want any more foreign students on campus.

Elsewhere in the world: In Germany police reported 2,285 acts of rightist violence in 1992, mostly against foreigners and including seven murders. On May 29, 1993 came the Neo-Nazi firebomb killing of five Turks—three young girls and two women—along with other violent attacks on Turkish refugee hostels, homes, and restaurants. A German clerk in a Berlin store falsely accused a Turkish resident of stealing; when the woman's daughter protested, the clerk said "We got rid of 6 million Jews, we'll get rid of you too." Chancellor Helmut Kohl refused to attend a memorial service for the firebombing victims and threatened Turks who might defend themselves. (Of Germany's 1.8 million Turks, many came here 30 years ago invited as guest workers; many were born in Germany.) The German parliament passed a law, which required changing the German constitution, that blocks most applicants for political asylum.

- In France attacks on North Africans have been common, with citizens complaining that Third World immigration "is changing the French way of life." Last June France's National Assembly overwhelmingly approved a new law authorizing police to carry out random identity checks to clamp down on undocumented immigrants.
- In Italy a group of North African immigrant workers were beaten and stabbed by 20 Nazi-skinheads in February 1992.

- Last spring Spain was reported to be increasingly xenophobic toward immigrants from Africa, who numbered 264,000 in Barcelona alone, as well as from South America. An African immigrant in Madrid was murdered last spring in an officially recognized hate crime. An appalling traffic bringing workers from North Africa to Spain by boat has led to 1000 deaths by drowning in the last five years, 300 in 1992 alone. Apparently nobody cares, again we find the zero value put on the life of a poor black person.
- In Hungary, with 50,000 refugees from the war in the Balkans, Gypsies have been a favorite target. One gypsy was beaten to death last Nov. 6 by skinheads.
- Britain sees constant attacks on "blacks" (which includes Indians and Pakistanis). One in three Britons does not want Arabs or Pakistanis as neighbors and two of three said in an October 1993 poll that they don't want to live near Gypsies.
- In Holland middle-class white flight from the schools increases as the immigrant population rises.
- Switzerland's 1991 elections showed rising animosity to immigration when the leader of a rightist party scored big election gains.
- Australia began enacting tough policies in 1992 to deal with an immigration "problem" that critics say does not really exist. And, in an ultimate irony for white folks, we find that immigrants from the Caucasus—yes, Caucasians—who have moved to Moscow since the Soviet Union disintegrated are resented, harassed and attacked as "blacks."

Three chilling commonalities surface in this geographic index. First, in almost every country the anti-immigrant attack coincides with and nurtures a rapid growth of neo-Nazi and far-right groups. But the New Right is not a fringe creature; it includes "respectable" reactionary politicians, with a number of them winning office on an anti-immigrant platform.

Second, many liberals join reactionary forces in scapegoating immigrants. Some major environmental organizations have formed an anti-immigration alliance and are loudly demanding curbs on immigration for its supposed ecological damage and excess population ("immigrant women have high fertility rates"). It seems that 2–4 percent of the U.S. population causes every evil from pollution to traffic jams.

Third, the attack on immigrants is usually racist (and often anti-Muslim). Paris's conservative mayor Jacques Chirac minced no words: they even have "smells" of their own, he said about immigrants. In the U.S. the very word "immigrant" means people of color in most people's minds; forget the many Europeans.

# WHY IS THE GUN BEING POINTED?

Immigrant-bashing and persecution embody a ruling class tactic going back centuries that blames "outsiders" for a society's woes. Today's message is: "Don't blame corporate interests, don't blame the Savings & Loan banks, don't blame the government or elected officials, do blame immigrants!"

"Operation Scapegoat" calls for the U.S.-born to see immigrants as individuals who have freely chosen to leave their homes and cultures, and not to see that most people migrate under the pressure of political, economic or social forces. Similarly the receiving country is seen as a passive victim of invading hordes, when in fact its policies may well "pull" migrants in various ways. The U.S. sent $6 billion in aid to El Salvador's government during the 1980s to crush the popular insurgency. Almost 500,000 destitute, frightened Salvadorans moved to Los Angeles, mostly during the 1980s. Could there be a connection?

Foreign policy including warfare is one answer to why people move across borders. Other politico-military reasons would be ethnic conflict, civil strife, and persecution. These have had devastating impact in recent years: the massive dislocation of people in Iraq and Kuwait caused by the Gulf War, the aftermath of the Berlin Wall's collapse, and effects of the disintegration of Yugoslavia and the Soviet Union.

The economic reasons for migration are no simple matter but we surely need to look at immigration in relation to global economic trends today. For centuries pressure from the failure of domestic structures to provide basic employment and subsistence has created economic refugees. We can see the effects of contemporary economic restructuring, intended by capitalists to restore their profit rates and to hell with millions of skilled steel workers, auto workers, and others. Arturo Santamaria Gomez, the Mexican professor and author, writes of how globalization has caused a deepening U.S. dependence on the Mexican immigrant work force, for example. "Globalization puts a competitive premium on pools of low-paid, 'flexible,' vulnerable workers," he said in a *Nation* article (Oct. 25). Mexican and other migrant labor—especially when undocumented—is key to restructuring the U.S. economy.

Historically that labor carries great advantages for the capitalist. It is vulnerable, especially if undocumented, and totally disenfranchised. Here is the most basic function of the border as a mechanism for defining and maintaining control over labor by the possession or lack of "legal" status. History is packed with experiences of deportation just when an undocumented worker was due to be paid or when workers began to organize for their rights; of low wages and terrible working conditions accepted because the alternative was deportation. Such crippling controls make the undocumented worker a very special kind of wage slave, more enslaved than waged.

But the growth of global economic integration involves more than cheap labor, as immigrant rights activist Maria Jimenez tells us. Why does the *Wall Street Journal* call for a totally open border, even as other voices from center to right demand tighter control? It seems possible the *Journal* understands that today countries belong to an inter-dependent collectivity shaped by global trends. That it questions the role of borders in an era of galloping, global economic integration. Why try to regulate immigration with border control at a time of energetic efforts to open up national economies and create trading blocs like NAFTA?

Saskia Sassen, of Columbia University, a longtime expert on immigration issues, has written about such contradictions. She points out, for example, the way overseas operations of firms have a migration impact. We can conclude, people are moved when investment moves. The real migrant is capital.

## WHAT IS THE GUN?

Instead of considering such realities, we are barraged with a repertory of hostile myths about immigrants. We hear regularly two key myths. (1) "Immigrants are taking away jobs."

In fact, in the U.S. the Rand Corporation, the Urban Institute and the Heritage Foundation—hardly dens of leftism—all concluded in various studies that immigrants do not take jobs from native workers and depress wages. *Newsweek* recently reported (and I would agree, from random observation of janitorial and other service work in a few cities) that during times of high unemployment there may be temporary displacement in some job sectors. But even if that happens, new jobs are soon created by the presence of immigrants with their needs for basic goods and services. This temporary displacement is numerically very small. Immigrants mostly work in jobs in highly exploitative sectors like the garment industry, as nannies, or in the fields, with the legalized working 2–5 hours more per day than the general population.

(2) "Immigrants use services but don't pay for them, and thus they drain local and state resources." But again numerous studies show the opposite: immigrants, including the undocumented, pay more in taxes than the cost of the services they use. *Business Week* (of July 13, 1992) reported that immigrants pay $90 billion in taxes each year, while receiving $5 billion in services. (This truth is masked by the fact that much of the tax money goes to the federal government, not the state providing the services.) Also, immigrants use fewer services than the native-born; for the undocumented, always fearful of capture and deportation, the percentage is tiny. The director of the National Immigration Forum says less than 1 percent of newly legalized immigrants received general assistance in 1987–88 and less than half a percent obtained food stamps and AFDC. As for social security taxes, since most immigrants are young they will pay a disproportionate amount of tax for an increasingly aging population.

The myths are intended to prove that the very real deprivation experienced today by the U.S.-born should be blamed on immigrants—that largely impoverished 2–4 percent of the population. In California, whose economic problems obviously rise from such setbacks as failed new industries and severe cuts in tax revenue under Prop. 13, this scapegoating seems ludicrous. Instead of swallowing it we should all protest the real causes of the crisis and immigrants should be demanding: No taxation without representation.

Politics is the first, obvious place to find the reasons for those myths. Governor Pete Wilson's approval rating rose seven points soon after his "get tough on immigrants" campaign warmed up. Immigrants have always been a favorite whipping boy and recruitment ploy for rightist forces. Such politics echo the anti-social services, anti-labor shift that has swamped much of the world over the last two decades.

A key part of this shift is the intensification of racism, and racism plays a key role in immigrant-bashing—so often that it's sometimes hard to separate one from the other. In France Jean-Marie LePen's rightist National Front Party has grown steadily for several years on a platform that would cut off immigration specifically of Arabs and Africans.

## FIGHTING BACK

In the long run, universally humane treatment of immigrants and refugees requires global changes in today's economic policies and the supra-national agencies like the World Bank or GATT who determine them. Meanwhile, we must deal urgently with the short run. That calls for two related kinds of action: building a new civil rights movement that includes immigrant and refugee rights, and combating forces that pit people of color or workers against each other by scapegoating immigrants.

On the first front we need to begin by defining immigrant and refugee rights as a civil rights issue around which all must unite. We need a new civil rights movement that recognizes immigrants are usually non-white and are made vulnerable to exploitation and abuse because they lack citizenship and knowledge of English. At the top of our civil rights list is getting the Border Patrol under some control. We need procedures, starting with H.R. 2119, the Immigration Enforcement Review Commission, to investigate complaints about this autonomous agency—the largest police department in the U.S., guilty of rape and murder of defenseless immigrant women and men, almost all Mexican or Central American.

Nothing is more difficult than combating the divisiveness that has pit [*sic*] people of color against each other. The mass media, right-wing organizations, politicians, and normally progressive voices have established a climate where 63 percent of 500 Latinos polled in California this year thought enforcing employer sanctions was the best way to curb illegal immigration and 73 percent of African Americans believe immigrants are taking their jobs, according to a Harris poll. The right-wing Federation for American Immigration Reform, FAIR, ran radio spots targeting black communities that blamed the problems there on those foreign hordes coming across the border. In a more subtle but equally venial way, TV gives us an automobile commercial in which an African American salesperson says: "Go see *Rising Sun,* then you'll know why you have to buy your car from me."

School children learn racist anti-immigrant epithets heard from parents or the media. To hear a Chicano kid sneer "Mexican" at a day laborer on the street corner is cause to grieve mightily. To hear African American children holler "wetback" at recently immigrated Latino kids who speak too little English for self-defense is also grievous. To hear Latinos object to protests about the bombing of an Asian rights center because "those people didn't have it hard like us" is sad indeed.

We need to set aside narrow, reactionary nationalisms that tell us to care only about our own. We need to welcome and encourage voices that try to expose the scapegoating, like that of Joe Williams III, an African American writing in the *Los Angeles Sentinel* last Sept. 9. Williams compared the current attacks on the undocumented to the harassment of blacks during the 1950s–1960s, when many moved north or west as southern agriculture declined. "They were accused of taking the jobs of the white man. They were accused [by whites] of undermining the salaries of union workers." But it's even worse today, Williams concludes, because mainstream politicians as well as segments of the black and Latino communities join the attacks. About Latino immigrants "We must realize that California and four other states were . . . part of Mexico," he says.

A new civil rights movement should not deny that class differences exist among immigrants, but those don't justify the current denial of civil/human rights across the board. A word must also be said to organized labor: it's time to reject that racist, elitist attitude toward immigrant workers, including the undocumented. Unions need to recognize the courageous determination of workers today like the Los Angeles drywallers—almost all Latinos—or the San Antonio garment workers' organization Fuerza Unida—almost all Latinas. It could do much to revive the U.S. labor movement. Civil rights, human rights, labor rights: all are needed.

We are left with a chilling question of our time: Will we unite to fight the divisive scapegoating of immigrants? At the very least that attack will move U.S. society still farther to the right. At worst, it can usher in neo-fascist tendencies.

The immigrant and refugee rights struggle points to our need for a whole new worldview. Does anybody really think the way to deal with an estimated one million migrants wandering the planet today is by locking some doors? There is no way that 19th-century nationalism can be useful. It is profoundly backward to go on seeing countries primarily as bordered nation-states which can resolve issues like immigration policy unilaterally. *No Hay Fronteras.*

# 14.

# Immigration and the Aliens Among Us

## Richard John Neuhaus

Like many American Jews, Martin Peretz, editor in chief of *The New Republic,* had until now a deep inhibition about ever, ever visiting Germany. But
he took the plunge and returns with some instructive observations about that
country, and ours. Germans, he suggests, have almost gone overboard to "mor-
tify themselves over anti-Semitism despite Germany having done more to purge
this poison than any other country in Europe." He writes admiringly of Germany
as Europe's "most responsible collective citizen" in responding to the masses of
refugees trekking Westward as a consequence of the turmoils following the collapse of Communism. Although shortly after his visit Berlin put new restrictions
on such mass immigration, one doubts that this would change Peretz's respect for
the German model as the world tries to cope with changing notions of citizenship
and nationhood.

"The advanced countries," Peretz writes, "are now having to choose
between being civic nations and ethnic nations, a choice they could elude so long
as huge masses of 'others' did not pass through their portals. It was easy to be a
civic nation of individuals until new ethnics with new demands for ethnic rights
put into question what 'we' meant. This is tinder-box material, especially when
ethnic and racial minorities demand cultural and political outcomes that they
want to deny to the defining or founding majorities. This has not quite occurred
in Germany, at least not yet, but it is happening in the United States."

The distinction between an ethnic and civic nation is important but not as
clear-cut as it may at first appear. Civic habits and presuppositions are not unrelated to what we have come to call ethnicity. The civic nation is not simply one
of "individuals" but of individuals tied to communities of memory, character, and
mutual help. But it is true that, from earlier discussions about the "melting pot"

From *First Things* (August/September 1993): 63–65. Reprinted by permission of the publisher.

through today's patter about "gorgeous mosaics," most Americans have insisted that the United States has never been an ethnic nation. That claim has frequently tended to overlook the degree to which the "founding and defining" majority in the American project was, at least until fairly recently, Anglo-Saxon and very Protestant. Scholars can dispute whether Anglo-Saxon—or even North European—qualifies as an ethnic group, but nobody moderately familiar with American beginnings doubts that the founders and definers were not, for example, Arab, American, or Japanese.

The synthesis of Puritan religion and the philosophy of John Locke that defined the civic nation presupposed cultural, moral, and even theological assumptions. The Puritan "errand in the wilderness" and sense of Providential mission, as well as the constitutional bid for a *novus ordo seclorum,* are the product of a singular cultural phenomenon that, somewhat paradoxically, imprinted upon the American mind both the conviction of universal purpose and the conviction of being a people apart. With what might be called the Protestant Descendency of the last century—a decline recently accelerated by new waves of immigration—these constituting convictions are being sorely tested. It is by no means clear that millions of new citizens can easily be educated to embrace the institutions and procedures of the civic nation without reference to the cultural-ethnic history that brought those institutions and procedures into being.

We should be disturbed but not surprised that there is today a rising agitation—mainly on the right but not only on the right—against massive, some say uncontrolled, immigration to the United States. There is little disagreement about the scandal of a great nation not being able to impose discipline upon access to its borders, notably its border with Mexico. But the present and building debate is about much more than that. It is once again becoming respectable to fret in public about the declining birth rate among Americans of native stock (the "founding and defining" part of the population that may soon no longer be a majority). The huge influx of Latin American, Asian, and Middle Eastern immigrants poses, it is argued, a possibly fatal threat to the civic nation, precisely because the civic nation depends upon undergirding habits and presuppositions that are historically and at present inseparable from cultural and ethnic experience. The great truths proclaimed by "We the People" presuppose some notion of the people involved. Are the "alien hordes" who have no real relationship to that people, aside from envy of their material success and wanting to share in it, capable of internalizing the civic nation's foundational truths that are inescapably derived from a particularist history of beliefs about, for instance, Nature and Nature's God?

These anxieties about immigration are hardly new, but neither are they dismissable simply as a replay of the Nativism of the last century. The Protestant Descendency, a felt threat in the nineteenth century, is now undeniable reality. The patterns and communities of adhesion that then made it possible to think of America as a nation have become increasingly tenuous. It is not unreasonable to worry that Madison, Jefferson, and others are being vindicated in their fear that our civic institutions were not designed for, and cannot survive, what they called a "vastly extended Republic." However right he was about slavery—and he was undoubtedly right about slavery—Lincoln may have been wrong in thinking that the war that effected its abolition could secure a nation "so conceived and so dedicated." The conception and dedication was the handiwork of the founding and defining leadership that, even in the 1860s, feared that it was losing its hold on the nation's future.

The arguments and agitations about immigration that are now gaining currency do indeed raise questions about what is meant by "we" and about the meaning of civic and cultural nationhood. This is "tinder-box material," but much of the anxiety is, in our view, misdirected. It is possible that the millions of new Americans arriving in recent years will turn out to be a force alien to and alienating from the American experiment. But that fear was much more politically potent, and perhaps plausible, in the late-nineteenth century when the country faced the invasion of "the great unwashed," composed mainly of Catholics, Jews, Slavs, and others who had not been part of the founding and defining moment. Such fears turned out to be unjustified as the nation rightly took pride in its demonstrated powers of assimilation, in its ability to "Americanize" the newcomers into a population that revivified the founding and defining ideas of the American enterprise.

The preponderance of evidence today suggests that immigrants continue to be a revivifying force in our national life. Asians in particular demonstrate an astonishing capacity to enter into the economic and educational dynamics of American opportunity. In polyglot immigrant communities such as those found in Queens, New York, where peoples from fifty or more nations live together in remarkable amity, the level of American patriotism is almost embarrassingly robust. As Linda Chavez has recently reminded us (*Out of the Barrio*), the largest immigrant group, the Hispanics, is in fact many distinct groups, almost all of whom enthusiastically embrace the chance to enter into the mainstream American experience. (The possible exception being Puerto Ricans, who, by virtue of their peculiar ties to the United States, have been infected by the mindset of being an alienated and victimized minority.)

Admittedly the story of the present chapter of immigrant history is still unfolding. It is possible that some of those from the most radically different religio-cultural background—Muslims come most immediately to mind—will assertively and collectively dissent from the foundational beliefs of our constitutional order. But this is highly speculative. Muslims are still a relatively small immigrant group. Despite higher and much publicized claims to the contrary, there are probably no more than a million Muslim immigrants in America. And to the extent that there is an organized Muslim immigrant community, its leadership is determined to demonstrate that Muslims are good Americans. Witness the still nascent but eager Muslim efforts to develop "dialogue" relationships along the lines of the long-standing Jewish-Christian dialogues.

A serious problem is posed by the aliens among us, but it is not the problem perceived by those who are agitating an anti-immigration agenda. The aliens among us are not the recent immigrants but sectors of the population that have been here for a very long time and have, for many and complex reasons, become alienated from the American experiment. One thinks, for instance, of the urban and mainly black underclass that is dangerously marginalized from the opportunities and responsibilities of the societal mainstream. Their alienation is exacerbated and exploited by a civil rights overclass that persists in preaching the calumny that the American experiment is inherently and incorrigibly racist. It is far from clear that the civil rights leadership really wants black Americans to be full participants in the society. The political alliance between the civil rights establishment and the gay and lesbian movement, for example, seems designed to guarantee that many blacks will continue to think of themselves as marginal, for homosexuals who constitute no more than 2 or 3 percent of the population are the very definition of social marginality.

More influential than the exploited black underclass are the aliens among us who are entrenched in elite positions of cultural leadership, notably in the media, the arts, and academe. In the nineteenth century, the cultural elites had few doubts about their responsibility to "Americanize" the newcomers to these shores. That is not the case today. It is commonly proposed among journalists, writers, academics, and a significant portion of the religious leadership that to be Americanized, to be assimilated into this putatively unjust social order, is to be victimized. The multicultural fevers that have seized upon almost the entirety of the American academy reflect an explicit and rancorous rejection of the core beliefs and institutions of the civic nation and the cultural experience that undergirds it.

If there is "tinder-box material" in problems posed by immigration, the fault lies not with the new immigrants but with members of the "defining and founding" population who have turned themselves into aliens in their own land. There are, however, countervailing forces to those in the societal elites who have abdicated their responsibility to transmit to new Americans the promise and obligations of the citizenship to which they aspire. The Protestant Descendency has been largely a decline of the oldline denominations, and in recent decades it has been at least partially countered by the ascendency of a newly assertive evangelical Protestantism that will no longer accept its exclusion from defining how we conduct business in the public square. These "new" Protestants are really the old Protestants redivivus. They are, for instance, quite prepared to pick up the religio-cultural task implicit in the Puritan perception that this is a covenanted nation devoted to "self-evident truths" about humanity and moral duty.

And there are sixty million Catholics, composed mainly of the descendents of the great unwashed, for whom the American dream has been generally vindicated. Perhaps in a quest for social status, some Catholics have followed the Protestant definers and founders into the wilderness of alienation from the American experience. But the general Catholic pattern gives credence to John Courtney Murray's musings of forty years ago that the day would come when Catholics would have to pick up from oldline Protestants in providing moral and religious legitimation for what he called "the American proposition." Catholics, who bore the stigma and realized the promise of the immigrant experience, are not likely candidates for the new anti-immigration campaign that may now be underway.

Nobody should argue against a more rational control of the flow of immigration to this country. A country that loses control of its borders loses something of its sovereignty and self-respect. But more rational control need not mean reduced immigration. The problem of immigration is posed not by the aliens who are coming but by the aliens who are among us. Americans who understand and affirm our defining and founding moment can confidently welcome and assist the millions who will in the years ahead come to seek their piece of that moment's promise. This will only happen, however, if we recognize that the choice is not between our being a civic nation of disengaged individuals or an ethnic nation of group solidarity. The time is long past when America had the option of being an ethnic nation. The hope is to be a civic nation, a community of communities, held together by the shared affirmation of the original definers and founders that "We hold these truths." Given the generally sorry record of nations trying to cope with the challenge of unity in diversity, America has not done at all badly in the past, and keeping that in mind can help it do even better in the future.

# PART V

# SHOULD ENGLISH BE
# THE NATIONAL LANGUAGE?

# 15.

# One Nation,
# One Common Language

## Linda Chavez

L uis Granados was a bright 5-year-old who could read simple English before he entered kindergarten in Sun Valley, Calif. But soon after the school year began, his mother was told that he couldn't keep up. Yolanda Granados was bewildered. "He knows his alphabet,' she assured the teacher.

"You don't understand," the teacher explained. "The use of both Spanish and English in the classroom is confusing him."

Yolanda Granados was born in Mexico but speaks excellent English. Simply because Spanish is sometimes spoken in her household, however, the school district—without consulting her—put her son in bilingual classes. "I sent Luis to school to learn *English*," she declares.

When she tried to put her boy into regular classes, she was given the runaround. "Every time I went to the school," she says, "the principal gave me some excuse." Finally, Granados figured out a way to get around the principal, who has since left the school.

Each school year, she had to meet with Luis' teachers to say she wanted her son taught solely in English. They cooperated with her, but Luis was still officially classified as a bilingual student until he entered the sixth grade.

Unfortunately, the Granados family's experience has become common around the country. When bilingual education was being considered by Congress, it had a limited mission: to teach children of Mexican descent in Spanish while they learned English. Instead it has become an expensive behemoth, often with a far-reaching political agenda: to promote Spanish among Hispanic children, regardless of whether they speak English, regardless of their parents' wishes and even without their knowledge. For instance:

• In New Jersey last year, Hispanic children were being assigned to Spanish-speaking classrooms, the result of a state law that mandated bilingual instruction. Angry parents demanded freedom of choice. But when a bill to end the mandate was introduced in the Legislature, a group of 50 bilingual advocates testified against it at a state board of education meeting.

"Why would we require parents unfamiliar with our educational system to make such a monumental decision when we are trained to make those decisions?" asked Joseph Ramos, then co-chairman of the North Jersey Bilingual Council.

• The Los Angeles Unified School District educates some 265,000 Spanish-speaking children, more than any other in the nation. It advises teachers, in the words of the district's *Bilingual Methodology Study Guide,* "not to encourage minority parents to switch to English in the home, but to encourage them to strongly promote development of the primary language." Incredibly, the guide also declares that "excessive use of English in bilingual classrooms tends to lower students' achievement in English."

• In Denver, 2,500 students from countries such as Russia and Vietnam learn grammar, vocabulary, and pronunciation in ESL (English as a Second Language). An English "immersion" program, ESL is the principal alternative to bilingual education. Within a few months, most ESL kids are taking mathematics, science, and social studies classes in English.

But the 11,000 Hispanic children in Denver public schools don't have the choice to participate in ESL full time. Instead, for their first few years they are taught most of the day in Spanish and are introduced only gradually to English. Jo Thomas, head of the bilingual ESL education program for the Denver public schools, estimates these kids will ultimately spend on average five to seven years in its bilingual program.

## ACTIVIST TAKEOVER

Bilingual education began in the late 1960s as a small, $7.5-million federal program for Mexican-American children, half of whom could not speak English when they entered first grade. The idea was to teach them in Spanish for a short period, until they got up to speed in their new language.

Sen. Ralph Yarborough (D-Tex.), a leading sponsor of the first federal bilingual law in 1968, explained that its intent was "to make children fully literate in English." Yarborough assured Congress that the purpose was "not to make the mother tongue dominant."

Unfortunately, bilingual-education policy soon fell under the sway of political activists demanding recognition of the "group rights" of cultural and linguistic minorities. By the late 1970s the federal civil-rights office was insisting that school districts offer bilingual education to Hispanic and other "language minority" students or face a cutoff of federal funds.

Most states followed suit, adopting bilingual mandates either by law or by bureaucratic edict. The result is that, nationally, most first-grade students from Spanish-speaking homes are taught to read and write in Spanish.

The purpose in many cases is no longer to bring immigrant children into the mainstream of American life. Some advocates see bilingual education as the first step in a radical transformation of the United States into a nation without one common language or fixed borders.

Spanish "should no longer be regarded as a 'foreign' language," according to Josué González, director of bilingual education in the Carter Administration and now a professor at Columbia University Teachers College. Instead, he writes in *Reinventing Urban Education,* Spanish should be "a second national language."

Others have even more extreme views. At the February 1995 annual conference of the National Association for Bilingual Education (a leading lobbying group for supporters of bilingual education) in Phoenix, several speakers challenged the idea of U.S. sovereignty and promoted the notion that the Southwest and northern Mexico form one cultural region, which they dub *La Frontera.*

Eugene Garcia, head of bilingual education at the U.S. Department of Education, declared to thunderous applause that "the border for many is nonexistent. For me, for intellectual reasons, that border shall be nonexistent." His statement might surprise President Clinton, who appointed Garcia and has vowed to beef up border protection to stem the flow of illegal aliens into the United States.

## "I WAS FURIOUS"

Bilingual education has grown tremendously from its modest start. Currently, some 2.4 million children are eligible for bilingual or ESL classes, with bilingual education alone costing over $5.5 billion. New York City, for instance, spends $400 million annually on its 147,500 bilingual students—$2,712 per pupil.

A great deal of this money is being wasted. "We don't even speak Spanish at home," says Miguel Alvarado of Sun Valley, Calif., yet his 8-year-old daughter, Emily, was put in a bilingual class. Alvarado concludes that this was done simply because he is bilingual.

When my son Pablo entered school in the District of Columbia, I received a letter notifying me that he would be placed in a bilingual program—even though Pablo didn't speak a word of Spanish, since I grew up not speaking it either. (My family has lived in what is now New Mexico since 1609.) I was able to decline the program without much trouble, but other Hispanic parents aren't always so fortunate.

When Rita Montero's son, Camilo, grew bored by the slow academic pace of his first-grade bilingual class in Denver, she requested a transfer. "The kids were doing work way below the regular grade level," says Montero. "I was furious." Officials argued they were under court order to place him in a bilingual class.

In fact, she was entitled to sign a waiver, but no one she met at school informed her of this. Ultimately she enrolled Camilo in a magnet school across town. Says Montero, "Only through determination and anger did I get my son in the classroom where he belonged." Most parents—especially immigrants— aren't so lucky. They're intimidated by the system, and their kids are stuck.

Most school districts with large Hispanic populations require parents with Spanish surnames to fill out a "home-language survey." If parents report that Spanish is used in the home, even occasionally, the school may place the child in bilingual classes. Unbeknownst to the parents, a Spanish-speaking grandparent living with the family may be enough to trigger placement, even if the grandchild speaks little or no Spanish.

Though parents are supposed to be able to opt out, bureaucrats have a vested interest in discouraging them, since the school will lose government funds. In some districts, funding for bilingual education exceeds that of mainstream classes by 20 percent or more. New York state, for example, doesn't allow Hispanic students to exit the bilingual program until they score above the 40th percentile on a standardized English test.

"There is a Catch-22, operating here," says Christine Rossell, a professor of political science at Boston University. She explains that such testing guarantees enrollment in the program, for "by definition, 40 percent of all students who take any standardized test will score at or below the 40th percentile."

## FAMILY'S BUSINESS

Bilingual programs are also wasted on children who do need help learning English. Studies often confirm what common sense would tell you: The less time you spend speaking a new language, the more slowly you'll learn it.

In 1994 bilingual and ESL programs in New York City were compared. Results: 92 percent of Korean, 87 percent of Russian, and 83 percent of Chinese children who started intensive ESL classes in kindergarten had made it into mainstream classes in three years or less. Of the Hispanic students in bilingual classes, only half made it to mainstream classes within three years. "How can anyone learn English in school when they speak Spanish four hours a day?" asks Gail Fiber, an elementary school teacher in Southern California. "In more than seven years' experience with bilingual education, I've never seen it done successfully."

Rosalie Pedalino Porter, former director of bilingual education in Newton, Mass., and now with the Institute for Research in English Acquisition and Development, reached a similar conclusion. "I felt that I was deliberately holding back the learning of English," she writes in her eloquent critique, *Forked Tongue: The Politics of Bilingual Education.*

Native-language instruction is not even necessary to academic performance, according to Boston University's Rossell. "Ninety-one percent of scientifically valid studies show bilingual education to be no better—or actually worse—than doing nothing." In other words, students who are allowed to sink or swim in all-English classes are actually better off than bilingual students.

The overwhelming majority of immigrants believe that it is a family's duty—not the school's—to help children maintain the native language. "If parents had an option," says Lila Ramirez, vice president of the Burbank, Calif.,

Human Relations Council, "they'd prefer all-English to all-Spanish." When a U.S. Department of Education survey asked Mexican and Cuban parents what they wanted, four-fifths declared their opposition to teaching children in their native language if it meant less time devoted to English.

## SENSE OF UNITY

It's time for federal and state legislators to overhaul this misbegotten program. The best policy for children—and for the country—is to teach English to immigrant children as quickly as possible. American-born Hispanics, who now make up more than half of all bilingual students, should be taught in English.

Bilingual education probably would end swiftly if more people knew about the November 1994 meeting of the Texas Association for Bilingual Education, in Austin. Both Mexican and U.S. flags adorned the stage at this gathering, and the attendees—mainly Texas teachers and administrators—stood as the national anthems of both countries were sung.

At least one educator present found the episode dismaying. "I stood, out of respect, when the Mexican anthem was played," says Odilia Leal, bilingual coordinator for the Temple Independent School District. "But I think we should just sing the U.S. anthem. My father, who was born in Mexico, taught me that the United States, not Mexico, is my country."

With 20 million immigrants now living in our country, it's more important than ever to teach newcomers to think of themselves as Americans if we hope to remain one people, not simply a conglomeration of different groups. And one of the most effective ways of forging that sense of unity is through a common language.

# 16.

# "English Only"

## ACLU Briefing Paper

From its inception, the United States has been a multilingual nation. At the time of the nation's founding, it was commonplace to hear as many as 20 languages spoken in daily life, including Dutch, French, German, and numerous Native American languages. Even the Articles of Confederation were printed in German, as well as English. During the 19th and early 20th centuries, the nation's linguistic diversity grew as successive waves of Europeans immigrated to these shores and U.S. territory expanded to include Puerto Rico, Hawaii, and the Philippines.

Just as languages other than English have always been a part of our history and culture, debate over establishing a national language dates back to the country's beginnings. John Adams proposed to the Continental Congress in 1780 that an official academy be created to "purify, develop, and dictate usage of," English. His proposal was rejected as undemocratic and a threat to individual liberty.

Nonetheless, restrictive language laws have been enacted periodically since the late 19th century, usually in response to new waves of immigration. These laws, in practice if not in intent, have punished immigrants for their foreignness and violated their rights.

In the early 1980s, again during a period of concern about new immigration, a movement arose that seeks the establishment of English as the nation's official language. The "English Only" movement promotes the enactment of legislation that restricts or prohibits the use of languages other than English by government agencies and, in some cases, by private businesses. The movement has met with some success, "English Only" laws having been passed in several states. And, for the first time in the nation's history, an English Language Amendment to the Constitution has been proposed.

The ACLU opposes "English Only" laws because they can abridge the rights

---

Courtesy of the American Civil Liberties Union (1990).

of individuals who are not proficient in English, and because they perpetuate false stereotypes of immigrants and non-English speakers. We believe, further, that such laws are contrary to the spirit of tolerance and diversity embodied in our Constitution. An English Language Amendment to the Constitution would transform that document from being a charter of liberties and individual freedom into a charter of restrictions that limits, rather than protects, individual rights.

Here are the ACLU's answers to some questions frequently asked by the public about "English Only" issues.

## What is an "English Only" law?

"English Only" laws vary. Some state statues simply declare English as the "official" language of the state. Other state and local edicts limit or bar government's provision of non-English language assistance and services. For example, some restrict bilingual education programs, prohibit multilingual ballots, or forbid non-English government services in general—including such services as courtroom translation or multilingual emergency police lines.

## Where have such laws been enacted?

Sixteen states have "English Only" laws, and many others are considering such laws. In some states, the laws were passed decades ago during upsurges of nativism, but most were passed within the last few years. The "English Only" states are Arizona, Arkansas, California, Colorado, Florida, Georgia, Illinois, Indiana, Kentucky, Mississippi, Nebraska, North Carolina, North Dakota, South Carolina, Tennessee, and Virginia.

## What are the consequences of "English Only" laws?

Some versions of the proposed English Language Amendment would void almost all state and federal laws that require the government to provide services in languages other than English. The services affected would include: health, education, and social welfare services; job training and translation assistance to crime victims and witnesses in court and administrative proceedings; voting assistance and ballots; drivers' licensing exams, and AIDS-prevention education.

Passage of an "English Only" ordinance by Florida's Dade County in 1980, barring public funding of activities that involved the use of languages other than English, resulted in the cancellation of all multicultural events and bilingual services, ranging from directional signs in the public transit system to medical services at the county hospital.

Where basic human needs are met by bilingual or multilingual services, the consequences of eliminating those services could be dire. For example, the

*Washington Times* reported in 1987 that a 911 emergency dispatcher was able to save the life of a Salvadoran woman's baby son, who had stopped breathing, by coaching the mother in Spanish over the telephone to administer mouth-to-mouth and cardiopulmonary resuscitation until the paramedics arrived.

## Do "English Only" laws affect only government services and programs?

"English Only" laws apply primarily to government programs. However, such laws can also affect private businesses. For example, several Southern California cities have passed ordinances that forbid or restrict the use of foreign languages on private business signs.

Some "English Only" advocates have opposed a telephone company's use of multilingual operators and multilingual directories, Federal Communications Commission licensing of Spanish-language radio stations, and bilingual menus at fast food restaurants.

## Who is affected by "English Only" laws?

"English Only" campaigns target primarily Latinos and Asians, who make up the majority of recent immigrants. Most language minority residents are Spanish-speaking, a result of the sharp rise in immigration from Latin America during the mid-1960s.

While the overwhelming majority of U.S. residents—96 percent—are fluent in English, approximately ten million residents are not fluent, according to the most recent census.

## How do "English Only" laws deprive people of their rights?

The ACLU believes that "English Only" laws are inconsistent with the Equal Protection Clause of the Fourteenth Amendment. For example, laws that have the effect of eliminating courtroom translation severely jeopardize the ability of people on trial to follow and comprehend the proceedings. "English Only" laws interfere with the right to vote by banning bilingual ballots, or with a child's right to education by restricting bilingual instruction. Such laws also interfere with the right of workers to be free of discrimination in workplaces where employers have imposed "speak English only" rules.

In 1987, the ACLU adopted a national policy opposing "English Only" laws or laws that would "characterize English as the official language in the United States . . . to the extent that [they] would mandate or encourage the erosion" of the rights of language minority persons.

## What kinds of language policies were adopted with regard to past generations of immigrants?

Our nation was tolerant of linguistic diversity up until the late 1800s, when an influx of Eastern and Southern Europeans, as well as Asians, aroused nativist sentiments and prompted the enactment of restrictive language laws. A 1911 Federal Immigration Commission report falsely argued that the "old" Scandinavian and German immigrants had  assimilated quickly, while the "new" Italian and Eastern European immigrants were inferior to their predecessors, less willing to learn English, and more prone to political subversion.

In order to "Americanize" the immigrants and exclude people thought to be of the lower classes and undesirable, English literacy requirements were established for public employment, naturalization, immigration, and suffrage. The New York State Constitution was amended to disfranchise over one million Yiddish-speaking citizens. The California Constitution was similarly amended to disfranchise Chinese, who were seen as a threat to the "purity of the ballot box."

Ironically, during the same period, the government sought to "Americanize" Native American Indian children by taking them from their families and forcing them to attend English-language boarding schools, where they were punished for speaking their indigenous languages.

The intense anti-German sentiment that accompanied the outbreak of World War I prompted several states, where bilingual schools had been commonplace, to enact extreme language laws. For example, Nebraska passed a law in 1919 prohibiting the use of any other language than English through the eighth grade. The Supreme Court subsequently declared the law an unconstitutional violation of due process.

Today, as in the past, "English Only" laws in the U.S. are founded on false stereotypes of immigrant groups. Such laws do not simply disparage the immigrants' native languages but assault the rights of the people who speak the languages.

## Why are bilingual ballots needed since citizenship is required to vote, English literacy is required for citizenship, and political campaigns are largely conducted in English?

Naturalization for U.S. citizenship does not require English literacy for people over 50, and/or who have been in the U.S. for 20 years or more. Thus, there are many elderly immigrant citizens whose ability to read English is limited, and who cannot exercise their right to vote without bilingual ballots and other voter materials. Moreover, bilingual campaign materials and ballots foster a better informed electorate by increasing the information available to people who lack English proficiency.

### Doesn't bilingual education slow immigrant children's learning of English, in contrast to the "sink or swim" method used in the past?

The primary purpose of bilingual programs in elementary and secondary schools, which use both English and a child's native language to teach all subjects, is to develop proficiency in English and, thus, facilitate the child's transition to all-English instruction. Although debate about this approach continues, the latest studies show that bilingual education definitely enhances a child's ability to acquire the second language. Some studies even show that the more extensive the native language instruction, the better students perform all around, and that the bilingual method engenders a positive self-image and self-respect by validating the child's native language and culture.

The "sink or swim" experience of past immigrants left more of them underwater than not. In 1911, the U.S. Immigration Service found that 77 percent of Italian, 60 percent of Russian, and 51 percent of German immigrant children were one or more grade levels behind in school compared to 28 percent of American-born white children. Moreover, those immigrants who did manage to "swim" unaided in the past, when agricultural and factory jobs were plentiful, might not do so well in today's "high-tech" economy, with its more rigorous educational requirements.

### But won't "English Only" laws speed up the assimilation of today's immigrants into our society and prevent their isolation?

In fact, contrary to what "English Only" advocates assume, the vast majority of today's Asian and Latino immigrants are acquiring English proficiency and assimilating as fast as did earlier generations of Italian, Russian, and German immigrants. For example, research studies show that over 95 percent of first generation Mexican Americans are English proficient, and that more than 50 percent of second generation Mexican Americans have lost their native tongue entirely.

In addition, census data reveal that nearly 90 percent of Latinos five years old or older speak English in their households. And 98 percent of Latinos surveyed said they felt it is "essential" that their children learn to read and write English "perfectly." Unfortunately, not enough educational resources are available for immigrants—over 40,000 are on the waiting list for over-enrolled adult English classes in Los Angeles. "English Only" laws do not increase resources to meet these needs.

The best insurance against social isolation of those who immigrate to our nation is acceptance—and celebration—of the differences that exist within our ethnically diverse citizenry. The bond that unites our nation is not linguistic or ethnic homogeneity but a shared commitment to democracy, liberty, and equality.

# 17.

# The Importance of Learning English: A National Survey of Hispanic Parents

## Center for Equal Opportunity

## INTRODUCTION

by Linda Chavez, President, Center for Equal Opportunity

One of the biggest challenges schools now face is educating a large and grow-ing population of children who cannot speak English. The Department of Education estimates that some 2.4 million children, nearly three-quarters of whom are Hispanic, have limited proficiency in English. For more than two decades, fed-eral policy has encouraged programs to teach these children in their native lan-guage for some or most of their academic subjects. According to a recent study by the American Legislative Exchange Council, 60 percent of state and locally funded programs for students with limited English proficiency are bilingual education programs which use the child's native language for at least part of the instruction.[1] Indeed, many prominent bilingual education advocates claim that learning to read first in the native tongue is necessary to develop optimal reading ability in the sec-ond language.[2] In practice, this often means that limited-English-proficient chil-dren will be kept in bilingual education programs for years. One recent study of New York City schools found that only about half of children who entered bilin-gual programs in kindergarten graduated into regular classes within three years, and only 22 percent of children who began such programs in second grade did so.[3]

Most methodologically sound studies of bilingual education, however, show that teaching a child in his or her native language is largely ineffective. The most comprehensive analysis of the academic literature on this subject, conducted by Christine Rossell and Keith Baker, shows that native language instruction is no

This survey was conducted by Market Development Inc., with analysis by Diversified Research Inc. Reprinted by permission of the Center for Equal Opportunity, which com-missioned this survey.

better than, or actually worse than, doing nothing at all for limited-English-proficient children. In place of bilingual education, Rossell recommends, "all-English instruction holds the least risk and usually the greatest benefit for limited-English-proficient children."[4]

But beyond the debate over the efficacy of bilingual education is the question of what parents of limited-English-proficient children really want for their own children. This question has been largely ignored in the research on bilingual education. As a practical matter, this issue primarily concerns Hispanic parents, who make up the overwhelming majority of children in bilingual programs. To date, only two national surveys of parents of limited-English-proficient children have been undertaken: a study by the Educational Testing Service for the U.S. Department of Education in 1988; and an opinion of of Hispanics on a variety of public policy topics, "The Latino National Political Survey," in 1992.[5] The former showed that the overwhelming majority of Hispanic parents—78 percent of Mexican Americans and 82 percent of Cubans—opposed teaching their children in Spanish if it meant less time for teaching English. Although the Latino National Political Survey showed strong support for bilingual education, less than 10 percent of respondents thought that the purpose of bilingual education was to maintain Spanish language and culture.[6]

The Center for Equal Opportunity commissioned the following survey of Hispanic parents in an effort to discern what they want their children to learn in school. The survey was conducted by Market Development Inc., a California-based polling firm that specializes in the Hispanic market. Survey results were analyzed by Diversified Research Inc., a national survey research firm based in New York.

The Center for Equal Opportunity is a non-partisan research institution, which studies the issues of race, ethnicity, and assimilation. This survey is part of an ongoing project on bilingual education.

## NOTES

1. American Legislative Exchange Council Foundation and U.S. English, "Bilingual Education in the United States 1991–1992; Special Supplement; The Report Card on American Education" (Washington, D.C.: 1994)

2. See Stephen Krashen and Douglas Biber, *On Course: Bilingual Education in California* (Sacramento: California Association for Bilingual Education, 1988); and Kenji Hakuta, *Mirror of Language: The Debate on Bilingualism* (New York: Basic Books, 1986).

3. New York City Board of Education, "Educational Progress of Students in Bilingual and English as a Second Language Programs: A Longitudinal Study, 1990–1994."

4. Christine H. Rossell and Keith Baker, *Bilingual Education in Massachusetts: The Emperor Has No Clothes* (Boston: Pioneer Institute, 1996).

5. Joan Baratz-Snowden, et al., "Parent Preference Study" (Princeton, N.J.: Educational Testing Service, 1988); Rudolfo O. de la Garza, et al., *Latino Voices: Mexican, Puerto Rican, and Cuban Perspectives on American Politics* (Boulder, Colo.: Westview Press, 1992).

6. Baratz-Snowden, 54; de la Garza, 99.

# EXECUTIVE SUMMARY

by Michael LaVelle, President, Diversified Research Inc.

This analysis summarizes the results of a survey of Hispanic parents of school-age children, conducted by Market Development Inc., on behalf of the Center for Equal Opportunity, during July–August 1996. The purpose of the survey was to document the experience of Hispanic parents with school programs designed for children needing help with English, and to ascertain Hispanic parents' attitudes regarding the goals and practices of such programs. Because Hispanics account for the majority of the clientele of U.S. school programs for children needing help with English, the present study should be of more than academic interest. In fact, the results of the survey have clear and important implications from a social policy planning viewpoint.

## Methodology

In all, 600 interviews were completed with Hispanic parents, each with one or more children currently in school (first grade through high school). Respondent selection occurred within five metropolitan areas in which Hispanics are relatively heavily concentrated, viz., Los Angeles, New York, Miami, San Antonio, and Houston. Questionnaires were administered via telephone, by professionally trained, bilingual interviewers calling from a central data collection facility located in San Diego, Calif. The results of a survey of 600 randomly selected respondents is statistically accurate to within plus or minus 4 percent at the 95 percent confidence level. This means that 95 times out of 100, the results will fall within a range of plus or minus 4 percentage points of the results one would obtain from interviewing the entire population from which the sample was drawn.

In addition to the substantive questions related to the goals and practices of school programs for children needing help with English, survey respondents were also asked a series of socio-demographic background questions. This allows the sample to be segmented for analysis purposes. For example, variations in responses can be systematically analyzed for patterns of similarity or difference based on age, gender, educational level, ethnicity, geographical region, length of time in the U.S., language spoken, etc.

## Summary of Results

Respondents were read, in random order, a list of five educational goals and asked to rank them by indicating which they considered to be most important, which second most important, etc. The five educational goals, listed in order of importance, as ranked by Hispanic parents, are as follows:

|  | Percentage of Hispanic Parents Ranking Each Goal: | |
| --- | --- | --- |
|  | **Most Important** | **Second Most Important** |
| Learning to read, write, and speak English | 51.0% | 18.8% |
| Learning academic subjects like math, history, science | 23.3% | 30.7% |
| Learning to read, write, and speak Spanish | 11.0% | 25.5% |
| Learning about Hispanic culture | 4.3% | 8.5% |
| Learning extras like music, arts, and sports | 3.7% | 8.8% |

As the table shows, the majority of Hispanic parents (51%) considered *learning to read, write, and speak English* to be most important among the five educational goals presented. Learning English was judged to be much more important than *learning other academic subjects, including math, history, and science* (23.3%). This, in and of itself, attests to the importance Hispanic parents place on learning English. Perhaps most telling, however, is the relative importance of learning English versus learning Spanish. Only 11 percent of all respondents designated *learning to read, write, and speak Spanish* as the most important goal, distantly followed by only 4.3 percent who think the top priority should be *learning about Hispanic culture.*

The greater priority placed on learning English versus learning Spanish occurred consistently across all major subgroupings of the sample population. **All** were more likely to rank learning English as a more important goal than learning Spanish: respondents in all five metropolitan areas, regardless of ethnic background; regardless of educational level; regardless of whether they currently, formerly, or never have had a child in a language program. Females were slightly more likely to prefer English than were males.

Since all interviewers were bilingual, respondents had the option of being interviewed in either English or Spanish. Interestingly, those interviewed in Spanish were actually more likely to rank learning English as most important (52.2%) than those interviewed in English (45.1%). This does not mean however that those interviewed in English were more likely to think that learning Spanish should be the top priority. In fact, only 4.9 percent of those interviewed in English ranked learning Spanish as the most important goal. Those interviewed in English were found to be relatively likely to place great importance on *learning other academic subjects like math, history, and science* (44.1 percent of those interviewed in English ranked this as the most important goal).

The relatively higher rankings attached to learning English versus learning Spanish provide strong evidence regarding the educational priorities of Hispanic parents. Another question on the survey addressed the issue not in terms of which is more important, but rather which should come first. The exact wording follows:

**In your opinion, should children of Hispanic background, living in the United States, be taught to read and write Spanish before they are taught English, or should they be taught English as soon as possible?**

|  | Percent |
|---|---|
| Spanish before English | 16.7% |
| English as soon as possible | 63.0% |
| Same time (volunteered) | 17.3% |
| Not sure | 3.0% |

Once again, the results are clear-cut. Hispanic parents are decisively more likely to prefer that their children be taught English as soon as possible, rather than postponing English instruction while they are being taught Spanish. Although there are variations in intensity, the pattern is broad-based with all sub-groupings of the sample in agreement on this issue. For example, among those interviewed in English, 81.4 percent favor teaching English as soon as possible. Among those interviewed in Spanish, a smaller but still significant majority (59.2%) choose this option (only 18.3 percent of those interviewed in Spanish would prefer that children learn Spanish first).

Intensity on this issue varies directly with educational level. The higher the educational level of the respondent, the more likely it is that he or she will prefer that English be taught as soon as possible. A similar pattern prevails with respect to the length of time respondents have lived in the United States. The longer they have been here, the more likely they are to favor English being taught as soon as possible. Cuban-Hispanics are especially adamant on this issue (70 percent want English as soon as possible).

A final question addressed the issue of how language instruction should interface with academic course instruction. The question was:

| In general, which of the following comes closest to your opinion? | Percent |
|---|---|
| 1. My child should be taught his/her academic courses in Spanish, even if it means he/she will spend less time learning English | 12.2% |
| 2. My child should be taught his/her academic courses in English, because he/she will spend more time learning English | 81.3% |
| 3. Unsure | 6.5% |

The overwhelming majority of Hispanic parents want their children's academic courses to be taught in English. This is true among all subcategories of the sample. Groups whose members are relatively most likely to insist on English include Cubans, in general, those in the United States the longest and those with the highest levels of education. Most interestingly, 82 percent of those with a child currently in a school program for children needing help with English would prefer that their children be taught in English.

In summary, this survey of Hispanic parents unequivocally shows that Hispanic parents place a nigher priority on their children learning English over learning Spanish; that they want their children to learn English first, that is, before they are taught to read, write, and speak Spanish. They want to reinforce their children's English skills and their children to be taught their academic courses in English rather than in Spanish. Furthermore, these finding are broad-based—all subgroupings of the sample population share these opinions.

This having been said, the findings of this survey do not in any way suggest that Hispanic parents do not want their children to learn Spanish. It only addresses the perceived relative importance of English versus Spanish, with English being considered the more important life skill for Hispanic children living in the United States.

The implications of these findings from a social policy planning viewpoint should be obvious. Hispanic parents may want their children to learn Spanish language skills, and to learn about Spanish culture, but they certainly do not want this to occur at the expense of learning to read, write, and speak English or before they learn these skills. School programs that provide Hispanic children with help in English should be designed with the findings of this study in mind.

### What Do Hispanic Parents Think Is Most Important?

Percentage of Hispanic Parents Ranking Each Goal:
Most Important

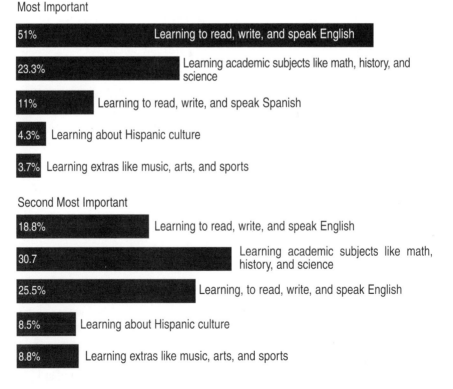

51%    Learning to read, write, and speak English

23.3%    Learning academic subjects like math, history, and science

11%    Learning to read, write, and speak Spanish

4.3%    Learning about Hispanic culture

3.7%    Learning extras like music, arts, and sports

Second Most Important

18.8%    Learning to read, write, and speak English

30.7    Learning academic subjects like math, history, and science

25.5%    Learning, to read, write, and speak English

8.5%    Learning about Hispanic culture

8.8%    Learning extras like music, arts, and sports

## How Soon Should Hispanic Children Be Taught English?

In your opinion, should children of Hispanic background, living in the United States, be taught to read and write Spanish before they are taught English, or should they be taught English as soon as possible?

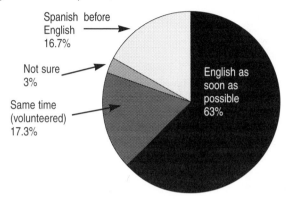

Spanish before English 16.7%

Not sure 3%

Same time (volunteered) 17.3%

English as soon as possible 63%

Percentage of parents who think Hispanic children should be taught English as soon as possible:

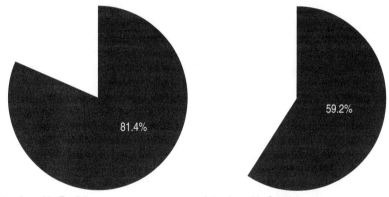
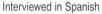

81.4%

59.2%

Interviewed in English

Interviewed in Spanish

Percentage of parents who think Hispanic children should be taught to read and write Spanish before they are taught English:

8.8%

18.3%

Interviewed in English

Interviewed in Spanish

## Should Academic Courses Be Taught in English or Spanish?

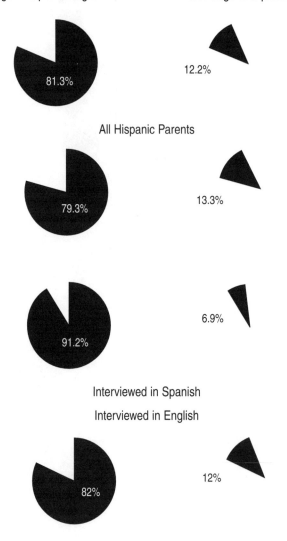

Percentage who prefer English:          Percentage who prefer Spanish:

81.3%                                    12.2%

All Hispanic Parents

79.3%                                    13.3%

91.2%                                    6.9%

Interviewed in Spanish

Interviewed in English

82%                                      12%

Currently with Children in program for those who need help in English

## Questionnaire

Question 1. How many school-age (first grade through high school) children do you have, who are living at home?

| | | |
|---|---|---|
| One | 38.7% | (232) |
| Two | 36.5% | (219) |
| Three | 17.2% | (103) |
| Four or more | 7.7% | (46) |
| Total responses | | (600) |

Question 2. Would you prefer that this interview be conducted in English or Spanish?

| | | |
|---|---|---|
| English | 17.0% | (102) |
| Spanish | 83.0% | (498) |
| Total responses | | (600) |

Question 3. Is your child (are any of your children) currently in, or ever been in, a program in school for children who need help with English?

| | | |
|---|---|---|
| Currently in | 8.3% | (50) |
| In past/not now | 7.2% | (43) |
| Never been in | 81.5% | (489) |
| Don't know | 3.0% | (18) |
| Total responses | | (600) |

Question 4. Was your child (were any of your children) ever asked to be in such a program?

| | | |
|---|---|---|
| Yes | 12.0% | (61) |
| No | 80.1% | (406) |
| Don't know | 7.9% | (40) |
| Total responses | | (507) |

Question 5. In what grade is your oldest child who is currently in such a program?

| | | |
|---|---|---|
| First | 10.0% | (5) |
| Second | 12.0% | (6) |
| Third | 8.0% | (4) |
| Fourth | 8.0% | (4) |
| Fifth | 10.0% | (5) |
| Sixth | 10.0% | (5) |
| Seventh | 8.0% | (4) |
| Eighth | 4.0% | (2) |
| Ninth | 8.0% | (4) |
| Tenth | 16.0% | (8) |
| Eleventh | 2.0% | (1) |
| Twelfth | 2.0% | (1) |
| Refused to answer | 2.0% | (1) |
| Total response | | (50) |

Question 6.  How many years ago was your child last in such a program?

| | | |
|---|---|---|
| One | 37.2% | (16) |
| Two | 11.6% | (5) |
| Three | 9.3% | (4) |
| Four | 9.3% | (4) |
| Five | 9.3% | (4) |
| Six or more | 18.6% | (8) |
| Don't know/refused to answer | 4.7% | (2) |
| Total responses | | (43) |

Question 7.  How many years has your child been in (was your child in) the program?

| | | |
|---|---|---|
| One | 30.1% | (28) |
| Two | 22.6% | (21) |
| Three | 21.5% | (20) |
| Four | 9.7% | (9) |
| Five | 5.4% | (5) |
| Six or more | 4.3% | (4) |
| Refused to answer | 6.5% | (6) |
| Total responses | | (93) |

Question 8.  Was your child in the program a boy or a girl?

| | | |
|---|---|---|
| Boy | 52.7% | (49) |
| Girl | 47.3% | (44) |
| Total responses | | (93) |

Question 9.  Was your child in the program born in the United States?

| | | |
|---|---|---|
| Yes | 45.2% | (42) |
| No | 54.8% | (51) |
| Total responses | | (93) |

Question 10.  At what age did your child come to the United States?

| | | |
|---|---|---|
| One | 13.7% | (7) |
| Two | 3.9% | (2) |
| Three | 11.8% | (6) |
| Four | 2.0% | (1) |
| Five | 2.0% | (1) |
| Six | 11.8% | (6) |
| Seven | 9.8% | (5) |
| Eight | 5.9% | (3) |
| Nine | 7.8% | (4) |
| Ten | 3.9% | (2) |
| Eleven | 2.0% | (1) |
| Twelve | 3.9% | (2) |
| Thirteen | 7.8% | (4) |
| Fourteen | 5.9% | (3) |
| Fifteen | 5.9% | (3) |
| Sixteen | 2.0% | (1) |
| Total responses | | (51) |

Question 11. When your child first entered the program, did he or she speak English?

| | | |
|---|---|---|
| Yes | 12.9% | (12) |
| No | 79.6% | (74) |
| Some | 7.5% | (7) |
| Total responses | | (93) |

Question 12. While in the program, how many of your child's lessons were taught in Spanish? Would you say most of the lessons were in Spanish, about half the lessons were in Spanish, only a small part of the lessons were in Spanish, or none of the lessons was in Spanish?

| | | |
|---|---|---|
| Most in Spanish | 26.9% | (25) |
| About half | 29.0% | (27) |
| Small part | 22.6% | (21) |
| No Spanish | 9.7% | (9) |
| Don't know/refused | 11.8% | (11) |
| Total responses | | (93) |

Question 13. Please rank the following things children might learn in school in order of importance:

*"learning to read, write, and speak English"*

| | | |
|---|---|---|
| (1) Most | 51.0% | (306) |
| (2) Second | 18.8% | (113) |
| (3) Third | 7.0% | (42) |
| (4) Fourth | 6.0% | (36) |
| (5) Least | 9.2% | (55) |
| Don't know/refused to answer | 8.0% | (48) |
| Total responses | | (600) |

*"learning to read, write, and speak Spanish"*

| | | |
|---|---|---|
| (1) Most | 11.0% | (66) |
| (2) Second | 25.5% | (153) |
| (3) Third | 21.8% | (131) |
| (4) Fourth | 16.8% | (101) |
| (5) Least | 15.7% | (94) |
| Don't know/refused to answer | 9.2% | (55) |
| Total responses | | (600) |

*"learning academic subjects, like math, history, science"*

| | | |
|---|---|---|
| (1) Most | 23.3% | (140) |
| (2) Second | 30.7% | (184) |
| (3) Third | 25.0% | (150) |
| (4) Fourth | 10.0% | (60) |
| (5) Least | 3.2% | (19) |
| Don't know/refused to answer | 7.8% | (47) |
| Total responses | | (600) |

*"learning about Hispanic culture"*

| | | |
|---|---|---|
| (1) Most | 4.3% | (26) |
| (2) Second | 8.5% | (51) |
| (3) Third | 19.7% | (118) |
| (4) Fourth | 36.8% | (221) |
| (5) Least | 22.2% | (133) |
| Don't know/refused to answer | 8.5% | (51) |
| Total responses | | (600) |

*"learning extras like music, art, and sports"*

| | | |
|---|---|---|
| (1) Most | 3.7% | (22) |
| (2) Second | 8.8% | (53) |
| (3) Third | 18.5% | (111) |
| (4) Fourth | 21.2% | (127) |
| (5) Least | 39.8% | (239) |
| Don't know/refused to answer | 8.0% | (48) |
| Total responses | | (600) |

Question 14. In your opinion, should children of Hispanic background, living in the United States, be taught to read and write Spanish before they are taught English, or should they be taught English as soon as possible?

| | | |
|---|---|---|
| Spanish before English | 16.7% | (100) |
| English soon/possible | 63.0% | (378) |
| Same time | 17.3% | (104) |
| Don't know/refused to answer | 3.0% | (18) |
| Total responses | | (600) |

Question 15. In general, which of the following comes closest to your opinion?
1. My child should be taught his/her academic courses in Spanish, even if it means he/she will spend less time learning English
2. My child should be taught his/her academic courses in English, because he/she will spend more time learning English

| | | |
|---|---|---|
| Spanish | 12.2% | (73) |
| English | 81.3% | (488) |
| Don't know/refused to answer | 6.5% | (39) |
| Total responses | | (600) |

Question 16. How many years of formal education have you had?

| | | |
|---|---|---|
| Some grade school | 10.3% | (62) |
| Finish grade school | 12.5% | (75) |
| Some high school | 22.8% | (137) |
| Finish high school | 21.8% | (131) |
| Commercial/tech | 3.5% | (21) |
| Some college | 11.8% | (71) |
| Finished college | 12.5% | (75) |
| Graduate studies | 3.0% | (18) |
| No school | 1.0% | (6) |
| Refused to answer | 0.7% | (4) |
| Total responses | | (600) |

Question 17.  What is your age?

| | | |
|---|---|---|
| 18–25 | 3.5% | (21) |
| 26–40 | 57.5% | (345) |
| 41–54 | 31.5% | (189) |
| 55–64 | 4.2% | (25) |
| 65 or older | 1.3% | (8) |
| Refused to answer | 2.0% | (12) |
| Total responses | | (600) |

Question 18.  What is your origin of descent?

| | | |
|---|---|---|
| United States | 11.0% | (66) |
| Mexico | 47.8% | (287) |
| Cuba | 8.3% | (50) |
| Puerto Rico | 6.8% | (41) |
| Dominican Republic | 4.2% | (25) |
| Spain | 0.8% | (5) |
| Other Central America | 10.5% | (63) |
| South America | 9.3% | (56) |
| Other | 0.3% | (2) |
| Refused to answer | 0.8% | (5) |
| Total responses | | (600) |

Question 19. How many years have you lived in the United States?

| | | |
|---|---|---|
| 10 years or less | 24.2% | (145) |
| 11–20 years | 31.3% | (188) |
| More than 20 | 22.2% | (133) |
| All my life | 20.5% | (123) |
| Refused to answer | 1.8% | (11) |
| Total responses | | (600) |

Question 20. Gender:

| | | |
|---|---|---|
| Male | 31.7% | (190) |
| Female | 68.3% | (410) |
| Total responses | | (600) |

Question 21. How well did respondent speak English? (Interviewers' evaluation of language skills)

| | | |
|---|---|---|
| Very well | 27.2% | (163) |
| Well | 20.7% | (124) |
| Not well | 35.5% | (213) |
| Not at all | 16.7% | (100) |
| Total responses | | (600) |

Question 22.  Market

| | |
|---|---|
| Los Angeles | (120) |
| Miami | (120) |
| New York | (120) |
| San Antonio | (120) |
| Houston | (120) |
| Total responses | (600) |

# 18.

# Bilingual Education in Massachusetts: The Emperor Has No Clothes

## Christine H. Rossell and Keith Baker

## THE EDUCATIONAL EFFECTIVENESS OF BILINGUAL EDUCATION

Despite the widespread acceptance of transitional bilingual education among policymakers, one question continues to be asked by those who read even a little of the research: Are TBE programs effective? Even well-known supporters of bilingual education have questioned its research foundations. Kenji Hakuta concludes, in *Mirror of Language,*

> There is a sober truth that even the ardent advocate of bilingual education would not deny. Evaluation studies of the effectiveness of bilingual education in improving either English or math scores have not been overwhelmingly in favor of bilingual education. . . . An awkward tension blankets the lack of empirical demonstration of the success of bilingual education programs. Someone promised bacon, but it's not there.[1]

Thomas Carter, despite being an advocate of bilingual education and an expert witness for LEP Hispanic plaintiffs in several bilingual education court cases over the last decade, begins a 1986 article with "Regardless of the many roots of the debate, one issue is unresolved. Does bilingual education work?"[2]

Christina Bratt Paulston, a well-known linguist and advocate of bilingual education, makes some telling points in her 1982 report to the National Swedish Board of Education. With regard to transitional bilingual education in the United States, she notes,

From *Bilingual Education in Massachusetts: The Emperor Has No Clothes,* Pioneer Institute Inc., © 1996, Boston, Mass. (http://www.pioneerinstitute.org)

The rationale for bilingual programs is that they are more efficient in teaching English although there is not much hard data to support such a view; it has however been the standard argument. . . . The Canadians believe, *with justification,* that fluent proficiency in the target language only occurs when that language is used as a medium of instruction [emphasis added].[3]

She also approvingly cites Toukomaa, another bilingual education advocate, who writes,

We wish to dissociate ourselves from those arguments, for teaching in the mother tongue, which attempt to frighten parents into choosing mother tongue-teaching by threatening emotional and intellectual under-development in those children who do not receive mother tongue-teaching. Teaching in the mother tongue does not seem to have the magical effect on the child's development, for good or for ill, which it has sometimes been ascribed.[4]

The Association for Supervision and Curriculum Development, an organization of 90,000 principals, school superintendents, teachers, and other educational leaders, noted in a 1987 report on bilingual education, "It is unclear which approach is better [teaching children in English or in their native tongue]."[5]

# RESEARCH REVIEWS

There have been a number of extensive reviews of the literature on the effectiveness of TBE for LEP students.[6] None of these reviews, however, has provided a definitive answer to the central question—Does TBE produce greater educational achievement in LEP children than any other education program? Indeed, we sometimes wonder, given the ideological fervor surrounding this issue and the limitations of social science research, whether a definitive answer can ever be provided to the satisfaction of both sides on the debate.

Rossell and Baker (1996) updates our previous reviews of the available research, conducted in the early and mid-1980s.[7] The strategy for Rossell and Baker (1996) was to begin with the studies reviewed in Baker and de Kanter (1983) and Rossell and Ross (1986) and to add to them.[8] The total number of studies and books we have read now numbers above 500, of which 300 are program evaluations, in the sense that their purpose is to evaluate the effectiveness of actual TBE practice or some other second language acquisition technique.

# METHODOLOGICAL APPROACH

Each of the 300 program evaluations[9] was assessed to determine if it addressed the relevant questions with a methodologically sound research design. Acceptable studies generally had the following characteristics:

(1) They were true experiments in which students were randomly assigned to "treatment" and control groups. Random assignment eliminates the bias that occurs when students are self-selected—when parents are permitted to volunteer their children for a program. It also eliminates the bias that occurs when a school district selects students for a program on the basis of achievement. If program participants were self-selected or selected by the district, the evaluator cannot be sure whether the outcomes observed are reflective of the program itself or biased by the selection process.

(2) If they had non-random assignment, they either matched students in the treatment and comparison groups on factors that influence achievement or statistically controlled for them. Among the important factors affecting the performance of language minority children in school, especially in learning English, are the following: age, socioeconomic status, ethnicity, student motivation and self-concept, parental support for the educational program, the language and environment of the community, cognitive ability, place of birth—immigrant or native-born—and degree of home-language dominance.[10] If the composition of one program is substantially different from that of another program on any of these dimensions, one cannot know if the outcomes are a result of the program or of these other factors unless one statistically controls for these other factors.

(3) Outcome measures were in English using NCEs (normal curve equivalents), raw scores, scale scores, percentiles, etc., but not grade equivalents.

(4) Additional educational interventions were non-existent, or the study controlled for them.

(5) Appropriate statistical tests were applied. There are statistical tests that are designed to take into account the number of subjects in each group, the size of the outcome difference between the groups, and the variation in outcomes within groups that must be performed in order to verify that the results are "statistically significant"—that they could not have happened by chance.

Analysis of covariance was by far the most common statistical method used to control for pre-existing differences in non-experimental studies.[11] Many statisticians have serious reservations about whether this method succeeds in properly adjusting pre-existing differences. Similarly there are doubts that matching students on important characteristics that influence achievement is entirely successful. Nevertheless, we generally accepted both methods unless there were serious defects in their application.

## FINDINGS

Seventy-two of the studies and program evaluations reviewed were deemed methodologically acceptable. These studies seek to demonstrate the effect of traditional bilingual education on second language (usually English) reading, language, and/or mathematics compared to (1) "submersion," i.e., doing nothing, (2) ESL, i.e., enrollment in a regular classroom with a pullout program of intensive English language instruction for a few hours a week, (3) structured immersion, i.e., enrollment in a self-contained classroom of second-language learners who are taught completely or almost completely in English at a pace they can understand, and (4) bilingual maintenance.

After reviewing the results of these studies, we find no consistent research support for transitional bilingual education as a superior instructional practice for improving the English language achievement of LEP children.

The results varied widely across the 72 studies. When TBE is compared to submersion, the most common finding is no difference in reading and math achievement between students in the two programs. The findings for TBE's effect on language (i.e., writing and knowledge of grammar) are somewhat worse than for TBE's effect on reading. This suggests that students may be less dependent on school for many of the skills learned in reading—decoding, vocabulary, and understanding concepts—than they are for grammar. It appears the fine rules of grammar are learned mostly in school, and, because they are more complex, are more influenced by school time spent on the task. There is, then, a risk that bilingual education students will incur a deficit in learning English grammatical rules because they have spent less time on them than have LEP children in an all-English environment.

One study showed transitional bilingual education produced significantly higher English reading achievement than maintenance bilingual education.[12]

None of the studies comparing reading achievement in TBE to the regular classroom with ESL pullout show TBE to be better. Five studies show no difference between TBE and ESL in reading, and two studies show TBE to be worse than the regular classroom with ESL pullout. Of the three studies that compared language achievement, none showed TBE to be superior, two showed no difference between TBE and ESL, and one showed TBE to be worse.

In developing math proficiency, TBE fared no better when compared to submersion or to regular classroom instruction with ESL pullout.

All but four of the studies of structured immersion compared to TBE or ESL are evaluations of the French immersion programs in English-speaking Canadian provinces, which come in several carefully documented types. When we use the terms "immersion" or "structured immersion" we are talking about the most common program type in Canada—total instruction in the second language during the early grades including learning to read and write in the second language. No studies showed TBE to be superior to structured immersion in reading, language, or math.

Most bilingual education advocates dispute the applicability of the Canadian studies to the United States. First, they argue that the studies are not relevant to the U.S. LEP student experience because the immersion and bilingual education programs in Canada involve mostly middle-class students. In fact, however, several early immersion experiments were conducted with children from low-income families and produced the same or better results.[13] Both the middle-class and poorer English-speaking students who were immersed in French in kindergarten and grade 1 were almost the equal of native-speaking French students until the curriculum became bilingual in grade 2, it which point the French ability of students from English-speaking families declined and continued to decline as English was increased. The time-on-task principle—that is, the amount of time spent learning a subject is the greatest predictor of achievement in that subject holds across classes in the programs where school is the only source of second language learning (French) for the native English-speaking children in the bilingual programs.

A second argument made to dismiss the Canadian French immersion experiments is that the students were self-selected. The fact that the students were self-selected means that they were probably better language learners than other students, all other things being equal. Yet, even for these "elite" students, the data show that the time-on-task principle holds. If self-selected students are so influenced by how much time is devoted to a language, it is hard to imagine that LEP children in the United States would not be affected at all.

Contrary to many interpretations of the Canadian experiments,[14] we think there is much we can learn about second language learning from these programs. It is clear, however, that immersion is not a program that can be imported without major modification to fit the U.S. situation where immigrant LEP children arrive at public school every day of the year and must be admitted regardless of their academic preparation.

Advocates of bilingual education have sometimes contended that the issue is learning *in* a language, not learning a language. These data, however, do not show TBE to be superior in either. Moreover, there is no research evidence on the effects of TBE on learning geography, social studies, and history because national standardized achievement tests are not given in these content areas. Any assertions regarding the superiority of TBE in these areas are anecdotal. Moreover, the math findings for TBE suggest an important problem: subject matter is taught in the native tongue, but the student is tested on his or her understanding of that subject *in English*. Many students find it quite difficult to translate into English what was learned in another language in the TBE program. This reduction in achievement caused by the "translation" problem may equal or surpass the reduction in achievement that may occur in the first few months of submersion before the second language is mastered enough to understand subject content.

## OTHER RESEARCH REVIEWS

Rossell and Baker (1996) is not the first to show a lack of research support for transitional bilingual education.[15] Given the evidence, on what basis have some reviewers of bilingual education research claimed superiority for the program? One technique, used by Zappert and Cruz (1977), is simply to redefine the word. As they argue,

> No significant difference should not be interpreted as a negative finding for bilingual education. . . . When one adds the fact that students in bilingual education classrooms learn two languages, their native language and a second lan-

guage, one can conclude that a statistically non-significant finding demonstrates the positive advantages of bilingual education.[16]

The problem with this argument is that the court decisions, the federal regulations, and Chapter 71A are based on the assumption that TBE produces greater English language achievement and content area mastery than doing nothing, not the *same* achievement. Doing nothing is considered a violation of a child's equal educational opportunity that transitional bilingual education is supposed to remedy.

Some research reviews make transitional bilingual education appear superior by including performance in Spanish language arts. Zappert and Cruz also do this. While facility in Spanish language arts is important, it is not the goal of government policy nor the stated object of the court decisions.

Interpretations of the same data differ greatly among researchers in the field of bilingual education. Advocates and opponents will frequently interpret data to suit their respective political agendas. Thus, reviewers of the research must carefully read each study and draw their own conclusions.

## SECOND LANGUAGE LEARNING THEORIES

Two competing theories of learning a second language lie at the center of the long debate over the value of transitional bilingual education programs. Proponents of bilingual education programs argue that children should be taught in their native tongue because learning the first language helps them to learn the second language. Critics of bilingual education programs, however, argue that the best way to learn English and subject matter in which one will be evaluated in English is to maximize the time spent hearing, speaking, and writing English. Both theories have problems, although for different reasons, and there is empirical research that appears to contradict each.

## THE FACILITATION THEORY

James Cummins is probably the principal proponent of the facilitation theory.[17] Cummins' initial (1978) theoretical work was designed to explain the conflicting findings in the empirical research. The facilitation theory has two components: (1) The "threshold" hypothesis states that a LEP child must attain a high level of linguistic competence in the native tongue before transitioning completely to English in order to avoid cognitive disadvantages. (2) The "developmental interdependence" hypothesis states that the acquisition of a second language is facilitated by reading skills already developed in the first language.

According to the first part of the facilitation theory, if LEP children taught bilingually reach the threshold in their native language, they will be capable of achieving greater proficiency in the second language than students taught entirely in the second language. On the other hand, if a child's bilingual education is abandoned before the threshold in the native language is reached, attainment in the second language will be inferior to that of students taught entirely in the second language. Although the theory is vague regarding the exact level of proficiency in the native language that constitutes the required threshold, the writings of Cummins imply that it takes considerable time—up to seven years—before the threshold in the native language is attained and the facilitation effect is manifested.

The second part of the facilitation theory claims that once a child has learned to read his or her native language, learning the second language is made easier because he or she has already mastered the "mechanics"—the hardest part—in the native language. Since it takes 3 to 4 years to acquire literacy in roman alphabet languages,[18] the facilitating effect will not become fully apparent until 5 to 7 years after bilingual instruction begins.

It is important to remember that bilingual education preceded the facilitation theory by more than a decade—the former began in 1968 with Title VII of the Elementary and Secondary Education Act and the latter with Cummins' first writing on the subject in 1978.[19] Indeed, the dominant component of second language learning theory in 1968 seems to have been the time-on-task principle. S. Izzo summarizes studies conducted in the late '60s and early '70s:

> The length of time spent in language study is, in fact, one of the most important factors in achievement. . . . [Moreover] it must be the total length of time spent in contact with the language that is of importance in determining second language proficiency.[20]

J. B. Carroll goes even further in summarizing the Canadian research evaluations as "eloquent confirmation of the statement that time is the most important factor in learning [a second language]."[21] These conclusions and theories dictated the practice of all-English instruction. Since all-English instruction had not eliminated the achievement differences between Hispanic and white children when the civil rights movement reached its peak in the late '60s, it was replaced by its opposite—native tongue instruction—which, it was argued, would raise the self-esteem and motivation of Hispanic children and ultimately their achievement. The facilitation hypothesis was then created by Cummins and others to provide an educational or linguistic justification for a policy already implemented on civil rights grounds.

## Research and the Facilitation Hypothesis

Is the facilitation theory valid? Much of the evidence Cummins cites to demonstrate its validity is either trivial—a study by Cummins and Mulcahy (1977) showing that fluent bilingual Ukrainians did better than either non-fluent bilingual Ukrainians or monolingual students on a test of ambiguities in sentence structure,[22] a study by Leslie (1977) showing that Native American children who scored high on *oral* Cree scored high on English reading[23]—or just plain contrary. Among the latter are studies by Hebert (1976) and Ramirez and Politzer

(1976) that show that instruction in the native tongue has no effect on achievement in the second language.[24]

The principal evidence Cummins cites for the effectiveness of transitional bilingual education programs, however, is Skutnabb-Kangas and Toukomaa (1976), who compared two groups of students who had immigrated from Finland to Sweden: those who immigrated before and those who immigrated after reaching the third grade.[25] Students who immigrated after third grade, who had been in school in Finland long enough to have first developed literacy in their native language (Finnish), supposedly performed better in Swedish than did the children who had moved to Sweden at a younger age and who presumably knew less Finnish and began learning Swedish at an earlier age. Both Cummins and Skutnabb-Kangas and Toukomaa argue that the greater ability of these older students in Swedish is it function of more years of instruction in Finnish.

There are major methodological problems with Skutnabb-Kangas and Toukomaa, however, and with the inference that their results support the facilitation hypothesis.[26] First, Skutnabb-Kangas and Toukomaa presented no statistical analysis of their data. Second, at the time of the Skutnabb-Kangas study, Swedish, the second official language of Finland, was a required subject in Finnish schools from the third grade on, a fact neither Skutnabb-Kangas and Toukomaa nor Cummins mention. Thus, if the simple descriptive data presented by Skutnabb-Kangas and Toukomaa show anything, it is that students who have a chance to study a second language before immigrating to the country where that language is spoken perform better than do students who had no such formal instruction before they immigrated. In short, contrary to Cummins' assertions, there is no empirical support in Skutnabb-Kangas and Toukomaa for the facilitation hypothesis and some support for the time-on-task principle.

Other research is sometimes misinterpreted as support for the facilitation hypothesis as well.[27] This research shows (1) that children can transfer skills learned in one language to another language[28] and (2) that older children are, contrary to popular belief, more "efficient" (i.e., faster) learners of languages.[29] Evidence that older learners who already knew how to read in their native language acquired a second language faster than younger learners has been interpreted as support for the facilitation effect.[30] When the proper analysis is conducted, however, the most important causal variable turns out to be age, not native language reading ability.[31] Moreover, while it is true that individuals who are literate in their native language have an easier time learning a second language, this tells us nothing about how non-literate individuals should be taught, nor in what language.

Perhaps the most important recent test of Cummins' facilitation theory is the Ramirez et al. (1991) national study. This is a methodologically acceptable study with a large national sample of 1,054 students. Although not much discussed in the final report, its design was specifically structured to test Cummins' facilitation theory.[32] The study sampled "early-exit" TBE classrooms, structured immersion, and "late-exit" bilingual maintenance classrooms across the United States. Only the TBE and immersion classrooms were directly compared to each other in statistical analysis.

In the transitional bilingual education and structured immersion program comparisons, Ramirez et al. found at the end of two years (kindergarten to grade one) a significant effect favoring TBE programs in reading, but not in language or math where there was no difference between programs. This advantage of bilingual instruction, however, had vanished by the end of four years in these programs. At that point structured immersion was favored in language arts, while in math and reading there was no significant difference between programs.

While there are enough problems with this study that it should be interpreted with great caution,[33] the fact that the early-exit program did as well as it did in comparison to immersion suggests the following possibility: bilingual education may be superior to all-English instruction in the very beginning when a student literally knows no English, but as the student's English language knowledge increases and English becomes more comprehensible, time on task in English becomes more important and more necessary because it is now *effective* time on task. Ramirez et al., on the other hand, shows *no* support for the facilitation effect. Contrary to the exaggerated claim made, the descriptive portion of the study shows that students who stayed in bilingual education the longest did the worst. While this apparently negative finding for bilingual education is not reliable given the lack of statistical control for student and classroom characteristics, it is definitively *not* positive evidence.

The Burkheimer et al. (1989) study, also funded by the U.S. Department of Education and critiqued by Meyer and Feinberg (1992), shows similar findings. It, too, is a methodologically acceptable study with a large national sample of more than 8,000 students. Not only did it show no facilitation effect, but the only positive effect of any kind from bilingual education in English language arts and math was found in the very beginning of a student's English language acquisition. Although, overall, teaching more English and less Spanish was positively related to achievement in English language arts over a one-year period, this finding varied by initial English proficiency. First graders with greater proficiency in English at the outset tended to improve more when there was more instruction in English. Those who were initially less proficient in English did better with more hours of native language arts instruction.[34]

Instruction in ethnic heritage *decreased* both the overall effect of more English language arts and the relative advantage for those with greater initial English proficiency. This is because as Burkheimer notes (but which is seldom acknowledged by others),

> ... Within a framework that constrains total instructional hours and is further constrained by legislated requirements for some courses, increased instruction in one particular subject area is typically accomplished at the expense of reduction in another subject area. ... As examples: maintenance of the child's native language skills is accomplished at the expense of reduction in another area; more hours devoted to Ethnic Heritage instruction reduced the remaining hours that could be devoted to other subjects. This reality is not a value judgment of what should or should not be taught (which is best determined by local conditions and goals), but simply a recognition that trade-offs are required (5.42–43).

Finally, the Burkheimer study included a seemingly contradictory finding: having a bilingual certified teacher had a *negative* effect on English language arts achievement for the first grade cohort, but having a teacher who is just familiar with the child's native language had a *positive* effect. It is not clear what this means, but if we assume that being bilingual certified means having a more advanced knowledge of the native tongue than not being bilingual certified, it may mean that some native tongue ability is good, but too much is not. This hypothesis is suggested by other research as well. Fillmore (1980), for example, examined different kinds of bilingual education classes for Chinese students and found that the teacher who was most successful in raising their English language achievement knew Cantonese, the native tongue of most of the students, but taught 90 percent of the time in English.[35] Similarly, the Austin Independent School District's TBE program, found to be superior to submersion, had teachers who used English as the medium of instruction 82 percent of the time.[36]

W. Tickunoff's (1983) descriptive study of successful bilingual instruction (58 teachers from six nationally representative sites) identified the following characteristics of successful programs: (1) 80 percent of time allocated to academic learning tasks, (2) the native tongue used by teachers primarily to clarify instructions, and (3) content areas such as math and social studies taught in *English*.[37] Two studies of the achievement gains of LEP children taught by bilingual and monolingual teachers found no difference between the two.[38] Similarly, the American Institutes for Research (AIR) national survey of bilingual education also found no relationship between whether a teacher was bilingual and the performance of his or her students.[39] Rossell (1990) found no difference in student achievement attributable to whether or not a teacher was bilingual certified.[40]

Moore and Parr (1978) found that teachers in the bilingual education program who were rated *less* competent had better student performance.[41] This finding is not as strange as it sounds if, as seems likely for a bilingual education program, the competence rating is primarily an evaluation of the teacher's ability in the non-English language. What all these studies suggest is that the psychological and perhaps initial pedagogical advantage one may gain from having a teacher fluent in the native tongue may be offset by the tendency of such teachers to teach too much and too long in the native tongue—in other words, to teach according to the facilitation theory.

## ENGLISH TIME ON TASK

Opponents of bilingual education programs argue that learning English is determined almost entirely by the time spent studying English.[42] This theory proposes that bilingual education programs are inferior to all-English instruction because bilingual education programs reduce the time spent on the task of learning English.

Any acceptable theory of teaching English to LEP students must account for the contradictory research evidence. Why is it that students in bilingual education programs with up to 30 percent native tongue instruction often do no worse than and sometimes do better than all-English programs? Why is it that monolingual teachers do no better than bilingual teachers?

If time on task were as important as its proponents suggest, all-English instruction would always be superior to any form of bilingual education, even programs where the native tongue is used only in small amounts, and monolingual English teachers would consistently produce greater achievement in their students than bilingual teachers. The scientifically valid studies indicate, however, that this is not the case.

Although some researchers find time on task to be the single greatest predictor of achievement in a subject, it is nevertheless only one of many instructional factors—such as classroom atmosphere, pace of instruction, and curriculum content—that influence academic achievement.[43] Karweit (1983), in a review of the time-on-task literature, concluded that the time-on-task effect, while significant, had been greatly overblown in importance. In reanalyzing the Beginning Teacher Evaluation Study (Fisher et al., 1980), Karweit estimates that an additional 60 minutes per day in time allocated to reading comprehension alone would be needed to increase reading comprehension scores by .25 standard deviations. If that were *effective* time on task, however, only a 10-minute increase would be required to improve mathematics achievement by .25 standard deviations.[44]

As Rossell and Ross (1986) suggested a decade ago, there are some mediating factors for time on task that explain why some methodologically sound research studies show TBE (i.e., less English language time on task) to be no different from or superior to submersion (i.e., more English language time on task). The first of these factors is the nature of the time spent in the English language environment. Much of the learning in a submersion situation is, at least initially, not *effective* learning because the students do not understand what is going on. A bilingual program that gives the children only half their education in English but structures the English so that it is understandable may provide more effective time in the English language than a program that is completely in English if only a small part of it is comprehensible. As English becomes more understandable, the greater time spent on English in the submersion situation would give these children an advantage during this later time period.[45] At the end of three years, students in both submersion and bilingual education may end up with the same amount of effective learning time in the English language, with TBE producing more at the beginning and submersion more at the end.

A second factor explaining the lack of harm of TBE in many good studies is that the supporters of bilingual education may be at least partially right—bilingual education may have important psychological effects that compensate for the reduced English language learning time. If students in submersion programs often feel alienated or inferior, and if a special program is a protected environment that, regardless of its academic utility, makes school more enjoyable, then they may come to school more often, stay longer, and pay more attention. Take, for example, a submersion situation in which students were taught 100 percent in English but only came to school 75 percent of the time, and only half of the instruction was comprehensible in the first year. They will have less effective

English language learning time for that year than if they had been in a bilingual program that taught them 50 percent in comprehensible English but motivated them to come to school 85 percent of the time.

Rossell's (1990) comparison in Berkeley, California, of TBE and all-English regular classroom instruction with ESL pullout has some interesting findings that are relevant to this discussion.[46] This study is a methodologically acceptable study of one school district. Rossell found no difference in student achievement between TBE and ESL in the first year's analysis. Interviews with teachers indicated that they used Spanish in the TBE program 30 to 50 percent of the time in kindergarten and first grade and not much after that except for individualized instruction with new non-English-speaking (NEP) students who entered in the later grades. The one TBE program in Berkeley that outperformed all the other school programs, including the regular classroom with ESL pullout programs, had given rise to the original court complaint; it was cited for using too much English. But, contrary to a strict time-on-task theory, the program did have some native tongue instruction.

Rossell conducted a second year evaluation of achievement in the year after the Berkeley Unified School District increased the use of Spanish in its bilingual program in response to pressure from the California State Department of Education. The analysis of the second year found that students in the bilingual program did worse than those in all-English instruction by about 12 to 15 points on reading, language, and math tests. The first year findings, in comparison to those of the second year, suggest some possible explanations: (1) there is some threshold *below* which native tongue instruction does not harm children (the reverse of the facilitation theory), or (2) there is some initial period of time when native tongue instruction actually benefits students. We do not yet have enough evidence to confirm or rule out either possibility, but we can theorize about what is at work here.

## SPACED LEARNING

There is a large body of research on the differential effects of learning material taught at once and continuously versus learning material taught in intervals with rest in between. One classic demonstration of the difference is Duncan (1951) who studied the acquisition of the skill of keeping a pen point on a moving target.[47] One group of subjects practiced for the entire learning time, while the other group was periodically interrupted for rest periods so that they were resting for two-thirds of the practice session. The group with less practice and more rest actually learned better.

A probable explanation for the superiority of spaced practice over continuous practice is that it takes time for the memory process to work. A constant barrage of material to learn overloads the memory process and interferes with learning. Rest, or doing something else between practice sessions, gives the memory process the time it needs to operate, resulting in more efficient learning.

Although learning a language is not exactly the same as learning a boring, repetitive task, there is enough similarity that these studies are suggestive of what might go on in language learning. Consider language learning for the school-aged, monolingual English-speaking child. The child already knows most of the words the teacher uses on any particular day. The few new words to be learned are interspersed with periods of no learning of new words, that is, rest. Language development in the child takes place through spaced, not continuous, practice.

The situation is initially quite different for the child learning a second language. Since all words are new at first, the situation is one of continuous practice. The student may actually make more progress learning the second language if rest is introduced into the constant stream of exposure to the unknown language.

How can rest occur in exposure to a new language? One, although by no means the only, way is to change the language of instruction to one the child already knows. Eventually, enough of the second language will be learned if it is part of the instructional program so that the second language learner will be able to get some "rest" between new words in all-English instruction.[48]

It is possible that bilingual education programs, because they provide a needed rest from constant exposure to the new language, can produce better learning at the early stages of learning a second language. Later on, however, instruction entirely in the second language probably works better than bilingual education, as English is comprehensible enough that new words are a minority.

## STUDENT'S SELF-ESTEEM, ATTENDANCE, AND ATTITUDES ABOUT SCHOOL

Advocates of bilingual education and bilingual teachers have argued that examining the effect of these program features on the academic achievement of students is too limited an analysis. They argue that bilingual education programs and bilingual teachers have a positive psychological effect on their students that is important in and of itself. Many of the teachers who teach in bilingual education programs believe that the purpose of these programs is to improve the self-esteem of children and by so doing improve their academic achievement. Despite the popularity of this theory, we could find very little research on this subject, scientific or otherwise.

## CONCLUSION

The facilitation hypothesis has been overwhelmingly accepted by educators in bilingual education as a proven fact and as the explanation for TBE's superiority to all other second language acquisition techniques, even though more than 15 years of research and literally thousands of studies have confirmed neither the theory nor the predicted effectiveness of bilingual education programs. Unfortunately, the latest scientifically designed research project, the Ramirez et al. (1991) study, costing millions of dollars, has made only a small contribution to our understanding of this issue. If anything, the Ramirez et al. (1991) and Burk-heimer et al. (1989) studies suggest to us that the threshold theory may work in reverse of Cummins' hypothesis. It seems more likely that a threshold in the second language, not the native language, needs to be passed before the second language instruction is consistently superior to native language instruction. Indeed, native language skills (after controlling for intelligence, something almost no one does) could be *irrelevant* to this process.

# NOTES

1. Kenji Hakuta, *Mirror of Language, The Debate on Bilingualism,* New York: Basic Books, 1986: 219.
2. T. P. Carter and M. L. Chatfield, "Effective Bilingual Schools: Implications for Policy and Practice," *American Journal of Education* (1986), 95: 210.
3. C. B. Paulston (ed.), *Swedish Research and Debate about Bilingualism: A Critical Review of the Swedish Research and Debate about Bilingualism and Bilingual Education in Sweden from an International Perspective,* Report to the National Swedish Board of Education, 1982: 47–48.
4. P. Toukomaa, "Education through the Medium of the Mother Tongue of Finnish Immigrant Children," in C. B. Paulston (ed.), *Swedish Research and Debate about Bilingualism,* 1982: 103.
5. *Building an Indivisible Nation: Bilingual Education in Context,* Alexandria, Va.: Association for Supervision and Curriculum Development, 1987: 35.
6. See R. Troike, "Research Evidence for the Effectiveness of Bilingual Education," *NABE Journal* (1978), 3 (1): 13–14; P. Engle, "The Use of the Vernacular Language in Education," Bilingual education series No. 2, Washington, D.C.: Center for Applied Linguistics, 1975; Iris Rotberg, "Federal Policy in Bilingual Education," *American Education* (1982), 52 (2): 30–40; Ann C. Willig, "A Meta-Analysis of Selected Studies on the Effectiveness of Bilingual Education," *Review of Educational Research* (1985), 55 (3): 269–317; J. Yates and A. Ortiz, "Baker & de Kanter Review: Inappropriate Conclusions on the Efficacy of Bilingual Education," *Journal of the National Association for Bilingual Education* (1983), 7 (3): 75–84; M. Peterson et al., "Assessment of the Status of Bilingual Vocational Training: Review of the Literature," *ERIC* (1976), 131: 683; General Accounting Office (GAO), *Bilingual Education: A New Look at the Research Evidence,* Briefing Report to the Chairman, Committee on Education and Labor, House of Representatives, 1987; R. Holland, *Bilingual Education: Recent Evaluations of Local School District Programs and Related Research on Second-Language Learning,* Washington, D.C.: Congressional Research Service, 1986; D. Ravitch, *The Troubled Crusade,* New York: Basic Books, 1983; H. Dulay and M. Burt, "From Research to Method in Bilingual Education," *Georgetown University Roundtable on Language and Linguistics,* Washington, D.C.: Georgetown University, 1978; L. T. Zappert and B. R. Cruz, *Bilingual Education: An Appraisal of Empirical Research,* Berkeley, Calif.: The Berkeley Unified School District, 1977; P. Zirkel, *An Evaluation of the Effectiveness of Selected Experimental Bilingual Education Programs in Connecticut,* Hartford, Conn.: Connecticut Department of Education, 1972.
7. This chapter is a condensed version of Christine H. Rossell and Keith Baker, "The Educational Effectiveness of Bilingual Education," *Research in the Teaching of*

*English* (February 1996), 30 (1): 7–74. The original contains more detailed discussions of our methodology and the results of specific studies mentioned here. It also contains complete lists of the studies we reviewed categorized as methodologically acceptable or unacceptable.

8. Christine Rossell and J. Michael Ross, "The Social Science Evidence on Bilingual Education," *Journal of Law and Education* (1986), 15: 385–419; Keith Baker and Adriana de Kanter, *The Effectiveness of Bilingual Education Programs: A Review of the Literature, Final Draft Report,* Washington, D.C.: U.S. Department of Education, 1981; Keith Baker and Adriana de Kanter, "An Answer from Research on Bilingual Education," *American Education* (1983), 56 (4): 157–69; Keith Baker and Adriana de Kanter, "Federal Policy and the Effectiveness of Bilingual Education," in Keith A. Baker, Adriana A. de Kanter (eds.), *Bilingual Education,* Lexington, Mass.: D. C. Heath and Company, 1983.

9. The initial list of studies on bilingual education was obtained from a search on the Educational Research Information Clearinghouse (ERIC) documents, the Boston University, MIT, Boston College, and the Boston Public Library card catalogues, Language and Language Behavior Abstracts, and the bibliographies of other reviews of the literature. The studies actually reviewed were those that could be obtained from (1) ERIC; (2) University Microfilms International; (3) the journal and book holdings of Boston University, MIT, Boston College, and the Boston Public Library; (4) the National Clearinghouse on Bilingual Education; (5) the Center for Applied Linguistics; (6) the Department of Education; (7) the authors themselves; (8) interlibrary loan; and (9) program evaluations for 1991–93 obtained by writing to school districts in the United States. Not all studies are documented, nor could all documented studies be obtained.

10. See Rossell and Baker (1996) for a list of studies that discuss each of these factors.

11. Analysis of covariance is a statistical technique that determines whether the difference in the mean outcome (e.g., achievement) for two or more groups (e.g., students in a bilingual education program compared to those in another program) is significantly different after adjusting for another variable (the covariate) thought to be correlated with the outcome, for example, the achievement of each student before entering the program.

12. Marcello Medina and Kathy Escamilla, "Evaluation of Transitional and Maintenance Bilingual Programs," *Urban Education* (1992), 27 (3): 263–90. Ramirez et al. (1991) also examined maintenance bilingual education (late-exit bilingual education) but unfortunately did not directly compare it to transitional bilingual education (contrary to media reports and his own conclusions). Although his graphs appeared to show that the students in late-exit bilingual education were doing worse than the students in transitional bilingual education, no statistical analysis was performed to verify that. J. Ramirez, S. Yuen, D. Ramey, and D. Pasta, *Final Report: Longitudinal Study of Structured English Immersion Strategy, Early-Exit and Late-Exit Transitional Bilingual Education Programs for Language-Minority Children,* Vol. I, prepared for U.S. Department of Education, San Mateo, Calif.: Aguirre International, 1991; J. Ramirez, D. Pasta, S. Yuen, D. Billings, and D. Ramey, *Final Report: Longitudinal Study of Structured English Immersion Strategy, Early-Exit and Late-Exit Transitional Bilingual Education Programs for Language-Minority Children,* Vol. II, prepared for U.S. Department of Education, San Mateo, Calif.: Aguirre International, 1991.

13. G. Richard Tucker, Wallace E. Lambert, and A. d'Anglejan, "French Immersion Programs: A Pilot Investigation," *Language Sciences* (1973), 25: 19–26; Margaret Bruck, Jola Jakimik, and G. Richard Tucker, "Are French Immersion Programs Suitable for Working-Class Children? A Follow-up Investigation," *Word* (1971), 27: 311–41; Gary A. Cziko, "The Effects of Different French Immersion Programs on the Language and Aca-

demic Skills of Children from Various Socioeconomic Backgrounds," M.A. thesis, McGill University, 1975; Fred Genesee, "The Suitability of Immersion Programs for all Children," *Canadian Modern Language Review* (1976), 32: 494–515.

14. Leonard A. Popp, "The English Competence of French Speaking Students in a Bilingual Setting," *Canadian Modern Language Review* (1976), 32: 365–77; G. Richard Tucker, "Implications for U.S. Bilingual Education: Evidence from Canadian Research," National Clearinghouse for Bilingual Education, *NCBE Focus* (1980), 2: 1–3; M. Swain, "Time and Timing in Bilingual Education," *Language Learning* (1981), 31: 1; Eduardo Hernandez-Chavez, "The Inadequacy of English Immersion Education as an Educational Approach for Language Minority Students in the United States," in *Studies on Immersion Education,* Sacramento: California State Department of Education, 1984.

15. Baker and de Kanter (1981, 1983a, 1983b), Engle (1975), Rotberg (1982), Holland (1986), Rossell and Ross (1986), and N. Epstein, *Language, Ethnicity and the Schools: Policy Alternatives for Bilingual Bicultural Education,* Washington, D.C.: Institute for Educational Leadership, 1977, have also concluded there is no research support for transitional bilingual education.

16. Zappert and Cruz, 1977: 8.

17. J. Cummins, "Educational Implications of Mother Tongue Maintenance in Minority Language Groups," *Canadian Modern Language Review* (1978), 34: 395–416; J. Cummins, "The Role of Primary Language Development in Promoting Educational Success for Language Minority Students," in California State Department of Education (Comp.), *Schooling and Language Minority Students: A Theoretical Framework,* Los Angeles: UCLA Evaluation, Dissemination, and Assessment Center, 1981; J. Cummins, "The Construct of Language Proficiency in Bilingual Education," in *Perspectives on Bilingualism and Bilingual Education,* Washington, D.C.: Georgetown University Press, 1985.

18. Perhaps one of the more serious flaws of the facilitation theory is its lack of attention to non-roman or non-alphabetic languages that have no similarity to English in appearance and take much longer to master. Learning to read in the native language may actually be harder in these languages than in the second language, if the latter is English or another roman alphabet language. We know of no non-roman alphabet bilingual programs in the United States that actually teach initial literacy in the native language, although many of them are nevertheless called bilingual education and receive bilingual education funding. Russian, for one, is apparently more difficult to master than English. Slobin (1966) found that the Russian-speaking child does not fully master his morphology until he is several years older than the age at which an English-speaking child does. Dan I. Slobin, "The Acquisition of Russian as a Native Language," in Frank Smith and George A. Miller (eds.), *The Genesis of Language,* Cambridge, Mass.: MIT Press, 1966: 129–52, cited in Izzo, 1981.

19. Cummins cites a UNESCO study, *The Use of the Vernacular Languages in Education* (Monographs on Fundamental Education, 1953), but there is no reference to this study in any of the legislation or literature of the 1960s.

20. S. Izzo, *Second Language Learning: A Review of Related Studies,* Virginia: National Clearinghouse for Bilingual Education, 1981: 51–52.

21. J. B. Carroll, "Commentary," in "The Ottawa-Carleton French Project: Issues, Conclusions, and Policy Implications," in H. H. Stern (ed.), *Canadian Modern Language Review* (1976), 32: 235.

22. J. Cummins and R. Mulcahy, *Orientation to Language in Ukrainian-English Bilinguals,* University of Alberta, 1977. Aside from the issue of the importance of the task, this study can tell us nothing about the kind of instruction LEP children should receive

since the fluent Ukrainian bilingual students not only did better than the monolingual controls, but they also did better than the non-fluent Ukrainian bilingual students who were receiving identical instruction. It is likely that other factors—such as intelligence levels—would explain these results.

23. D. Leslie, "Bilingual Education and Native Canadians," research report, University of Alberta, 1977. This only further underscores the extent to which these studies simply test native intelligence since there is no pedagogical theory that argues high native tongue *oral* fluency stimulates higher second language *reading* levels.

24. E. Hebert and Others, "Academic Achievement, Language of Instruction, and the Franco-Manitoban Student," College Universitaire de St. Boniface: Centre de Recherches, 1976; A. G. Ramirez and R. L. Politzer, "The Acquisition of English and the Maintenance of Spanish in a Bilingual Education Program," in J. Atlatis and Twaddell (eds.), *English as a Second Language in Bilingual Education,* Washington, D.C.: Teachers of English to Speakers of Other Languages, 1976. Although Cummins' theories are widely cited in the United States as evidence for the superiority of TBE, he relies on research on *bilingualism* conducted in Canada, where the educational process of creating bilinguals is the reverse of the United States. There, in the most common and successful program, students are taught completely in the second language in kindergarten and first grade and gradually transitioned to mostly the native tongue by high school. Although everyone believes these programs to be quite successful, Cummins continues to be cited as evidence for the superiority of the U.S. version of bilingual education—the native tongue first and a gradual transition to the second language.

25. Tove Skutnabb-Kangas and P. Toukomaa, "Teaching Migrant Children's Mother Tongue and Learning the Language of the Host Country in the Context of the Socio-Cultural Situation of the Migrant Family," New York: UNESCO, 1976.

26. See Baker and de Kanter, 1981.

27. Collier has conducted one of the few studies that directly attempts to test Cummins' hypotheses and, as with many studies of bilingual education, her data contradict the theory she purports to have proved. Because it is widely cited as support for the facilitation theory, however, it is worth discussing here although we have classified it as methodologically unacceptable in Rossell and Baker (1996). Collier tested Cummins' hypothesis that there is a facilitation effect of the native tongue on the second language with 20 pseudo-learning curves derived from cross-sectional achievement data of students who had been in the United States for varying amounts of time. (She incorrectly describes these as "rates" of learning. Since they are cross-sectional rather than longitudinal data, she cannot show rates of learning but only levels of achievement at a particular point in time.) If the facilitation hypothesis is correct, these curves should be negatively accelerated—that is the shorter the length of residence in the Untied States for students 8 years or older, the higher the achievement in English. Of the 20 curves, however, only two (or perhaps three) clearly show negative acceleration. About eight curves show *positive* acceleration. If one simplifies the problem of interpreting the curves by asking only if the two end points of the curve show negative acceleration, there are eight that support the hypothesis and eight that contradict it.

There is a second way in which Collier's results contradict Cummins. Collier claimed evidence of the facilitation effect for children aged 8 to 11 because she could not find it in children aged 12 to 16, which is where Cummins says it occurs. Thus, one of the few researchers to directly test Cummins' theory finds contrary evidence, but, because of the importance of the facilitation effect for transitional bilingual education, urges us to discount her findings instead. V. Collier, *The Effect of Age on Acquisition of a Second Lan-*

*guage for School,* Washington, D.C.: National Clearinghouse for Bilingual Education, 1987; V. Collier, "Age and Rate of Acquisition of Second Language for Academic Purposes," *TESOL Quarterly* (1987), 214: 617–41.

Several other researchers have directly or indirectly tested the facilitation effect. The Eastman Project is perhaps the major effort to demonstrate the facilitation hypothesis. Although Krashen and Biber claim to support the facilitation hypothesis, their analysis is so severely flawed that no conclusions can be drawn from it. S. Krashen and D. Biber, "On Course: Bilingual Education's Success in California," Sacramento: California Association for Bilingual Education, 1988. For a critique of Krashen and Biber, see Keith Baker, "Bilingual Education's 20-Year Failure to Provide Civil Rights Protection for Language Minority Students," in A. Barona and E. Garcia (eds.), *Children at Risk: Poverty, Minority Status, and Other Issues in Educational Equity,* Washington, D.C.: National Association of School Psychologists, 1990.

28. W. E. Lambert and G. R. Tucker, *Bilingual Education of Children: The St. Lambert Experience,* Rowley, Mass.: Newbury House, 1972; H. Barik and M. Swain, "Three Year Evaluation of a Large Scale Early Grade French Immersion Program: The Ottawa Study," *Language Learning* (1975), 25 (1); M. Bruck, W. Lambert, and R. Tucker, "Cognitive Consequences of Bilingual Schooling: The St. Lambert Project Through Grade Six," *Linguistics* (1977): 13–32.

29. D. Ausubel, "Adults versus Children in Second Language Learning," *Modern Language Journal* (1964), 48: 420; B. Taylor, "Toward a Theory of Language Acquisition," *Language Learning* (1974), 24: 23; S. Ervin-Tripp, "Is Second Language Learning Like the First?" *TESOL Quarterly* (1974), 8: 11; H. Stern, C. Burstall, and B. Harley, *French from Age Eight, or Eleven?* Toronto, Ont.: Ontario Ministry of Education, 1975; L. H. Eckstrand, "Age and Length of Residence as Variables Related to the Adjustments of Migrant Children with Special Reference to Second Language Learning," paper presented at the Association Internationale de Linguistique Appliquee Congress, Stuttgart, 1975; A. G. Ramirez and R. L. Politzer, "Comprehension and Production in English as a Second Language by Elementary School Children and Adolescents," in E. M. Hatch (ed.), *Second Language Acquisition: A Book of Readings,* 1978; Swain, 1981.

30. See, for example, P. Rosier and M. Farella, "Bilingual Education at Rock Point: Some Early Results," *TESOL Quarterly* (1976), 10: 379; P. Rosier and W. Holm, *The Rock Point Experience: A Longitudinal Study of a Navajo School Program* (saad naaki been na'nitin), Arlington, Va.: Center for Applied Linguistics, 1980; Skutnabb-Kangas and Toukomaa, 1976.

31. See Izzo, 1981.

32. Ramirez et al., 1991. Keith Baker was the project officer at the U.S. Department of Education for the Ramirez et al. (1991) study.

33. One of the two main mistakes of the Ramirez et al. (1991) study was the use of nominal program designation—early-exit TBE, late-exit TBE, and structure immersion—as the treatment variable rather than the percentage of English used in instruction, which varied considerably within nominal program categories and by subject matter. The second mistake was the failure to directly compare with statistical analyses the late-exit program to the early-exit and immersion programs. See Christine Rossell, "Nothing Matters? A Critique of the Ramirez et al. Longitudinal Study of Instructional Programs for Language-Minority Children," *Bilingual Research Journal* (1992), 16 (1&2): 159–86; Keith Baker, "Ramirez et al.: Led by Bad Theory," *Bilingual Research Journal* (1992), 16 (1&2): 91–104; M. Meyer and S. Fienberg (eds.), *Assessing Evaluation Studies: The Case of Bilingual Education Strategies,* Washington, D.C.: National Academy Press, 1992.

34. G. J. Burkheimer Jr., A. Conger, G. Dunteman, B. Elliott, and K. Mowbray, "Effectiveness of Services for Language Minority Limited English Proficient Students," Raleigh-Durham, N.C.: Research Triangle Institute, 1989: 5, 43.

35. L. W. Fillmore, "Learning a Second Language: Chinese Children in the American Classroom," *Georgetown University Roundtable on Language and Linguistics,* Washington, D.C.: Georgetown University Press, 1980.

36. K. Carsrud and J. Curtis, *ESEA Title VII Bilingual Program: Final Report,* Austin, Tex.: Austin Independent School District, 1980.

37. W. J. Tickunoff, *An Emerging Description of Successful Bilingual Instruction: Executive Summary of Part I of the SBIF Study,* San Francisco: Far West Laboratory for Educational Research and Development, 1983.

38. G. Ligon et al., *ESAA Bilingual/Bicultural Project,* 1973–74 evaluation report, Austin, Tex.: Austin Independent School District, 1974; J. Curtis, "Identification of Exemplary Teachers of LEP Students," paper presented at the annual meeting of the American Educational Research Association, New Orleans, April 1984.

39. Malcolm N. Danoff, Beatiz M. Arias, Gary J. Coles et al., *Evaluation of the Impact of ESEA Title VII Spanish/English Bilingual Education Program,* Palo Alto: American Institutes for Research, 1977; Malcolm N. Danoff, Gary J. Coles, Donald H. McLaughlin, and Dorothy J. Reynolds, *Evaluation of the Impact of ESEA Title VII Spanish/ English Bilingual Education Program,* Palo Alto: American Institutes for Research, 1978.

40. Christine Rossell, "The Effectiveness of Educational Alternatives for Limited-English-Proficient Children," in *Learning in Two Languages,* New Brunswick: Transaction Publishers, 1990.

41. F. B. Moore and G. D. Parr, "Models of Bilingual Education: Comparisons of Effectiveness," *The Elementary School Journal* (1978), 79: 93–97.

42. For the most recent example of this, see Rosalie Porter, *Forked Tongue,* New York: Basic Books, 1990; Rosalie Porter, "Reflections on the Politics of Bilingual Education," *Journal of Law and Politics* (1990), 6 (3): 573–99.

43. For example, D. Wiley, "Another Hour, Another Day: Quantity of Schooling, a Potent Path for Society," in W. Sewell, R. Hauser, and D. Featherman (eds.), *Schooling and Achievement in American Society,* New York: Academic Press, 1976; B. V. Rosenshine, "Content, Time and Direct Instruction," in P. Peterson and H. Walberg (eds.), *Research on Teaching: Concepts, Findings and Implications,* Berkeley: McCutcheon, 1979; K. Clauset and A. Gaynor, *Closing the Learning Gap: Effective Schooling for Initially Low Achievers,* Boston University, 1980.

44. C. W. Fisher et al., "Teaching Behaviors, Academic Learning Time and Student Achievement: An Overview," in C. Denham and A. Leiberman (eds.), *Time to Learn,* Washington, D.C.: Department of Health, Education, and Welfare, National Institute of Education, 1980; N. Karweit, *Time on Task: A Research Review,* Washington, D.C.: National Commission on Educational Excellence, 1983.

45. See also S. Krashen, "The Input Hypothesis," in J. Alatis (ed.), *Georgetown University Round Table on Language and Linguistics,* Washington, D.C.: Georgetown University, 1980; M. Long, "Input, Interaction and Second Language Acquisition," *Annals of the New York Academy of Science,* New York: New York Academy of Science, 1981; M. Swain, "Communicative Competence. Some Roles of Comprehensible Input and Comprehensible Output in Its Development," paper presented at the Second Language Research Forum, University of California, Los Angeles, November 1983.

46. Rossell, 1990.

47. C. Duncan, "The Effect of Unequal Amounts of Practice on Motor Learning Before and After Rest," *Journal of Experimental Psychology* (1951), 42: 257–64.

48. Because of the influence of the facilitation theory, however, it is not always the case that English will be part of the instructional program. Christine Rossell has personally observed dozens of kindergarten, and to a lesser extent first grade, classrooms in Massachusetts where almost no English at all is used in instruction. The teachers justify this on the grounds that their students need a long time to develop a high level of native tongue proficiency—a prerequisite to future academic success in the all-English classroom. In short, they are true believers of the facilitation theory even if they may not know its name.

# 19.

# Bilingual Education: Separating Fact from Fiction

## Richard V. López

**Fiction:** *"Studies prove that bilingual education doesn't work."*[1]

**Fact:** There is a consensus in the research community both on the soundness of the theory and effectiveness of bilingual education. The culmination of the research consensus is reflected in two studies, covering thousands of Spanish-speaking limited-English proficient (LEP) students, validated by the National Academy of Sciences (NAS) in 1992.

In 1990, the Department of Education asked the NAS to review these studies and critique their findings. The NAS is the most prestigious research body in the world. Composed of researchers and social scientists recognized by their peers as the best in their fields, the NAS is considered the "all-star team" of the research community. When an NAS review Committee can agree on the validity of research, it is believed that a research consensus has been reached.

The NAS review affirmed the finding that LEP students in bilingual education programs made greater academic gains in content areas, like math, than the students who received all instruction in English.[2]

**Fiction:** *"Many 'bilingual' programs use the student's native language almost exclusively in the first few years. Students aren't learning English."*[3]

**Fact:** This often-heard claim is wholly refuted by the studies validated by the NAS. The studies found that English was used the majority of [the] time in bilingual education programs and by the fourth grade only 3 percent of instruction was in the student's native language. Specifically, the studies found that in transitional bilingual education classrooms, English was used 65.8% of the time in Kindergarten, 69.1% in Grade 1, 74.5% in Grade 2, 80.3% in Grade 3, and 97.3%

Reprinted by permission of the National Association for Bilingual Education.

in Grade 4. Even in developmental bilingual programs, where the goal is fluency in both languages, English was used a majority of the time in Grades 3–6. Every bilingual education program has an English as a second language (ESL) component. That is, every bilingual education program includes significant coursework in teaching English language skills.[4]

**Fiction:** *"Studies confirm what common sense would tell you: the less time you spend speaking a new language, the more slowly you'll learn it."*[5]

**Fact:** The studies validated by the NAS directly addressed and refuted this claim. "The study concluded that providing LEP students with substantial instruction in their primary languages does not interfere with or delay their acquisition of English language skills, but helps them to 'catch up' to their English-speaking peers in English language arts, English reading, and math. In contrast, providing LEP students with almost exclusive instruction in English does not accelerate their acquisition of English language arts, reading or math, i.e., they do not appear to be 'catching up.' The data suggest that by grade six, students provided with English-only instruction may actually fall further behind their English-speaking peers. Data also document that learning a second language will take six or more years [regardless of the instructional approach, English-only or bilingual education]."[6]

Students in bilingual education classes posted superior test scores because bilingual education students were allowed to continue to academically and cognitively develop as soon as they entered school through the use of their native language. Bilingual education students were able to problem solve, analyze, and apply critical thinking skills earlier than LEP students in monolingual English settings because they could explore challenging content matter long before students in monolingual English classrooms.

To use an example from Washington, D.C., Public Schools, students at the Oyster Bilingual Elementary School—where the student body is composed of roughly equal numbers of native English- and native Spanish-speakers—are taught half of the time in English and half of the time in Spanish. Sixth grade students at the school posted scores equivalent to twelfth grade students in English language arts on the California Test of Basic Skills. In other words, sixth grade bilingual education students were not only performing at the level of high school seniors in English, they were also fully literate in Spanish.[7]

**Fiction:** *"How difficult can it be to learn English if Berlitz can teach someone to speak English in 30 days?"*[8]

**Fact:** There is a great difference between the conversational phrases taught by Berlitz and the high-level academic English needed to succeed in school, college, and high-skills job market. The conversational phrases taught at Berlitz and other short-term language programs permit the student to order food, make hotel reservations, or locate a train station. They do not claim to equip students with the ability to write a high school paper, for example, on the symbolism of the white whale in Herman Melville's *Moby Dick,* at the same level as a native English speaker.

In a soon-to-be-published study that mirrors the findings of studies validated by the NAS and many, many others on the length of time for English acquisition, two researchers from George Mason University examined school records of approximately 24,000 language-minority student records per school year with six to ten years of data on achievement in standardized tests, performance assessment measures, grade point averages, and high school courses in which enrolled. Students reached English fluency, as measured by the 50th percentile on an English standardized test, in 5 to 10 years if taught in English only and in 4 to 7 years if taught in bilingual education.[9]

**Fiction:** *"Language-minority parents and communities oppose bilingual education."*

**Fact:** Polls show that language-minority communities solidly support bilingual education. For example, more than 80% of the Latinos interviewed back bilingual education, according to a poll by the *Los Angeles Times.*[10]

Surveys cited by bilingual education opponents always use loaded questions that border on silliness. For example, English First, a national lobbying organization that helps to funnel campaign contributions to English-only supporters, offers this survey question result in their promotional material: "the great majority of Hispanic parents—more than three-fourths of Mexican-American parents and more than four-fifths of Cuban-American parents—are opposed to the teaching of Spanish *at the expense of English*" (emphasis added). It is almost surprising that only 75 percent of Hispanics affirmatively answered such a loaded question that way. The question is not whether Hispanic or other language-minority communities want their children to speak Spanish or another native language *only,* but rather what is the best way to teach an LEP student and does it produce students who speak both English and their native tongue. As this document shows, bilingual education teaches English and is the most effective way to teach children academic content areas.[11]

**Fiction:** *"Kids are being placed in bilingual education who can already speak English fluently just because they have a Hispanic or ethnic minority surname."*[12]

**Fact:** Anecdotes of inappropriate misplacement of non-LEP students in bilingual education are tragic. They reflect terrible education policy that no bilingual educator would condone and are against federal law. There have been no national studies nor evaluations that have even suggested that inappropriate misplacement of non-LEP students into bilingual education is anything but an abhorrent aberration.[13]

What has been well documented is that there are millions of LEP students who are not provided at all with services that enable them to understand instruction. More than a quarter (26.6 percent) of LEP students currently receives no tailored educational services to allow them to understand instruction, in violation of federal law.[14]

Even more troubling is the misplacement of LEP students into special education classes. A class action suit on behalf of over 1,000 Asian immigrant families accused the City of Philadelphia of misplacing their LEP children into special education classes without parental knowledge or consent in the late 1980s. In the initial case that led to the class action, an Asian refugee child was transferred to three separate middle schools but never received any assistance in learning English, in violation of state and federal law. After years in which the child failed to make any academic progress, the school tested him, found him to be mentally disabled, and placed him in a special education class, all without the knowledge or consent of his parents.[15]

**Fiction:** *"LEP dropout rates remain very high despite the widespread application of bilingual education."*[16]

**Fact:** High dropout rates of limited-English proficient (LEP) students cannot be blamed on bilingual education because over three-quarters of LEP students are not taught through bilingual education. Bilingual education is used to instruct only about one in four LEP students. English as a Second Language (ESL) instruction, in which the student's native language is not used for academic instruction, is used to teach just less than half of LEP students. Over a quarter of LEP students receive neither services to teach them English nor assistance tailored to help them understand what is being taught to them. This is often called a "sink-or-swim" approach to teaching LEP students and is in violation of federal law. If a reading of this data suggests anything, it is that *lack* of bilingual education, an overreliance on ESL, and the prevalence of sink-or-swim approaches to teaching LEP students may be the real culprits in high LEP dropout rates.[17]

**Fiction:** *"Bilingual education is impractical because it costs $8 to $11 billion and there are 180 languages spoken by America's students."*[18]

**Fact:** The $8 to $11 billion estimates of the costs of bilingual education offered by opponents are outrageous but simple to understand. The number reflects the cost of educating LEP students whether or not they are taught using bilingual education instructional techniques. There are approximately 2.3 million LEP students in the U.S., according to the U.S. Department of Education. If this number of students is multiplied by the average cost of educating a student in the U.S., about $5,000, one arrives at the often repeated $8 to $11 billion estimates. As one can see, $8 to $11 billion would be spent on instructing LEP children even if every school in the U.S. chose to use neither bilingual education nor ESL. The true cost of bilingual education is the additional amount of funds that a school expends to change a monolingual English program to a bilingual educational program. This additional cost is limited primarily to the purchase of additional instructional materials, which is marginal.[19]

The large number of language groups would only be a problem for schools if each school had to instruct students from many different language groups. While it is true that most major school districts have many language groups, most schools are linguistically homogeneous. For example, there are over 75 languages represented in the Tucson public schools, however, no single school has more than four languages represented. In Denver, there are 60 identified language groups, yet not more than three languages are spoken in any given school. In these situations, there is no question that bilingual education can, and should, be provided. Nationally, only one quarter of LEP students attends schools in which the numbers and diversity of LEP students would make it impossible to carry out a bilingual education program, according to data from the General Accounting Office.

Even when the numbers are not large and certified teachers sparse, there are many ways to use the students' native language and culture by drawing upon the resources of the language minority communities. In Fountain Valley, California, for example, Project GLAD students, who come from 12 different language groups, receive one hour each day of content and literacy instruction in the native language, taught by paraprofessionals from their communities. Bilingual education in most U.S. schools is not only desirable, but is also possible.

More important, arguments against the practicality of bilingual education forward the absurd proposition that because one LEP student cannot be served, no LEP students should be served. The Supreme Court in *Lau v. Nichols,* the landmark case that requires schools to ensure that LEP students can understand instruction, wrote that states can and should consider the numbers and diversity of their LEP students when considering what services schools can reasonably offer LEP students.[20]

**Fiction:** *"My grandparents were immigrants and made it without bilingual education or any other special help."*

**Fact:** While there are surely extraordinary cases, examples of turn-of-the-century immigrants learning English and succeeding in the American job market are exceptions to the rule that are usually inapplicable to today's high-skills, high-technology labor market. Contrary to the widely accepted myth that earlier immigrant groups manage without special programs, most immigrant children who entered schools were more likely to sink than swim in English-only classrooms. In 1908, for example, just 13% of the twelve-year-olds enrolled in New York public schools, and whose parents were foreign-born, went on to high school, compared with 32% of white children whose parents were native born. Some immigrants with limited English skills and formal education could succeed because the economy, with its industrial and agricultural base, relied on uneducated and unskilled labor. For example, an immigrant factory worker could do quite well for himself with conversational English skills, but the same immigrant with the same conversational English skills would have much greater difficulty securing even an entry level job today with IBM.[21]

**Fiction:** *"Bilingual education is a 1960s creation of the federal government."*²²

**Fact:** There is a tradition of bilingual education in the U.S. that dates from early nineteenth-century American schools. In the public schools of many states between 1839 and 1880—including Ohio, Louisiana, and New Mexico—German, French, and Spanish were used for instruction. Between 1880 and 1917, German-English bilingual schools, in which both languages were used for instruction, operated in Ohio, Minnesota, and Maryland. In several other states, German was included in the curriculum as a subject rather than as a means of instruction. The same is true for Norwegian, Italian, Czech, Dutch, and Polish.

In private schools, mostly parochial, German-English bilingual education flourished throughout the United States before 1800. Also, during this period, many French schools were established in the northeastern United States (precursors of the modern-day Lycée Français found in New York City, for example) and Scandinavian and Dutch schools were formed in the Midwest.²³

**Fiction:** *"Ethnic leaders use bilingual education as a way to keep their constituencies easily manipulated and disenfranchised."*²⁴

**Fact:** Of all the claims made against bilingual education, this is the single most ridiculous. The nation's highest language-minority elected officials—Members of Congress—are democratically elected every two years to represent the largest language-minority communities nationwide and millions of Latino voters. All Latino, all Native American, and the overwhelming majority of Asian American members of Congress support bilingual education as a key to educational and life success. In contrast, those individuals who accuse Latino leaders of disenfranchising their constituencies are usually not democratically elected officials and therefore in a poor position to represent the views of language minorities across the country.

Elected officials critical of language-minority leaders invariably do not represent significant numbers of language-minority voters (they hail from places like Wisconsin, Missouri, Kansas, or Georgia) and therefore are in no position to assert the "true" sentiments of language-minority communities. On the other hand, those non-language-minority elected officials who do represent language-minority communities are some of bilingual education's strongest supporters. Indeed, the claim seems to suggest that language-minority voters are incapable of electing representative leaders.

# NOTES

1. For example, "No evidence exists to back up the claim that teaching children predominantly in their native tongues is better than other instructional models using intensive English, such as English as a Second Language." From Rosalie Pedalino Porter, "Bilingual Ed Flunks Out," *The American Experiment: A Quarterly Publication of the*

*Center for Equal Opportunity,* Spring 1995, p. 1. Porter is Chair of the Research in English Acquisition and Development, Inc. (READ Institute) and is editor of the *READ Perspectives* publication. READ was founded with funds and assistance from U.S. English, a national lobbying group devoted to making English the official, federal language.

2. Michael M. Myer and Stephen E. Feinberg, eds., *Assessing Evaluation Studies: The Case of Bilingual Education,* Panel to Review Evaluation Studies of Bilingual Education, Committee on National Statistics, and Commission on Behavioral and Social Sciences and Education, National Research Council (National Academy Press: Washington, D.C., 1992). The two Department of Education studies reviewed by the NAS are entitled: *The National Longitudinal Study of the Evaluation of the Effectiveness of Services for Language Minority Limited-English Proficient Students* and *The Longitudinal Study of Immersion Strategy, Early-exit and Late-exit Transitional Bilingual Education Programs for Language-Minority Students.*

3. Linda Chavez, "Bilingual Ed the Real Culprit," *USA Today,* September 6, 1995, p. 13A. Linda Chavez is president of the Center for Equal Opportunity (CEO) and former executive director of U.S. English.

4. *The Longitudinal Study of Immersion Strategy, Early-exit and Late-exit Transitional Bilingual Education Programs for Language-Minority Students,* pp. 90–91, as validated by the NAS review.

5. Linda Chavez, "One Nation, One Common Language," *Reader's Digest,* August 1995, p. 90.

6. Executive Summary, *The Longitudinal Study of Immersion Strategy, Early-exit and Late-exit Transitional Bilingual Education Programs for Language-Minority Students,* p. 1, as validated by the NAS review.

7. Results reported in D.C. Public Elementary Schools Median Scores and Percentiles from May 1991 Examinations of Comprehensive Test of Basic Skills. The sixth grade students from Oyster Bilingual Elementary School scored at the 12.2 grade level, grade equivalent scores based on national norms.

8. Paraphrasing of Jim Boulet, executive director, English First, on numerous radio talk shows.

9. Wayne P. Thomas and Virginia P. Collier, "Research Summary of Study in Progress: Language Minority Student Achievement and Program Effectiveness," George Mason University, 1995. Publications to come on this series of studies: Report by Lynn Schnaiberg, *Education Week,* September or October 1995; research monograph by Thomas and Collier for the National Clearinghouse on Bilingual Education, late fall 1995; articles in *Bilingual Research Journal* and other education journals in 1996. For other studies on the length of time to acquire academic mastery of a second language see V. P. Collier, "Age and rate of acquisition of second language for academic purposes, *TESOL Quarterly* 21: 617–41; Collier, "How Long? A Synthesis of research on academic achievement in second language," *TESOL Quarterly* 23: 509–31; Collier, "A synthesis of Studies examining long-term language-minority student data on academic achievement," *Bilingual Research Journal* 16, nos. 1–2: 187–212; Collier and Thomas, "How quickly can immigrants become proficient in school English," *Journal of Educational Issues of Language Minority Students* 5; James Cummins, "The Role of Primary Language Development in Promoting Educational Success for Language Minority Students," *Schooling and Language Minority Students,* California Department of Education, 1981, and "Interdependence of first- and second-language proficient in bilingual children," in Bialystok, ed., *Language Processing and Bilingual Children,* Cambridge University Press, 1991, and "Bilingual Education and English Immersion: The Ramirez Report in Theoretical Per-

spective," *Bilingual Research Journal* 16, nos. 1–2; and F. Genesee, *Learning through two languages: Studies of Immersion and Bilingual Education,* Cambridge, Mass.: Newbury House, 1987.

10. Poll reported in the *Los Angeles Times,* December 7, 1992.

11. English First, "Statement of English First in Opposition to S.B. 88." The president of English First is Larry Pratt, also president of Gun Owners of America.

12. Jorge Amselle, "When one language is better than two," Opinion Editorial in the *Washington Times,* August 24, 1995, p. A19. He writes: "Bilingual education today means three to five years in a program where as much as 90 percent of child's [*sic*] is spent in the native language, even if it isn't his or her native language. I have spoken to many parents and teachers all over the country who have similar horror stories."

13. "Students shall not be admitted to or excluded from any federally assisted education program merely on the basis of a surname or a language-minority status." Section 7502(b)(4) of the Improving America's Schools Act.

14. Data from the California Department of Education as reported by Reynaldo Macias, "More LEP Students Receive No Special Services," University of California Language Minority Research Institute, Volume 4, Number 2, p. 1. Data from California, which enrolls 42.1 percent of all LEP students, gives the best description of educational services to LEP students.

15. United States District Court, Eastern District of Pennsylvania, Class Action Complaint, *Y.S., a minor, by his father, Yin S., and Yin S. and Lim C., individually and on behalf of all others similarly situated, Plaintiffs,* v. *School District of Philadelphia, Defendant,* No. CA 85–6924.

16. For example, see Porter, "Bilingual Ed Flunks Out," p. 5. She writes: "Spanish speaking LEP students who have had the heaviest engagement in bilingual programs still have the highest dropout rates in the country at nearly 50 percent, compared to about 10 percent for English speakers."

17. Data from the California Department of Education as reported by Reynaldo Macias, "More LEP Students Receive No Special Services," University of California Language Minority Research Institute, Volume 4, Number 2, p. 1. Data from California, which enrolls 42.1 percent of all LEP students, gives the best description of educational services to LEP students.

18. Rep. Toby Roth and Jim Boulet in English First promotional materials.

19. Figures from the Office of Bilingual Education and Minority Language Affairs of the U.S. Department of Education for 1992 as reported by State Education Agencies.

20. Data cited by Senator Edward Kennedy during reauthorization of the Elementary and Secondary Education Act, 1992. *Lau* v. *Nichols* (1974).

21. U.S. Department of Education, *The Condition of Bilingual Education in the Nation: A Report to the Congress and the President,* Office of the Secretary, U.S. Department of Education, Washington, D.C.: 1991, p. 2.

22. Rep. Peter King, press release entitled, "Rep. King Introduces English Language Bill," Spring-Summer 1995. King writes: "Beginning in 1968, however, the federal government began to reverse this proven policy by mandating bilingual education in our schools which meant that students would be taught in their native language rather than in English." Rep. King is author of HR 1005, a bill that would make English the official, federal language of the United States and eliminate bilingual education.

23. See James Crawford, *Hold Your Tongue: Bilingualism and the Politics of "English-Only,"* Reading, Mass.: Addison-Wesley, 1992; Arnold H. Leibovitz, *The Bilingual Education Act: A Legislative Analysis,* Washington, D.C.: InterAmerica Research Associ-

ates, Inc., 1980; Diego Castellanos with Pamela Leggio, *The Best of Both Worlds: Bilingual-Bicultural Education in the U.S.,* Trenton, N.J.: New Jersey State Department of Education, 1983; and Bill Piatt, *Only English? Law & Language Policy in the United States,* Albuquerque: University of New Mexico Press, 1990.

24. For example, see Rep. Newt Gingrich, "English Literacy Is the Coin of the Realm," Opinion Editorial in the *Los Angeles Times,* August 4, 1995. He writes, "Sadly, there are some ethnic leaders who prefer bilingualism because it keeps their voters and supporters isolated from the rest of America, ghettoized into groups more easily manipulated for political purposes often by self-appointed leaders."

# Appendix

# The Index of Leading Immigration Indicators

## John J. Miller and Stephen Moore

**Number of Immigrant Arrivals by Decade, 1820–1990**

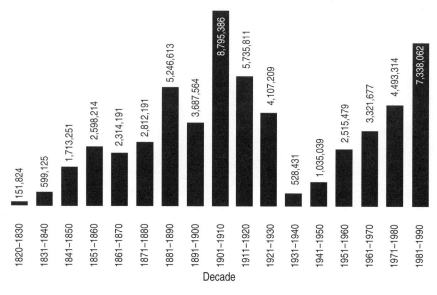

Source: Statistical Yearbook of the Immigration and Naturalization Service, 1992

In 1993, the United States admitted more than 904,000 legal immigrants. As many as 300,000 illegal immigrants also settled permanently.

## Rate of Immigration by Decade, 1820–1990

Number of immigrants per 1,000 U.S. residents

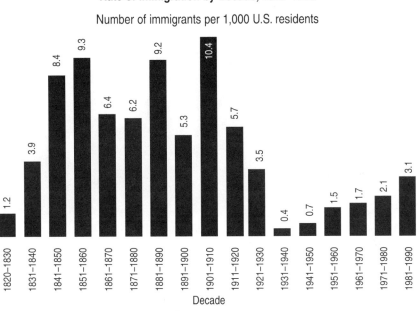

Source: Statistical Abstract of the United States, 1992

Recent decades have seen large numbers of immigrants arrive in the United States, but their numbers are relatively low as a percentage of the population.

## Total Size of the Foreign-Born Population, 1850–1990

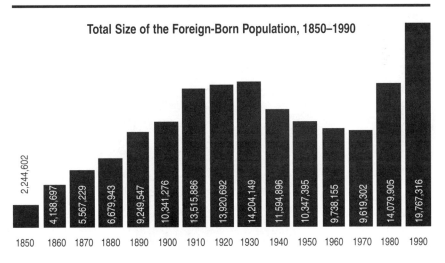

Source: Census data

Since 1850, the size of the foreign-born population has increased nearly nine times over.

Today's foreign-born population outnumbers the entire U.S. population of the 1840s.

## Immigrants as a Percentage of the Population, 1850–1990

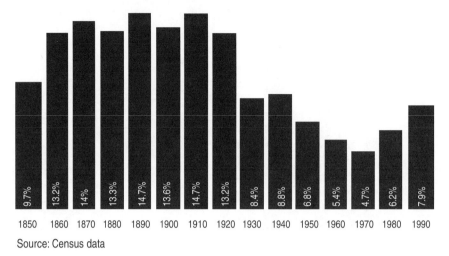

| 1850 | 1860 | 1870 | 1880 | 1890 | 1900 | 1910 | 1920 | 1930 | 1940 | 1950 | 1960 | 1970 | 1980 | 1990 |

9.7%  13.2%  14%  13.3%  14.7%  13.6%  14.7%  13.2%  8.4%  8.8%  6.8%  5.4%  4.7%  6.2%  7.9%

Source: Census data

Record numbers of immigrants live in the United States today, but their share of the total population is relatively small.

Since 1900, the total population has more than tripled, but the total immigrant population has not yet doubled.

## Legal Status of the Foreign-Born Population, 1990

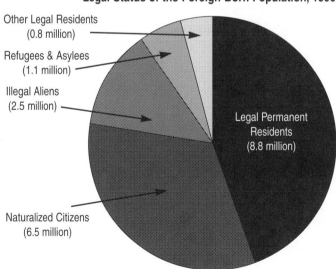

Other Legal Residents (0.8 million)

Refugees & Asylees (1.1 million)

Illegal Aliens (2.5 million)

Legal Permanent Residents (8.8 million)

Naturalized Citizens (6.5 million)

Source: Urban Institute estimates

In 1993, 68 percent of Americans agreed that "most of the people who have moved to the United States in the last few years are here illegally," according to a New York Times/CBS News poll. That same year, legal immigrants outnumbered illegal immigrants by about three-to-one.

## Legal Immigration by Country or Region, 1951–1990

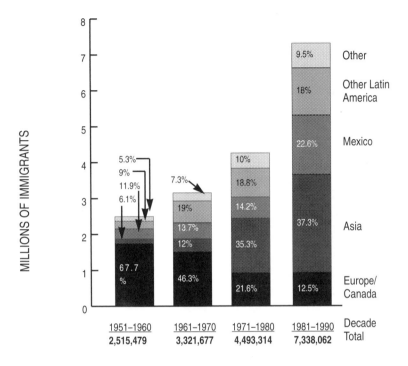

Source: Statistical Yearbook of the Immigration and Naturalization Service, 1992

*Percentages may not add up to 100 due to rounding.

Not only has the size of the immigrant population changed, but so has its racial and ethnic make-up. About three-fourths of all immigrants come from Asia or Latin America.

The number of sending countries with at least 100,000 foreign-born residents in the U.S. rose from 21 in 1970 to 41 in 1990.

## Immigrants Admitted by Place of Birth and City of Intended Residence, 1993

Over 904,000 legal immigrants entered the U.S. in 1993, and 55 percent of them settled in these 12 metropolitan areas.

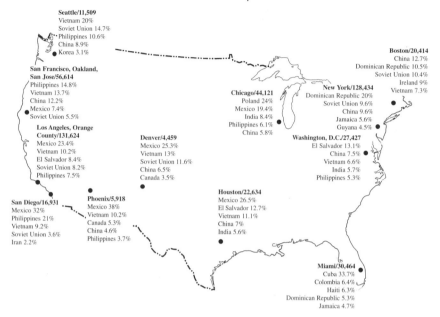

**Seattle/11,509**
Vietnam 20%
Soviet Union 14.7%
Philippines 10.6%
China 8.9%
Korea 3.1%

**San Francisco, Oakland, San Jose/56,614**
Philippines 14.8%
Vietnam 13.7%
China 12.2%
Mexico 7.4%
Soviet Union 5.5%

**Los Angeles, Orange County/131,624**
Mexico 23.4%
Vietnam 10.2%
El Salvador 8.4%
Soviet Union 8.2%
Philippines 7.5%

**San Diego/16,931**
Mexico 32%
Philippines 21%
Vietnam 9.2%
Soviet Union 3.6%
Iran 2.2%

**Phoenix/5,918**
Mexico 38%
Vietnam 10.2%
Canada 5.3%
China 4.6%
Philippines 3.7%

**Denver/4,459**
Mexico 25.3%
Vietnam 13%
Soviet Union 11.6%
China 6.5%
Canada 3.5%

**Houston/22,634**
Mexico 26.5%
El Salvador 12.7%
Vietnam 11.1%
China 7%
India 5.6%

**Chicago/44,121**
Poland 24%
Mexico 19.4%
India 8.4%
Philippines 6.1%
China 5.8%

**New York/128,434**
Dominican Republic 20%
Soviet Union 9.6%
China 9.6%
Jamaica 5.6%
Guyana 4.5%

**Washington, D.C./27,427**
El Salvador 13.1%
China 7.5%
Vietnam 6.6%
India 5.7%
Philippines 5.3%

**Boston/20,414**
China 12.7%
Dominican Republic 10.5%
Soviet Union 10.4%
Ireland 9%
Vietnam 7.3%

**Miami/30,464**
Cuba 33.7%
Colombia 6.4%
Haiti 6.3%
Dominican Republic 5.3%
Jamaica 4.7%

Source: Statistical Yearbook of the Immigration and Naturalization Service, 1993

The immigrant population varies wildly from city to city across the United States. Although Mexicans dominate immigration in the Southwest, their numbers along the eastern seaboard are relatively small.

## Immigrant Destination by State, 1982–1993

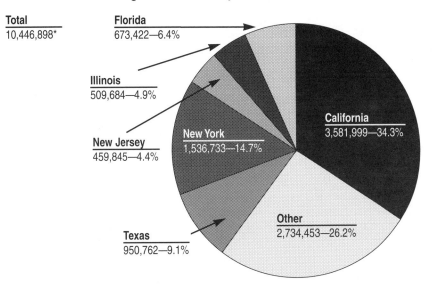

**Total**
10,446,898*

**Florida**
673,422—6.4%

**Illinois**
509,684—4.9%

**New Jersey**
459,845—4.4%

**New York**
1,536,733—14.7%

**California**
3,581,999—34.3%

**Texas**
950,762—9.1%

**Other**
2,734,453—26.2%

Source: Statistical Yearbook of the Immigration and Naturalization Service, 1990 & 1993

*Includes persons amnestied under provisions of the Immigration Reform and Control Act of 1986.

Immigrants tend to settle near other immigrants—often friends and family. More than 90 percent move into cities, and many live in highly visible ethnic enclaves.

## Households Composed of Families, 1990

Total Population: 70.7%

Total Native-Born: 70.2%

Total Foreign-Born: 76%

Non-Hispanic White: 69.6%

Black: 71%

Asian: 78%

Asian Foreign-Born: 81.1%

Hispanic: 81.3%

Hispanic Foreign-Born: 85.2%

Source: 1990 Census

Immigrant households tend to be larger than those of the native-born: 40 percent live in homes with four or more persons, compared to 25 percent of natives.

Immigrants are on average older than natives: 37.3 years versus 32.5 years. But they are also much more likely to be of working age: 71.4 percent are 18–59 years, compared to 56.4 percent of natives.

## Households Composed of Married Couples with Minor-Age Children, 1990

Total Population: 26.3%

Total Native-Born: 25.6%

Total Foreign-Born: 34.6%

Non-Hispanic White: 26.1%

Black: 18.8%

Asian: 40.4%

Asian Foreign-Born: 44.9%

Hispanic: 37.5%

Hispanic Foreign-Born: 43.7%

Source: 1990 Census

Foreign-born women have an average of 2.25 children, versus 1.93 children for U.S.-born women.

**Female-Headed Households with Minor-Age Children, No Husband Present, 1990**

Total Population: 6.3%

Total Native-Born: 6.4%

Total Foreign-Born: 6%

Non-Hispanic White: 4.3%

Black: 19.1%

Asian: 4.8%

Asian Foreign-Born: 4.7%

Hispanic: 11.6%

Hispanic Foreign-Born: 9.3%

Source: 1990 Census

Immigrants are more likely to marry and stay married. Sixty percent are married, versus 55 percent of natives. Almost 11 percent of natives are divorced or separated, compared to 8.3 percent of the foreign-born.

## Educational Attainment for Persons 25 and Older, 1990

### Percent with at least a college degree

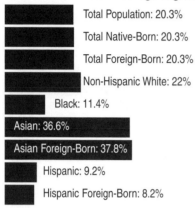

Total Population: 20.3%

Total Native-Born: 20.3%

Total Foreign-Born: 20.3%

Non-Hispanic White: 22%

Black: 11.4%

Asian: 36.6%

Asian Foreign-Born: 37.8%

Hispanic: 9.2%

Hispanic Foreign-Born: 8.2%

### Percent not finishing high school

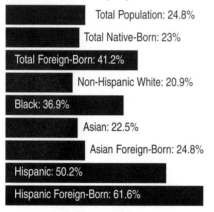

Total Population: 24.8%

Total Native-Born: 23%

Total Foreign-Born: 41.2%

Non-Hispanic White: 20.9%

Black: 36.9%

Asian: 22.5%

Asian Foreign-Born: 24.8%

Hispanic: 50.2%

Hispanic Foreign-Born: 61.6%

Source: 1990 Census

Although a large share of immigrants have not completed a high school education, they are also twice as likely as natives to hold a Ph.D.

Immigrant education levels rose during the 1980s. Among immigrants arriving 1980–1990, 23.6 percent hold at least a college degree. For those entering 1987–1990, 29 percent do.

**Ability to Speak English "Very Well," Persons 5 and Older, 1990**

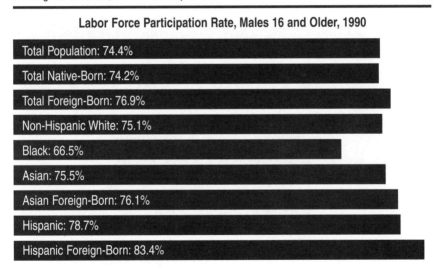

Total Population: 93.9%

Total Native-Born: 97.7%

Total Foreign-Born: 53%

Non-Hispanic White: 98.2%

Black: 97.6%

Asian: 61.6%

Asian Foreign-Born: 48.7%

Hispanic: 60.6%

Hispanic Foreign-Born: 33.5%

Source: 1990 Census

About 28 percent of immigrants over age 5 live in "linguistically isolated households," in which no member of the household over 14 speaks English "very well." For immigrants arriving before 1980, the rate is 18 percent.

**Labor Force Participation Rate, Males 16 and Older, 1990**

Total Population: 74.4%

Total Native-Born: 74.2%

Total Foreign-Born: 76.9%

Non-Hispanic White: 75.1%

Black: 66.5%

Asian: 75.5%

Asian Foreign-Born: 76.1%

Hispanic: 78.7%

Hispanic Foreign-Born: 83.4%

Source: 1990 Census

Immigrants are less likely than natives to work for the government: 9.8 percent versus 15.7 percent. This is true for both legal residents and naturalized citizens.

Rates of self-employment for immigrants and natives are roughly the same at just under 7 percent. Immigrants who arrived before 1980, however, are slightly more likely than natives to be self-employed.

**Income Levels, 1989**

Total Population
Median Household/$30,056
Per Capita/$14,420

Total Native-Born
Median Household/$30,176
Per Capita/$14,367

Total Foreign-Born
Median Household/$28,314
Per Capita/$15,033

Non-Hispanic White
Median Household/$31,672
Per Capita/$16,074

Black
Median Household/$19,7
Per Capita/$8,859

Asian
Median Household/$36,784
Per Capita/$13,638

Asian Foreign-Born
Median Household/$35,521
Per Capita/$15,937

Hispanic
Median Household/$24,156
Per Capita/$8,400

Hispanic Foreign-Born
Median Household/$23,723
Per Capita/$10,173

Source: 1990 Census

Immigrant incomes rise over time. For those entering the U.S. before 1980, median household income in 1989 was $35,733 and per capita income was $19,423. Asian immigrants arriving before 1980 earned $45,048 in household income and $23,464 in per capita income in 1989. Those from Latin America earned $25,783 and $13,836, respectively.

## Immigration and Unemployment

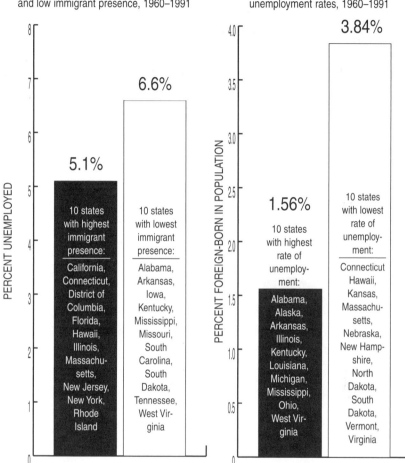

Median unemployment rate in states with high and low immigrant presence, 1960–1991

Immigrant presence in states with high and low unemployment rates, 1960–1991

Source: Vedder, Gallaway, and Moore, 1994

Immigrants do not lead to higher unemployment rates for U.S. workers, largely because they create jobs with their businesses and consumer spending.

## Immigrant Prison Rates, 1992

California

14.9

10.4

Florida

7.3

7

███ % Aliens in general population

▒▒▒ % Aliens in state prison population

Illinois

4.6

1

New York

8.6

12.4

Texas

5.9

4.3

Source: National Institute of Corrections, 1992; 1990 Census

The 1991 Survey of State Prison Inmates found that about 4 percent of state prison inmates were not U.S. citizens. In the 1990 Census, 4.7 percent of all U.S. residents were not citizens.

Federal prisons have a much higher rate of foreign-born inmates: 25 percent. But this fig-ure is largely due to the incarceration of drug smugglers and other international criminals, not immigrants.

**Welfare Use, 1989**

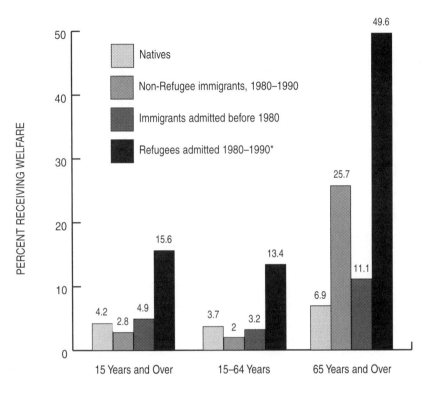

Source: Urban Institute tabulations of 1 percent sample from 1990 Census

*Refugees are defined as immigrants from Afghanistan, Albania, Cambodia, Cuba, Ethiopia, Iraq, Laos, Poland, Romania, Soviet Union, and Vietnam.

Immigrants are more likely than natives to receive welfare, but that is due mainly to very high rates of welfare use among refugees and the elderly. Non-refugee immigrants of working age are less prone to welfare than natives.

## Public Opinion on Level of Immigration, 1955–1993

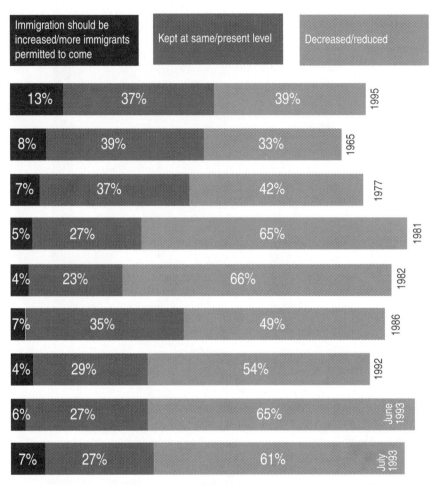

Source: National Opinion Research Center, 1955; Gallup, 1965, 1977, July 1993; NBC News/AP, 1981; Roper, 1982, 1992; New York Times/CBS News, 1986, June 1993

Over the last 40 years, almost always a plurality and sometimes a majority of Americans have wanted to reduce the flow of immigrants.

### Public Opinion on Immigrants by Ethnicity, 1985–1993

Percent saying these nationalities generally benefit the country or create problems.

| | Benefit Country | | Create Problems | |
|---|---|---|---|---|
| | **1985** | **1993** | **1985** | **1993** |
| Irish | 78% | 76% | 5% | 11% |
| Poles | 72% | 65% | 7% | 15% |
| Chinese | 69% | 59% | 13% | 31% |
| Koreans | 52% | 53% | 23% | 33% |
| Vietnamese | 47% | 41% | 30% | 46% |
| Mexicans | 44% | 29% | 37% | 59% |
| Haitians | 31% | 19% | 35% | 65% |
| Iranians | 32% | 20% | 40% | 68% |
| Cubans | 29% | 24% | 55% | 64% |

Source: USA Today/CNN, 1993

This poll also found that 74 percent of Americans think Asian immigrants "work very hard," and 77 percent think they "have strong family values." Regarding Hispanic immigrants, 65 percent believe they "work very hard," and 72 percent feel they "have strong family values."

## Public Opinion on Benefits of Immigration, 1993

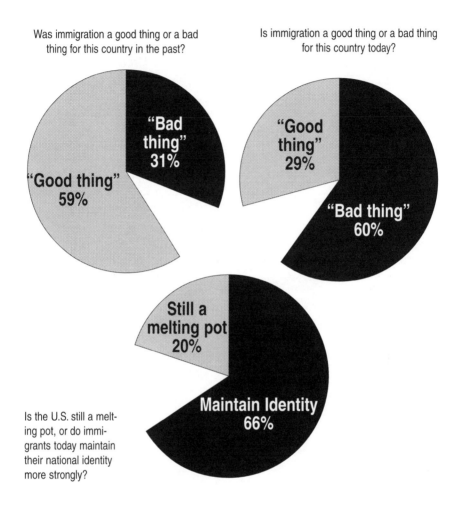

Was immigration a good thing or a bad thing for this country in the past?

"Bad thing" 31%

"Good thing" 59%

Is immigration a good thing or a bad thing for this country today?

"Good thing" 29%

"Bad thing" 60%

Is the U.S. still a melting pot, or do immigrants today maintain their national identity more strongly?

Still a melting pot 20%

Maintain Identity 66%

Source: Newsweek, 1993

# Contributors

KEITH BAKER is a consultant and a former administrator in the U.S. Department of Education.

GEORGE J. BORJAS is professor of economics at the University of California, San Diego.

LEON F. BOUVIER is adjunct professor of demography at Tulane University.

VERNON M. BRIGGS JR. is professor of labor economics at the New York State School of Labor and Industrial Relations at Cornell University.

PETER BRIMELOW is senior editor, *Forbes* and *National Review.*

LINDA CHAVEZ is president of the Center for Equal Opportunity (CEO) and the former director of the U.S. Commission on Civil Rights.

LOUIS DESIPIO is professor of political science at the University of Illinois at Urbana-Champaign.

CLAUDIA DREIFUS is a contributing writer for the *New York Times Sunday Magazine* and a Distinguished Visiting Professor in the Graduate Creative Writing Program of the City College of New York.

MARION MONCURE DUNCAN was president general of the Daughters of the American Revolution (DAR) from 1962 to 1965.

PETE HAMILL is the editor of the New York *Daily News.*

JOHN F. KENNEDY was president of the United States from 1961 to 1963.

RICHARD V. LÓPEZ is the associate director for legislation, policy, and public affairs at the National Association for Bilingual Education (NABE).

ELIZABETH MARTINEZ is a writer, teacher, and activist based in the San Francisco area. She is the author of six books, including *Five Hundred Years of Chicano History.*

DORIS MEISSNER is head of the U.S. Immigration and Naturalization Service (INS).

JOHN J. MILLER is vice president of the Center for Equal Opportunity.

STEPHEN MOORE is the director of fiscal policy studies at the Cato Institute.

NADIA NEDZEL is an attorney and former clerk to the Hon. Carl E. Stewart of the U.S. Fifth Circuit Court of Appeals.

RICHARD JOHN NEUHAUS is president of the Institute on Religion and Public Life, a nonpartisan interreligious research and education institute in New York City.

HARRY PACHON is Kenan Professor of Politics, Pitzer College and Claremont Graduate School. He is also the president of the Tomás Rivera Policy Institute.

CHRISTINE H. ROSSELL is professor of political science at Boston University.

ARTHUR M. SCHLESINGER JR. is a historian, author, and educator.

PETER H. SCHUCK is Simeon E. Baldwin Professor of Law, Yale Law School.